Dambeck

995
Cess 18%

8.96

THE THEATRE IN THE
MIDDLE AGES

Property of
Charles A. Owen Jr.
Medieval Studies Library

THE THEATRE IN THE MIDDLE AGES

WESTERN EUROPEAN STAGE CONDITIONS, c.800–1576

WILLIAM TYDEMAN

Senior Lecturer in English
University College of North Wales

CAMBRIDGE UNIVERSITY PRESS

Cambridge

London · New York · Melbourne

Published by the Syndics of the Cambridge University Press
The Pitt Building, Trumpington Street, Cambridge CB2 1RP
Bentley House, 200 Euston Road, London NW1 2DB
32 East 57th Street, New York, NY 10022, USA
296 Beaconsfield Parade, Middle Park, Melbourne 3206, Australia

© Cambridge University Press 1978

First published 1978

Printed in Malta by Interprint (Malta) Ltd.

Library of Congress cataloguing in publication data

Tydeman, William.
The theatre in the Middle Ages.

Bibliography: p.

Includes index.

1. Theater — History — Medieval, 500-1500. I. Title.
PN2152.T9   792′.09′02   77-85683

ISBN 0 521 21891 8   hard covers
ISBN 0 521 29304 9   paperback

CONTENTS

In Memory of
HENRY MARCUS TYDEMAN
(1902–1975)

ILLUSTRATIONS

* Illustrations 4, 6, 9, 11 and 14 are based on drawings by Jacqueline Tydeman.

PREFACE

'I mus' say,' said Kipps, 'I don't quite like a play in a theayter. It seems sort of
unreal, some'ow.'
 'But most plays are written for the stage,' said Helen, looking at the
sugar.
 'I know,' admitted Kipps.

H. G. Wells, *Kipps*

This book offers its readers a concise and therefore over-simplified survey of medieval stage conditions in Britain, France, Germany and
Spain. It was originally intended to include Italy, but the Italian stage
developed in such individual and indeed unique ways that it has
proved impossible to cope adequately with it in a small compass, and I
have only paid it occasional attention. Not that other countries have
received comprehensive coverage: paradoxically the problems of suc-
cinctly surveying such a wide area have been complicated by the
energetic researches conducted in this field in recent years. Scholarly
interpretations of the available evidence now tend to diverge more
and more sharply, as long-accepted theories and explanations have
been thankfully or reluctantly abandoned. With almost every aspect of
his topic now subject to bombardment by the heavy artillery of rival
authorities, the writer striving to produce an acceptable account of the
medieval theatre inevitably finds himself caught in the cross-fire. To
avoid controversial matters altogether reduces the value of even a
general summary, yet to linger too lovingly over the learned conjectures
of experts risks alienating the non-specialist for whom this book is
chiefly intended. I have therefore compromised by dealing with
disputed matters more briefly than they deserve, and by pointing out in
the notes where fuller discussions of complex problems may be found.
My keenest wish is that readers will treat this book as a sketch-map
of a rich and absorbing region into which they will later venture in the
company of the genuine explorers.
 In compiling my survey I have drawn extensively on published
criticism and research by leading figures in the field of medieval theatre
studies: my sense of indebtedness is, I trust, everywhere acknowledged,
for it is certainly immense. Indeed, it may be legitimately argued that

ix

'I have but gathered a nosegay of strange flowres, and have put nothing of mine unto it but the thred to binde them', but because 'a spark is often kindled by the mere juxtaposition of facts long familiar in isolation', I have felt justified in binding a quantity of other men's facts within the covers of a single volume. Regrettably A. M. Nagler's salutary reappraisal, *The Medieval Religious Stage* (1976), came to hand only when my survey was almost finished.

Translations in the text unless otherwise indicated are my own and, although I have received expert guidance, any errors of interpretation or meaning which remain are my sole responsibility. I have reproduced a foreign original where I felt it to be of interest; in the case of Middle English and early Tudor writings, texts have been printed as they stand, apart from some changes to punctuation, abbreviations, manuscript errors, and spelling, to make them less perplexing for a modern reader. I have also given all proper- and place-names in their most familiar English form, although dates, currency, and measurements have not been converted to conform to a common system.

Specific debts to scholarly authorities are gratefully recorded in the appropriate places; other thanks are more personal but no less important. Gordon Honeycombe first stimulated my practical interest in medieval drama, and Peter Bayley and Glynne Wickham have shown me many kindnesses over the years. I also hope to have profited from the opportunity to direct my own adaptations of the English cycle plays in Bangor Cathedral on two occasions: for this my gratitude is expressed to the Dean and Cathedral Chapter, and to Alun R. Jones and the late John F. Danby for their support and encouragement. I must thank the Librarian of the University College of North Wales and his staff for indulging an apparently insatiable appetite for obscure titles; to my colleagues John Bednall, Michael Heath, Ruth Anne Henderson, David Hollister, Martin Smith, and Laurence Wright I tender thanks for their willingness to give freely of their time and expertise. Joyce Williams and Lesley Savage have cheerfully typed a tortuous manuscript with their customary efficiency and uncanny intuition, and the book has greatly benefited from the experience and care of the staff of the Cambridge University Press in general, and Diane Speakman in particular. My wife Jacqueline has again sweetened the rigours of authorship with loving assistance tempered with shrewd advice, while our children Josephine and Rosalind have displayed exemplary tolerance towards a preoccupied parent. Finally, this book is dedicated to the memory of one whose sterling example has been a constant source of sustenance.

Bangor, Gwynedd, June 1977   *William Tydeman*

Map of Western Europe, showing the principal places mentioned in the text

Map of Britain, showing the principal places mentioned in the text

1

RITUAL SURVIVALS

The Art of the Theatre has sprung from action — movement — dance.

Gordon Craig, *The Art of the Theatre*

A probably apocryphal Second World War story from Oxford University relates how an open-air production of a Shakespearean play was interrupted one fine summer evening by the appearance of a V2 rocket which 'cut out' sufficiently near the playing area to bring the action to a halt: as cast and spectators raced for shelter, a solitary voice was heard to remark, 'Thank God for war!' Such an attitude towards dramatic activities must be relegated firmly to the back of the mind when exploring the ancient and medieval stage. For pre-Renaissance man, drama had not yet lost its associations with tribal rituals, with the seasonal cycle of growth and decay, with the common need for worship, celebration, and refreshment; his theatre was a collaboration in which the whole community, both performers and spectators, participated.

If we wish to escape the contemporary connotations of drama, the most easily available route, more accessible to the layman than that provided by anthropological surveys of the habits of primitive tribes, is by way of the customs and taboos of young children. (Parents will be aware of other analogies with primitive tribes.) Re-entering that childhood region, where a certain sequence of actions or a verbal formula must be followed before sleep will come, where holding one's collar as an ambulance passes ensures immunity against injury, and where a bus-ticket whose digits add up to twenty-one is a talisman of mystic significance, we may still share the fears of early or natural man confronted by a largely unknown and potentially hostile world, and seeking to render it less menacing. So children placate the unknown with pieces of protective magic, not only the established ones of touching wood or throwing salt over the shoulder or not walking under ladders, but others unique to the individual: for several years the present writer would always avoid treading on the top step of the stairs, to keep at bay some vague nameless terror.

1

Children's games offer a slightly different route, for they follow set patterns and preordained rules, not so much as acts of propitiation to ensure that no harm will befall, but as an assurance that recalcitrant nature can be tamed and reduced to manageable proportions so long as one observes the obligatory laws. In this way children through playing gain control over chaos by imposing the needful form on it; they take possession of what seems alien by organising it into a manageable shape. Games, which are after all only formalised play, are a popular art-form, and 'All art', says André Malraux, 'is a means to gain a hold on fate.'

A basic aspect of both art and play is imitation. Some games like 'Follow my leader' or 'Simon says' depend on corporate mimicry of an individual's actions, while countless others involve tracing a motif such as a skipping-rhyme or a trail of chalked arrows, initially established by somebody else. Rather more sophisticated and much more inventive are such children's 'play-acting' games as 'Mothers and Fathers' or 'Doctors' (so beautifully handled in Laurie Lee's reminiscences, *Cider with Rosie*), where the actions of others are not necessarily literally mimicked but where adult behaviour and conversation are reflected in a more flexible manner. Imitation is of course a basic human pleasure, but it signifies much more than amusement. Children's imitation-games represent the tentative beginnings of growing-up; such attempts to assimilate the larger world of mature concerns and responsibilities again render it less strange and more explicable, and level the balance as it were. 'Let's pretend,' said my younger daughter when three years old, 'that you're a tiny little boy and I'm a great big lady.'

If such actions still have currency in urbanised Western society, how much more potent is their significance for primitive or prehistoric communities, where human beings lacking the protective comforts of modern technological civilisation must fight desperately to survive a harsh, unstable universe. As Gilbert Murray observes

Under ancient conditions, it was anxious work for every human group, when the harvest was over, to face the winter, when all life seemed gone, followed by the spring when . . . 'it blooms but there is not enough to eat'. Men could live only in the hope that a living and fruitful world would eventually be reborn. If there was no rebirth, there was famine. We scarcely realize today how close primitive communities stood to that recurring danger.[1]

In inimical environments the need for plentiful supplies of food and manpower ordains that men must both propitiate the gods in order to ensure their favour, and tame and harness the forces of the natural world by their own deliberate efforts. The civilisation of ancient

Mexico offers many examples of man's belief in the necessity for placating the gods: the Aztecs recognised the vital importance of nourishing their tribal deities and retaining their good-will, devising a whole range of ceremonies which involved human sacrifice, for only by this means could they present their gods with the most precious gifts they knew of: the human heart and human blood. Human sacrifice was the paramount rite which secured divine favours and the continued existence of the race. Jacques Soustelle writes of the whole elaborate system of ceremonials:

For the ancient Mexicans there was nothing more vitally important than these motions, these songs, dances, sacrifices, and traditional actions, because as they saw it, these things assured the regular succession of the seasons, the coming of the rains, the springing of the plants upon which they lived, and the resurrection of the sun. The Mexican nation, and above all the priests and the dignitaries, was engaged day after day in a continually renewed white-magic operation, a perpetual collective effort without which nature itself would be destroyed. It was therefore the gravest of life's occupations, the most imperative of duties.[2]

Both art and ritual spring in large measure from this universal need for the continuance of nature's seasonal rhythms which guaranteed the fertility of the crops and the propagation of the species. The rituals involved have two main aspects, often referred to as those of *Kenosis* and of *Plerosis*, Greek terms for the emptying and filling of the vessels of corporate vitality. Associated with the former are such rites of mortification as fasting or other forms of self-denial and abstinence, often preceded by a 'vacant period' when no work is done and the customary order of society is reversed. Associated with *Plerosis* are preliminary ceremonies of purgation, through which the community rids itself of its accumulated contagions and evils, physical and moral; rites of invigoration, which include mock-combats and ceremonial mating; rites of jubilation, requiring little definition.[3]

An excellent illustration of the prime importance of imitation in such acts of collaboration between man and the gods, man and nature, is found in W. E. Harney's *Brimming Billabongs*, an account of the life and thoughts of an Australian aborigine of the Uwadga tribe, who remarks:

I want to tell you about old Benji, the painter . . . Benji's paintings on sheets of bark were always strange, for he painted the fishes not as you see them but as though you could see through their skin and flesh. He painted every bone in the fish's body, with its liver, heart, and different fats all in their proper places. As he finished painting one fish Benji would put it aside and then go on with another; and when I asked him why, he told me that by making all these pictures he was helping the fish to be plentiful in the sea.

White people may smile and think we aborigines are fools; but we believe in such things. We believe that if we want rain, the rain man of the tribe must imitate the rain by squirting water from his mouth, and the painters must re-trace the age-old paintings at the cave of the water totem. We believe that we can get things done by imitating with magic those things we want done. We feel that we are part of this earth beneath our feet; that it and the trees upon it are alive and can do things for us if we approach them in the right way.[4]

Painter and rain man dedicate their talents to the service of the tribe: in performing mimetic acts of 'sympathetic magic' intended to influence natural events, both strive to mirror through their art the fundamental desires and emotions of the group. The aborigine painter creates from material substances imitation fish to encourage the proliferation of real fish, and similar examples can be found among primitive artefacts. Archaeologists have unearthed a number of prehistoric statuettes of animals, through which holes have been bored or on which the outlines of spears or arrows have been scratched, examples of imitative magic intended to cause death for reasons of security or nutrition. Analogous is the practice in witchcraft of moulding a wax figure of an enemy which, stuck through with pins or set to melt by the fire, is believed to inflict real sufferings on the victim.

The rain man described by W. E. Harney shapes the actions of his own body to imitate rainfall in the belief that it will bring down actual rain. Such physical mimicry of nature can occasionally be found in prehistoric art; among the celebrated Palaeolithic cave-paintings at Les Trois Frères on the Franco-Spanish border, two frescoes depict a hunter or sorcerer clad in an animal's skin, complete in one case with a cow's horns, and in another with a stag's antlers, standing upright as if taking part in some dramatic dance, perhaps the enactment of a mimed hunt and capture, intended through 'sympathetic magic' to ensure success in the real hunt to follow (Illustration 1). The Gonds, an aboriginal hill-race from central India, perform a bison-hunting dance, in which one of their number dons horns and a bison skin. The wearing of animal accoutrements has additional interest: it has been suggested that the human performer in such rites does not simply impersonate individual aspects of nature, but the general powers of fertility in nature. In ancient Mexico during the second month of the Feast of Xipe Totec, the god of seedtime and the spring rains, captive prisoners were shot to death with arrows (their dropping blood symbolising the

1   A skin-clad man wearing antlers, Cave of Les Trois Frères (after the Abbé Breuil)

desired rainfall) and then flayed, the priests performing a dance, in which the skins were worn to represent the earth's new clothing of spring vegetation. One may compare the less drastic forms adopted by the masked and leaf-clad clown who appears in the Fijian club-dance or the leaf-covered figures of western European festivals such as the 'wild men' and 'wild women' of medieval processions and tableaux (see p. 76 below), the English 'Jack-in-the-Green' or Italian *pagghiera* of folk-rituals, or the legendary 'Green Man' who features in folklore, in the Middle English *Sir Gawayne and the Grene Knight*, and in the more mundane setting of present-day inn-signs. All these disguised figures stem from the presenters of 'the demonic agents of nature', phallic demons and fertility gods; in medieval Europe those participating in such rites often wore black masks or blackened their faces, sometimes being mistaken for true devils.[5]

The importance of mimetic dance in the genesis and evolution of drama cannot be over stressed: typical is the expression of a variety of communal desires in the colourful dances of the Red Indians of the Plains with their strong imitative element, or the springing, leaping dances which follow the sowing of the spring crops in some parts of Europe, where the dancers copy the required upward thrust of the young grain, inciting it to emulate in its turn the action demonstrated.

It might be argued that such ceremonials provide us with true examples of early drama, but Theodor Gaster claims that ritual only develops into drama when it becomes linked with myth, whose function is 'to translate the real into terms of the ideal', to endow functional ritual procedures with a more transcendental *raison d'être*, whereby the presenters not only take on themselves the rôles of the gods, but are considered to imitate their very deeds and actions: 'The participants are no longer protagonists of a direct experience but mere actors or guisers (*personae*) reproducing an ideal or imaginary situation and impersonating characters other than themselves. Dramatic ritual then becomes drama proper.'[6]

Myths embodying the basic seasonal phenomena of *Kenosis* and *Plerosis*, the death and rebirth of nature, are found throughout the world from the earliest times. The Greek gods Dionysus and Adonis, the Egyptian Osiris, and the Babylonian Tammuz, were all deemed to have been slain in violent combat against a spirit of darkness, drought, or winter, and subsequently to have been reincarnated either in their own persons or in that of an heir. Such myths flourished in dramatic form through plays which featured conflict between the god and his archetypal adversary often followed by the slain deity's restoration to life, symbolising the initial demise and later renaissance of earth's fertile potential. The great Egyptian Memphite creation drama, performed annually on the first day of spring, featured the contest between Horus (the re-embodiment of the defeated Osiris) and his opponent Set, and the death and resurrection of Osiris.[7]

Ritual-combat routines occur in religious and folk drama down the ages, involving the initial defeat or death of a popular hero, who eventually arises in resurrected form to avenge himself on his murderer and triumph in reincarnation. The custom of mock battles between the forces of Life and Death, or Light and Darkness is well attested, even up to the present day, and in Europe it often forms part of the celebrations associated with Shrove Tuesday or May Day. Such a provenance certainly explains, for example, the sequence of events followed in surviving dramatic ceremonies such as the traditional British Mummers' Play of St George, or the springtime Pace-Egging Play still enacted in the Calder Valley, Yorkshire, during the Easter period, in which the central core of the action is the battle between the 'good spirit' (St George or another) and a rival champion such as the Turkish Knight. Corrupted by centuries of adaptation and interpolation, these rudimentary late plays still preserve the 'death' of the hero, and his eventual triumph over his foe following his restoration to life.[8] Further examples of dramatic combats indebted to the pattern of *Kenosis* and *Plerosis* are found in the Horn Dance from Abbot's Bromley in Staffordshire, in which three black-antlered and three white-antlered dancers clash their 'horns' in mock conflict, or in the Basque carnival contest between 'les Rouges' and 'les Noires' at La Soule in southern France; in Guatemala a mock battle is fought between dancers wearing animal heads and skins, always culminating in victory for those bearing the heads of deer.

The Middle Ages also provide illustrations of the popularity of mimed contests and battle-play. One of the earliest comes from *De ceremoniis*, a manual of ceremonies to be observed at the Byzantine Court, compiled by the tenth-century Emperor Constantinus Porphyrogenitus (913-59), in which a Twelfth Night diversion of about 953 is described. After dinner two teams of masked warriors in reindeer-skin cloaks and armed with staves and shields presented a dance-combat in a circular playing-area of the emperor's dining-hall, accompanied by stringed music, the clash of the weapons, and their own battle-songs. The performance concluded with the chanting of heroic verses in both Gothic and Latin, extolling Gothic and Old Testament warriors and terminating with a tribute to the emperor himself.[9] Arnulfus of Orléans, a twelfth-century commentator on Ovid's *Fasti*, links the performance of religious drama with a Roman ceremony involving mock battle:

Once a year the Romans gathered together on the Campus Martius and there presented that massacre once carried out by Sulla, just as we now present the slaughter of the innocents.
Romani singulis annis conveniebant in Martium Campum et ibi representabant illam interfectionem a Silla [sic] *olim factam, sicut nos modo representamus interfectionem innocentum.*[10]

A similar action was incorporated into a winter play depicting the Old Testament prophets at Riga in Latvia in 1204, when armed men under Gideon fought with the Philistine army (see pp. 223-4 below).[11]

Mock combat also features in the English 'hocking' customs, when battle was joined between the sexes, and village men and women attempted to 'hock' (lassoo and trip) each other, exacting after capture some forfeit such as a kiss, no doubt a relic from some rite of invigoration. Such an origin might be the reason for banning the practice in the Worcester diocese in 1450, but in the Coventry area at least the usage survived long enough to be revived in July 1575 as part of the 'Princely Pleasures' organised for the delight of Elizabeth I at Kenilworth, although by this time the ritual had become inextricably entangled with a belief that it commemorated a battle between the English and Danish invaders of 1002.[12]

A mock killing, especially by beheading, is a widespread feature of many dramatic conflicts, for example those which feature in some European types of sword dance. The popularity of this dance can be traced back at least as far as Tacitus, who in his *Germania* describes how agile young Germanic warriors would dance naked among swords and spears for sport;[13] centuries later the sword dance was still common at German Shrovetide festivals, and Olaus Magnus's *Historia de gentibus septentrionalibus (History of the People of the Northern Regions*, 1555) observes that

The Goths and the Swedes of the northern regions have another sport for training their young men, in which they dance [*exerceant saltu*] among naked swords and menacing blades or spears, and they also learn from experts to do this in an athletic manner and with precision, at successive ages, and to leap about while singing: and they present this sport chiefly at Shrovetide, entitled by the Italians 'the time of masking'.[14]

A frequent pattern in the modern sword dance is for the dancers to select one of their number as a victim for 'slaughter' between the linked blades (the 'knot' or 'lock') of their weapons as a sacrifice to the seasonal forces of destruction or as a symbol of the departure of winter and the old year. A similar motivation lies behind the popular Teutonic and Slavonic custom of transforming the departing year into an evil effigy of Death or Winter who, as a scapegoat for the people's ills, is eradicated from the community in a purgation ritual of banishment, beheading, burial, burning, hanging, or drowning, often on Shrove Tuesday or Ash Wednesday, leaving the way free for the Summer to be 'brought in' in the form of a tree or a leafy branch.[15] An even more innocuous version enjoys vigorous life in the game 'Oranges and lemons' involving a series of 'beheadings' and a final tug-of-war between two contending forces. In many mock-killing routines the 'slain' victim is restored to life by a quack doctor in the same way that

St George is resurrected in the mumming play so that, despite frequently festive or burlesque presentation, these rituals look back to the reaffirmation of the seasonal pattern — Summer's recurrent strife with Winter, Life's battle with Death.

There were five great seasonal festivals of the Celto-Germanic races corresponding to critical moments in the European agricultural cycle. They comprised a ploughing and sowing feast towards the end of winter (mid-January to mid-February); a spring ceremony in mid-March; a high summer rite in mid-May to mid-July; a harvest celebration in mid-September; a winter festival (Yule) about the middle of November. With the establishment of the Roman calendar and the spread of Roman cultural influence, many Celto-Germanic customs became assimilated into the Latin pattern. Winter celebrations were now absorbed into a variety of Roman festivals including the *Brumalia* (24 November), the *Saturnalia* (17—19 December), the Mithraic feast of *Sol Invictus* (25 December), and the *Kalendae* (1 January). Spring rites took place in April at the annual *Ambarvalia*, while the high summer celebrations were divided to coincide with the Roman *Floralia* (28 May — 3 June) dedicated to the goddess of spring and flowers, and the summer solstice commemorated on 21 June.[16]

Many customs associated with these pagan festivals have retained their ancient vigour to the present day. On 1 May, in particular, countless traditional celebrations have marked the rebirth of nature, another children's game, 'Here we come gathering nuts in May' ('nuts' meaning 'knots' or posies) being a survivor of rituals extending back to pagan times. The long-cherished custom for young men and women to take to the woods at dawn or during the previous evening to cut may blossom and bring it in to decorate the streets and houses is remembered in the English processional dance-song 'Hal an' Tow' (heel and toe):

> Hal an' Tow — Jolly rumbelow —
> We were up — long before the day-o
> To welcome in the summer —
> To welcome in the may-o
> For summer is a-comen in —
> And winter gone away-o![17]

A wealth of dance-songs greeting the arrival of spring is associated with European Mayday festivals: some places in Britain still retain the traditional round-dances performed around the newly erected maypole, which recalls the pagan custom of setting up an evergreen tree in ancient temples as a symbol of fecundity.

The most famous English survivor of the processional dance-song is the Helston Furry or Floral Dance, said to have originated in honour of the goddess Flora and now held on or near 8 May, when teams of dancers wind their way through the streets, and in and out of houses, their song having close affinities with 'Hal an' Tow'. Related to it is the Mayday song from Padstow in Cornwall, which belongs to one of the most fascinating folk-ceremonies to survive in Britain. The Padstow 'Oss, a beast composed of fierce dragon-like mask and black skirts billowing down from a wide hoop borne on a man's shoulders, gambols through the town accompanied by dancers and singers, to the chant of lively verses and a catchy chorus:

> Unite and unite, and let us all unite,
> For summer is a-comen today,
> And whither we are going, we all will unite,
> In the merry morning of the May!

Death and resurrection also feature here, for the 'Oss periodically slumps to the ground as if dead, only to be roused up again by his attendant known as the 'Teaser' to carry on the dance. Only at the end of the day does the 'Oss finally 'die' for the duration of a year.[18]

Other links with some fertility cult are clear; part of the original ritual enabled the 'Oss on its travels occasionally to catch a young girl by throwing its voluminous skirts over her, a sign that she would be married by Christmas, although such a mark of fortune's favour was evidently supplemented with a liberal coating of soot from a bag concealed under the skirt. Even this was not idle slapstick but sustained the notion of fruitfulness, for, as has been observed, black masks or blackened faces were the marks of the phallic demons of primitive rites: black-faced 'Moggies' still appear at Maytime festivities in Ickwell Green, Bedfordshire, while others perform the famous Nutters' Dance every Easter Saturday at Bacup in Lancashire. The English Jack-in-the-Green should correctly be played by a chimney-sweep, now the traditional bearer of generalised 'good luck' but once no doubt a fertility figure, as suggested by surviving rites in which sweeps may claim kisses from girls at upstairs windows on May morning.

A common Maytime ceremonial is the crowning of a May queen, occasionally, though rarely nowadays, joined by a May king. In fact the May king is the more ancient figure, and the selection of Albert Herring as May king in Britten's opera is not a revolutionary innovation, but the revival of a hallowed tradition. The choice of a king can be traced back to societies where the physical vigour of the ruler serves as an index of the success and welfare of his tribe (as in the Arthurian legend of the Fisher King and his waste land), and his eventual slaughter and the substitution of a new monarch has links with the alternating cycle of growth and decay. The creation of a substitute ruler who 'plays the part' of the true king during a token reign, receiving homage, and then is sacrificed to propitiate the gods and spare the real sovereign, is common to many civilisations. The Aztecs at their feast of Toxcatl sacrificed a prisoner of war who had spent a year living in luxury not as an earthly king but as the god Tezcatlipoca, whose identity he assumed and whose sacrifice ensured the continued movement of the sun.

However, the regular appearance of a May queen alongside the king, and mock weddings between them, suggest some earlier sexual connection, although the queen in former days was frequently a boy in woman's clothing; the two figures are often referred to as 'the lord' and 'the lady' (one wonders if Shakespeare drew on this tradition for Christopher Sly's 'wife' in *The Taming of the Shrew*)[19] or as 'Robin Hood' and 'Maid Marian', possibly because Mayday activities were associated with forays into 'the merry green wood'. E. K. Chambers suggests that the traditional shepherds' names of 'Robin' and 'Marian' may have been adapted from the French *fêtes du Mai* through the agency of Norman minstrels, and bestowed on the mythic figures,[20] but whatever the reason for his name, Robin Hood long remained part of early summer celebrations, usually as the leader of a money-raising expedition, or *quête*, but in some areas as the hero of a Mayday play (see pp. 20—1 below).

Other seasonal festivals maintained their programme of attendant rituals: the most significant perhaps are those connected with the harvest festival and the New Year, although ploughing and sowing time and the arrival of midsummer also had a plentiful share of celebrations, including the custom of yoking unmarried women to the plough to draw it through the streets, or presenting a Plough Monday play in which an ox was ritually 'slain', and the lighting of votive bonfires and the burning of effigies at midsummer. Harvest practices such as the selection of a harvest 'king' or 'lord' lingered on into the present century; Ronald Blythe's recent study of Suffolk village life, *Akenfield*, shows that farm labourers would choose a harvest lord to negotiate the price of reaping with the farmer, and that the privilege of riding on top of the final load to be carried was his.[21] In earlier times his 'privileges' may have included the dubious honour of being murdered as the type of substitute-king or god already mentioned. Occasionally the 'king' was a figure made from the corn itself, and either burnt *in situ* or preserved for destruction the following spring as a scapegoat, a ritual recalled in the construction of a Corn Dolly, which derives from a custom of weaving the last stalks into a 'dolly' which was kept until the next year's sowing. In some regions, at harvest, a stranger was caught and held prisoner, sometimes inside a sheaf of corn, until a ransom was paid, while in ancient Phrygia a stranger, seized at the end of harvest, was beheaded with a sickle in the field, to ensure that a replenished crop would arise next spring.

New Year customs included ceremonies involving a sheaf retained from the previous harvesting, but there were also fertility rituals centred on winter-defying evergreens and miraculously flowering shrubs such as the Glastonbury Thorn; bonfires were lit and Yule kings or lords elected; animals were again impersonated, the most interesting survival here being the familiar hobby-horse which features in other dramatic ceremonies. In parts of South Wales today a 'horse' known as the 'Mari Lwyd' (grey Mary) is still a congenial Christmas or New Year visitor to the houses and hill-farms, where its entry is followed by singing, dancing, eating and drinking.[22]

When Christianity began to spread through Europe, it endeavoured to assimilate the old heathen festivals into the new patterns of worship by ensuring that the dates on which the Church commemorated the significant events in the Christian calendar coincided with the old pre-Christian ceremonies. The revelry and licence of the Roman *Saturnalia*, marked from 17 to 19 December by a suspension of work and trading and an exchange of places between master and slave (a staple ingredient of Roman comedy), and the welcome extended to the New Year at the *Kalendae*, were incorporated into the period of 'misrule' around the feast of Christmas. The release of energy and vitality stimulated by the pagan spring festival was transposed to Easter, the culmination of the Christian year, while the traditional period of ritual mortification and the ceremonial expulsion of evil, common before rites of invigoration and jubilation could begin, was appropriated by the Church and consecrated as the period of abstention and self-examination Christians know as Lent. A period of hectic revelry was retained before Lent in the customs of Shrovetide, the three days preceding Ash Wednesday, which on the Continent became known as Carnival and extended over a longer period. Carnival under its various titles is still associated in parts of Europe with dressing up, drinking, parties, processions, and various rites associated with the creation of the figure of Carnival himself whose features are well known from Pieter Brue-

ghel's famous painting of *The Battle between Carnival and Lent*; in Italy
he is the central figure in purgation ceremonies in which a dummy is
given a mock funeral, and then 'put to death' in some violent way.[23]

The spirit in which many of the traditional rituals inspired by pagan
beliefs or half beliefs still lingered on after the coming of Christianity
may be gleaned from the Venerable Bede's account in his *History of the
English Church and People* (c. 731) of the behaviour of King Redwald of
the East Angles, converted to Christianity and baptised in Kent early
in the seventh century,

but to no good purpose; for on his return home, his wife and certain perverse
advisers persuaded him to apostatize from the true Faith. So his last state was
worse than the first, for, like the ancient Samaritans, he tried to serve both
Christ and the ancient gods, and he had in the same temple an altar for the
holy Sacrifice of Christ side by side with an altar on which victims were
offered to devils.[24]

In something of the same frame of mind many inhabitants of western
Europe received the new faith, content to pay lip-service to its observances and doctrines, provided that they were also permitted to continue the older rites.

It was fruitless for missionaries to persuade men to jettison their old
gods overnight, and in 601 Pope Gregory the Great specifically advised
St Augustine not to destroy the temples of heathen idols in Britain,
but rather to adapt them for Christian worship. Bede quotes the instructions to Augustine:

He is to destroy the idols, but the temples themselves are to be aspersed with
holy water, altars set up, and relics enclosed in them. For if these temples are
well built, they are to be purified from devil-worship, and dedicated to the
service of the true God. In this way, we hope that the people, seeing that its
temples are not destroyed, may abandon idolatry and resort to these places
as before, and may come to know and adore the true God ... For it is certainly
impossible to eradicate all errors from obstinate minds at one stroke, and
whoever wishes to climb to a mountain top climbs gradually step by step,
and not in one leap.[25]

Nevertheless, the Christian faith gained ground in men's hearts only
by degrees, and the gradual uprooting of pagan rituals took longer to
achieve than even the most pessimistic missionary could have imagined; while actual sacrifice to the old gods was proscribed and only
practised in secret, many other heathen customs were all too blatantly
observed, even if purged of those features most repellent to the new
faithful. We hear from Rudolfus, a twelfth-century monk from St Trond
(now St Truiden in the Belgian province of Limburg), that in 1133 men

from the Jülich district of north-west Germany built a ship on wheels in honour of the Teutonic wood-goddess Freya, and drew it about the region, to Aachen (Aix-la-Chappelle) and to Maastrict whence, with the addition of mast and sail, it proceeded up river to Tongres (Tongeren) and beyond, being met and escorted in every place by crowds of exultant people who, wherever the ship halted, sang triumphal songs and danced wildly round it late into the night. Such ships on wheels provide us with the etymological source of the word Carnival (from Latin *carrus navalis*, ship-cart), and less ambitious ship-processions persisted in such German towns as Ulm and Oldenburg until comparatively recently.[26]

Ceremonies like these indicate that one important aspect of the medieval stage involved forms which had at their base rites of pagan provenance.[27] Literary texts which survive often hint at dramatic presentation. Medieval European literature is rich in delightful 'songs for dancing', celebrating the coming of spring and the joys of love,[28] and not only are many of these lyrics couched in dialogue-form, but actually appear to have been performed with mimed actions, as in traditional children's games such as 'The farmer's in his den' or 'Here we go round the mulberry bush' today. Dance-songs often took the form of alternating choruses, or of solo verse and chorus refrain, familiar as the pattern of sea-shanties and other work-songs, and the accompanying dramatic action might involve interplay between chorus members and soloist, or between those dancing in a circle and those standing outside it. The thirteenth-century manuscript from Benediktbeuern Abbey in Upper Bavaria whose contents include the *Carmina Burana* contains one lyric in which girls dancing in a ring seem to tease the young men into joining them:

> *Swaz hie gât umbe,*
> *daz sint alle megede,*
> *die wellent an man*
> *alle disen sumer gân!*

Those circling about here, all of them are girls who all want to go after a man this summer!

The business of pairing up is a frequent feature of dance-songs: Peter Dronke cites as 'the oldest surviving secular Latin dance-song' a lyric from a manuscript collection known as the Cambridge Songs (*c.*1050), in which a female dancer gaily invites her man to make love to her, while the chorus suggestively mimic her probable reactions.[29] Several other European dance-songs, including the mysterious Middle English

14

'Maiden in the mor lay', may have been given an extra dimension through mimed action. Another notable reference comes from *Le Tournoi de Chauvency*, a *chanson de geste* by Jacques Bretel, describing a tournament and attendant festivities held in a small French town in 1285, in which the action of a dance-play entitled the *Chapelet* (garland) is set forth, the chief participant being the Countess of Luxembourg whose solo dance and dialogue with her minstrel leads to the selection of one of the assembled knights as her partner.[30]

Some mimed dance-songs met not with aristocratic favour but with clerical disapproval, for Pope Gregory's policy of rededicating the old shrines to the Christian god meant that it was to these former sites of pagan worship that the faithful returned for their devotions. Hence the occurence of so many medieval indictments of 'wanton' dance and song in churches and churchyards, the best-known appearing in *Handlyng Synne*, Robert Mannyng's thirteenth-century adaptation of the Anglo-Norman *Manuel des Pechiez* by William of Waddington,[31] which relates an eleventh-century legend from Kölbigk in Saxony, in which a priest, disturbed in the celebration of Christmas Mass by the noise of revellers including his own daughter Ava, singing and dancing a *karolle* (round dance) about the church, laid a curse on them so that they were compelled to continue their dance for a year without respite.

> As sone as the preste hadde so spoke,
> Every handle yn outher so fast was loke,
> That no man myght with no wundyr
> That twelvemonthe parte hem asundyr.   (9087—90)

The words sung by the dancers of Kölbigk imply that a dramatic element was present: Mannyng's version of the Latin lyric reads:

> By the *leved* wode rode Bevolyne,   leafy
> Wyth hym he ledde feyre Merswyne;
> Why stonde we? why go we noght?   (9049—51)

which suggests that two dancers mimed the parts of Bevolyne and Merswyne.

Giraldus Cambrensis tells of churchyard revels in his *Gemma Ecclesiastica* (c. 1195), where a priest from Worcestershire, having been kept awake all night by the amorous songs and dances in his churchyard, began the morning service by singing the refrain 'Swete lamman, dhin are [Sweet lover, have mercy]' instead of the customary '*Dominus vobiscum* [The Lord be with you]'. This shocking incident led his bishop to pronounce an anathema upon anyone ever heard singing the song again within the diocese.[32] In his *Itinerarium Cambriae* (c. 1188)

15

Giraldus also draws attention to a Breconshire custom at the festival of St Elined or Almedda in August, linking dance-song and mimetic action: here men and women could then be seen dancing and singing in church and churchyard, falling as if in a trance, then leaping up to mime labours unlawfully performed on feast days. One man ploughed, another goaded oxen forward, another pursued the cobbler's craft, another that of the tanner, one girl drew thread from the distaff and wound it on the spindle, another arranged threads for the web, another appeared to weave. On being brought into church before the altar, they suddenly came to themselves again.

Dance-songs were performed in churches and churchyards of Europe during the whole medieval period; Chambers cites instances of clerical denunciations of these acts of sacrilege going back to the sixth century.[33] A decree of the Council of Rome in 826 is typical of them all: 'there are certain people, chiefly women, who on festivals, holy days, and saints' days, are not delighted to attend because of desire for those things by which they ought to be delighted, but are concerned to come in order to dance, to sing shameful words, to perform choric dances, behaving just like pagans'. Not only the laity strayed from the narrow paths of righteousness: according to *The Chronicle of Lanercost*, in 1282 one John, a priest, compelled the young girls of his parish of Inverkeithing to join in a processional dance-song in honour of Priapus during Easter week, while he not only carried at the head of the dancers a pole topped with the phallus, but joining in the dancing himself, stirred the spectators 'to wantonness by mimed actions and shameless words'.[34] Today clerical aberrations of a similar kind, while not unknown, are less ingenuously revealed.

It was possibly to divert tendencies like Father John's that in parts of Europe, notably in France and Flanders, the medieval Church permitted official clerical festivities such as the Christmas week Feast of Fools or of Asses, and the ceremony of selecting a Boy Bishop, enabling minor clergy and choristers to relax liturgical discipline a little. However, the permissible celebrations frequently went beyond the bounds of propriety.[35] The Feast of Fools took place at the Festival of the Circumcision on 1 January, when sub-deacons conducted the church services, much as a Lord of Misrule at court or in noble households presided over the licensed anarchy during the twelve days of Christmas. This vacation from adherence to the regular observances allowed the minor clergy to make 'unauthorised' additions to the services, often as parodies of the set liturgy: a donkey would be brought into the cathedral or monastery church, providing an excuse for a burlesque extension of the service in the 'Prose of the Ass', a pastiche Christian hymn sung with a chorus of 'hee-haws'. Sometimes the liturgical responses came in the form of braying or gibberish. Drinking was freely carried on and the altar censed not with incense but with smoke from puddings, sausages, or the soles of an old pair of shoes. The participants wore hideous and monstrous masks, fools' clothing or female costume might be adopted, mock precentors were drenched with buckets of genuine water, lewd songs were sung, clerics danced, ran or leapt about the church, and similar antics were performed in the streets, where the clergy rode round in shabby carts using indecent gestures and filthy language to amuse the people. It is hardly surprising that the Church was constantly fighting to control the proceedings in the interest of decency.

Choirboys were often allowed to enjoy less outrageous revels on the Feast of the Holy Innocents (28 December), when they took control of the liturgical proceedings, led by one of their number who had been elected Boy Bishop (*Episcopus Puerorum*) usually on St Nicholas's Day (6 December). This rather endearing figure was especially popular in France and England: he presided over the services of the day, often preaching a Mass sermon, and carried out a number of episcopal functions, processing to various appropriate establishments such as the palace of the true bishop, local convents and hospitals, where refreshments suitable for choirboys were frequently provided. In the liturgical Rouen prophet play or *Festum Asinorum* (see p. 43 below), in which figures (among them Balaam's ass and the Erythraean Sibyl) appear prophesying the birth of the Messiah, an acting part is assigned to the Boy Bishop. Not only cathedrals but religious houses too had their Boy Bishop, and nunneries were known to elect a mock abbess.

Similarly uninhibited activities were commonplace, though not always countenanced, throughout the Middle Ages.[36] Articles drawn up in connection with the Provisions of Oxford in 1253 condemn the playing of *ludi* (whose meaning includes plays as well as games) among other abuses of consecrated places, and prohibitions from the Synods of Exeter in 1287 and York in 1367, from the chapter of Wells Cathedral *c.* 1338, and from William of Wykeham, Bishop of Winchester, in 1384, testify to the Church's difficulties in trying to stamp out the use of church premises and precincts for the pastimes and entertainments of an apparently impervious laity. The Exeter decree speaks of 'wrestling-matches, dancing to the singing of songs, or other disgraceful games . . . theatrical plays and shows by jesters [*ludos theatrales et ludibriorium spectacula*]'. *Handlyng Synne* is explicit, if leaden footed on the subject:

> Karolles, wrastlynges, or *somour* games,   summer
> Who-so ever haunteth any swyche shames
> Yn cherche, other yn chercheyerd,
> Of sacrylage he may be a-ferd;
> Or entyrludes, or syngynge,
> Or tabure bete, or other pypynge,
> Alle swyche thyng forbodyn es,
> Whyle the prest stondeth at messe.   (8987—94)[37]

As late as 1576 Archbishop Edmund Grindal in his Visitation Articles of that year still found it necessary to enquire

whether the minister and churchwardens have suffered any lords of misrule or summer lords or ladies, or any disguised persons, or others, in Christmas or at May-games, or any morris-dancers, or at any other times, to come unreverently into the church or churchyard, and there to dance, or play any unseemly parts, with scoffs, jests, wanton gestures, or ribald talk, *namely* in the time of Common Prayer.[38]

*especially

Presumably Grindal, no witch-hunter but an 'establishment liberal',[39] had evidence that such activities were actually taking place.

It was not only games, dance-songs, and plays in churchyards and churches that won clerical disapproval: the choice of location merely compounded offences already heinous enough. A sermon preserved in an early thirteenth-century manuscript (Trinity College, Cambridge MS B 1.45) takes for its text a couplet from a love-song of its day, and the comment which follows suggests that secular amusements, wherever they might be enjoyed, were looked on askance by the clergy and the pious-minded:

> Atte wrastlinge my lemman i *ches*   chose
> and atte ston-kasting i *him for-les*   let him go

... Mi *leve* frend, wilde wimmen & †golme† ‡i mi contreie‡,, wan §he§ gon o the ring, among manie othere songis that ‖litil ben wort ‖ that ¶tei ¶ singin, so sein thei thus.[40]

*dear †men ‡in my region §they ‖are worthless ¶they

Later in the same century Robert Grosseteste, Bishop of Lincoln from 1235 to 1253, issued prohibitions against secular diversions common in his diocese,[41] which evidently included wrestling for the ram, a village sport Chaucer refers to in describing the Miller in the Prologue to *The Canterbury Tales*:

> At wrastling he wolde have alwey the ram   (548).

A fifteenth-century Robin Hood play from East Anglia reveals that wrestling was a popular ingredient in drama in the Middle Ages; Shakespeare may have drawn on the tradition in *As You Like It*. Wrestling occurs in the Chester cycle play of the shepherds (Play 7) where bouts fought between the shepherds and their boy, who overthrows them, symbolise the Christ child's victory over sin and death.

In a letter of *c.* 1244 Bishop Grosseteste forbids his clergy to appear in 'plays [games?] which they call the Bringing-forth of May, or of Autumn [*ludos quos vocant Inductionem Maii, sive Autumni*], wording which suggests that the bishop may be referring to traditional pagan spring and harvest customs. Grosseteste links to this disapproval of diocesan clerics performing in 'plays which they call miracles [*ludos quos vocant miracula*]'. Bishop Walter de Chanteloup of Worcester anticipated Grosseteste's attitude to popular sports in his own prohibitions of 1240, instructing his clergy 'that they should not countenance the production of "King and Queen" plays, nor ram-raisings, nor the holding of public wrestling contests, nor disgusting gild-ales [*nec sustineant ludos fieri de Rege et Regina, nec arietas levari, nec palaestras publicas fieri, nec gildales inhonestas*]', the 'King and Queen' plays possibly being analogous to Grosseteste's *Inductio Maii*. (The 'ram raising' may be a reference to setting rams' horns on the top of a maypole, as Glynne Wickham suggests,[42] or it may have been some kind of trial of strength involving a ram.) A 'somerkyng' received twelve pence reward at Winchester College in 1412. Another 'mockery king' ritual was being enacted at Norwich in 1443 when a riot took place during a ride by the 'kyng of Crestmesse' with a crown and sceptre, one John Gladman of the 'Bachery guild', the citizens being fined 1000 marks. Gladman (has the name any significance?)

who was ever, and at thys *our* is, a man of †sad† disposition, and trewe and feythfull to God and to the Kyng, of disporte as hath ben acustomed in ony cite or burgh thorowe alle this realme, on Tuesday in the last ende of Cristemesse, viz, ‡Fastyngonge Tuesday‡, mad a disport with his neyghbours, havyng his hors §trappyd§ with tynefoyle and other nyse disgisyn things, corouned as kyng of Cristemesse, in tokyn that all mirthis that seson shuld end, with the twelve monthes of the yere afore hym, yche moneth disguysyd after the seson requiryd, and Lenton clad in whyte and redheryngs skynnys, and his hors trapped with oyster shell after him, in tokyn that sadnese shuld folowe, and an holy tyme, and so rod in diverse stretis of the cite, with other peple with hym disguysyd, makyng myrth and disportes and plays.[43]

*hour †serious ‡Shrove Tuesday §adorned

Similar customs had not died out by 1572 when a letter to the Mayor of York from Archbishop Grindal and his Ecclesiastical Commissioners dated 13 November of that year, forbade the continuance of

a verie rude and barbarouse custome mainteyned in this citie, And in no other citie or towne of this Realme to our knowledge, that yerelie upon *St Thomas Daie* before Christmas two disguised persons called Yule and Yules wief should ryde thorow the cite verey undecentlie and uncomelie Drawyng great concurses of people after them to gaise, often times committinge other enormities.[44]

*21 December

Plays associated with Robin Hood also persisted late. In a letter of 16 April 1473 Sir John Paston regretted his excessive generosity to his servants, including one W. Woode who had promised to stay with him and whose talents as an amateur actor he had valued: 'I have kepyd hym thys iij yere to pleye Seynt Jorge *and* Robynhod *and* Shryff off Notyngham, and now when I wolde have good horse [horsemen], he is goon in-to Bernysdale, and I wyth-owt a kepere'.[45] A fragment of what is probably the summer play which Woode performed has been preserved (see p. 19 above); in it Robin Hood engages in a series of sporting contests with a knight, competing at archery, stone-throwing, wrestling, and finally in a sword-fight, as a result of which Robin beheads his opponent. The play also reveals the close links once binding drama and what we now think of as sport — links perpetuated by the cinema which has created films purely to exhibit the feats of athletic heroes.

Robin Hood plays and games continued in vogue for much of the sixteenth century; in the first year of Henry VIII's reign the king and some companions invaded the queen's chamber at Westminster as Edward Hall recounts:

his grace therles of Essex, Wilshire, and other noble menne, to the nombre, of twelve, came sodainly in a mornyng, into the Quenes Chambre, all appareled in shorte cotes, of Kentish Kendal, with hodes on their heddes, and hosen of the same, every one of them, his bowe and arrowes, and a sworde and a bucklar, like outlawes, or Robyn Hodes men, whereof the Quene, the Ladies, and al other there, were abashed, as well for the straunge sight, as also for their sodain commyng, and after certain daunces, and pastime made, thei departed.[46]

Richard Morison, a Protestant polemicist, writing in about 1535 deplored the popularity of Robin Hood plays which led in his view not only to 'lewdness and ribaldry' but encouraged civil disobedience: 'these good bloodes go about for to take from the shiref of Notyngham one that for offendyng the lawes shulde have suffered execution.'[47] Hugh Latimer, in a sermon preached before Edward VI in April 1549, pays rueful tribute to the popularity of the ritual fund-collecting tour that went on in Robin Hood's name on 1 May:

I came once my selfe to a place, rydyng on a jornay homewarde from London, and I sente worde over nyghte into the toune that I would preach there in ye morninge because it was holyday; and me thought it was an holye dayes woreke, The church stode in my waye, and I toke my horsse, and my companye, and went thither, I thoughte I shoulde have founde a greate companye in the church, and when I came there, the churche dore was faste locked.

I tarried there halfe an houer and more, at last the keye was founde, and one of the parishe commes to me and sayes, 'Syr thys is a busye daye with us, we can not heare you, it is Robyn Hoodes daye The parishe are gone abrode to gather for Robyn Hoode, I praye you *let* them not.' I was fayne there to geve place to Robyn Hoode, I thought my †rochet† shoulde have bene regarded, thoughe I were not, but it woulde not serve, it was fayn to geve place to Robyn Hoodes men.

It is no laughynge matter, my friendes, it is a wepyng matter, a heavy matter, a heavy matter, under the pretence of gatherynge for Robyn Hoode, a traytore, and a thefe, to put out a preacher, to have hys office lesse estemed, to prefer Robyn Hod before the ministracion of Gods word.[48]

*hinder †surplice

Thirty years later George Gilpin, satirising Roman Catholic observances in *The Bee hive of the Romishe Churche*, could still allude to the plays' popularity: 'a man doeth often spende a pennie or two, to see a play of Robin Hood, or a Morisse daunse, which were a great deale better bestowed uppon these apishe toies of these good Priests, which counterfeite all these matters so handsomlie, that it will do a man as much good to see them, as in frostie weather to goe naked'.[49]

Any account of medieval stage conditions must acknowledge the presence of these and similar traditional ceremonies, stemming from primitive pagan rites, and never quite assimilated or extinguished by Church or State. Alongside the newer acceptable forms of drama, the older forms retained much of their disreputable vigour and continuity. Possibly undue zeal is bestowed periodically on researches linking these pagan customs and survivals with the rise of medieval religious drama,[50] but such labours at least serve to remind us that dramatic activity in the Middle Ages was not solely confined to the dissemination of Christian doctrine or the entertainment of royalty. The common people had their theatre too.

2

CLASSIC AND CHRISTIAN

Acting in Song, especially in *Dialogues*, hath an extreme Good Grace: I say *Acting*, not *Dancing* (For that is a Meane and Vulgar Thing;) . . .

Francis Bacon, *Of Maskes and Triumphs*

Contemporary observers eager to relate the moral decline of the West to its apparently degenerating tastes in entertainment are quick to find support for their diagnosis in the fate of the Roman Empire. Certainly, whether regarded as the cause or effect of decadence, for several centuries before the partition of the empire in AD 395 the Roman stage was creatively moribund. Under the emperors a penchant for display, slaughter, and conspicuous licence and expense testified to its decline: the elder Pliny writes of a temporary playhouse of 58 BC able to accommodate 80,000 spectators, and of two theatres which could be swung round on pivots to form one vast amphitheatre,[1] and when Pompey had the first permanent theatre built at Rome in 55 BC, Cicero was moved to ask rhetorically:

what pleasure can there be in the sight of six hundred mules in the *Clytaemnestra*, or of three thousand bowls in the *Trojan Horse* or of the varied accoutrements of foot and horse in some big battle? . . . what pleasure can it possibly be to a man of culture, when either a puny human being is mangled by a most powerful beast, or a splendid beast is transfixed with a hunting-spear?[2]

For the ruling class, the provision of such spectacles was perhaps a necessary factor in ensuring the quiescence of an unruly populace, but although the theatre played an important part in the life of imperial Rome, the quality of its dramatic offerings was manifestly inferior to what had gone before. Little if any original straight drama was produced under the emperors, most Latin authors, like many mid-Victorians, regarding writing for the public stage as beneath the dignity of a respectable literary figure. The chief dramatic species in imperial Rome, outside the athletic extravaganzas of arena, circus, and stadium, were traditional popular farces or *fabulae Atellanae*, the newer genre of pantomime officially introduced in its elaborated form in 22 BC, and mime, probably the most widespread type of Roman stage entertainment.

22

The *fabulae Atellanae*, short farcical plays of rustic origin surviving from republican days, featured stock comic characters — fool, malicious hunchback, yokel, old man — wearing grotesque masks; their varied content might include animal impersonation, political satire and mythological burlesque, but untoward occurences in everyday life provided the principal subject-matter; the most significant ingredient was probably the players' use of popular improvisatory techniques such as extempore topical allusions and off-the-cuff repartee. Pantomime originated with dance, and the central figure was invariably, as in the Japanese Noh theatre, a masked dancer miming on a stage to specially composed words sung by a chorus, accompanied by musicians playing flutes, pipes and cymbals. The player might appear in several different rôles in a single piece, a skilled performer priding himself on his histrionic versatility as well as on his physical agility and interpretative flair. Lucian of Samosata, writing in the second century, praises the pantomime artist: 'Wondrous art! — on the same day, he is mad Athamas and shrinking Ino; he is Atreus, and again he is Thyestes, and next Aegisthus or Aerope; all one man's work.'[3] Generally the subjects of pantomime were elegantly and stylishly treated, even when elements of lasciviousness and deliberate titillation predominated.

Mime, the most primitive, flexible, and permanent of Roman stage diversions, originated in shows given by bands of itinerant players, travelling from town to town and setting up their simple platform-stage backed by a curtain wherever they found a suitable playing-place and a potential paying audience. The genre always embraced a wide range of performers, and programmes might involve juggling or acrobatics, acts of mimicry, dancing, and singing, as well as the staging of short amusing sketches partly improvised on stock themes. As time went by, mimes came to be staged at regular theatres as well as in the homes of private citizens, and some nobles even maintained their own troupes, but although winning favour from educated and influential citizens, mime's principal aim was to amuse the common people, and its traditional subjects, while including romantic themes such as that of Hero and Leander, ranged through political satire, burlesque of the pagan gods, and farcically stupid behaviour, to adultery and sexual inversion, while its language and tone were unrefined and frequently lewd. Its tendency towards the physically explicit culminated in the second century AD with the Emperor Heliogabalus's reputed order that the sex act should no longer be simulated but should take place in actuality on the mime stage.[4]

Heliogabalus was not the only Roman emperor to further stage activities: Julius Caesar, Augustus Caesar and Caligula all encouraged theatrical presentation of different types, while Nero is reported to have given solo impersonations including one of Canace in labour,[5] and the Emperor Commodus (AD 180–92), himself apparently an expert dancer and singer, was not only a generous patron of popular entertainers but appeared as a gladiator in the public arena. The elder Gordian in AD 238 had stage plays produced at his own expense in the main cities of Campania, Etruria, and Picenum; Aurelian (270–5) 'took a strange delight in the mimes', while the same authority informs us that the palace of Carinus (284–5) was crowded with performers of mime and pantomime, singers, courtesans, and bawds. An account of Julian the Apostate (360–3) providing dramatic performances for the soldiers during the Persian campaign of 363 is also extant, although he left on record his personal view that priests of Mithras and pious laymen should avoid the public theatres altogether.[6]

By Julian's time Christianity was well established as a force in Roman life, Constantine the Great issuing the edict permitting its toleration as a state religion in 313; in 378 it was adopted as the official Roman belief, but during the centuries while it was gaining support, it offered a tempting target to the mime stage. An account survives of a mime mocking a fool's death-bed conversion to Christianity, which includes a burlesque christening in a deep tub of tepid water amid much comic horseplay: unfortunately for theatre historians, though not for hagiographers, the account breaks off to describe how sundry performers became genuinely inspired by the faith they were ridiculing, and made an instant affirmation of Christian belief, suffering martyrdom at the hands of the authorities. A tale from the Egyptian town of Antinoe, in the third century, involves a *mimus* named Philemon who for amusement's sake agreed to save from official persecution a Christian priest enjoined to make sacrifice at the altar of the pagan gods. The disguised Philemon, performing the appropriate rites in the civic prefect's presence on behalf of the timid cleric, suddenly became filled with divine inspiration, and not only revealed himself to the watching crowd for the man he really was, but declared his instantaneous belief in the sacred truth which he had been prepared to treat flippantly. Adamant in his assertion that he now believed in Christ, he too was put to death, rejoicing in his new-found faith.[7]

The mime stage was no more antagonistic to the Christian religion than it had been to pagan beliefs and ceremonies, ridiculing the older classical deities quite as frequently as it did the absurdities of the newer faith, but the early Christians deplored levity about solemn matters, and founded an enduring tradition of censure for a form of art which permitted these things to be shown. Christianity, 'emerging from Syria with a prejudice against disguisings' (Chambers), and with strict Hebraic notions concerning the divisions between truth and falsehood, found its suspicions confirmed by what it saw as the dubious morality of Roman theatrical entertainments and of those who supplied them, and that the mime stage did not shrink from ridiculing even the most sacred of truths was surely final confirmation that here indeed was the devil's own personal and peculiar dwelling-place. Typical are the sentiments of Tertullian (*c.* 155 − *c.* 222) in his *De Spectaculis* of *c.* 200, in which he fulminates not merely against the immorality and cruelties of the Roman stage, but against the very art of acting itself:

Will God be pleased with the man who alters his appearance with a razor, [mime actors often shaved their heads] betraying his own face, which, not content with making it resemble Saturn, and Isis, and Bacchus, he exposes to the additional insult of slapping, as if mocking the Lord's command [i.e. to turn the other cheek] ... In the same way the devil raised the tragic actor up on his buskins, since 'no man can add one cubit to his stature' and he wants to make Christ a liar. Again I ask whether this business of masks in fact pleases God, who forbids the making of any likeness, his own image in particular? The Author of Truth hates whatever is untrue; in his sight everything fabricated is corrupt. In the same way he will not approve of an assumed voice, sex, or age, or anyone who displays love, anger, sighs, and tears: for he condemns every kind of falsehood. Moreover, when in his law he ordains that the man who wears female dress is accursed, how will he judge the pantomime actor who sways around in imitation of a woman?[8]

Yet, given the objectivity of hindsight, it would be wrong to accept a totally negative picture of the Roman stage. While we can only regret that so much of what it offered its audiences was evidently tasteless, trivial, and even depraved, we cannot necessarily argue that it was technically inept or artistically incompetent. The leading performers of mime and pantomime were highly praised for their skill and grace, and their ability to please and delight their audiences, which would suggest that, while their material possessed little aesthetic worth, its presentation was not without merit. Whatever the deficiencies of its drama as literature, and its stage as a moral force, the Roman Empire did support a flourishing and talented stage profession which commanded a wide variety of theatrical skills and worked within popular traditions of considerable vitality. All but the finest tastes appear to have been catered for in its repertoire, and while farce, pantomime, and mime were all open to abuse, their techniques ensured that the tradition of the professional stage was somehow maintained throughout the early Christian centuries. Whatever the cause, by some means a legacy of song, dance, mimicry, and comedy was bequeathed to the popular entertainers of the Middle Ages.

Some evidence for the continuance of stage entertainments following the fall of the Western Roman Empire in the fifth century is available, but often the chief problem is to decide which particular branch of the theatrical arts is alluded to. The early Middle Ages had an extensive range of Latin terms for entertainers, *mimi, histriones, scenici,* and *joculatores* among them, but since such titles are not applied consistently from writer to writer, place to place, or century to century, it is often impossible to determine whether we are glimpsing a minstrel diverting guests at a feast, a speaker or singer of recitations, an actor taking part in a play, or what we should now think of as a variety or cabaret artist. Terms used for entertainments are equally ambivalent, and it is unlikely that any passage can be said to indicate that what we should recognise as a play was being presented. Yet some may find the simple equation that 'legitimate drama' died more or less completely after the fall of the Roman Empire in the West, and miraculously sprang up again like the Padstow 'Oss hard to accept.

Many authorities now believe that the Roman actors of mimes again joined forces with the main body of nomadic performers whose activities can be traced all through the period,[9] and strictures about their conduct and appearance from disapproving ecclesiastics and conciliar sources, as well as some pictorial evidence, testify to the continuing vitality of the mime players. Masters of improvisation, accustomed to adapt themselves to varying circumstances, in demand as much for private functions such as banquets and other festivities as they were for shows on street-corners and at fairs, it is unlikely that the *mimi* failed to weather barbarian assaults on cities where they enjoyed so much prestige, even if they now had to 'rub shoulders and contend for *denarii* with jugglers and with rope-dancers, with out-at-elbows gladiators and beast-tamers'.[10] There was a thriving theatre in the Eastern Empire, and even in the West, though the conquering Germanic kings regarded the professional stage with suspicion, they allowed themselves to be diverted by its performers. When Attila gave a banquet in 448 for an embassy from Constantinople, his guests were treated to a recital narrating heroic deeds of valour, followed by buffoonery from a Scythian and a Moorish clown, while Theodoric II, Visigoth king of Gaul (*c.* 460) occasionally permitted entertainers to perform before him at supper so long as they forced none of his guests to endure scurrilities, and ensured that 'virtue should charm the soul as much as singing did the ear [*non minus mulcet virtus animum quam cantus auditum*]'.[11]

Records now show a gap of some two hundred years, but the evidence suggests that dramatic performances by mime players continued: the English clergy were warned at the Council of Rome in 679 not to maintain the services of musicians or to permit revels or plays (*iocos vel ludos*) to be staged for their benefit, while one of the canons promulgated at Clovesho in 747 warns bishops to beware that monasteries do not become the resort of what sound like travelling troupes of variety entertainers. A Carolingian capitulary of 789 threatens any player donning clerical clothing with corporal punishment and exile, while a biographer in about 835 tells us that the Emperor Louis I consented to be entertained at his banquets by performers including *mimi*; fairly positive evidence comes from Edgar, the reformist king of the English, in about 960 when he complains that English monasteries are so decadent that the *mimi* mock them in song and dance (action?) in the market-places (*mimi cantant et saltant in triviis*).

When true drama re-emerges from the shadows and precise details of its presentation are recorded, it is firmly under the auspices of the Roman Catholic Church, but even then we must not ignore the survival of classical influence, most particularly in the plays of Hrotswitha (*c.* 935—*c.* 1002), a Benedictine Abbess of Gandersheim, now in Lower Saxony, who composed six energetic religious dramas said to have been inspired by her desire to emulate the Latin comedies of Terence.[12] Whether or not Hrotswitha had actually witnessed professional performances of Roman comedy, her plays reveal a good deal of understanding of the playwright's craft, and the claim that they were written merely for recitation or as 'closet dramas' has lost ground in recent years. Indications that Terence's plays *were* in fact acted during the period stem from a ninth- or tenth-century fragment known as *Terentius et Delusor (Terence and the Detractor*, or possibly *the Player*), which may have served as a prologue to a revival (recitation or stage performance?) of one of the Roman's comedies.[13] In the fragment, the figure of the Latin playwright steps on stage to answer the charge that his plays are old fashioned and boring, and possibly he proceeded to give a performance of his own work in refutation, reciting the words while actors mimed out the action, in the manner thought to be characteristic of actual Roman performances. Richard Axton suggests that this mode of separation between actors and narrator would mean that the cast (probably professional players) would not need to learn complicated

Latin speeches, simply improvising to the narrator's story-line, while the learned author or narrator avoided the stigma of too close an association with the acting fraternity. While we might find it incongruous today to have dramatic narrative and action handled by different participants, oral recitation was the most familiar medieval method of disseminating literature, and the impersonation of different voices in passages of dialogue would have been quite usual.[14] Similar methods of presentation occur in ancient rituals,[15] and a combination of recitation and mimetic action seemed later quite an acceptable method of presenting medieval drama (cf. pp. 29, 31, 48–9, 66, 75, 91–2, 186 below).

Hrotswitha's plays could have been performed in this manner or staged in the conventional way; possibly they were only meant for reading aloud or as spirited literary exercises. Yet their stagecraft and dramatic potentialities make it hard to accept the latter view, and while they contain farcical and even erotic ingredients, these did not necessarily render it impossible for an educated aristocratic tenth-century canoness and her fellows to have them staged in their convent, although admittedly, Hrotswitha's aim in writing her plays was to reconcile the fatal appeal of Terence with a Christian message, and she never speaks of any desire to see her plays physically staged. About Hrotswitha's familiarity with a living tradition of performance, there must always be some doubt, but her apparently isolated achievement reminds us that six colourful and effective medieval religious dramas were inspired not by the Roman Catholic liturgy (the prescribed forms of worship), but by a classical playwright, and possibly by actors who had inherited classical theatre traditions.

Around the twelfth century, when church-drama was strongly developed, another revival of interest in the classical theatre occured with attempts to recreate the spirit if not the form of Latin comedy by the composition of about twenty so-called 'elegiac comedies' in the scholarly schools of England and northern France, which include elements very close to those of the mime tradition. Though often referred to as *comoediae*, these were Latin poems rather than plays, consisting of a mixture of narrative and dialogue, as Hrotswitha's plays do not. The best known is the *Geta*, attributed to Vitalis of Blois, on the theme of adultery and indirectly based on Plautus's *Amphitruo* (later adapted by Shakespeare in *The Comedy of Errors*); it introduces comic routines for two servants, the sprightly Geta and the stolid Birria, which have a popular flavour. The piece still has a narrative framework, including the use of 'he said', 'he asked', to introduce direct speech, but we should not regard this as evidence against live performance. As Grace Frank suggests, this popular school-book could have proved suitable for presentation 'by ambitious masters and their pupils'.[16]

From about the same period come the *comoediae Horatianae*, dramatic monologues with narrative links, a few of which eliminate the links altogether; the best are undoubtedly the farces *Babio* and *Pamphilus*, both of which blend acquaintance with classical authors such as Plautus and Ovid with keen first-hand observation of day-to-day domestic disturbances, as does the early Tudor comedy *Gammer Gurton's Nedle*. It has been argued[17] that these dramas, like Hrotswitha's, despite their learned affiliations, reveal a debt to live acted drama, and although a paucity of stage directions makes it difficult to accept such a view without question, ascriptions of speeches and a few stage directions in some manuscripts do indicate that they may have been later adapted for professional performance. The action is certainly lively: in *Babio* the stupid old farmer of the title vainly tries to seduce the young girl Viola, but is sadly duped, not only through losing Viola to the young squire, but also by his own wife Petula, who in his absence takes his servant Fodius as her own lover; *Pamphilus* relates how a young man with the assistance of an old woman as go-between persuades his not-too-reluctant girl-friend to sleep with him, a theme found in numerous medieval tales, among them the Middle English poem *Dame Sirith* and the fragmentary *Interludium de Clerico et Puella* (*The Interlude of the Clerk and the Girl*). There are certainly grounds for thinking that a number of routines from earlier mime drama found their way into both *Babio* and *Pamphilus*.

A number of later medieval farces also seem to owe a debt to the traditions of the classical mime. *The Interlude of the Clerk and the Girl* is one of a regrettably small group of existing pieces employing mime techniques, which includes the Flemish *Le Garçon et l'Aveugle* (*The Boy and the Blind Man, c. 1270*) — a routine in which an old blind rogue is cheated by a young sighted one — as well as some excellent farces of everyday domestic life from France, Spain, Germany, and Holland. These, although late, are probably linked with the popular entertainments of medieval Europe and those of imperial Rome. That drama discovered a new point of departure under the auspices of the Church is probable, but we must not dismiss the possibility that Latin dramas were performed, nor disregard the continued existence of professional entertainers of the kind known to classical Rome. Indeed some of those secular and comic elements which came to extend the appeal of medieval drama possibly derive from popular mime dramas: Benjamin

Hunningher has gone so far as to suggest that it was professional *mimi* rather than clerics who performed the first religious plays, being employed by the Church for that very purpose.[18] Whatever one makes of this somewhat eccentric view (see pp. 189–90 below) it seems clear that while the Church provided the main impetus towards a new mode of dramatic expression, classical stage traditions in the medieval period were far from moribund.

Although outraged prelates and fathers might inveigh against the scurrilities and obscenities of the Roman *mimi* and *pantomimi*, there is little doubt that, from a fairly early date, the Christian Church sought to incorporate man's histrionic instincts into its worship rather than to suppress them. Tertullian in *De Spectaculis*, after castigating the entertainments offered in circus and amphitheatre, urges Christians to seek their theatrical pleasures within the church itself, and to slake their thirst for *spectacula* in the faith they profess:

What greater pleasure is there than scorn for pleasure, contempt for the times, true freedom, a clear conscience, a full life, with no fear of death? What greater pleasure than to trample the gods of the people underfoot, to cast out demons, to heal diseases, to seek revelations, to live for God? These are the pleasures and the spectacles fit for Christians, holy, eternal, and free; take these for your circus games, contemplate the chariot race of the years, the seasons slipping past, count the completed circuits, look for the finishing post of the final consummation, guard the fellowship of the church, rise at God's starting-signal, stand to attention at the angelic trumpet, and glory in the palms of martyrdom.[19]

But as the centuries passed, the Church felt the need to celebrate some of its festal days by giving scope to the mimetic urge within the framework of its liturgy, the officially prescribed canon of worship, the chief feature of which was the observance of Divine Offices including the Mass. Whether or not the impetus came from a desire deliberately to combat the influence of pagan, classical, or popular kinds of theatre, such a policy would certainly not be inconsistent with the evangelising practices of the Church throughout the medieval period.

The manner in which Latin church-drama evolved from certain musical and literary developments within the services for Easter Day has now found general if not complete acceptance among scholars,[20] but the existence of several alternatives warns us to be cautious in proclaiming any account of the rise of medieval religious drama to be definitive.

One puzzle is created by the presence in the Old English poem *Christ*, which is partly attributed to Cynewulf (*c.* 750 – *c.* 850), of a thirty-line passage of dialogue between Joseph and Mary, unpunctuated by any third-person narrative and reading exactly like dramatic speech. Pre-dating any other piece of English dramatic literature, it could well derive from some unknown play, and support a theory that religious drama was known in the West at least a century earlier than the earliest extant liturgical play-text.[21] Also noteworthy is an eighth-century fragment on Christ's Harrowing of Hell, a text of sixty lines forming part of the so-called *Book of Cerne*, an Anglo-Saxon miscellany of *c*. 800—25, and recently claimed as the earliest example of a Latin liturgical drama extant.[22] Unfortunately, the work does not appear to be a liturgical text at all, but a passage of private non-liturgical devotion. Nor is the piece irrefutably an acted drama, for choruses of supplication and thanksgiving by the souls in Hell, and similar speeches by Adam and Eve are interspersed with narrative passages in the form of instructional rubrics picked out in red ink, but not couched in the present tense as true stage-directions would surely be. However, it is difficult when one reads of the tearful voices of suppliant souls, of Adam throwing himself at Christ's feet, and of Eve persisting with her weeping, to resist the view that these are intimations to actors performing roles, and although certain portions read more like third-person narration than stage directions, it is arguable that they still govern a performance containing movements and gestures, perhaps something approaching the concert performance of an opera rather than a fully staged play. Since the tone of the fragment is dramatic, it does at least suggest that we should never accept a simple, single explanation of the rise of medieval religious drama.

Similarly an account of the Passion in another Cambridge University manuscript, an eighth-century text of the Gospel of St Luke and St John, has been divided up by a later hand, as if for two soloists, one handling the descriptive portions, the other the words of Christ. Such a practice is found in texts dating from a later period, notably in versions of the sermon *Contra Judaeos, Paganos et Arianos* erroneously attributed to St Augustine, one section of which, quoting prophecies of Christ's coming from Jewish and pagan sources, and subsequently developing into the dramatic *Ordo Prophetarum*, formed a separate *lectio* (reading) frequently used at Christmas Matins, and is occasionally found apportioned among a number of different readers, one of whom reads the main narrative, the others speaking the words of the prophets.[23] The divisions shown in Cambridge manuscripts of the Gospels suggests that this method of delivery may be much older than was once thought, and that liturgical drama may have been influenced by it.

Suggestions that the originals of analogous dramas are not western European but stem from the Byzantine Empire in the East have been advanced for some decades.[24] At least four theatres flourished in Constantinople, offering the same kind of fare as proved popular at Rome, but it has been argued, on slender evidence, that there was a parallel interest in composing Christian literary dramas, evolved from dramatic homilies of the sixth century into live theatrical performances in the church of Hagia Sophia in about 950. It has even been claimed that Byzantine drama influenced the development of religious plays in the West. Its best surviving play, *Christos Paschon* (*Christ's Suffering*), an attempt, dating from a time between the fourth and the twelfth centuries, to write a Christian tragedy on the Passion, is a patchwork utilising scraps from Euripides and other Greek playwrights, which scholars now regard as a literary drama not intended for stage production. However, if the aim were public recitation, a very common form of medieval presentation, it is possible that the play did receive some form of performance. Although links between the Byzantine theatre and that of western Europe are not strong, new evidence for their existence may yet come to light.

That a certain tendency towards drama was present in the ceremonies of the Christian religion from an early date must be granted; when Christians were no longer forced to make their devotions in secret, habits of public worship created many of the conditions from which drama might develop. As Rosemary Woolf points out, the Christian Church possessed 'the outward phenomena of a theatrical performance, a building, an audience, and men speaking or singing words to be listened to and performing actions to be watched ... Action as well as words could have a dramatic character.'[25] Nor were acts of worship confined to church buildings: at some time between 381 and 395 a noble Galician nun named Etheria made a pilgrimage to Palestine and in Jerusalem joined in a Palm Sunday procession to the Mount of Olives led by the bishop;[26] after a reading of the Gospel account of the first Palm Sunday, the procession returning to the city recreated the biblical event by singing 'Blessed is He that cometh in the Name of the Lord', the children carrying palms and olive branches. Similarly on Epiphany eve worshippers made the journey from Jerusalem to Bethlehem, and sang the night service at the grotto of the Holy Manger.

One of the most significant ceremonies described by Etheria is that of the Adoration of the Cross on Good Friday at the church of Golgotha on Mount Calvary: during the service a relic of the true cross was fetched, and while the bishop held the casket containing the relic firmly in his hands, all the people present filed past one by one, bowing down to touch the relic with their foreheads and eyes, finally kissing it before passing on. This eastern custom formed a regular part of the Roman usage by the seventh century, and spreading through the churches of the West, had become very fervently and devoutly practised by the tenth century, by which time the ceremony had come to include the showing of a veiled cross or crucifix to the congregation, the singing of Christ's Reproaches from the cross (the *Improperia*), the unwrapping of the cross, and its placing on the altar.[27]

Associated with the Adoration of the cross (the *Adoratio*) were the originally separate ceremonies known as the *Depositio Crucis* and the *Elevatio Crucis*, in which the cross or crucifix kissed by the congregation would be first wrapped in a napkin or *sudarium* representing Christ's grave-clothes and then symbolically 'buried' by being conveyed to some appropriate resting-place, possibly under the altar, until it was 'elevated' in time for the first Mass of Easter Day. Originally it would seem as if it were customary to hide and restore the communion Host, a ritual doubtless stemming from the practice of reserving the sacrament from the Mass of Maundy Thursday until the Mass of the Presanctified on Good Friday, when the sacrament would be brought from its special place of reservation to the altar, consecration of the Bread and Wine being avoided on Good Friday. Whatever was left of the elements after the service was then wrapped in a cloth and solemnly returned to the place of reservation, a ceremonial which came to symbolise the burial of Christ's shrouded body in the tomb: the earliest evidence for such a custom comes from Augsburg in the middle of the tenth century, but the rite is probably a good deal earlier in origin. Early on Easter morning the remainder of the sacrament was brought out once again for the Mass of Easter, although the evidence from Augsburg is less clear on this point. It is uncertain at what time or in what place a cross or crucifix became substituted for the Host as the central object of the *Depositio* and *Elevatio* ceremonies, or why the exchange was made: suffice it to say that the cross came in time to link together the three rituals of *Adoratio*, *Depositio*, and *Elevatio*, and that the cloth in which it was wrapped, and which remained in the place of reservation when the cross was returned to the altar, became the central feature of another originally separate ceremony performed in some churches and called the *Visitatio*. This took place before the *Te Deum* at the end of Easter Matins, when the clergy processed with lit candles to the 'sepulchre' to recover the *sudarium*. Some scholars believe that part of this ceremony came to consist of a sung dialogue between one or more of the monastic brethren chanting the words of the angel at the tomb on Easter morning, and others responding with the words of the three Marys, and that as small mimetic touches were added, the procession by the whole choir was dropped, the resulting brief exchange between Marys and angel retaining the name *Visitatio Sepulchri.*

The words and music providing the sung dialogue for the scene are an example of what is known to musicologists as a trope, the Latin term *tropus* being used to denote any verbal or musical embellishment to the regular liturgical office.[28] In the ninth and tenth centuries additional words and melodies found their way into the traditional Gregorian liturgy, these new texts amplifying and explaining the sense of passages already present in the office, so that the added tropes were still integral to their context. Troping became a popular fashion, exemplifying the tendency for the sung services to move away from simple plain-chant, which allocated one musical note to one verbal syllable of a sung text, in favour of more elaborate styles where a syllable might acquire several notes, or a whole new melody might be assigned to the last syllable of a word, for example, the final '*-a*' of '*Alleluia*' or the 'mus' of '*Benedicamus*'. The long melodies composed to follow the final '*-a*' of the '*Alleluia*' became so elaborate and important that they seem to have acquired words to assist the singers to remember them, and this particular form of troping became known as a sequence, some of the most famous hymns of the Church — the *Dies Irae*, the *Stabat Mater*, and the *Victimae Paschali* among them — originating in this way.

The precise origins of the vogue for troping are still obscure, but the Benedictine monasteries of St Gall (St Gallen) in Switzerland and St Martial at Limoges in France were the two most important centres of the art, although the technique may have developed first in northern Italy. The composition of the first sequence is attributed to a monk of St Gall, Notker Balbulus ('the Little Stammerer', *c.* 840–912), although he claimed to have learnt the skill from a service-book brought to St Gall from the abbey of Jumièges in Normandy, which had been sacked by the Norsemen in 851.[29] The trope which chiefly interests us here as providing the text of the *Visitatio*, the *Quem Quaeritis* (its name taken from the angelic question to the Marys at Christ's tomb: 'Whom do you seek?'), may be Italian in origin and exists in several other extant texts, but appears earliest in manuscript versions from St Martial and St Gall dating from 920–50, that from St Martial probably pre-dating slightly that from St Gall. Both tropes appear as part of the Mass service, leading into the Introit of the Easter Mass, but neither makes it clear whether the *Quem Quaeritis* trope was originally composed specially for the *Visitatio* at Matins, and then taken into the Mass service, or whether the reverse process occurred. It may be that the *Visitatio* 'borrowed' and expanded a trope first created to embellish and lead into the Introit, as it does in both the earliest versions. Alternatively, the Mass may be borrowed from the previously established *Visitatio* ceremony, reducing the *Quem Quaeritis* text in length in doing so.[30]

Whatever the truth, it seems that by the tenth century the ritual actions of the *Visitatio* ceremonial and the sung words of the *Quem Quaeritis* trope had been brought together to form a basic liturgical unit. The earliest unequivocal evidence for the performance of such a ceremony is found in an English manuscript, the *Regularis Concordia* (*c.* 965–75), a code of rules drawn up by St Æthelwold, Bishop of Winchester from 963–84, for the governance of the Benedictine monastic houses in England, part of which is devoted to the way in which the Divine Office was to be observed in monastic churches. Æthelwold who, with St Dunstan and St Oswald, was responsible for the great revival of Benedictine monasticism in England during the second half of the tenth century,[31] was assisted in compiling the *Regularis Concordia* by monks from the two great foundations at Fleury and Ghent, with the result that the observances laid down derived from a wide variety of western European practices, especially those of Fleury, and are in no way specifically English. However, it has been argued that the *Visitatio Sepulchri* is an original piece of composition specially compiled by the authors of the *Regularis Concordia*,[32] and certainly it is a manuscript from England which contains the earliest extant version of the *Visitatio Sepulchri* to be set out as a piece of Latin church-music drama.

The passage giving the dialogue and instructing the participants is scheduled not as an introduction to the Introit of the Mass, but for a position towards the end of Matins for Easter Day, that is to say, as part of the earliest of the eight separate canonical offices of the day, sung in religious communities between 2 and 2.30 a.m.; some scholars argue that only through its transference from the Mass itself to the Matins service was the trope free to develop into the performance of a play in the sense that we understand the term. In the *Regularis Concordia* and most other versions of the *Visitatio*, the dialogue is placed after a reading of the third and final lesson (*lectio*) of the Matins service with its verse and response (*responsio*), and before the final joyful singing of the *Te Deum*. Its text runs as follows:

While the third lesson is read, four brothers robe themselves, one of whom dressed in an alb enters as if for another purpose and discreetly goes to the place where the sepulchre is, and sits there quietly with a palm in his hand. While the third response is being sung, the remaining three come forward, every one dressed in a cope, carrying thuribles with incense in their hands, and hesitantly like people seeking something, come to the site of the sepulchre. For these things are performed in imitation of the angel sitting in the tomb, and of the women coming with spices to anoint Jesus's body. Consequently when the one sitting there sees the three nearing him, just like people straying about seeking something, he begins to sing sweetly in a moderate voice:

Quem quaeritis in sepulchro, o Christicolae? [Whom do you seek in the tomb, o dwellers in Christ?]

When this has been sung all through, the three reply in unison:

Ihesum Nazarenum crucifixum, o cœlicola. [The crucified Jesus of Nazareth, o dweller in heaven.]

He answers them thus:

Non est hic, surrexit sicut praedixerat; ite, nuntiate quia surrexit a mortuis. [He is not here; he has risen as he foretold; go, announce that he has risen from the dead.]

At his command the three turn to the choir, saying:

Alleluia, resurrexit Dominus, hodie resurrexit leo fortis, Christus, filius Dei. Deo gratias, dicite eia! [Alleluia, the Lord has risen, today the strong lion, Christ the son of God, has risen. Cry joyfully, thanks be to God!]

This being sung, the seated one as if calling them back sings the antiphon:

Venite et videte locum ubi positus erat Dominus, alleluia. [Come and see the place where the Lord was laid, alleluia.]

Singing these words he rises and lifts the curtain, and shows them the place with the cross gone but with the linen cloths in which the cross was wrapped lying there. Having seen this, they put down the thuribles which they carried to the sepulchre, and take up the linen, and spread it out in the sight of the clergy, as if making it plain that the Lord has arisen and is not wrapped in the grave-clothes now; they sing this antiphon:

Surrexit Dominis de sepulchro, qui pro nobis pependit in ligno, alleluia. [The Lord has risen from the tomb, who for our sake hung upon the cross, alleluia.]

And they place the linen upon the altar cloth. When the antiphon is finished, the prior, rejoicing with them in the triumph of our king, who arose after conquering death, begins the hymn *Te Deum laudamus.* [We praise thee, O God]. When this has begun, all the bells peal out together.[33]

The descriptive rubrics make it at least arguable that by about 970 the *Visitatio* had come to be regarded no longer as a liturgical ceremony but as a piece of ritual drama, in which the participants sought (to a necessarily limited extent) to 'play the parts' of the angel and the three Marys, and not merely to carry out actions symbolic of the original happenings. Although no attempt was made to disguise the fact that the three Marys were male clerics in vestments (see Illustration 2), that the ointments carried to anoint Christ's body were in fact censers containing incense, and that the 'place where the sepulchre is' was an altar, or some kind of ornamental structure built into a wall, the 'stage

2   Clerics performing the *Visitatio Sepulchri*: relief from the church at Gustorf, *c.* 1130

directions' suggest a deliberate attempt to convey through mime something resembling lifelike motivation for the women's behaviour. Although others have argued against such a view, it has been maintained that through combining sung dialogue and mimed action for the purpose of worship, Latin liturgical drama had been brought into being.

The most thorough and well-documented opposition to this generally accepted account is that of O. B. Hardison Jr, in his closely argued *Christian Rite and Christian Drama in the Middle Ages*; he believes that we are too prone to make a non-existent distinction between Christian ritual and Christian drama, arguing that liturgical ritual *was* the drama of the early Middle Ages, and that the Mass, the central Roman rite, was already thought of in dramatic terms before the middle of the ninth century, when its symbolism was made to suggest eternal truths by means analogous to those employed in drama. The classic expression of such allegorical interpretations of liturgy is found in the writings of Amalarius, Bishop of Metz (*c.* 780–850), notably in the third book of his *Liber Officialis*, which went through three editions between 821 and 835. His view of the Mass stresses the rising and falling emotional rhythms which give the 'plot' its pattern, the parallels between the celebrant and Christ, the 'supporting roles' of the minor clergy, and the importance of the part played by the congregation, and for Hardison it is these elements which enable us to speak of the Mass itself as ritual drama. To objections that the priest does not actually *impersonate* the figure of Christ, Hardison answers that impersonation is too modern a criterion for determining at what point liturgical ritual becomes drama

(cf. p. 6 above), claiming that by no means every actor accepts impersonation as a necessary ingredient of his art, preferring to think of
himself as identifying with and so *becoming* the character he portrays.
It might be retorted that, even on Hardison's premise, every actor,
whatever his own inner convictions, seeks to persuade us that he cur-
rently represents somebody other than himself whose new if temporary
existence he expects us to accept. This is a different phenomenon from
a priest who, while imitating Christ by performing certain symbolic
actions or by quoting Christ's words at the Last Supper during the consecration of the elements at Mass, does not expect us to accept that he
himself has become Christ. Nor, some have argued, did the priests
taking the rôles of the three Marys in the *Visitatio* play just described,
but their actions in 'straying about as if seeking something' or being
called back by the angel, indicate a degree of representation missing
from the Mass 'play'. A good deal of scholarly argument for and against
this view has been heard in recent years, and it is now frequently
claimed that the *Visitatio* is non-representational and non-dramatic.
As we have already seen, the line between religious celebrations and
drama is very tenuous (see p. 6 above), but many would still argue
that the liturgical 'drama' of the Mass and the semi-dramatic performance of the *Visitatio* lie on different sides of it.

Hardison is also sceptical of the received account of the liturgical
origins of the *Quem Quaeritis* text: he believes that the *Quem Quaeritis*
dialogue was not originally a trope at all, but a liturgical ceremony
first performed as part of the so-called Vigil Mass celebrated before
the dawning of Easter Day, and then shortened and transferred to the
Easter Mass itself as a trope of the Introit (its position in the Limoges
and St Gall texts), and finally, as the text of the *Visitatio* play, to Easter
Matins as in the *Regularis Concordia*. Hardison's arguments derive from
the fact that the Easter Vigil was the last crucial phase of the Lenten
period, culminating in the baptism and confirmation of the cate-
chumens, and a ceremony of illumination in which candles were
kindled and blessed (The Blessing of New Fire), and that to connect
the faithful keeping watch and the Marys visiting the tomb was a
commonplace of the period. Although Hardison's elaborate hypothesis
can never be totally refuted, several musicologists have questioned its
validity, in particular William Smoldon who has shown that the *Quem
Quaeritis* dialogue has all the distinguishing marks of a trope, and
therefore is unlikely to have formed part of the earlier Gregorian
musical traditions to which the Easter Vigil adhered.[34] It is also significant that in Arab-ruled Spanish Castile, where the liturgical rite was

Mozarabic (or, more accurately, Hispanic) and neither trope- nor sequence-writing developed, liturgical drama was unknown.[35]

Hardison is on less disputed ground when he discusses the history of medieval religious drama as a whole, criticising both E. K. Chambers and Karl Young for their proneness to assert or imply that this drama developed in Darwinian style through evolutionary growth, whether by steady organic expansion or by a series of sudden mutations. For both these scholars, liturgical drama evolved in linear fashion from simple beginnings to adopt increasingly complex and elaborate modes, while Chambers, in particular, implied that as it advanced so it developed into vernacular forms, and acquired more 'secular' elements (and by implication became more worthy of attention), and that the final triumph of such a process of 'secularisation' came when drama broke free of the repressive stranglehold of the Church, and, expelled into the open-air because of its demotic indecorousness, reached its apotheosis in the vernacular cycle sequences of Germany, France and, in particular, England. Hardison was able to demonstrate that the simplest types of liturgical drama are not necessarily the earliest, any more than some of its most complex forms are late, and that the vernacular traditions of religious drama did not necessarily develop logically out of Latin. Already other writers had begun to show that the tendency to include secular elements had not in fact been the reason for religious drama's departure from church buildings into the market-place.[36] Moreover, the motives behind the so-called 'secularisation' of the plays were shown to have been quite misunderstood and misinterpreted, the Church only ceasing to support the staging of religious drama at the point when, in England at least, Protestant reformers intervened to suppress the presentation of religious plays entirely.

The precise development of the liturgical drama is impossible to chart. It does seem that the *Visitatio* exchanges, known to England, France and Germany by 1000, remained more or less unaltered for roughly a century; by about the end of the eleventh century some churches, possibly influenced by comparable plays of the Christmas season developed by analogy with the *Quem Quaeritis* dialogue, had created new versions of the plays by drawing on further gospel material for their subject-matter. The Marys' purchase of spices from a spice-seller (*unguentarius*) (St Mark 16. 1) first occurs in a book of tropes from Ripoll in Spain of around 1100,[37] while the earliest version of the scene in which Mary Magdalen mistakes the newly risen Christ for the gardener (St John 20. 11–18), known as the *Hortulanus*, is probably that found in a Norman manuscript used in Sicily dated *c.* 1135,[38] where it is introduced into the *Peregrinus* (*The Pilgrim,* or perhaps *The Traveller*), one of a number of Easter plays depicting Christ's appearance to the disciples on the road to Emmaus (St Luke 24. 13–32).[39] Another element, the race between Peter and John to reach the empty sepulchre (St John 20. 2–10), first occurs in a manuscript from Augsburg of about 1100, although speaking parts are not yet assigned to the apostles, their actions being mimed while a descriptive antiphon is sung;[40] the other principal extension involves the introduction of Pontius Pilate and his placing of a guard on the tomb as related in St Matthew's Gospel, and found in the four most comprehensive plays printed by Young under the title *Ludus Paschalis* (*The Play of Easter*).[41] It must be emphasised that such developments are not simply expansions or cumulative versions of an original nucleus,[42] and not every *Quem Quaeritis* dialogue became incorporated into an 'Easter play'; nor did any of the elaborate plays necessarily evolve from some simpler version according to a regular pattern. But a number of ambitious representations did materialise, such a play often being entitled an *Ordo* or *Officium* (service or office), indicating its continued function as part of the liturgical scheme. The most elaborate *Ludus Paschalis* is a French version from Tours, which only exists in a very confused and fragmentary text, in which the Marys buy spices from two merchants, one an apprentice; another specimen containing vernacular episodes comes from the women's abbey of Origny-Sainte-Benoîte, near St Quentin in France (*c.* 1284), where the three Marys were played by nuns which would obviously have resulted in greater verisimilitude.

Plays are also found treating Christ's Ascension and the events of Pentecost (Whitsunday), while the liturgy of Christ's Passion also produced drama, despite the fact that the church ceremonies themselves were already highly dramatic. There was some development of the *planctus*, a hymn of grief assigned to the Virgin Mary at the foot of the cross, as in the *Planctus Mariae* from the cathedral of Cividale del Friuli in north-west Italy, which contains a wealth of stage-directions in its accompanying rubrics;[43] the *Carmina Burana* manuscript from Benediktbeuern contains two versions of a Passion play,[44] the longer and more elaborate of which also features a *planctus*, some of its stanzas in German. It also contains an entirely original sequence, occupying almost a third of the existing text, in which Mary Magdalen, under diabolical influence, goes with her friends to buy cosmetics to attract a lover, singing as she does so a vernacular chorus song:

Chramer, gip die varwe mier,
div min wengel roete,
da mit ich di iungen man
an ir danch der minnenliebe noete.

Merchant, give me rouge to redden my cheeks, so that I can make the young men fall in love, in spite of themselves.

This has clear affinities with the dance-songs of folk tradition, helping to point up Mary's human worldliness and enabling a secular audience to identify with her.[45]

An even earlier and more elaborate Latin Passion drama was brought to light with the discovery of a play from the Benedictine monastery of Monte Cassino in Italy dated *c*. 1150, at least a hundred years prior to the *Carmina Burana* plays.[46] The incomplete text offers twelve scenes, beginning with Judas's betrayal of Christ and ending with a fragmentary Italian *planctus* from the Virgin Mary at the foot of the cross. A close relationship exists between the Monte Cassino text and a Passion play from Sulmona Cathedral, surviving as a script copied out for the actor playing the part of the Fourth Soldier,[47] indicating that the Sulmona play was greater in scope than even the Monte Cassino work, contained a multiplicity of scenes, and required an elaborate organisation to mount it. The staging of Passion plays, probably of a similar type, is recorded from Siena, Italy, *c*. 1200, and Padua in 1243 or 1244; of the Siena performance we are told that it was presented on Good Friday by decree of the Commune and that the actors were paid out of public funds.[48]

The Christmas season developed its own ceremonial customs just as that of Easter did, though none of them was charged with quite the tension and fervour of the Holy Week ceremonies of *Adoratio, Depositio, Elevatio,* and *Visitatio.* Christmas scenes, similar to the *Quem Quaeritis* exchanges, seem to have developed by analogy in the second half of the eleventh century, taking as their starting-point a trope modelled on that of *Quem Quaeritis*, taking the form of question and answer between singers, later identified as midwives and the shepherds bringing their gifts to the crib:

Quem quaeritis in presepe, pastores, dicite? [Whom do you seek in the manger, shepherds, say?]
Salvatorem Christum Dominum, infantem pannis involutum, secundum sermonem angelicum. [The Saviour Christ the Lord, the child wrapped in swaddling clothes, just as the angel said.]

Eleventh-century texts of this trope diverge little from one another, and the staging details they supply are minimal: it seems clear from one text from Novalesa[49] that two deacons in dalmatics (as midwives?) stood behind the altar which represented the manger, while two cantors from the choir replied for the shepherds. Christmas presentations were freer to expand than those of the Easter season, and Hardison argues that the development of Christmas performances encouraged a comparable growth in the Easter plays, but only a few short plays featuring the shepherds, known as the *Officia Pastorum*, are extant:[50] two versions from Rouen are the fullest and most explicit with regard to theatrical detail. Five or seven youths played the shepherds, two priests the midwives, a choirboy the angel, while others formed the heavenly host. At the Mass which followed, the shepherds took a leading part in the singing of the responses and at the office of Lauds they responded in character once more to the choir's question '*Quem vidistis, pastores, dicite*? [Whom have you seen, shepherds, say?]' with the words '*Natum vidimus et choros angelorum* [We have seen Him who is born, and the angelic chorus]'. Indeed, it was at Lauds that the *pastores* played their fullest role in the liturgical celebrations of Christmas: in Toledo, according to a fourteenth-century breviary, choirboys dressed as shepherds appeared at this service.[51]

It was not the *Officium Pastorum* of Christmas that proved the most popular dramatic subject at this season, but the *Officium Stellae*, the *Ordo Rachelis*, and the *Ordo Prophetarum*.[52] The *Officium Stellae* (*The Play of the Star*), associated with Epiphany (6 January) and the visit of the three Magi to the stable at Bethlehem, possibly developed from two liturgical ceremonies, one connected with the Mass oblation or offertory (the 'collection') in which three cantors dressed as the kings proceeded to the altar with their gifts, guided by a star on a cord, the other linked to the dramatisation of parts of the gospel (*Evangelium*) of the Mass of Epiphany. In both cases the altar represented the manger. Unfortunately, manuscripts in which these ceremonies occur are of uncertain date, and it cannot be proved that Epiphany plays did not take shape without them. Of the versions printed by Young, several incorporate the *pastores* into the action by means of an encounter between the shepherds departing from the stable and the kings approaching it, in which the inquiry '*Quem vidistis, pastores, dicite?*' is transferred to the kings. Some of these plays are the first to feature Herod, an eleventh-century text from Freising Cathedral in Germany being perhaps the earliest to present him as the irate and violent tyrant of later medieval tradition, uttering arrogant boasts, dashing a book of prophecies to the floor, and brandishing his sword.[53]

Two later examples of an Epiphany play are found in the thirteenth-century manuscript, the so-called 'Fleury Play-book' from the monastery of St-Benoît-sur-Loire at Fleury,[54] and in the comprehensive Christmas play from the monastery of Benediktbeuern in Bavaria.[55] Freising and Fleury possess separate plays on the Massacre of the Innocents, known as the *Ordo Rachelis*, the name deriving from St Matthew's Gospel (2. 18) which recalls Jeremiah's prophecy concerning Rachel mourning for her children. An *Officium Stellae* from Laon Cathedral in north-east France incorporates the Massacre, but the monastery of St Martial at Limoges, the Benedictine house at Fleury, and the cathedral at Freising appear to be the only places possessing separate and independent texts of the *Ordo Rachelis*, the latter pair being the most developed of the four versions.

The other branch of Christmas drama was the *Ordo Prophetarum* (see p. 31 above), in which a sequence of Old Testament and pagan prophecies of Christ's coming, taken from the pseudo-Augustinian sermon *Contra Judaeos* and divided among several readers as part of the liturgy of the Christmas period, was turned into an elementary drama, mainly by the suppression of the intervening narrative. Only three full texts exist, from Limoges, Laon, and Rouen, the latter elaborated to the point where twenty-eight prophets are presented; two cases (those of Balaam and Nebuchadnezzar) are made subjects for quite extensive treatment. Prophet plays also appear to have been staged at Tours and the abbey of Einsiedeln in Switzerland and they were particularly popular in France and Spain.

The Benediktbeuern Christmas play combines the *Ordo Prophetarum* with the rest of its Christmas scenes, employing only five prophets, but making much of a semi-comic debate between the turbulent chief of the Jewish synagogue (*Archisynagogus*) and St Augustine, while the shepherd scene is given dramatic tension by the presence of the devil who tries to undermine the angel's joyful tidings, recalling the competition over Mary Magdalen's soul in the Easter play from the same manuscript. A number of predominantly Latin liturgical works contain a small admixture of the vernacular, among them the Benediktbeuern and Monte Cassino Passion plays, and the Origny *Ludus Paschalis*, and Young suggested that these passages may have been introduced as literary ornaments rather than as aids to the uneducated;[56] it is now argued that they reflect that radical shift of piety in the twelfth century which accentuated Christ's humanity and suffering in contrast to his power and majesty. However, when the first wholly non-Latin religious plays appear, they usually keep very close to liturgical models, although many commentators now favour the view that such vernacular works developed alongside, rather than out of, the Latin plays.

A play which combines ancient and modern tongues is the *Sponsus* (*The Bridegroom*), a Latin—Provençal treatment (*c.* 1100) of the parable of the five wise and five foolish virgins (Matthew 25. 1–13), found in a manuscript of the monastery of Limoges.[57] Some scholars suggest that the work began as a Latin liturgical *ordo*, and the demotic lines are mere amplifications; others dissent.[58] The opening hymn is in Latin, but the angel Gabriel speaks to the virgins in Provençal, employing the verbal and musical idiom of the troubadour dawn-song or *alba*, with a refrain

> *Gaire noi dormet!*
> *Aisel espos que vos hor atendet*

Sleep here no longer! Behold, the bridegroom who awaits you here

Exchanges between the wise and foolish virgins are mainly in Latin, but with a vernacular refrain '*Dolentas, chaitivas, trop i avem (avet) dormit!* [Wretched and unhappy ones, we (you) have slept too long!]' When the foolish virgins approach the merchants, they are answered (in Provençal) that they should return as the bridegroom is coming; despite their pleas to be admitted to the marriage feast, the foolish virgins are seized and thrown into Hell by demons, the first known appearance of these essential figures in medieval drama.

The *Sponsus*, like the Benediktbeuern Passion play, is an excellent illustration of the way two languages could be employed for dramatic purposes, the formal solemnity of the Latin contrasting with the homely poignancy of the *langue d'oc*, just as the inexorability of the parable's doctrinal message is counterbalanced by the pathos of the unprepared virgins. Their irremediable plight in a fourteenth-century German play on the same subject, performed by scholars and clergy of Eisenach on 4 May 1322, was the indirect cause of the death of Margrave Frederick of Meissen who found its theology so distasteful that he was moved to great anger and eventually suffered a stroke from which he never recovered:[59] the Eisenach virgins' behaviour is given a more naturalistic aspect in keeping with its non-liturgical setting, for they dance and play with a ball when they should trim their lamps, and even the Virgin Mary's intercession cannot save them from Hell-fire.[60]

Plays extensively in macaronics (more than one language) are not so common as medieval lyrics which employ the same device: the most impressive example, the *Ludus Paschalis* from the abbey at Origny-Sainte-Benoîte, also mingles liturgical with popular elements, most notably secular songs of the era, and as in the Benediktbeuern Passion, the human relevance of the redemption is thus emphasised. But liturgical feeling is still strong and, although by 1284 religious plays in the vernacular were well established, Latin liturgical plays continued to be performed in Europe for several centuries. Interesting evidence for plays composed partly in Latin and partly in English, and probably presented in Lichfield Cathedral in about 1300, is found in the 'Shrewsbury Fragments', which consist of one actor's part and cues in an *Officium Pastorum*, a *Visitatio Sepulchri*, and a *Peregrinus*.[61] He played the parts of the Third Shepherd, the Third Mary, and Cleophas, one of the travellers to Emmaus; although most of the lines are in English, Latin liturgical passages also occur. Another striking piece of evidence comes from a fourteenth-century manuscript from Trier (Trèves) in Germany in the form of a Latin *Visitatio* with the speeches translated and paraphrased into German; it is possible that these were offered as an alternative version.[62]

Not all vernacular drama was independent of the liturgy: a change to the native tongue was by no means invariably accompanied by a move away from liturgical methods of dramatising the Gospel narrative. The northern English play known as *Christ's Burial and Ressurection* (c. 1430–50)[63] remains close to the traditional formalities of the genre: the settings are those associated with church production; there is much use of hallowed antiphons, responses, and hymns; there are no comic ingredients, the play conforms to the liturgical situation and much of the conventional material of the *planctus*, the *Quem Quaeritis* exchanges, the *Hortulanus*, is present. Such a work seems merely an amplification of a form of drama which rarely strayed outside its original church setting.

3

INDOOR THEATRE

The whole frame of the world is the Theatre, and every creature the stage, the *medium*, the glasse in which we may see God.

John Donne, Sermon, Easter Day, 1628

It is unlikely that purpose-built theatre buildings existed in the Middle Ages, although the Latin words *theatrum* and *scaena* are employed quite freely in the writings of the period.[1] But the continued use of such Latin nouns did not mean that the objects they once signified survived.[2] The word *theatrum* was applied to any public place, indoors or out, where entertainments were held, and if a church or a churchyard, a monastery refectory or a noble banquet-hall, became the site of a staged spectacle, then it was temporarily a *theatrum*, 'a place for seeing', in the original Latin sense. But the word did not carry this meaning alone: it was, for example, the term for a brothel, as when Caesarium of Heisterbach reported that in *c.* 1222 twenty men were killed but a priest miraculously spared when lightning struck a *theatrum*,[3] or when Chaucer, translating Boethius in about 1380, speaks of 'thise comune strompettis of swich a place that men clepen the theatre'.[4] The word was certainly not employed exclusively to refer to a playhouse.

That the function of Roman amphitheatres was understood in the Middle Ages seems clear: Giraldus Cambrensis visiting the ruins of Caerleon in South Wales in 1188 recognised theatre-sites (*loca theatralia*), while Alexander Neckham in an elegy of 1211 mourned the ruined amphitheatre at Paris in terms indicating that he knew its function. Yet there is no evidence that such structures ever housed medieval performances, being more usually employed as quarries, barracks, and forts, when not 'crumbling, overgrown or built over'. However, the arena at Verona was apparently used as a tournament-site for a time, and bull-fights were staged at the Colosseum in Rome early in the fourteenth century, and it was on the foundations of a Roman amphitheatre that the citizens of Bourges built a circular structure to present *Les Actes des Apôtres* in 1536, so that it is not impossible that some Roman theatres were reclaimed for theatrical purposes in the Middle Ages. But as yet it has not been proved.

More problematic are those medieval descriptions which appear to refer to contemporary theatres: a fragmentary ninth-century glossary from the German abbey of Werden describes a *theatrum* as a place 'built of wood where men play [present tense] and create spectacles [*theatrum de lignis sit ubi ludunt homines et spectacula faciunt*]'.[5] When John of Garland (*c.* 1195 — *c.* 1272) writes in his *Equivoca* that *theatrum* derives from *theorare*, 'that is "to see", namely a spectacle or a place in which men, standing or seated, can see and hear easily actions performed and the utterances or anyone singing, reading, or playing a part', he may have contemporary performance in mind.[6] Significant too may be the description of a circular theatre contained in the *Flores Historiarum* of Roger de Wendover (d. 1236), in which an Essex peasant, Thurkill, is carried off to Hell in a vision and sees a large arena surrounded by seats from which demonic spectators watch the damned mime out the sinful deeds of their mortal lives. Some commentators suggest that this imaginative *tour de force* was based not simply on an awareness of the Roman amphitheatre but on personal experience of attending entertainments in similar buildings.[7] Most commonly, however, references to *theatra* allude to open-air public places as in Bishop Grandisson's letters of July 1348 and August 1352,[8] in the first of which we hear how young men of Exeter roamed the city streets dressed as monks, holding clergy and laity to ransom, and setting up a lunatic as an abbot *in theatro* to be revered there. On the second occasion the bishop prohibited an indecorous *ludus* satirising the city's leather-dressers, planned for performance *in Theatro nostrae Civitatis*, which suggests an outdoor place of public resort: an indecorous play lampooning the *bourgeoisie* does not sound like the ideal vehicle for some prototype civic theatre.

Before we leave the term *theatrum*, we must not lose sight of the mime players whose flexible methods of presentation almost certainly survived into the Middle Ages. Even before they appeared in the permanent theatres of imperial Rome, they were accustomed to set up their movable booth-stage, with its rear curtain or *siparium* serving to mask exits and changes of costume, in public squares or private houses with equal unconcern. Their equipment of portable platform and back curtain enabled them to continue presenting entertainments at the courts of kings, the homes of noblemen, the refectories of monasteries, as well as in the open air. Their appearance in monasteries and the homes of prominent ecclesiastics is deplored by the stricter clergy throughout the Middle Ages,[9] but few allusions tell us anything about the conditions in which they performed: a cartulary of King Edgar of England (see p. 27 above) claims that the *mimi* make songs and dances

publicising monastic abuses, in the market-place (*in triviis*); all such
locations by our definition may be legitimately termed *theatra*.

The Latin term *scaena* has an interesting semantic history which
helps to explain one of the dominant misconceptions about the classical
theatre prevalent in the Middle Ages:[10] Archbishop Isidore of Seville
(*c.* 560–636) was one of the first to describe in his *Originum sive etymologiarum* (*c.* 620) the *scaena* not as a raised platform but as 'built in
the form of a house, with a platform which was called the orchestra'.
He later explains that the *orchestra* (in Rome a flat arena before the
theatre stage) 'was a stage platform where a dancer [player?] could perform, or two people present a dispute between themselves; there comic
and tragic poets went up to take part in the contest, and while these
men recited, the others relayed the content by gestures. [*Orchestra
autem pulpitus erat scenae, ubi saltator agere posset, aut duo inter se disputare.
Ibi enim poetae comoedi et tragoedi ad certamen conscendebant, hisque canen-
tibus alii gestus edebant.*]'

The notion of the *scaena* as a little shelter or booth where the poet
recited while actors mimed the actions he described was gradually
accorded the status of reliable fact. Thus Hugutius (Ugiccione) of Pisa,
Bishop of Ferrara from 1190–1210, defines *scaena* in his *Magnae
Derivationes* as

a little shelter, actually a hidden place in the theatre and concealed by curtains just like merchants' stalls covered with poles and hangings, and secondly
it may be said that it is a house on the stage, since it is built in the style of a
house. In this little shelter masked characters were hidden, who came out to
make their gestures at the sound of the narrator's voice.

Nicholas Trevet (*c.* 1258 – *c.* 1328), an English Dominican chronicler
and commentator, conflated Isidore's view of the *scaena* as a house and
Hugutius's notion of a shelter for hidden actors, and gave ultimate
expression to the misconception of the classical theatre which dominated medieval thinking. In his commentary on Seneca's *Hercules
Furens* Trevet wrote that

The *theatrum* was a semi-circular open space, in the middle of which was a
small house called the *scena*, in which there was a platform on which the poet
stood to recite his works. Outside the house were the *mimi* who performed
bodily movements while the pieces were being recited, by adapting themselves to whatever character the poet was speaking of.

This method of performance was certainly claimed for the work of
Terence, whose reputed friend Calliopus was said to be the speaker to
whose narration the actors mimed.[11] The error attained its most

graphic expression in the frequently reproduced illustrations forming the frontispieces to two Terence manuscripts, the so-called Terence des Ducs in the Bibliothèque de l'Arsenal in Paris, and another in the Bibliothèque Nationale (see Illustration 3).[12] The first shows four masked *joculatores* performing in a circular amphitheatre (labelled *theatrum*) before the people of Rome, while in a curtained booth marked *scena* (from which the fifth masked player is making an energetic entry) sits Calliopus with an open text before him. It is hard to resist the view that here is Isidore's 'singer', Hugutius's 'narrator', and Trevet's 'poet', recounting the action as it proceeds. John Lydgate's *Troy Book* (c. 1412–20) speaks of performances of tragedies in Priam's Trojan theatre in terms of medieval notions of classical theatrical practice:

> Whan thei wer *rad* or songyn, as I fynde,   read
> In the theatre ther was a smal auter
> Amyddes set, that was half circuler,
> Whiche in-to the Est of custom was directe;
> Up-on the whiche a pulpet was erecte,
> And ther-in stod an awncien poete,
> For to reherse by *rethorikes swete*   elegantly phrased expressions
> The noble dedis, that wer historial,
> Of kynges, princes for a memorial,
> And of thes olde, worthi Emperours,
> The grete emprises eke of conquerours . . .
> And whil that he in the pulpit stood,
> With dedly face al devoide of blood,
> Singinge his dites, with muses al to-rent,
> Amydde the theatre schrowdid in a tent,
> Ther cam out men *gastful of her cheris*,   with fearful faces
> Disfigurid her facis with *viseris*,   visors, masks
> Pleying by signes in the peples sight,
> That the poete songon hath on hight;
> So that ther was no maner discordaunce
> Atwen his dites and her contenaunce.   (862–72, 897–906).[13]

However, while it is no longer tenable to argue that medieval readers of Latin plays believed that they were straightforward recitations in dialogue form never intended for performance, there is little to suggest that medieval man was inspired to erect his own custom-built theatres as a result of trying to reconstruct ancient practice. We may be fairly confident that for the greater part of the medieval period places of worship, halls and chambers of royal palaces, castles, and noble houses, refectories or chapter-houses in nunneries and monasteries, were the principal indoor sites for dramatic performances.

Liturgical drama in performance necessarily had to accommodate it-

3 Calliopus and mime players performing in a circular theatre

self to pre-existing conditions: the physical shapes of churches and their architectural features determined the basic setting for church-drama, just as Christian ritual supplied the plays' original *raison d'être* and governed their textual content. The scope for ambitious production was inevitably conditioned by the ecclesiastical environment, but we must never look on this as necessarily irksome or repressive, for the prescribed framework compelled the director, usually the choir-master of the cathedral or monastic school and often no doubt the composer of the play, to concentrate on the imaginative integrity and spiritual intensity of his presentation rather than strain after meretricious extraneous 'effects'.

Without some appreciation of the development of church-building in both western and eastern Europe between 600 and 1200, even a conjectural assessment of liturgical performances is impossible.[14] Christian church-design in the West mainly derives from the rectangular Roman basilica, and early examples such as Sta Sabina in Rome (*c.* 425) consist of a long nave, divided by columns to form at least two side-aisles, which culminates in a semicircular vaulted apse containing the altar. This division between the 'public area' and what Philip Larkin has called 'the holy end' has been long maintained in traditional Christian edifices, even when the length of the eastern section, made up of various combinations of apse, choir, chancel, presbytery, and sanctuary, rivals that of the nave. Rapidly assuming cruciform shape by the addition of north and south transepts, the basilican plan became the model for the great monastic churches and episcopal cathedrals of the Middle Ages, and 'in the larger Romanesque churches of western Europe, the aisled basilica was practically universal'.[15] But a fairly common type of early church was built on the polygonal or circular plan adopted by early Christians for housing baptismal pools, and hence known as baptisteries. These structures were chiefly used for baptisms, as shrines for relics, or as chapels to hold a tomb, but soon complete churches on the round or polygonal plan were constructed, their outstanding feature being an arcaded aisle or ambulatory encircling an open central area. Notable are those of San Stefano Rotondo at Rome (*c.* 475), the octagonal church of San Vitale in Ravenna (526—47), and Charlemagne's sixteen-sided palatine chapel and mausoleum (*c.* 800) at Asachen and now the cathedral there. The outstanding example in the East is of course Justinian's magnificent Sta Sophia at Constantinople, consecrated in 537. The existence of places of worship having their focal point in an open central area suitable as an acting-site should alert us to the possibility of a rather different orientation for church-plays

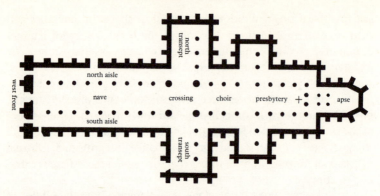

4 Plan of a typical medieval cathedral, showing the principal areas

than the one usually imagined, and offers us the exciting hypothesis that at some centres liturgical drama may have been presented as theatre-in-the-round.[16]

Our primary concern, however, must be with basilican-type buildings, and with examining just which areas of a Romanesque or Gothic cathedral offered themselves as performance-sites during the period (see Illustration 4). The assessment of potential locations raises questions concerning spectators, too, for not all parts of a medieval church, whether a regular (or monastic) or secular establishment, were freely accessible or even visible to the laity. The east or sanctuary end where stood the high altar, although it might be raised a few feet above the nave, was invariably separated off by some means from it, while the choirs of the priests and singers, which in early Italian basilicas consisted simply of benches set around the curve of the apse behind the altar, were partitioned off by stone *cancelli* or low screens, which still permitted the clerics to be seen. Later the clergy- and choir-seats were placed in a railed-off space at the east end of the nave, as at Odo's newly restored cathedral at Canterbury (c. 940–60); and, during the post-Carolingian period, church architecture became more elaborate, and choirs (of which there might be as many as four, as at St Riquier in Picardy) were completely concealed from view by means of *pulpita*, solid stone screens across the east end of the nave. Probably the earliest European reference to such a structure is found in a description of Aldred, Archbishop of York from 1060–9, adding a new presbytery to the church at Beverley in Yorkshire: 'Above the choir-door he also caused to be made a *pulpitum* of incomparable work of bronze and gold and silver.' By the twelfth century this custom of terminating the choir at its west end by a screen topped with a parapet was common, especially in the greater churches of England and Spain and since pilgrims *en route* for the apse on their visits to the tombs or shrines of saints and martyrs passed near the choirs of monastic churches, it became essential to ensure that the clergy were not disturbed at their frequent devotions. In many monastic churches therefore, a rood- or parclose-screen supplemented or replaced the *pulpitum*, while choir-screens to the north and south shielded clerics from the intrusive gaze of pilgrim bands. A nave altar was often set up before the rood-screen which acted as a reredos or backing to it, and Masses for the laity would be celebrated there. Rood-screens are largely a thirteenth-century fashion, but liturgical plays continued to be staged after their erection, and we can never be sure that plays performed entirely in the choir would not be hidden from lay eyes, and those intended exclusively for popular edification would certainly have had to be presented in the nave,[17] which of course in medieval times would have been quite devoid of pews or benches, the laity standing or kneeling throughout the services. On some occasions the people might even have followed the dramatic action from place to place.

The most vital feature of the church interior for dramatic as well as sacramental purposes was the high altar, site of the sepulchre for the Easter *Visitatio*: the long-established identification of the altar with the tomb, often sanctioned by the presence of saintly remains sealed into the altar or buried below it, was fortunate for the presenters of the Easter ceremony. Relics were also often placed in a cavity at the top of the stone altar-table known as a *sepulchrum*, and it became the custom to place fragments of the consecrated communion wafer here, too. A medieval high altar was not backed by a reredos, so that action could take place behind it without difficulty. The dialogue between the three Marys and the angel was thus presented not only at the most appropriate focal area in the church building, but at the site agreed to represent Christ's burial-place most fittingly.[18] Where no *sepulchrum* existed, one might be simulated, as the earliest text of the *Depositio Crucis*, contained in the *Regularis Concordia*, suggests: 'On one side of the altar, where there is space, there should be some likeness of the sepulchre, with a veil stretched all round it. [*Sit autem in una parte altaris, qua vacuum fuerit, quedam assimilatio Sepulchri, velamenque quoddam in gyro tensum.*]'[19] The same structure no doubt also served for the *Visitatio* since the angel at the tomb, after singing the antiphon *Venite et videte locum ubi positus erat Dominus*, rises to draw or lift the curtain, 'and shows them the place with the cross gone'. Similarly, we read in a fourteenth-century text from Cividale Cathedral that '*Angelus levat cortinam*', while at Senlis the angels raise the altar-cloth (*palam altaris*) as they chant *Non est hic*; elsewhere the cloth is entirely removed to show the *sudarium* (napkin) lying in the 'tomb'. At Narbonne a structure was formed on the altar from silver-bound books to represent the sepulchre, and a cloth placed over it was removed by the angels.

Permanent architectural representations of the sepulchre became popular in the tenth and eleventh centuries, and may have been built as focal points for the ceremonies of the *Depositio, Elevatio*, and *Visitatio*.[20] Circular or polygonal in shape, often with cone-shaped roofs, these so-called *monumenta* which contained the *sepulchrum*, a sarcophagus with a lid, were frequently large enough to hold several people. A twelfth-century text from Augsburg stations two deacons as angels in such a *monumentum*, and requires two priests playing the Marys to enter it as well. Aquilèia Cathedral contains an eleventh-century monument large enough to accommodate a deacon playing the angel and cantors representing Peter and John; according to Karl Young, it measures about 3.8 metres (12½ feet) in diameter and just over 2 metres (6½ feet) in height; there is a door in one side, and inside are a niche and an altar, the former possibly to take the grave-clothes and *sudarium*. But permanent edifices were more often dispensed with: at Bamberg a curtained area was set aside as a temporary sepulchre during the ceremonies of Passion Week, and a fourteenth-century *Visitatio* from Essen mentions a *tentorium* or curtained structure in which an *archa* (coffer or chest) is placed to represent the sepulchre, pointing out that the angels inside will need books and light to see them by. Wooden structures, too, easily erected in the choir and removed when no longer required, were known, and seem to have been employed for Easter plays at Fleury and St Quentin.

Permanent or temporary sepulchres occupied a variety of positions in the church, and the choir or presbytery was often chosen; in England they were nearly always located on the north side of the choir or chancel, possibly to facilitate use in drama. In Germany and related countries, they were often found in an ancillary chapel or even the crypt. Thus, even if liturgical drama had never required the use of more than a *sepulchrum* and its associated *monumentum*, its presentation would have occurred at a number of alternative sites.[21] In fact, the playwright-composer-directors of liturgical plays soon availed themselves of the staging opportunities offered by large buildings with plenty of floor-space, a variety of separate acting-areas, and several levels in the form of galleries, pulpits, and often a raised sanctuary beyond the choir. Even without supplementing these facilities with platforms and built structures, a clerical producer might set his action in the choir or sanctuary, in the body of the church using the nave and the bays between arcades, in one or both of the transepts before the side-altars, in the 'crossing' before the chancel arch where nave met transept, or around the west door. He could exploit architectural features such as archways, flights of steps, chapels and shrines, and for all these uses he could find precedents in ceremonies of the kind we have already observed.

Although the increasingly elaborate architectural complexity of medieval church buildings may have encouraged more ambitious staging, plays featuring movement, such as journeys by the Magi and by the travellers (*peregrini*) to Emmaus, may have chiefly influenced the liturgical drama towards greater freedom. The need to suggest travel no doubt stimulated the use of separate areas of the building to create a sense of space. In the thirteenth-century *Visitatio* from Toul the three Marys first appear before one of the church entrances (*ante hostium ecclesie*) and before proceeding to the sepulchre, visit a side-altar where they collect vessels, no doubt the embryo from which evolved the women's encounter with the *unguentarius* or *apotecarius* from whom they buy ointments. Texts from Ripoll and Prague provide for the spice-seller to appear in person, and it is reasonable to suppose that he had his own position or *sedes* (literally 'seat'), possibly a side-altar on which to place his wares. At Trier the Marys descended to the crypt to visit the sepulchre, and later parts of the action took place on the crypt steps, at the tomb of Archbishop Theodoric, and in the choir. At Essen the curtained *tentorium* was set up before the altar of St Michael, on the raised gallery of the choir at the west end of the collegiate church. Angels and Marys made dramatic use of this upper level and its galleries to north and south, the performers ascending to the organ-loft to make triumphant announcements. At Le Mans three young clerks playing the Marys processed to the sepulchre at the main altar, visiting every subsidiary altar in turn, kissing any they chose, and occasionally repeating '*Surrexit, non est hic.* [He has risen, he is not here.]'

Processions from the west door, or the entrance vestibule or *narthex*, were a common feature of the *Visitatio Sepulchri*, which at Fleury requires the Marys to sing nine stanzas as they advance down the nave;[22] in a similar manner the two disciples in the Rouen *Peregrinus* enter at the west door and walk down the church to join the choir in the middle of the nave. In many *Peregrinus* plays the inn at Emmaus or a table to represent it is set up in the centre of the nave, although in the versions from Saintes and Sicily the 'inn' is firmly located at the altar.[23] In the

Fleury rendering of *Herod* and *The Massacre of the Innocents*[24] full use is made of the nave and its open space, especially for the travels of the Shepherds and the Magi, and for the procession of the Innocents who pass chanting through the nave, having assembled in the monastery cloister. The Magi, attracted towards the high altar by the *stella*, probably on a wire (see pp. 167–8 below) make their way to the choir from different parts of the church, symbolising their different countries of origin, while the Holy Family may have passed down the nave to the *narthex* to simulate the Flight into Egypt. The Beauvais *Daniel*[25] would also have taken advantage of the nave for its lavish processional entries and exits, and in the Beauvais *Peregrinus*[26] the two disciples scour the entire church in their search for the vanished Christ. The nave also provided the location for the race between Peter and John to reach the sepulchre.

Choir and chancel were often the sites for the culminating scenes of these dramas: in the Fleury *Peregrinus*[27] the choir appropriately forms the setting for Christ's appearance to the apostles in Jerusalem, and in the *Massacre* from the same collection the Holy Innocents pass into the choir singing, following their slaughter and apotheosis. In the miracle play of St Nicholas, the *Filius Getronis*,[28] the chancel represents the church of St Nicholas with its choristers and clergy in attendance; this play also makes use of north and south transepts, and these areas are brought into play in the *Planctus Mariae* at Cividale,[29] where the appearance of the shallow north transept with its wall-crucifix remains relatively unchanged today. Also intact is the larger southern transept of Padua Cathedral (the Duomo), where the fourteenth-century plays of the Annunciation and the Purification were performed; in both these pieces Gabriel made an impressive entry from outside the church carried on a portable throne or *cathedra* borne by four bearers, being costumed in the baptistery close to the Duomo and making his appearance by a door in the south side of the nave. Side-doors are also used for dramatic effect in the *Filius Getronis*, women singing from a door leading to the cloisters of the monastery. Special effects of this kind are also deployed from elevated positions in the church: in the Rouen *Pastores* (*Shepherds*)[30] seven choristers sing the message of the angels 'in a high place [*in alto loco*]', probably a raised gallery or simply the slightly elevated area of the sanctuary, either of which could be used by the angel in the Beauvais *Daniel* who appears suddenly to sing a Christmas hymn. Similarly the voice from on high (*vox ex alto*) which strikes down Saul in the Fleury *Conversion of St Paul*[31] might emanate from here.

Supplementation of the available resources by means of simple furnishings and constructed facilities was, however, inevitable. While it is doubtful if scenic requirements in the form of benches or low platforms (*sedes*) and simple 'houses' (often referred to by the Latin term *domus* and later by the French *mansion*) were very complex, a particular stage area (*locus*) could be given stronger definition and a heightened reality if it were raised from the floor, or embellished with a small house-like structure or a table and benches. Furthermore, as more laymen, especially the nobility, came to witness liturgical plays, so their need to see the action became a crucial factor in planning its staging. Earlier, the small standing audience of spectators could, if necessary, follow the performers from area to area on foot, but soon there were too many onlookers for mobile viewing to be viable, and since many present were men of importance and influence, seats had to be provided without restricting vision. Thus the benches supplied for spectators were mounted on platforms (the English 'pew' is related to the Latin *podium* and the French *puy*, both of which indicate an elevation), and the actors were placed on *sedes* which enabled them to be seen. The *sedes* could be distributed through the church, usually at the salient spots occupied by dramatic action in the past — choir-entrance, central nave, west door.

In this way evolved, doubtless, the system of both indoor and outdoor staging which dominates the medieval period, and is known most often as *mansion*-staging. Its essential feature is the simultaneous appearance on the playing-site of a number of juxtaposed scenic locations (*sedes, locus, domus, mansion* are the usual terms) grouped around or across an open playing-area ('the place', in Latin *platea*) frequently but not invariably on its periphery, and remaining in view throughout the action, during which several locations may be in use concurrently. The individal scenic locations may be simple platforms or elaborate 'houses', but the distinction between *platea* and *locus* is invariable: specific places are identified by the presence of a structure or a character, while the *platea* takes on a variety of identities, being earmarked for pieces of action not assigned to designated locations, such as open country or the street, and for journeys undertaken between the various specific locales.

Information concerning the appearance of the scenic structures for church-drama is lacking: Fletcher Collins has argued that the *sedes* were curtained at the sides and rear, and in a few instances, a curtained platform would be advantageous: versions of the *Peregrinus* require Christ to disappear suddenly from sight and to reappear with equal speed, and a curtained platform with a split rear curtain would permit this. The Rouen and Fleury versions call for special structures in the nave, the Rouen text speaking of a raised *tabernaculum* in the likeness of the Château (*castellum*) at Emmaus prepared in the middle of the church, and Fleury describes Christ and the disciples *sessum in sedibus ad hoc preparatis* (seated in places prepared for the purpose).

Other Fleury plays are more demanding: the *Herod* and the *Massacre* require only two fixed locations, the manger at the monastery doors and Herod's court on a platform at the entrance to the choir, but the *Resuscitatio Lazari* (*The Raising of Lazarus*)[32] employs three *sedes*, the tomb flanked by a structure representing Galilee and another standing for both the house of Simon the Leper and that of Lazarus, containing tables and benches to suggest a dwelling. The *platea* acts as the inter-vening space between the three *sedes* and can loosely be thought of as the road on which the parties travel: much of the action occurs on the *platea*, and Collins argues that its area covered the nave before the choir, the whole of the crossing, and both transepts. A considerable *platea* is also needed for the Fleury *Conversion of St Paul*, extending between four scenic structures representing two buildings in Jerusalem and two in Damascus, a couch for Ananias being set up between the latter pair. Thus five locations are on view simultaneously, the action flowing from one to another across the *platea*. The most intriguing stage-direction calls for Paul to be lowered in a basket to the ground 'from a high place' by the disciples, but Collins nips in the bud notions of winches in the galleries and triforia by stating that this incident could never have been physically staged.

Some of the most ambitious stage effects in the liturgical repertoire are found in two plays on the prophet Daniel, the first by Hilarius (*c.* 1130), one of the celebrated *vagantes* or wandering scholars, a pupil of Abelard, and probably an Englishman, and the second composed by students of the choir-school at Beauvais for Christmas performance, *c.* 1180. Hilarius's is an attractive rendering of the tale of Daniel,[33] but the Beauvais version is generally regarded as superior in theatrical and musical impact. It contains eight choral processions as bridges between its nineteen separate episodes, but the play only demands three *sedes* consisting of the royal palace, Daniel's house, and the lion's den. The palace setting requires a throne (*solium*) and a banqueting-table at which Belshazzar's feast is held; no doubt this important loca-tion held the centre of the playing-area, while Daniel's *domus* was a simple skeletal structure of roof and pillars enabling the prophet to be seen clearly when within, the pit (*lacus*) or den for the lions was presumably on the other side of the palace, possibly surrounded by a parapet low enough to permit the lions (each played by a pair of choirboys suitably costumed and masked) to perform their parts not only to their own but their audience's satisfaction. Some technical device might have been employed to contrive the writing of the fatal words on Belshazzar's palace-wall, even though the slow unrolling of a scroll might have satisfied a medieval audience's desire for verisimilitude; however, the text emphasises the appearance of a right hand (*Interim apparebit dextra*), and a number of medieval illustrations show one in action.

Several plays describing miracles wrought by St Nicholas make interesting use of the *mansion*-convention:[34] the Hildesheim *Tres Clerici (Three Clerks)*[35] in which the saint restores three clerks to life after their murder by an avaricious inn-keeper, is simple to stage, one room in an inn being sufficient, although the bedchamber may also have been shown. The more elaborate Fleury version[36] treats the *platea* as the highway outside the inn, as well as depicting the inn's main room and bedroom. Two *loca* are needed to stage Hilarius's *Ludus super Iconia Sancti Nicolai (The Play of St Nicholas's Image)*,[37] one the interior of the room occupied by the heathen Barbarus who entrusts his treasure to the image of the saint, the other the hide-out of the robbers from whom Nicholas exacts restitution of the plunder. In the *Filius Getronis (The Son of Getron)*, also from Fleury, two main locations are involved, probably on opposite sides of the crossing: the court of Marmorinus the heathen king complete with throne and armed attendants, and Getron's home in the city of Excoranda from which his son Adeodatus is abducted, this *sedes* having 'in its eastern part' St Nicholas's church, probably represented by the choir of the monastery church at Fleury. Once again journeys between one geographical location and another are symbolised by movement across the *platea*: the king's soldiers cross the stage to attack Excoranda and seize the boy, and at the *dénouement* Adeodatus is conveyed across the *platea* from court to his own home by a saintly miracle. The simultaneous existence on stage of two or more contrasted *loca* is very effective in theatrical terms; the homely piety of Getron's simple home is literally set over against the grandiose splendours of the pagan court.[38] In the same way the presence in the Fleury *Herod* of the Christ child in his simple manger and Herod on his barbaric throne reinforces the contrast between spiritual and temporal kingship, and to watch Daniel praying in his humble house while the jealous counsellors complain to Darius on the palace *sedes*, is a further benefit of simultaneous staging at Beauvais.

The scenic principles thus established were capable of infinite extension in wider ranging plays: the *Ludus Paschalis* from Klosterneuburg in Austria (*c.* 1204)[39] requires *loca* for Pilate, the sepulchre, Hell, and possibly others for the spice-merchant (*specionarius*) and for the apostles. Little elaboration was demanded, although the gates of Hell, broken down by Christ, must have been built for the purpose. More demanding was the Monte Cassino Passion play of *c.* 1150,[40] staged within the monastery church, with its need for at least two 'built' structures, Caiaphas's house and a room in Pilate's house; if the complete text had survived, it would certainly have included a *sedes* for Herod, and some form of sepulchre. Other locations such as Pilate's Judgement Hall and Calvary may have been simply areas of the *platea* either given temporary identity or retaining their status throughout the action by continued use of the same furnishings or players. Medieval audiences found nothing incongruous in silent, static performers occupying their own *sedes* or *loca* while the dramatic action was pursued elsewhere on stage.

The shorter Passion play from Benediktbeuern also demands a generous playing-area: simultaneous action may be presumed in at least one instance, when Judas bargains with the priests and Jews on one part of the stage while the Last Supper continues partly in dumb-show on another. The lengthier and more ambitious Benediktbeuern *Passion* employs a greater range of *sedes*, since Pilate, Herod, the High Priests, the Merchant and his wife, Mary Magdalen, Lazarus's tomb, the Last Supper, and the Crucifixion seem to require their own locations, although it may have been possible to share some *sedes* if the characters did not occupy the stage all the time.[41]

The most extensive early use of scenic stations is found in the liturgical-cum-political *Ludus de Antichristo* (*The Play of Antichrist*) from Tegernsee in the Bavarian Alps,[42] which seems to have originated at the court of the Holy Roman Emperor Frederick Barbarossa in about 1160. The play indicates that eight *sedes* will be needed, arranged about a *platea* which with them represents virtually the entire universe; the eight structures comprise the Temple of the Lord, and a stage for the King of Jerusalem and Synagoga to the east; to the west *sedes* for the Emperor (with space enough for the imperial troops), the Pope and his clergy, Ecclesia, Misericordia, and Justitia (The Church, Mercy and Justice), the Teuton King, and the King of the Franks; to the south are *sedes* for the King of the Greeks (Byzantium), and another shared by the King of Babylonia and the spirit of heathendom, Gentilitas. Spectators probably occupied the northern side of the *platea*. Processions at entry and movements between scaffolds play an important rôle in the action, and equally vital to the play's impact are the various battles waged in the *platea* between the rival powers searching for dominance, and between the forces of Antichrist and those he comes to compel into submission. It was these or similar representations of conflict which Gerhoh of Reichersberg condemned in his *De Investigatione Antichristi* of *c.* 1162, deploring clerical participation in performances of this kind.[43]

The Anglo-Norman play, *La Seinte Resureccion* (*c.* 1175), which calls for at least forty-two actors, offers far fewer details of presentation.[44] The texts make it clear that the play was intended for performance before the common people (*devant le peuple*) which might suggest open-air staging, but there seems to be nothing to prevent its *lius* (simple platforms?) and its *mansions* (built structures?) being set up in the nave of a church for *le peuple* to witness. Certainly *La Seinte Resureccion* makes no apparent use of the external facilities of the church in the way that *Le Jeu d'Adam* does (see pp. 64 and 121—4 below), but equally there are no choral or liturgical elements in the play itself. However, it is much more ambitious in its scenic demands. Whether presented outside or within a church, a simultaneous 'polyscenic' setting is involved, with as many as seven different structures (*maisuns*) juxtaposed: the Crucifix, the tomb, a gaol, Hell, Heaven, the Tower of David and Bartholomew, and the inn at Emmaus in the centre of the *platea*. These unoccupied *maisuns* are distinguished from eight *lius* or *estals* (stalls), probably simple platforms or floor-areas, where such characters as Pilate, Caiaphas, Joseph of Arimathea, Nicodemus, the Disciples, and the three Marys stand. Galilee is to be in 'the middle of the *platea*' (*en mi la place*), alongside Emmaus, since the prologue reads '*Iemaus uncore i seit fait* [Emmaus should also be constructed there]'. It is not clear how this structure avoided interfering with the line of vision for some spectators, although if the play were staged in a church nave, seats may have been raised and tiered, or the play viewed from above, as suggested by Richard Leacroft. The number of acting areas simultaneously required, and the range of movements taking place between them, suggests that ample total playing-space was needed, and that a nave with an audience seated or standing on both sides or above, is the only possible church setting for it.

Although the best church-dramas had probably been composed at least by 1275, church performances of traditional and new liturgical pieces still continued to be given: one of the most fully described is the *Presentation of the Blessed Virgin Mary in the Temple* devised by Philippe de Mézières around 1372, when a performance appears to have been given in the church of the Friars Minor at Avignon.[45] The action demanded the erection of two special stages within the church, one in the nave between the west portal and the choir, the other against the north wall of the choir, between the choir-stalls and the high altar. Twenty-two characters including a three- or four-year-old Mary, put on their costumes in the chapter-house and, led by the bishop, processed through the cloisters, entering the nave by the west door and advancing down the central aisle protected by spearmen. Although this piece utilises several areas of the church, it does not employ the *mansion* principle in quite the same way as the earlier liturgical pieces: stages are not identified with particular locations, the platforms and the space between are never conceived as co-existing, and stage actions are never simultaneous.

Liturgical drama was presented in churches throughout the Continent, and in England Lichfield and Lincoln Cathedrals and York Minster are known to have presented *Pastores, Stella*, or *Peregrinus* plays by the fourteenth century, while a *Visitatio* play is found in Dublin during the same period.[46] From the nunnery of Barking in Essex comes a *Visitatio* associated with *Depositio* and *Elevatio* ceremonies from the period 1363–76: nuns play the Marys as at St Quentin in 1284, and members of the clergy play the disciples.[47] Catalonia in north-east Spain was particularly rich in Easter and Christmas plays,[48] a Gerona book of observances or *consueta* of 1360 containing provision for eight Latin liturgical plays in the course of the year, its *Visitatio* being a very advanced affair demanding a cast of nine ecclesiastics. Palma in Mallorca also presented an Easter play featuring a Mary Magdalen in colourful vestments questioned by twelve priests; as she sang in Catalan a song referring to corpses rising from the dead, seven or eight choirboys rolled from beneath the main altar as if resurrected; shortly afterwards the angel, in a large pair of wings aglow with candlelight, appeared, accompanied by a loud noise.

Mallorca also possesses an important codex of religious plays, some dating from the fifteenth century, perhaps intended for performance in Palma Cathedral;[49] they include a vernacular music-drama, the *Consueta del Rey Asuero*, requiring five scaffolds or platforms (*cadefals*) probably set up at the nave crossing, and representing King Ahasuerus's banquet-hall, Queen Vashti's apartments a council-chamber, a site for Haman which will later contain a gallows, and, a little apart from the rest, 'the house of Esther'. Possibly grouped in a half-circle, the platforms face the audience in the nave, while the floor-space serves as the *platea*. Another play, the *Consueta de Sant Crespí y Sant Crespinià*, demands three large platforms, on one of which stands the palace of the

Moorish king, a nearby chapel with a crucifix, and a church with a bell-tower. King Maximià's palace, a structure with wide doors, occupies the whole of the second platform, although a 'royal governor' is nearby, and possibly indicates the presence of another built structure. The third scaffold is large enough to hold a shop at each extremity, houses for two hermits, and the saintly shoemakers' hut, containing a table and two chairs: plenty of space is called for to enable free passage between platforms. All the settings are of course visible (and possibly occupied) simultaneously.

Not only those who attended presentations in churches and cathedrals were able to enjoy their drama in the relative comfort of a building. Performances in religious houses were certainly popular throughout the period, and, while some were provided by secular entertainers whose presence was frequently frowned on, accounts of more seemly spectacles survive. A striking instance comes from the first decade of the twelfth century when a Norman schoolmaster, Geoffrey of Le Mans, staged an ill-fated production of a Latin (or Anglo-Norman) miracle or saint play, the *Ludus de Sancta Katherina*, at Dunstable in Bedfordshire, his pupils at the choir-school probably forming the cast.[50] He borrowed from the nearby abbey of St Albans a number of copes, and when a fire accidentally destroyed them while in his care, Geoffrey entered the abbey as a mark of contrition, and by 1119 had become its abbot. If the St Albans Psalter (*c.* 1123) portrays actual stage performances, as scholars claim, Geoffrey encouraged further productions at his abbey, a tribute to his persistence if not perhaps his prudence.[51] Roughly contemporary evidence comes from Gerhoh of Reichersberg (1093–1169) who, in a commentary on the Psalms, censures the monks of Augsburg for never sleeping in their dormitory or using the refectory during Gerhoh's term as *magister scholae* 'except on rare festive occasions, chiefly when they represented Herod the persecutor of Christ, the murderer of the Innocents, or at the exhibiting of other plays or what were virtually theatrical spectacles...'[52] Such testimony is supported by that of Herrad of Landsberg, abbess of a nunnery at Hohenberg from 1167 to 1195, who complains that plays, formerly presented to strengthen the Christian faith and instruct the unbeliever, have now degenerated into opportunities for horseplay and lewdness:

What happens nowadays? What is presented in certain churches in our time? Not a pattern of religion or divine veneration and a source of reverence, but the impassioned licence of irreligion and dissoluteness is practised. Clerical dress is changed, a military system is established, no distinction is made bet-

ween priest and soldier, the house of God is turned upside down by the mixing
of laity and clergy, revellings, drunken orgies, buffooneries, harmful jests, plays
in which weapons clash and only please the performers, a gathering-together
of debaucheries, an undisciplined assault by all kinds of vanity.[53]

Possibly, like Gerhoh in the *De Investigatione Antichristi*, Herrad had
the Tegernsee *Antichrist* in mind, which might well have been staged in
some monastic refectory rather than in a church or in some great
imperial hall or banquet-chamber.

More likely to have been staged within monastic premises is Hildegard of Bingen's *Ordo Virtutum* (*c*. 1155),[54] which takes as its theme the
battle between the Virtues and the Devil for control of the human soul,
anticipating the theme of the English morality play *The Castel of Perseverance* by almost three hundred years. It is far from impossible that
Hildegard's drama was staged in her convent on the Rupertsburg where
the German mystic was abbess from 1147 until her death in 1179, for
despite its academic tone, it is a genuine piece of living theatre and
not a chamber-drama.

In almost the same year that Hildegard composed the *Ordo Virtutum*,
the first extant piece of western European religious drama composed
in the vernacular appeared: a play in Old Castilian entitled *Reyes
Magos* (*The Magi Kings*)[55] alerts us to the decreasing dependence of
Christian drama on the liturgy which nurtured its earliest phase. The
liturgical plays were in Latin and sung; the *Reyes Magos* seems to have
been spoken, the story is told with more vivacity, and while associated
with a particular church festival, the play no longer exists purely to
ornament rituals attendant on worship. But the place of performance,
if the piece were actually staged (it contains no stage directions), is still
likely to have been a religious edifice, Toledo Cathedral.

At about the same time, highly developed religious plays in the vernacular begin to appear in France and England; two outstanding plays
in Anglo-Norman dating from 1146–74 almost certainly represent the
culmination of an established literary tradition. *Le Mystère* (or *Jeu*)
d'Adam (or the *Ordo Representacionis Adae*) and *La Seinte Resureccion*
already referred to,[56] like the *Reyes Magos*, appear to stand clear of
liturgical drama in characterisation and purpose, most notably *Adam*
with the freedom of its dialogue and subtle psychology. But the most
exciting aspect of *Adam* is that it is the first known example of a Christian drama clearly intended for open-air staging (see pp. 121–4 below).

The explanation chiefly favoured by scholars for the development of
religious plays outside places of worship in the twelfth century is that
outdoor performance offered far greater opportunities for accom-

modating a large audience comfortably and conveniently, without the restrictions created by church buildings. There is certainly unlikely to have been greater scope for stage effects in such an exodus. Indeed, to move plays outside an edifice probably meant some loss of flexibility for director and cast, in that many valuable architectural features such as the altar and *narthex* were lost, along with their symbolic associations. The chief advantage was that to shift productions to the *parvis* or open space before a religious building enabled more people to view the action.

There is certainly no validity in the view that the plays were becoming unsuitable for church presentation because of the infiltration of 'secular' elements (see p. 39 above): the Church rarely ceased to be involved with the plays even after their departure from church premises, both in her official capacity and in the varied services rendered by individual churchmen as authors, directors, organisers, and performers. It is also completely incorrect to suggest that the secular arm commandeered the plays once they left the confines of buildings and developed them in drastic worldly ways not approved of by Mother Church.

At the same time, it is not entirely without foundation to suggest that some church authorities were relieved to see the plays go. Plays inside churches were not universally frowned on: Herrad of Landsberg was careful to distinguish between godly and restrained representations and those which got out of hand (see p. 63 above), and the same kind of discrimination is found in a famous Decretal (1234) of Pope Gregory IX (1227–41) clarifying an earlier ruling by Innocent III (1198–1216) by exempting piously presented *ludi* from papal disapproval:

However, it is not forbidden to perform *The Manger of the Lord*, the *Herod* play, the *Magi*, and *Rachel Weeping for her Sons*, and those other plays which are linked to those festivals of which mention is made here, since such plays touch men's consciences rather than lead them to wantonness or evil desires, just as at Easter *The Sepulchre of the Lord* and other plays are staged to arouse devotion.[57]

Yet the strong temptation existed to over-embellish formerly chaste ceremonies and to create histrionic opportunities beyond those necessary for arousing devotion and it may have been a factor in the decision to transfer the more elaborate and ambitious religious plays to the open air where they might develop on freer and more naturalistic lines.

Yet indoor performances continued to be given: in Italy the rise of the 'Disciplinati di Gesu Cristo', fraternities evolved from the popular religious revival in Umbria of the late 1250s, gave a fresh impetus to church-performances.[58] The vernacular hymns of adoration known as *laudi*, sung by peripatetic bands of flagellants, included lyrics of spiritual conflict in dialogue form, and, when the wave of processional self-chastisement was spent, the Disciplinati continued to sing the dramatic *laudi* in semidramatic form in their churches and chapels, assigning the different rôles among themselves. Initially the performers simply chanted their parts while remaining in their places, but recitation developed into costumed impersonation. Sung either after Mass on Sundays and festivals or incorporated into the service itself, these *devozioni* or *laude drammatiche* soon spread through Italy, and paved the way for the more elaborate *sacre rappresentazioni* of the fifteenth century. Wardrobes of clothing and stocks of scenery were built up to support performances which seem to have taken the familiar form of recitation-with-mime, a common style of presentation. A clerical narrator would no doubt have taken his place on a small stage in the nave and to one side of a larger platform where the players would perform the necessary motions and movements.

The degree of technical sophistication which the sacred drama ultimately attained in Italy is best illustrated from the famous account of an Annunciation play witnessed by the Russian bishop, Abraham of Souzdal, in the Church of the Annunciation at Florence on 25 March 1439;[59] here a curtained platform representing Heaven was erected above the church door, containing God seated in majesty and an attendant band of children surrounded by seven globes enclosing oil lamps to represent the planets. Below, in the middle of the church before the rood-screen, was another curtained platform on one side of which a bed and a large chair were placed to represent the home of the Virgin Mary, while in the centre stood four prophets with long beards and scrolls, and their disputation occupied the first half hour of the action. Then the curtains on the upper stage parted amid the sound of thunder, and Gabriel descended from Heaven by means of a harness on small wheels attached to two ropes extending to the stage in the nave, his flight being controlled by stagehands out of sight of the spectators. His return after the Annunciation was also engineered in the same way, and was followed by a further crack of thunder and the descent of 'a flaming and crackling fire' which seemed to fill the whole church, and light the lamps as if by divine agency (see pp. 168–9 below). On 14 May 1439 the bishop witnessed a performance of the Ascension at the Church of the Carmine, in which Christ ascended to Heaven by much the same means, but here scenic devices including a castle representing Jerusalem and the Mount of Olives covered with rose silk were featured, as well as the curtained platform 17 metres (56 feet) high symbolising Paradise. Numerous small lamps, cut-out angels and human actors created a scene of heavenly splendour towards which Christ ascended on a cloud which ran on seven separate ropes: the cloud bore two boys dressed as angels with wings of gold; God the Father was also suspended miraculously in the air.

Two important groups of plays intended for indoor performance are found in fourteenth-century France, where associations known as *puys* or *confréries* were set up to stage plays (see pp. 200—1 below). The Parisian Confrérie de la Passion's repertoire appears to have been preserved in MS 1131 of the Bibliothèque Ste Geneviève, a miscellany of biblical plays and others dealing with the lives and miracles of saints.[60] Another ambitious collection of miracle plays, known as *Les Miracles de Nostre Dame* and comprising forty texts dating from 1339—82, seems to have been designed for annual presentation by the Guild of the Goldsmiths of Paris, many demonstrating how the Virgin Mary assists those who seek her aid, making telling use of surprise and suspense in depicting the frailties of humanity, and employing realistic stage devices to depict physical suffering, violence, and depravity.[61]

The predecessor of such indoor performances appears to be Jean Bodel's remarkable and original *Le Jeu de Saint-Nicolas* (*c.* 1200),[62] whose presentation on the night of St Nicholas's Eve (December 5) precludes an outdoor site. The play, which recounts the traditional legend of a pagan king robbed of the treasure placed in the saint's protection, calls for several distinct *loca*, and derives much of its pace from swift-moving shifts of scene, although the text itself only contains one actual stage-direction ('Now the Saracens kill all the Christians'). Locations include the Saracen king's palace with a throne and a site for his idol Tervagan up a flight of steps; the tavern at Arras, with a door at the rear where the thieves gather to drink and dice; a prison, complete with instruments of torture; four areas probably on the edge of the *platea* inhabited by the vassal Emirs; an open space for a battlefield (probably the main *platea*); a *manoque* (a hut or oratory) serving as a place for Preudom (the Good Man), who is found praying there after the battle; Paradise, possibly in the form of a high tower. The vitality and variety of Bodel's play are well reflected in the range of its settings, and its stock of properties which include the contrasted images of Christian saint and pagan idol, the king's treasure and the multiple paraphernalia of the tavern — pots, wine-bottles, candles, dice, and dice-board whose level has to be tested with a pea.

In the same indoor tradition stands *Le Miracle de Théophile* (*c.* 1261)[63] by the Parisian *trouvère* Rutebeuf (*fl.* 1245–85), which calls for six *mansions* in recounting the legend of this sixth-century bishop who made a pact with the devil in order to retain his bishopric. Théophile's *domus* would surely have occupied the central position on the *platea*, since the battle for the bishop's erring soul is the focal point of the action; on its left would be the house of the wily necromancer Salatin, and from Hell to the left of that Satan would emerge at Salatin's invocation. On Théophile's right would lie the *mansion* of the bishop and his clerks, while right of that would be the abode of the Virgin Mary who saves Théophile from damnation by her intervention. Again, a symmetrical stage arrangement centred on the dramatic protagonist mirrors the play's theological polarities, and reinforces its doctrinal impact.

Despite their lack of stage directions, *Les Miracles de Nostre Dame* and the Ste Geneviève plays probably received a very similar style of presentation, being staged indoors at the end of a large hall on a raised platform, employing the conventions of *mansion*-staging. The place chosen was doubtless a hall where the guild held its meetings or one rented specially; in the case of the Confrérie de la Passion the Hôpital de la Trinité was probably employed. A stage was set up across one end of the hall (the Trinité was only 12 metres (40 feet) wide), curtained at the rear and possibly the sides, and elevated sufficiently from the floor for trap-doors and a basin of water representing the sea or a lake to be included.

The likeliest disposition of the scenic locations in such an environment is in a semi-circle fringing the stage foreground (termed the *champ* or *parloir*) which serves as the *platea* or main acting area. Dorothy Penn deduces that the *Miracles de Nostre Dame* make increasing use of *mansions* as their dramatic technique becomes more assured so that, where the earliest scripts use between four and seven *mansions*, the later plays require between six and ten, and more elaboration is called for as the writers' ambitions expand.[64] The first play, the *Miracle de l'enfant donné au diable* (*The Child Given Away to the Devil*) requires seven structures, but most of them appear to have been formed from simple archways backed by tapestries and containing an appropriate object such as a throne or an altar; Heaven is the only built location needed, a platform 2 metres (6 feet) from the ground approached by a flight of steps front and rear. A later *miracle*, *La Fille d'un Roy* (*The King's Daughter*), one of the most elaborately staged of the series, demands nine structures, including a castle divided into two rooms, a church or *moustier* (monastery), the Temple of Jerusalem, a forest, Heaven with two stair-ways, a 'sea' complete with a boat which will hold five actors, an inn with tables and chairs, the emperor's palace and a church at Constantinople, plus a prison, not to mention a small pool and an area of the *parloir* designated as a battlefield! On a stage estimated by Dorothy Penn as being 12 metres (40 feet) wide by 6 (20) deep, this play must have taxed even the resourcefulness of an experienced guild and its stage technicians.

Only two plays call for the construction of a Hell, not the dragon's mouth of the *mystères* but simply a tower with an iron door and grating through which smoke and fire probably poured. In the *miracle* of Oton, King of Spain, a representation of Burgos was called for, and later the city gates went up in flames; in the play of St Jehan de Paulu, the hermit burns his hut to the ground in full view. In several plays hunting scenes, complete with dogs and horses, occur; while in the *Miracle de la marquise de la Gaudine* a horse and cart make a brief appearance. Nautical effects were also popular, with ships involved in six of the plays, and tempests enlivening the action on several occasions. In two plays an innocent victim is abandoned to the mercy of the waves in a boat without sail or rudder, and with the *miracle* of the Empress of Rome, the 'sensation drama' of the Victorians is anticipated when the empress is marooned on a rock in mid-ocean and left to her fate, which needless to say is divinely averted.

The plays of the Ste Geneviève manuscript were presented on a large indoor stage apparently 42 × 12 metres (138 × 40 feet): simplicity appears to have been the keynote of performance, although the Confrérie de la Passion no doubt exploited the limits of simultaneous staging in arranging their settings. The saints' plays ask for simple *mansion* sets: *maisons*, a prison, taverns, churches with altars, a hermit-age, a boat, while Heaven is often set at the side of the stage opposite Hell, although it can be placed on a higher level than the main stage with Hell on a lower level. The biblical plays, such as the *Nativité*, the *Passion*, the *Résurrection* also demand the usual wide range of locations: temples, palaces, the sepulchre, and other appropriate *sedes*. In the Passion and Resurrection plays the interior of Hell is shown, but the famous dragon's head could be used where space was less limited. Later the famous Parisian amateurs, the Enfants sans souci, used the Hôpital de la Trinité for their farces and secular moralities, most of which are similarly unambitious in their staging, although some call for Heaven and Hell to be shown, *Bien Avisé et Mal Avisé* (*Well-Advised and Ill-Advised*) not only featuring an elaborate Hell but also a revolving wheel of fortune. *La Condamnacion de Banquet* (*The Sentencing of Gluttony*) is probably the most complex *moralité*, demanding several 'houses', two with windows and one with a kitchen as well as a dining-area, a number of tables, a prison, and a gibbet. These were no doubt grouped about the platform in the traditional manner associated with simultaneous *mansion* staging.

The time has come to shift our attention from drama in church, chapel, and guild premises to the banquet-halls and chambers of emperors, kings, and noblemen, where indoor drama took the form of elaborate spectacles and 'dressing-up games'. The planning and execution of such ambitious ventures, the development of technical expertise in building stages, arranging spectator accommodation, and evolving elaborate machinery, the organisation of large casts and complicated performance schedules, are all important aspects of the stagecraft of the age. Furthermore, such festivities served an important social and psychological function; as Johan Huizinga writes:

it is important to realize the function of festivals in the society of that time. They still preserved something of the meaning they have in primitive societies, that of the supreme expression of their culture, the highest mode of a collective enjoyment and an assertion of solidarity ... at a time when the highest pleasures were neither numerous nor accessible to all, people felt the need of such collective rejoicings as festivals. The more crushing the misery of daily life, the stronger the stimulants that will be needed to produce that intoxication with beauty and delight without which life would be unbearable.[65]

We may begin most fruitfully with court banqueting entertainments provided by professionals, when the aristocratic amateurs who would take part in court 'mommeries' and disguisings of a later period were no doubt otherwise occupied. An early example of a miniature pageant or *entremés* is found in an account of the coronation banquet of Alfonso IV of Aragon on Easter Day 1328, when each course of the meal was introduced by the performance of a specially composed dance accompanied by singing.[66] '*Un bell entremés*' was also featured at the coronation banquet of Doña Sibila, Queen of Aragon, in 1381, but this time more elaboration was introduced in the form of a peacock bearing verses and surrounded by other fowl, who was presented to the queen to the strains of instrumental music.

Three years before, on Twelfth Night 1378, a celebrated spectacle took place in the Palais de la Cité in Paris, devised for the delectation of Charles V of France and his uncle the Emperor Charles IV by Philippe de Mézières, diplomat, traveller, crusader, and tutor to the future

Charles VI. The event depicted in the banquet-hall was the conquest of Jerusalem in 1099 by Godfrey of Bouillon, and its scenic marvels attracted wide attention (see Illustration 5). One device was a ship with sails and a mast, presumably mounted on wheels and related to the ship-carts of pagan processions, which bore armed men into the hall, along with Peter the Hermit as narrator. The other *entremés* (French *entremet*) was in the form of the city of Jerusalem, its temple topped by a high tower, from which a Saracen called others to prayer in Arabic, almost touching the ceiling as he did so. The warriors from the ship set about besieging the tower which was defended by other armed Saracens, while the crusaders ran up ladders, fell from them, and finally captured the city.[67] Froissart records another *entremés* in June 1389 at the Palais de la Cité, where the set-pieces again included a lofty castle 12 metres (40 feet) high, with four towers in the corners and a higher one in the centre, representing Troy, with the high tower as the 'citadel of Ilion'. The whole structure moved on four hidden wheels, as did two similar vehicles, one an assault-tower occupied by Greeks, the other a splendidly constructed ship capable of holding 100 soldiers. Those from ship and tower mounted an assault on the castle, but the combat had to be called to a premature halt by the king because the heat and over-crowding upset so many of the onlookers.

The fame of French scenic devices must have reached Geoffrey Chaucer for in *The Franklin's Tale* he alludes to the skill of 'subtile tregetoures' (magicians) who bring such things to pass:[68]

> For ofte at feestes have I wel herd seye
> That tregetours, withinne an halle large,
> Have maad come in a water and a barge,
> And in the halle rowen up and doun.
> Somtyme hath semed come a grym leoun;
> And somtyme floures sprynge as in a *mede*;   meadow
> Somtyme a vyne, and grapes white and rede;
> Somtyme a castel, al of lym and stoon;
> And whan hem lyked, voyded it anon.
> Thus semed it to every mannes sighte. (1142–51)

A variety of spectacular effects[69] graced the coronation banquet of Martin I of Aragon in Saragossa in 1399: an angel descending on a cloud from an elevated Heaven served the king with delicacies and sang, accompanied by musicians concealed in the heavens; one dish was preceded to the table by a great golden eagle, another by a fire-breathing snake which was attacked and killed by armed men. The *pièce de résistance* was the entry of a huge lioness crouched on a large rock out of which came hares, rabbits, doves, partridges, other birds

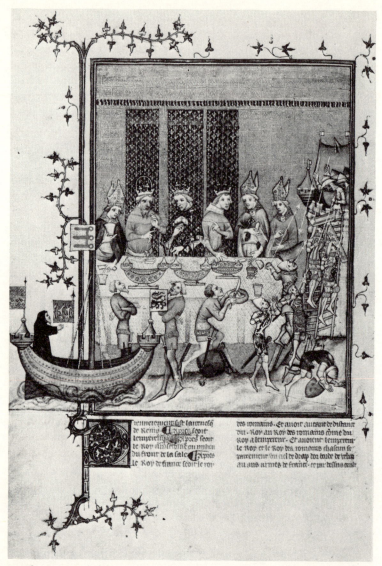

5   The conquest of Jerusalem performed as an *entremet*, Palais de la Cité, Paris, 1378

and wild bears. A battle ensued between armed men who tried to kill the lioness and 'wild men' (*salvajes*) defending her; from a wound made in the lioness's shoulder a crowned child in the royal arms appeared, bearing a drawn sword and singing sweetly. The coronation celebrations of Fernando, 'el Honesto', in 1414 included a banquet with a range of elaborate *entreméses* including a flame-breathing gryphon as large as a horse which literally blazed a trail for dishes of food carried through the crowd. The main built-structure was a decorated platform representing Heaven, in the middle of which three wheels, set one above the other and filled with angels in gold wings and white masks, revolved in opposite directions, while the angels sang and played on instruments. On the highest level of all, a child dressed in cloth of gold crowned another representing the Virgin Mary. The wheels turned, hymns and the *Te Deum* were sung, an angel on a cloud descended and returned, the Vices and the Virtues addressed the company, and then Death ('a man dressed in close-fitting yellow leather so that his body and his head looked like those of a skeleton, all gaunt and fleshless and without eyes, looking very ugly and very terrifying, and with his hands making gestures in every direction beckoning to some and to others') descended on a cloud which also bore snakes, skulls, and tortoises. At a later performance courtiers terrified a court jester by tying a rope round him and getting Death to haul him up to his cloud, so that the jester, weeping with fear as he hung suspended above the diners, urinated on the heads of those below, 'and the king looked on and had great enjoyment'. The second course was introduced by the appearance of a large *roca* (probably meaning a pageant-waggon) in the form of a painted wooden castle which moved on wheels, containing six singing girls and a golden eagle.

At the so-called Banquet of the Pheasant's Vows at Lille given by Philip the Good of Burgundy in 1454, the lavish scenic structures included a church with a cross, windows, an organ, four singers, and 'a bell that rang', a rigged and ornamented boat filled with sailors and merchandise, a meadow with trees, rocks, and a fountain, and a castle, from two of whose towers streams of orange water fell into a moat: also featured was a gigantic pie containing twenty-eight musicians.[70] At the marriage feast of Philip's son, Charles the Bold, and Margaret of York at Bruges in 1468, a pastoral *entremet* was staged, in which princesses of the past were seen dressed as shepherdesses guarding their flocks. In Portugal in 1490 at Evora, two roasted oxen with gilded hooves and horns drew a golden cart containing roasted sheep into the hall so that the guests might serve themselves: later black-faced dancers (see p. 6 above) and three giants appeared.

A bridge between such professional entertainments and those in which the court itself participated is provided by the mumming; mumming seems to be a sophisticated survival of a pagan folk-ritual, or of the

Roman Saturnalia, and a prerogative of the *bourgeoisie* rather than the nobility. It consists of a processional visit on a winter night to a private house by masked and silent figures who may dance and play dice with, or bring gifts to, their host. John Stow writes of an early mumming at Kennington in 1377 before Richard II, who had succeeded to the throne as a boy of ten only that year: 'in ye night were 130 men disguizedly aparailed and well mounted on horsebacke to goe on mumming to ye said prince, riding from Newgate through Cheape whear many people saw them with great noyse and minstralsye, trumpets, cornets and shawmes and great plenty of waxe torches lighted.'[71]

The disguises adopted by the citizens included that of an emperor attended by esquires and knights, and a pope accompanied by cardinals, who were followed by '8 or 10 arayed and with black vizardes [masks] like devils appearing nothing amiable seeming like legates' which suggests some anti-papal satire was intended. When they had ridden over London Bridge and arrived at Kennington, the mummers dismounted and entered the palace where the king, his mother, and other nobles met them in the hall

and ye said mummers saluted them, shewing a pair of dice upon a table to play with ye prince, which dice were subtilly made that when ye prince shold cast he shold winne and ye said players and mummers set before ye prince three jewels each after other: and first a balle of gould, then a gould ring, ye which ye said prince wonne at thre castes as before it was appointed ... And then ye prince caused to bring ye wyne and they dronk with great joye, commanding ye minstrels to play and ye trompets began to sound and other instruments to pipe & c. And ye prince and ye lordes dansed on ye one syde, and ye mummers on ye other a great while and then they drank and tooke their leave and so departed toward London.

Whether this was a new venture or not is hard to say: as early as Christmas 1347 Edward III's Royal Wardrobe supplied for Christmas *ludi* at Guildford 42 'viseres' in the likenesses of women, men with beards, and heads of silver angels, as well as 28 'crestes' and peacock, swan, and dragon or serpent costumes, but it is possible that these refer to equipment for tournaments or court revels of some other kind.[72] Documents referring to similar items for Christmas 1348 and Epiphany 1349 simply tell us they were required '*ad faciendum ludos domini regis* [for making the revels of the Lord King]'.

Mumming continued in vogue for some time:[73] several fifteenth-century chroniclers claimed that in 1400 a plot was laid to kill Henry IV 'undir the coloure of mummeris in Christmasse tyme'; Stow again records that in 1401 when the king was entertaining the Emperor of Constantinople at Eltham Palace, the 'men of London maden a gret mommying to hym of xij aldermen and there sons, for whiche they hadde gret thanks'. But mummings in the London streets came under interdict in 1418 when it was proclaimed 'that no manere persone, of what astate, degre, or condicioun that evere he be, duryng this holy tyme of Christemes be so hardy in eny wyse to walk by nyght in any manere mommyng, pleyes, enterludes, or eny other disgisynges with eny feynyd berdis, peynted visers, diffourmyd or colourid visages in eny wyse'.

A similar prohibition was issued in Bristol in 1479, and as late as 1511 an *Acte against disguysed persons and Wearing of Visours* states that

lately wythin this realme dyvers persons have disgysed and appareld theym, and covert theyr fayces with Vysours and other thynge in such manner that they sholde nott be knowen and divers of theym in a Companye togeder namyng them selfe Mummers have commyn to the dwellyng place of divers men of honor and other substanciall persones; and so departed unknowen.

The opportunities for trouble-making and crime offered by such un-invited visitations were obviously tempting, and mummers were often suspected of ulterior motives: in 1414 Sir John Oldcastle and the Lollards were accused of using a mumming at Eltham 'to have destryte the Kynge and Hooly Chyrche', and it is appropriate that the anony-mous Elizabethan author of *Woodstock* depicts Thomas of Gloucester as betrayed to his enemies through his genial action in admitting masked entertainers to his house in Essex. However, at court and in some noble households mummings continued on a less haphazard footing, changing their nature from the semi-spontaneous dice-playing to more refined theatrical and allegorical acts of homage, yet still often presented by citizens at the time of seasonal festivities.[74] Of this type are several 'momeries' attributed to the poet John Lydgate (*c.* 1370– *c.* 1450),[75] in which presumably the identity of the players was known, and their arrival scheduled in advance. Audiences for such pieces included the king and queen, the mayor of London, the city sheriffs and aldermen and the great estates of the realm, and they were staged on Mayday, at Christmas, Twelfth Night, and New Year's Eve. The performers still remained silent, the text of their entertainment being recited by a narrator while they mimed the action, which often amounted simply to posing on stage in costume, a mode of presenta-tion recalling the method possibly employed earlier for other plays (pp. 27–9, 31, 48–9, 66, 91–2, 186). Several mummings involved the presentation of gifts, and Wickham suggests[76] that this is the main factor in distinguishing the mumming from the 'disguising', the generic term for this kind of entertainment until the word 'masque' came to supplant it during the sixteenth century. Certainly Lydgate's New Year's Eve disguisings at London and Hertford do not involve gifts, but nor does his Christmas diversion at Windsor which is entitled a Mumming! Two of the mummings were presented by the London Goldsmiths' and the Mercers' Companies respectively, but it is quite possible that the casts included professional performers.

The staging of Lydgate's dramatic poems is of interest: in his mumming for the Mercers' Company three mechanical ships of the recognised type enter the hall very much as in the French *entremet*; the mumming at Windsor requires a church as at Lille in 1454, a hermitage, and a 'Heaven', while in the London disguising Fortune's 'hall' is described as a structure with two sides, one ugly and ruined, the other rich with gold, silver, and precious stones.

At what point in time royalty and nobility began to take a part in court dramatics is uncertain, but obviously the tendency gathered momentum as the mumming lost its element of surprise, and became a visitation by disguised friends or performers whose arrival was expected. Aristocratic participation probably derived from the evening celebrations following medieval tournaments, and Froissart describes a banquet given by Edward III in 1364 at which 'the young Lord de Couci danced and sang splendidly when his turn came'; it was a small step from this to appearance in a mumming or disguising. An account of the most notorious of such mommeries, staged in January 1393 to enliven a fashionable wedding at the court of Charles VI of France, we owe to Froissart: the performers were five nobles of the court and the king himself, who secretly masked and dressed themselves in pitch-coated costumes stuck with flax as 'wild men' so beloved of organisers of tableaux and pageants, and then entered the hall yelping and dancing crazily before the assembled court who did not recognise them. Unfortunately, Louis Duke of Orleans was over-eager to discover the revellers' identities:

he put one of the torches that his servantes helde so nere, that the heate of the fyre entred into the flaxe, wherin if fyre take there is no remedy, and sodaynly was on a bright flame, and so eche of them set fyre on other; the pytche was so fastened to the lynen clothe, and their shyrtes so drye and fyne, and so joynynge to their flesshe, that they began to brenne and to cry for helpe. None durste come nere theym; they that dyd, brente their handes, by reason of the heate of the pytche ... there was two brente to dethe in the place, and other two ... borne to their lodgynges, and dyed within two dayes after in gret mysery and payne. Thus the feast of this maryage brake up in hevynesse ...[77]

In 1461 the Constable of Castile and his wife organised festivities in which members of their household appeared disguised as strangers, wearing masks and dressed in light green, who claimed that they had been released from captivity to dance at the feast.[78] In another entertainment pages pretending to be strangers were projected into the hall by the belch of a fiery serpent who was supposed to have swallowed them; they emerged apparently on fire, their costumes having been drenched in spirit. In 1463 'momos' arrived following a banquet, wearing masks and costumes decorated with flames; at Christmas 1464 the Constable diced with citizens of Jaén, although there is no evidence that they were disguised as were the Kennington mummers of 1377, or that the Constable himself dressed up to participate. However, a momerie composed by Gómez Manrique for the birthday of Prince Alfonso in November 1467, involves not only the traditional bearing of gifts associated with some of Lydgate's mummings, but Princess Isabel herself took part in the performance, while the masquers who played the nine Muses were all her court ladies. These performers were silent, but as in Lydgate's momeries, the words were spoken by a presenter, probably the princess herself. After this introduction, each lady, dressed in white 'with beautiful plumes', presented a birthday gift to the fourteen-year-old prince.

At Lisbon in 1500 masked mummers were accompanied by a wheeled device of the *entremés* type, a garden of love guarded by a three-headed dragon coiled about a quince tree in whose branches were lighted candles. About the tree, bearing flaming torches, sat six ladies, one of whom addressed a petition to the queen who sat on a dais in the hall; after the garden was trundled away, the king and twenty gentlemen, all in masks, appeared and danced, after which the king removed his mask to dance with the queen. Subsequently pilgrims in a boat, a giant, eight devils, eight ghosts, a wheeled pageant-waggon topped by a wilderness and another bearing a cave appeared.

By this time such costumed scenic diversions were well established at the English court of Henry VII: at Epiphany 1494 William Cornish, poet-composer and later Master of the Children of the Chapel Royal, devised a prologue in which he appeared on horseback as St George, accompanied by 'a fair virgin' leading 'a terrible and huge red dragon'. His speech was followed by dancing by twelve gentlemen and twelve ladies, who may have been courtiers.[79] In 1501 elaborate disguisings performed by the Gentlemen of the Chapel Royal in Westminster Hall and Richmond Palace formed part of the lavish celebrations to mark the marriage of Henry VII's eldest son Arthur to Katherine of Aragon. A 'moost goodly and pleasaunt disguysing' at Westminster involved three 'pagens proper and subtil', one the inevitable castle on wheels drawn in by a gold and a silver lion, a hart, and an ibex, containing eight ladies looking out of windows and four singing children in the turrets. The second structure was the well-known wheeled ship, bearing 'a goodly and faire lady, in her apparell like unto the Princess of Hispayne'. From the ship came Hope and Desire 'as ambassadours from Knights of the Mownte of Love unto the ladies within the castell', and on the ladies' refusal to grant the knights their favours, a third pageant 'in the likeness of a great hill' came in, from which eight knights 'right freshly disguysed' came forth, and assaulted the castle 'in such wise that the ladies, yeldyng themselvys, descendid from the seid castell" and dancing between knights and ladies followed. Later the pageant-waggons and performers departed, and the royal spectators danced, the young Duke of York (then aged ten) throwing off his gown and dancing in his jacket. Ten years later, in February 1511 when the young Duke had become Henry VIII and himself married Katherine of Aragon, 'a pageaunt upon wheles' representing a garden of trees and flowers, in which sat four knights who had taken part in a joust earlier in the day, was featured in celebrations to mark the birth of a son to the royal pair.

Such disguisings were superseded by the masque which reached England in 1512, the fact being recorded thus in Hall's *Chronicle*:[80]

On the daie of the Epiphanie at night, the kyng with a xi [eleven] other were disguised, after the maner of Italie, called a maske, a thyng not seen afore in Englande, thei were appareled in garmentes long and brode, wrought all with gold, with visers and cappes of gold & after the banket doen, these Maskers came in, with sixe gentlemen disguised in silke bearyng staffe torches, and desired the ladies to daunce, some were content, and some that knewe the fashion of it refused, because it was not a thyng commonly seen. And after thei daunced and commoned together, as the fashion of the Maske is, thei tooke their leave and departed.

The masque's principal novelty probably lay not in the participation of the king and courtiers but in the fact that they were disguised with masks and special costumes and yet mingled with the noble spectators as part of the dramatic action: the more usual practice would seem to have been for the mummers to dance separately as at Kennington in 1377. The convention was rapidly assimilated, and in the account of a masque performed at Greenwich in 1527[81] by Henry VIII and several of his courtiers, disguised 'in maskyng apparel of cloth of gold and purple tinsel satin' and masks with golden beards, we are told that 'these viii noble personages entred and daunsed long with the ladies, and when they had daunsed there fill, then the quene plucked of the kynges visar, and so did the Ladies the visars of the other Lordes, and then all were knowen'.[82]

It may be doubted whether the presentation of genuine plays at the early Tudor court was as sumptuous: while talented devisers, directors, performers, and designers were occupied in supplying the Tudor kings with suitably lavish banquet entertainments, Henry VII also had in his employment four 'pleyers of the Kyngs enterluds' and his son increased that number to eight. Whether a clear line was drawn between the style of show they staged and those mounted for instance by William Cornish cannot be ascertained. Certainly in 1501 John English, Master of the King's Players, devised one of the disguisings presented, which suggests some identity of artistic purpose with Cornish who devised three entertainments. Yet interlude-players were usually called on to supply dramatic fare very different from that involving pre-constructed scenic devices which could be wheeled into the hall, or established in advance of the banquet.

Not all late medieval indoor entertainments were of a splendid and complex type; in England performances of plays were mounted in halls and chambers of varying degrees of modesty, not only in palaces and noble houses for the enjoyment of aristocrats and their private households, but in colleges, schools, and Inns of Court for the pleasure of students and scholars, and in the squire's manor or the town house of some merchant for family enjoyment. Indeed, anyone willing to pay the players for their pains could command a performance in the comfort and convenience of his own dwelling. Such presentations were staged generally in the principal room of the house or institution, usually the Great Hall, the focal area for social activity among royalty, nobles, gentry, students and civic dignitaries alike.[83]

Methods of staging were as always dependent on conditions confronting the players when they arrived to perform: what they could be virtually certain of finding in the average hall was a raised dais at one end where stood the 'high table' reserved for the leading members of the community and their guests, as at Oxford and Cambridge colleges today. The performance had to be given in an area which permitted the chief spectators to watch the action without discomfort or disturbance. Thus the hall-floor in front of the dais offered the obvious playing-space, with the audience ranged on three sides of it around the walls of the room, standing or seated at tables during or after their meal. The entertainment (usually known as an interlude) thus evolved as a histrionic addition to the menu: this was not a performance to which spectators had come of their own volition, but one which had been brought to them, and which had to adapt itself to the function required of it. The players could not expect to disrupt the normal social processes with their artistic demands: their offering formed the *apéritif* or dessert, not the main course.

Two principal forms of stage were open to them: they could erect a platform on trestles at the lower end of the hall, of the booth-stage type used in market-place and town-square, backed by curtains to hide the assembly- and changing-area behind the platform. Such stages were traditional, stretching back to the *mimi*, and may have received additional sanction from the classical revival, since it has been argued that the illustrations for the Lyon edition of Terence's comedies (1493) reveal such a system in use, although T. E. Lawrenson and Helen Purkis have cautioned theatre historians from placing too much reliance on the early Terence illustrations as pieces of factual data.[84] However, for hall or chamber purposes, the booth-stage seems an obvious device.

On the other hand, there is little evidence that raised and curtained platforms were set up in halls before the second half of the sixteenth century,[85] and most scholarly attention has focussed on an alternative method, which took advantage of the usual structure of a Tudor hall,[86] where the lower end leading off to the kitchens and servants' quarters was partially or completely partitioned off with screens from the main body of the hall, so that a kind of passage-way was formed, sometimes called 'the entry'. Part of the purpose of the screens was to shield those dining from the eyes of those crossing the lower end of the hall (just as the screens in medieval churches had done); their other main function was to protect the inmates from draughts from doors at each end of the passage-way. By the mid-fourteenth century some entry passages were roofed over so that a musicians' gallery might be formed, as at Penshurst Place in Kent. Usually the screens were pierced by two openings, closed off with curtains or doors, which allowed those serving the meal to pass to and from the kitchens. To a travelling company staging its play at the lower end of the hall, this feature was ideally suited to its needs. Actors could costume themselves in the servants' rooms; the entry passage could serve as an assembly-area; entrances and exits could be made through the openings in the screen. The traditional *platea* was supplied by the central floor between the tables, and architectural features or furnishings could be incorporated into the action, just as the proximity of the spectators enabled them to be addressed directly or even brought into the action itself, if only by being requested in the course of the drama not to obstruct the access to the stage through the screen-passage.

It is uncertain how many late fifteenth-century and early sixteenth-century plays can be safely assigned to theatrical settings similar to the one described, but this mode of performance was probably fundamental to the fifty or so short English plays generally referred to as interludes. This elastic term is employed throughout the late Middle Ages in England to denote a wide range of diversions, from party-games to farces and religious plays, but it comes to indicate principally brief dramatic entertainments popular in the Tudor period. These comprise didactic pieces such as *Mundus et Infans*, expounding Christian doctrine and conduct, political moralities (*Magnyfycence*, *Respublica*), debating-plays on humanistic topics (*The Mariage of Witte and Science*, *The Nature of the Four Elements*), humorous farces such as those of John Heywood, and bitter polemics on religious doctrine. Frequently unrewarding to read, these plays often blossom into life in the warmth of actual presentation. Few depended for their effect on built scenic structures such as *mansions*, or on grandiose stage devices; when we consider the limited means, both financial and technical, available to the itinerant performers mostly associated with these pieces, we shall understand why their forte was improvisation and 'doing without'. Only perhaps in the more lavish productions mounted in court circles, in colleges, and in the Inns of Court, could adequate funds be found for ambitious scenery or costumes. Even in these cases scenic aids must have been of a fairly elementary kind;[87] the screen doorways were often used to denote houses, and where there is unequivocal evidence that built structures were employed, they seem to have been principally devised for court, university, or school performances of such plays as *Thersytes* (c. 1537), *Ralph Roister Doister* (c. 1553), *Gammer Gurton's Nedle* (c. 1553), and *Horestes* (1567–8), some of which may reveal knowledge of the 'classical' style of presentation fashionable in humanistic circles. *Thersytes* requires Mulciber to have 'a shop made in the place', probably a light temporary framework set up on the hall floor, and another location is prepared for Thersytes's Mother (possibly in the form of a traverse curtain) where her son may hide; Custance in *Roister Doister* needs a house in which she and her servants may be besieged by Ralph and his companions; the text of *Gammer Gurton's Nedle* suggests that two houses and a street in the ancient comedic mode were constructed to cope with the bifocal action which shifts between the homes of Dame Chat and Gammer Gurton, although Richard Southern has demonstrated just how many problems arise from an attempt to erect

a stage and two houses at one end of a college hall.[88] In *Horestes*
a central structure representing a castle gate is employed for several
purposes: Clytemnestra appears, to speak 'over ye wal' above the gate;
Aegisthus is hanged from the battlements; the city is assaulted and
later entered through the gate. A gated structure also seems to feature
in *Wyt and Science* dating from the same year, and may have been specially built, since the permanent hall-screen could scarcely have been
employed for the purpose.

Other scenic devices used in the exceptional interludes requiring
scenery include a practical tree which has to be climbed in *Common
Conditions* (c. 1576), and possibly a wall bisecting the stage from front
to rear in Thomas Garter's *Vertuous and Godlye Susanna* (c. 1569).[89]
The wall requires a door to allow entrance to the orchard where
Susanna takes her fateful bath, the remainder of the stage being
variously used for those episodes manifestly not taking place in the
orchard. Richard Southern envisages a low stage, placed between the
entrance doors, on which the Elders stand plotting Susanna's downfall (see Illustration 6), and interprets the stage direction 'Here they
go afore into the Orchard' as a reference to stepping *down* into the main
body of the hall, where a fenced-off area with a gate in it represents
the orchard with its pool, thus enabling Susanna and her maids to
'come upon the stage' simultaneously. Southern sees the erection of this
low platform at the screen-end of the hall as an important innovation,
and one with great future potential; it is also an excellent example of
the medieval tradition whereby a stage location changes identity
according to the characters who occupy it. The orchard area is a
further instance of the survival from the past of fixed scenic locations,
although Southern raises the possibility that this area was later dispensed with by removing the fence, thus freeing an area where the
stake for Susanna's threatened execution could be set up.

But in many instances scenery for performances of interludes had to
be dispensed with: apart from its cost and the inconvenience of
setting up even the simplest of *sedes* in a banquet-hall or council
chamber, space was at a premium. Playing-conditions were cramped,
as texts make plain: the boastful Thersytes thrusts his way into the
hall, exclaiming:

> Abacke, geve me roume, in my way do ye not stand —
> For if ye do, I wyll soone laye yow lowe!

And when Merry Report, Jupiter's Messenger in John Heywood's
Play of the Wether prepares to leave the hall, he advertises the fact with

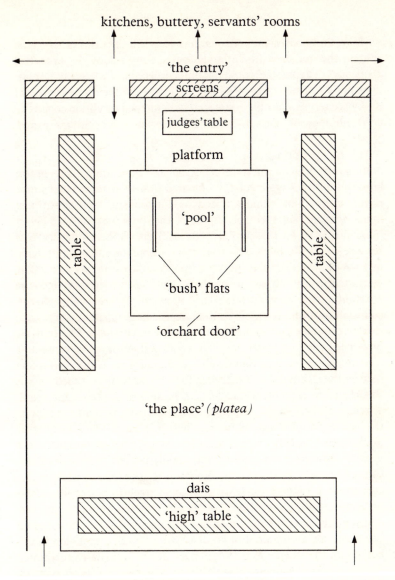

kitchens, buttery, servants' rooms

'the entry'

screens

judges' table

platform

'pool'

table

table

'bush' flats

'orchard door'

'the place' *(platea)*

dais

'high' table

6   A conjectural reconstruction of the staging of *Susanna* in a Tudor hall, *c.* 1569 (after Richard Southern)

a request that the crowd of spectators should clear the way:

> Frendes, *a* fellyshyppe let me go by ye!   out of
> Thynke ye I may stand thrustyng amonge you there?

As T. W. Craik observes,[90] only aggressive or self-important characters address the audience in this style, never the virtuous; yet even 'the comic and disreputable' could not order others out of their way, if there were not a sufficient press of people present to give their remarks point. Bulky scenery could only result in more cramped conditions or a reduced number of spectators, neither of which the players would relish.

The hall-performances so far discussed may be regarded as predominantly private entertainments, but the travelling players of the late Middle Ages were equally prepared to display their talents to a paying clientèle of ordinary citizens, and indoor sites were sometimes made available for such performances, the town- or guild-hall being frequently used for this purpose. Although special performances may have been given solely for the mayor and corporation, as at Canterbury in 1486−7 when the site was the Swan Inn, the commons were often permitted to watch plays in city-halls: in 1538−9 the Canterbury corporation gave a 'reward to my Lord Protector's pleyers pleyng in the courthall over and besydes the benevolence of the peple'.[91]

Where indoor performances were given in city-halls,[92] it seems to have been the custom to erect a temporary stage at the lower end of the hall, as in some private dwellings: an entry referring to an interlude in the Chamberlain's accounts for 1541−2 from Norwich makes this clear: 'to ii laborers that fetchyd barrells and tymber and made a scaffold then − ii^d'. A later reference (1542−3) indicates that the venue was the assembly chamber of the guild-hall, and that a platform was raised on this occasion on 'fourmes' or benches. Next year six labourers 'caryed xii long popill [poplar] planks from the comon' to make a stage in the Common Hall at Norwich, and in the accounts for 1546−7 we learn that for a stage to be set up 'at the ende of the halle', the 'tabyles, trustylls, & forymes' had to be removed and replaced after the performance. At Gloucester in 1559−60 money was paid 'for an hundred of borde-nayles to make a scaffolde in the bothall for the Quenes Majesties players' and to 'John Battye, carpinter and his fellowe for the makinge of the said scaffolde'; at Nottingham in 1571−2 a hire charge in connection with a visit from the same company of players reads: 'to William Marshall for bordes that was borowed for to make a scaffold to the Halle when the Quen's Maiestyes players dyd play'. In 1577−8 the Bristol accounts refer to a play given in the 'Yeld Hall before Mr. Mayor and the Aldermen'; in the course of arranging this damage evidently occured, for an additional entry reads 'for men, one party 3 days, one 2 days, for mending the bord in the Yeld hall and the doers [doors] there, after my L of Leycesters players who had leave to play there. . . . '

But by now companies like the Earl of Leicester's Men were less dependent on the hospitality of halls and houses, or indeed on the availability of any building primarily intended for some other purpose than the housing of drama. By the new year of 1577 their leader James Burbage, joiner, actor, and impresario, had opened his timber-built Theatre north of Bishopsgate in London, and the players had a permanent home of their own at last.

4

STREET THEATRE

We can wait with our stools and our sausages.
What comes first? Can you see? Tell us.

T. S. Eliot, 'Triumphal March' from *Coriolan*

It is not easy for an age which has resolutely turned its back on ceremony and ritual to attune itself to an age which set great store by them.
At a period when the fireside chat commands more attention than the
Speech from the Throne, when we arrange weddings and funerals to
cause minimal disruption to our daily routine, and when we pride
ourselves on our informality and lack of display, the medieval or
Renaissance predilection for the very opposites of such things can only
seem puzzling. At that date, as Johan Huizinga writes,

Every event, every action, was still embodied in expressive and solemn forms,
which raised them to the dignity of a ritual. For it was not merely the great
facts of birth, marriage, and death which, by the sacredness of the sacrament,
were raised to the rank of mysteries: incidents of less importance, like a journey, a task, a visit, were equally attended by a thousand formalities: benedic-
tions, ceremonies, formulas.[1]

One reason for this preponderance of ceremonial customs and ritual
routines in medieval times is perhaps that in an epoch which feared
keenly the outbreak of anarchy, the imminence of chaos, and the un-
certainty of the future, a period too frequently made aware of the
violence and cruelty underlying civilisation's thin veneer, society
tended to hallow precious notions by endowing them with idealised
forms. As Chapter 1 argues, a universally felt desire to impose order on
disorder finds expression in traditional rites and patterns and it is likely
that such medieval ideals as chivalry, feudalism, monasticism, and
courtly love germinated in similar soil to that which nourished ritual
drama.

This was also an era which evinced a strong need for the concrete
presentation of abstract ideas, as the rich allegorical literature of the
Middle Ages constantly makes us aware. Just as medieval man could
best understand the human struggle to overcome spiritual temptations

86

if it were presented to him as a physical battle between personified Virtues and Vices, and preferred to follow a complicated narrative of courtship in the metaphor of a lover's vicissitudes in trying to pluck a rosebud, so magnificent public displays of homage, loyalty, religious faith, or temporal power brought home to him through his own eyes the meaning of those abstract concepts. Moreover, since, to the greater part of the medieval population of Europe, literature was literally a closed book, illiteracy being widespread, visual imagery constituted a major element in the popular experience of art and drama, even if it had to be acquired after a long wait in a chilly street, or by craning one's neck in a crowded market-place or throne-room.

Closely related to drama in their spirit and iconography were the rituals associated with the medieval tournaments, an activity which began as a series of training exercises for war, and culminated in a complex and spectacular ceremonial governed by a highly developed system of ethical and aesthetic notions.[2] Indeed it has been claimed that the tournament was the source of much dramatic imagery employed in court and street theatre presentations. Purged of brutality and indiscipline, the tournament came to represent the apotheosis of the cult of the medieval knight, and one of the chief arenas in which the ideals of chivalry and *courtoisie* could be deployed. Whether in the form of single combat between warriors known as the Joust (which involved either tilting on horseback with lances or fighting across a wooden barrier on foot with swords, axes, or spears), in Tourneying, where rival troops of horsemen engaged each other in swordfight, or in the *Pas d'Armes* (passage of arms), where one troop would defend a natural or artificial obstacle such as a mountain pass or a bridge, a tower or a castle, from attack by an equal number of challengers, exhibitions of knightly prowess were usually accompanied by attendant rites and observances. 'The actual combats would be sandwiched between long ceremonial processions of entry into the lists and departure from them',[3] and participants might assume allegorical identities reinforced by their dress and behaviour, playing quasi-dramatic rôles which they might maintain into evening festivities which followed a day's combat in the lists. Although chivalric conflict could become a deadly earnest affair, the lists became a natural setting for symbolic games of elaborate make-believe, to which allegorical scenic devices, inscriptions, costumes, action, impersonation, and even dialogue contributed.

Conscious imitation of chivalric literature is indicated by the foundation of Round Tables in western Europe during the late thirteenth century;[4] such a gathering of knights was held at Kenilworth in 1279, and another at Nefyn in North Wales in 1284. By 1330 the burghers of Tournai in Belgium had a Round Table society and were inviting other towns to attend jousts imitative of those of King Arthur and his knights, though whether impersonation was demanded is unclear. In September 1331, however, we learn that Edward III and his court processed to the lists in Cheapside 'all dressed in shining armour and masked in the likeness of Tartars'. These street-jousts lasted three days; Stow informs us that a wooden scaffold set up to accommodate spectators collapsed, injuring those below, and that the king had a permanent stone structure set up to replace it.[5] Dressing-up was also a feature of 'solemne justs' held at Smithfield in 1343, where one challenger dressed as the pope was accompanied by twelve others wearing 'garments like to cardinals', resembling garbs adopted by some of the mummers who visited Richard II in 1377 (see pp. 73–4 above). Stow again informs us that in 1374 a joust began with a costumed procession: 'Dame *Alice Perrers* (the kings Concubine) as Lady of the Sunne, rode from the Tower of London, through Cheape, accompanied of many Lords and Ladies, every Lady leading a Lord by his horse bridle, till they came into west Smithfield, and then began a great Just, which endured seven dayes after.'[6]

Continental tournaments also involved pageantry and wearing disguises: at Jaén at Epiphany 1462 the Constable of Castile and his guests tilted at the ring, wearing crowns and masks in honour of the Magi, while in 1463 one hundred knights dressed as Christians fought against one hundred dressed as Moors with false beards, whose challenge was borne by the figure of Mahomet riding a mule and carrying the Koran and books of the Law. Another impersonated the King of Morocco.[7] Another such tournament-drama was devised for Henry IV of Castile: on the road to Madrid he and his entourage were confronted by a wooden barrier defended by '*salvajes*', the wild men so beloved of courtly entertainers, who issued the king's gentlemen with a challenge to joust. An account exists of the *Pas de la Bergière* (*The Shepherd's 'Pas'*) from Tarascon in Provençe,[8] organised by René I (1409–80), Duke of Anjou, titular King of Naples and Sicily, and father-in-law of England's Henry VI, in which two knights dressed as shepherds defended a shepherdess and her flocks against all-comers who struck a white or a black shield to indicate their willingness to joust. The shepherdess was in fact Jeanne de Laval, René's second wife, who rode round the lists on a horse led by two young men dressed as shepherds; her crook was topped with silver, and at her side hung a drinking-barrel also of silver; she also had a little basket of goods.[9] René appears to have excelled at stage-managing such devices; when his daughter Margaret left for England to marry Henry VI in 1445, an *Emprise du dragon* was celebrated, the melancholy king appearing dressed entirely in black, 'and his whole outfit, caparison, horse and all, down to the wood of his lance, was of the same colour'.[10]

From Ghent in 1469 derives a tournament-drama known as the *Pas d'Armes de la Sauvaige Dame (The 'Pas' of the Wild Woman),*[11] in which a knightly challenger fought on behalf of a wild woman who had supposedly saved his life; the *pas* to be defended was a gateway topped with a mountain surmounted by an artificial forest in which a cave sheltered the 'Dame Sauvaige' attended by wild men and women.[12] She was, we are told, 'covered in a life-like manner on every part of her body with long hairs, the loveliest and most blonde that one might see, with no other clothing, having on her head a most beautiful crown of little flowery twigs'. At the ensuing feast this wild woman, like Jeanne de Laval earlier, distributed prizes to the winning jousters, a commonly recorded ceremony accompanied by courtly revels in which the day's tournament-devices often reappeared. As the prelude to a tournament at Evora in 1490 the Portuguese king appeared as the Knight of the Swan and made his entry with eight companions, all in separate boats on wheels complete with artillery.[13] After the ships had withdrawn, another mobile *entremés* entered the hall, in the form of a fortress between a rock and a grove of trees; wild men guarded the gates, but were defeated, whereupon the fortress's gates opened, its drawbridge was let down, and the players came out into the hall, along with a number of live partridges and other birds.

The chronicles of the early Tudor court offer several similar descriptions:[14] when Prince Arthur married Katherine of Aragon in 1501 Henry VII arranged a number of sumptuous tournaments in her honour at Westminster Palace, the scenic structures differing little from those already encountered. In 1511 four knights of the realm of Coeur Noble bearing allegorical names (including Henry VIII himself as Coeur Loyal) obtained permission to fight a tournament entitled *Les quater Chevalers de la forrest salvigne (The Four Knights of the Fiercesome Forest),* a *Pas d'Armes* for which the participants entered in a pageant car, bearing a magnificent forest scene

with rockes, hilles and dales, with divers sundrie trees, floures, hathornes, ferne and grasse. In the middes of this forrest was a castell standing, made of golde, and before the Castel gate sat a gentleman freshly appareiled, makynge a garlande of Roses for the *pryce*. This forrest was drawen, as it were by strength of twoo great beastes, a Lyon and an Antelop.[15]

*prize

Similar allegorical tableaux and devices feature in those street theatres which were frequently set up along the length of the main thoroughfares of medieval towns and cities, to grace royal entries and welcome visiting celebrities, or to mark notable occasions such as royal births, weddings, coronations, funerals, or victories. Honoured guests would progress past displays where live performers would pose in sumptuous settings, and occasionally deliver brief speeches to the chief dignitary. The ingenuity and magnificence of these set-pieces were valued as demonstrations of the wealth and loyalty of the community, a great deal of skill, care, and expense being devoted to their planning and execution. Such lavish exhibitions, primarily intended to flatter the royal or noble visitor, frequently had some ulterior political or economic motive, as when the burghers of Bristol in 1486 urged the new king, Henry VII, to halt the decline in their city's industrial fortunes, or when in 1515 the young Charles, Count of Flanders (later the Emperor Charles V), entered Bruges where the tableaux past which he rode drew his attention to the exodus of business interests from Bruges to Antwerp, depriving the city of its former prosperity.[16] Street theatres compelled their chief spectator to familiarise himself with and address himself to pressing municipal problems, as he travelled past the specially erected stages that lined his route.

Sometimes a visiting great one would be treated to a special performance of a pre-existing entertainment,[17] but it was more usual for the pageants and tableaux with which cities and towns greeted notabilities or expressed their joy on important national occasions to be specially devised. Such tableaux would often be centred on prominent city landmarks past which the distinguished visitor had to ride or be conveyed, at each of which some fresh spectacle would be staged for his delectation or indoctrination. In addition, a series of platforms might be set up along the royal route: thus, when Henry V entered Paris on 17 November 1420, we are told that the scaffolds on which 'a very moving mystery play of the Passion' was presented stretched 'almost a hundred paces in length', running from the 'Rue de la Kalande' right up to the walls of the Palais, while Alain Chartier tells us that when Charles VII of France entered the city in November 1437 richly draped scaffolds were set up all along the 'grande rue S. Denis' 'almost within a stone's throw of each other'.[18]

One of the earliest and simplest entries on record is the reception in London in 1207 of the Emperor Otho IV, the guest of King John, for which the citizens simply arrayed themselves solemnly in long cloaks and went to meet the Emperor,[19] but by 1236 when the London streets were decorated for the wedding of Henry III and Eleanor of Provence, there were on view 'certain wonderful devices and marvels [*quibusdam prodigiosis ingeniis et portentis*]'.[20] When in 1269 the King of Castile was entertained with *jochs* (diversions) at Valencia,[21] they were accompanied by tournaments and martial exercises, and featured the ubiquitous wild men and armed vessels on wheels dragged along by minions dressed as seamen. Two armed ships (*dos lenys armats*) appeared at the coronation of Alfonso III of Aragon in 1286 at Saragossa, and the peace of Tarascon in 1290 called forth *jochs*, tournaments, and dances in Barcelona.[22] By 1313 when King Philippe IV of France welcomed Edward II of England to Paris, the king saw the presentation along the route of what were probably stage tableaux, some depicting incidents from the life of Christ: the title usually given to such a spectacle is *mystère mimé*.[23] One similar performance was presented before John, Duke of Bedford, on his entry to Paris in 1424, described as

ung moult bel mystère du Vieil Testament et du Nouvel, que les enffens de Paris firent; et fut fait sans parler et sans signer, comme ce feussent ymaiges enlevez contre ung mur.[24]
a very beautiful mystery play of the Old and New Testament, which the children of Paris put on: and it was staged without speech and without movement, just as if they were figures set up against a wall.

The Confrérie de la Passion offered a similar spectacle to Charles VII in 1437, although on this occasion, while 'the characters did not speak', they used gestures to portray Christ's Passion and the treachery of Judas; in July 1484 when it was Charles VIII's turn to enter Paris, the custom was still being maintained:

People thought highly of the splendidly costumed Satan and God the Father, performing on trestle-top stages, before the gate of St Denis and under the church porches, mimed plays in almost motionless tableaux.
On admira Satan et Dieu le Père, en grand costume, sur des treteaux, devant la porte Saint-Denis et sous les porches des Eglises, jouant des pantomimes en tableaux presque immobiles.

Henri Rey-Flaud is inclined to attach great importance to these *mystères mimés* and their staging before dignitaries at royal entries.[25] During the entry a *rhétoricien* or some other man of letters and learning, chosen for his fluent speech, would often explain the significance of what was being presented before the honoured visitor as he wended his way past tableaux composed of mute actors: such a figure appeared at Philip the Good's entry into Mons in 1455, when *un homme éloquent* accompanied the Duke and gave him an explanation of the allegorical felicities of each successive scaffold as the parties came up to it. Rey-

Flaud thinks the early vernacular religious plays were presented in the same way by a presiding narrator who would read or recite the entire piece while the often inexperienced actors would be required only to mime the action (pp. 27–9, 31, 48–9, 66, 75, 186); this did not preclude a more conventional style of presentation should the cast be sufficiently competent to learn and speak their lines themselves, when the *lecteur* could confine himself to passages of pure narrative and indirect dialogue. The account of the Riga prophet play of 1204 (see pp. 223–4 below)[26] may preserve an early record of such a performance, since this piece, given in order that the heathen might learn the rudiments of the Christian faith, was carefully explained to them, as well as to the neophytes, by an interpreter (*interpres*); many German plays contain an expositor to explicate the action.[27] At all events, Rey-Flaud believes that such a manner of presentation not only accounts for narrative passages in the early vernacular religious plays, but also illustrates the gradual transformation of the *mystères mimés* into the spoken *mystères* of fourteenth-century France.

Secular diversions also featured in Edward II's 1313 entry into Paris; indeed, a curious medley of religious and non-sacred pageantry seems to have been devised for presentation at street theatres. While the history of Christ from birth to resurrection was lavishly supplied with at least ninety angels and over a hundred devils, according to Godefroi de Paris one might also witness.

> *Herod et Cayphas en mitre*
> *Et Renard chanter une epistre.*

Herod, and Caiphas in his mitre, and Reynard the Fox chanting the epistle.[28]

Even if these diversions were not juxtaposed quite so blatantly as this account suggests, the medieval ability to blend secular and sacred elements without any sense of incongruity could scarcely receive more striking testimony.

The rôle played by municipal business interests in the royal entry is clear: in London Edward I's victory over William Wallace at Falkirk in 1298 was signalled on his return by a parade of the trade guilds, a ceremony closely related to similar Spanish receptions;[29] John Stow records that the citizens.

according to their severall trade, made their severall shew, but specially the Fishmongers, which in a solemne Procession passed through the Citie, having amongest other Pageants and shews, foure Sturgeons guilt, caried on four horses; then foure Salmons of silver on foure horses, and after them six and fortie armed knights riding on horses, made like *Luces* of the sea, and then one representing Saint †*Magnes*†, because it was upon S. Magnes day.

*pike   †Magnus

It was also the Fishmongers who in 1313 marked the birth of Edward III the previous November with the construction of a ship in full sail bearing the heraldic blazons of England and France, taking their device to Westminster, almost certainly on wheels, and then on to Eltham Palace.[30] Later, scaffolds were erected in the streets to stage tableaux of a more ambitious kind, although usually employing the traditional set-pieces. For the coronation of Richard II in 1377 at the upper end of the Cheapside at the Great Conduit 'a sort of castle had been made, having four turrets ... from which castle wine flowed abundantly on two sides'; in each of the towers stood a lovely girl of about the king's age and stature, dressed in white. On the king's approach they wafted gold leaves (*aurea folia in eius faciem efflaverunt*), showered him with imitation gold sovereigns, and then offered him and his retinue wine in gold cups. A golden angel bearing a gold crown, who had stood between and above the four turrets, then bent down and held out the crown to the king.[31]

Froissart has left a memorable account of the street-pageants which greeted Isabeau of Bavaria's entry into Paris in August 1389:[32] we again find children dressed as angels, a fountain running wine with a richly dressed choir of girls offering the liquor in golden cups and goblets, a castle complete with men-at-arms and a courtyard full of varied livestock, while there is an angelic descent from Paradise with a crown, contrived to look like genuine flight. The occasion's most purely theatrical event was the performance of a historical tournament-drama, the *Pas Saladin*,[33] probably based on a French poem describing how Richard Coeur de Lion and twelve companions during the Third Crusade fought a *Pas* against Saladin, who retired on learning their illustrious names from a spy. The performance was given on a raised platform (*eschafault*) overlooking the street, bearing a castle, before which the Christian and Saracen knights did battle; the role of Richard I included some dialogue:

As the Queen's litter came opposite the platform, King Richard stepped forward from among his companions, went up to the King of France, and asked permission to attack the Saracens. When it had been given, he went back to his twelve companions who drew up in battle order and immediately moved to the attack of Saladin and his Saracens. A fierce mock battle took place, which lasted for some time and delighted the spectators.

A wooden castle on wheels bearing singers dressed as angels features at the coronation procession of Martin I of Aragon in 1399;[34] another graced the coronation of Fernando, 'el Honesto', in 1414,[35] each of its five towers bearing a great candle. A similar structure was also employed at the celebrations afterwards, its central tower bearing a huge revolving wheel on which were seated four maidens representing claimants to the throne who rose and fell with the wheel. Another device of the same kind is found in Barcelona in 1481,[36] when three heavens were made to turn one against another, and St Eulalia and angels came down from a tower singing.

Such marvels were a constant feature of royal entries throughout the fifteeenth and sixteenth centuries, and George Kernodle has amassed examples from well into the 1600s, in support of his assertion that the pageant theatres of the streets made a considerable contribution to the visual appearance of the public theatres of the Renaissance. Glynne Wickham, too, has emphasised the importance of the street theatres for assessing the staging of English drama in the sixteenth century. Changes of emphasis can be observed in the later entries, for the spoken word plays an increasing part, while the stress on Biblical figures and scenes in some of the earlier spectacles comes to be shared first by the iconography of historical chivalry, and then by that of classical mythology and literature. In 1468 Charles the Bold witnessed a tableau at Lille depicting the Judgement of Paris, with Juno, Minerva, and Venus represented by three naked girls,[37] and other favourite subjects included the Nine Worthies, or Apollo and the Nine Muses which featured in Anne Boleyn's pre-coronation procession in 1533, along with another Judgement of Paris, or Jason and the Golden Fleece which appropriately greeted the Emperor Charles V in numerous imperial towns and cities. But despite the fresh ingredients, the mode of presentation and the same familiar set-pieces remain:[38] wheeled castles and ships; forests, mountains, trees, fountains and gardens, separately or in combination; knight-champions, wild men and women, children dressed as angels; birds and beasts, lions and dragons of tradition. A London pageant devised by John Rastell to greet Charles V in June 1522 consisted of

a pageaunte off an ylonde betokenyng the Ile off Englonde compassede all abowte with water made in silver and *byce* lyke to waves off the see and rockys jonyng therto, watelde abowte with roddys off silver and golde and wythyn them †champion† contrey, mountayns and wooddys where were dyvers bestes goyng abowte the mountayns by ‡vyces‡ and dyvers maner off trees, herbys and flowres as roses, dayses, gyloflowres, daffadeles, and other so craftely made thatt hitt was harde to knowe them from very naturall flowres, and in the mountayns pondys off fressh water with fisshe. And att the comyng off the §emprowr§ the bestys dyd move and goo, the fisshes dyd sprynge, the byrdes dyd synge rejoysing the comyng off the ‖ij‖ princes, the emprowr and the kynges grace.[39]

*azure †open ‡machinery §emperor ‖two.

Apart from the more sophisticated technical wonders in the form of figures worked by machinery, none of the visual splendours described here would have been considered remarkable a hundred and fifty years before.

While clearly a basic form of semi-dramatic activity, the procession takes on a particular importance in the context of the street theatres, not only because of its relationship to such liturgical performances as the *Visitatio*, but because processional playing is the mode of theatrical presentation most firmly impressed on the popular imagination as typical of the vernacular religious drama of the Middle Ages. While performances presented in this manner were almost certainly the exception rather than the rule, some important presentations of medieval plays did involve the use of mobile pageant-waggons, especially in England.[40]

The origins and psychological motivations of processions are buried sufficiently deep in antiquity and anthropology not to detain us here: in terms of human behaviour to move in procession contributes to a strong sense of identification with a common purpose (witness the 'protest march'), and playwrights have long been aware of the strong theatrical potentialities of the processional form. Medieval citizens could witness and participate in a far wider variety of processional spectacles than is the case today: Rudwin[41] points out that one of the longest-enduring medieval German processions was the Nuremberg *Schumbartlauf*, derived from the folk custom of running and leaping to ensure the crops' fertility: men and women wearing animal heads or devil-masks or dressed as leaf-clad savages took part, bearing lighted torches, evergreens, and spears. Ship processions, too, continued in popular vogue at least until the sixteenth century, the boat and its crew of dummy figures being burnt at the end of the ceremony, and such sources account for the presence of the 'wild men and women' and wheeled ships at royal entries and *entremets*.

More relevant to our present theme are the official civic processions of urban dignitaries marching or on horseback, known in Britain as ridings or watches, which took place annually or on special occasions in the municipal year, and which in the fourteenth and fifteenth centuries came to serve as manifestations of the increasing power and wealth of prosperous communities and of their trade and craft guilds.[42] An early prototype of such celebratory ridings is that of the London Fishmongers who, in 1298, rode out to meet Edward I 'in a solemne Procession ... through the Citie', accompanied by 'Pageants and shews'. Elaborate visual devices were not always in evidence: Richard Maydiston's lengthy verse description of Richard II's entry into London in 1392[43] outlines the preparations for welcoming the king, which include a procession of clergy from every city church, and a riding by representatives of the craft guilds in their ceremonial liveries, but although we read of the order of advance that

The keys being taken up and the sword of the city too, the Mayor leads forth the chief citizens, and they follow close behind him. A gaily dressed crowd from every craft guild you can think of follows these; each guild clearly keeps its station according to procedure. These are the workers in silver, these the fishmongers, just as this group contains mercers, and this wine-sellers[44]

the poem contains no reference to emblems or devices accompanying the actual riding.

However, visual symbolism played a large part in such proceedings during the following centuries: not only did members of the guilds proclaim their identity by means of their regalia and liveries, but they bore or had borne alongside them flaming torches and banners displaying appropriate emblems. By the sixteenth century at least many exotic fabrications were being included: the Norwich accounts of 1542/3 include expenditure on the annual Whitsun fair procession for 'makyng of a Tevell [Devil]', 'newe peyntyng of the gorgyn [Gorgon]', and 'canwas and peyntynge of ij apryns for ij giantes', while the Midsummer Watch celebrated at Coventry also featured a huge giant and his wife made from wicker-work. Devices for the Chester Midsummer Watch or 'Show', annually supported by both city authorities and guilds, included by 1564 'foure Jeans [giants] . . . won Camell, won Asse, won dragon, sixe hobby horses and sixtene naked boyes'.[45]

Of greater significance is the guilds' involvement in predominantly religious processions, and their use of visual images more sophisticated than banners or even model fishes or ships. Processions through the streets on various church festivals and saints' days were a feature of medieval life, and in Britain there were Palm Sunday, Whitsun, and Rogation processions, as well as others held on St Anne's Day (Lincoln), St Helen's Day (Beverley), and St George's Day, celebrated in many towns and cities including Dublin, Newcastle, Norwich, and York. Aberdeen had a Candlemas procession on 2 February, the Feast of the Purification of the Virgin Mary; this was marked by the Beverley Guild of St Mary with a procession terminating in a short dramatic routine, described in terms which enable us to see how readily parade might merge into play:

one of the gild shall be clad in comely fashion as a queen, like to the glorious Virgin Mary, having what may seem a son in her arms; and two others shall be clad like to Joseph and Simeon; and two shall go as angels, carrying a candle-bearer, on which shall be twenty-four thick wax lights. With these and other great lights borne before them, and with much music and gladness, the pageant Virgin with her son, and Joseph and Simeon, shall go in procession to the church. And all the sisteren of the gild shall follow the Virgin; and afterwards all the bretheren; and each of them shall carry a wax light weighing half a pound. And they shall go two and two, slowly pacing to the church; and when they have got there, the pageant Virgin shall offer her son to Simeon at the high altar; and all the sisteren and bretheren shall offer their wax lights, to-gether with a penny each. All this having been solemnly done, they shall go home again with gladness.[46]

The most generally observed and widely popular religious procession was that held to celebrate the Feast of Corpus Christi. This important feast in honour of the Real Presence of Christ in the Eucharist, celebrat-ing God's gift of the Holy Sacrament to mankind, was observed on the Thursday after Trinity Sunday, which meant that its date could vary from 23 May to 24 June. Its institution is attributed to the efforts of St Juliana (*c.* 1193 —*c.* 1258), a Belgian prioress from Mont Cornillon, near Liège. A former archdeacon of Liège, Jacques Pantaléon, became Pope Urban IV in 1261, and ordered the whole Church in 1264 to celebrate the new festival for which St Thomas Aquinas composed the liturgical office. However, Urban's death on 2 October 1264 meant that his decree was generally ignored until ratified by Pope Clement V at the Council of Vienne in 1311—12, when the Church was required to adopt the Feast of Corpus Christi forthwith. By the fifteenth century it was a principal church feast in western Europe, generous indulgences being granted to those who participated in its rites. The central feature of this great festive ceremony was a procession by the civic and religious leaders of the community in which the consecrated Sacrament or Host was par-aded with great solemnity through the streets, pausing at certain sites for worship and culminating in a service at the parish church or cathed-ral (see Illustration 7). Among the functionaries participating would be representatives of the craft and trade guilds and the religious fraterni-ties of the town, attended by armed men or retainers bearing lighted torches, banners, and other pictorial accessories, items of the type being referred to in the Chamberlains' accounts for York in 1397:

pro vexillo novo cum apparatu, xijs ijd. [for a new banner with its accoutre-ments, 12s. 2d.]
pro pictura pagine, ijs. [for the pageant picture, 2s.][47]

By the last quarter of the fourteenth century certain guildsmen at

7   A Corpus Christi procession of the fifteenth century

least were parading with more than single banners and pictures in
the York Corpus Christi ceremony, for an entry in a memorandum
book recording rents received for 1376 suggests that, indeed, storage
space was required for rather more elaborate forms of 'pageant':

De uno tenemento in quo tres pagine Corporis Christi ponuntur, per annum, ijs.
For a building in which three Corpus Christi pageants were placed, 2s. a year.[48]

If special accommodation were now needed, presumably guildsmen
were displaying such objects as effigies or tableaux of wooden figures in
the procession; the likeliest course of development is that devices symbolising crafts and trades (such as the Fishmongers' sturgeons and sal-
mon of 1298 and their fully rigged ship of 1313), originally paraded as
part of a civic procession, were very rapidly assimilated into the Corpus
Christi procession as part of the ceremonial. The idea may have occured
to the guilds that their usual banners, visual devices, and walking
figures (such as St Magnus in 1298) might be appropriately supplemented by displays having scriptural significance — Noah's Ark, the
Tree of Knowledge, the Manger at Bethlehem — especially if a particu-

lar biblical tableau were appropriate to the trade responsible for its mounting; for example the Water Drawers of Dee at Chester who came in time to perform the cycle play known as *Noes Fludde* possibly began by bearing in the procession a banner or a tabernacle depicting this incident. From these simple beginnings it was no doubt a logical step for the guilds to include in the parade wheeled floats carrying human figures in costume (possibly deriving from the walking impersonators) to depict scenes from the Old and New Testaments in dumbshow, and so create mobile versions of the French *mystères mimés*; after a while the characters on the vehicles possibly began to deliver brief speeches either as they travelled or when the floats came to a halt. It is probable that from this germ may be traced the growth of the spoken processional cycle plays of the British Isles.

Support for such a theory is found in Spain, where the Corpus Christi play apparently began as a series of static scriptural tableaux formed with wooden figures mounted on draped floats and borne in the procession by men hidden beneath the draperies.[49] A reference from Barcelona in 1391 indicates that instrumentalists accompanying the Host on foot were by this time costumed as angels in masks, diadems and tinfoil wigs. In 1400 the walking Corpus Christi parade at Valencia included not only figures of angels, but apostles, patriarchs, prophets, virgins, saints, dragons, Noah's Ark, St Bartholomew's silver cross, St Nicholas's ship, and St Peter's keys. In 1404 a float depicting the Garden of Eden bore carved figures of Eve and Adam; an eagle and assorted dragons, made of canvas on a wooden frame, also appeared, with men concealed within to animate their movements; on several occasions men were paid to dress as lions and accompany the figure of Daniel as he walked. The principal attractions, however, were the wheeled or men-borne floats (*rochas* or *rocas*) on which the scenery or appropriate decoration was constructed,[50] and by 1435 the authorities at Valencia were building a special *Casa de les Roques* to house the increasing number of floats required for the procession, their cost and maintenance being borne by the participating religious congregations and the trade guilds, with subsidies from the municipality and rich citizens. An order of procession from Barcelona dated 1424[51] indicates that 108 *representacions* were then involved in the Corpus Christi celebrations, a medley of scriptural tableaux and Christian saints on foot being led by the banners of the various city parishes, guild devices, crosses from the churches, and the clergy; it seems likely that some type of performance was given along the route, although it may only have been a dumb show, similar to that preserved in a document of 1453 which provides for the construction of new floats of the Creation and the Nativity.[52] In this year the Nativity float consisted of four angels on pillars supporting a heaven set with stars and clouds with God in the midst from whom rays of light or fire descended to the Christ Child in the manger, on each side of whom knelt Joseph and Mary. The 'action' comprised the Magi riding up to the float, dismounting, and going up the steps to worship the child. As far as one can tell, dialogue was not involved. Similarly at Seville the following year, when a *roca* bearing a similar heaven was introduced complete with sun, moon, stars, and clouds, accompanied by angels and the four Evangelists (St John holding an eagle), no speeches were indicated, the accent being on such scenic wonders as the heaven opening and closing by a mechanism controlled by the angels. A *castillo* or float was also required, possibly to carry a Nativity scene, since by 1530 this was certainly its function: borne by twelve men, the scene was presented by Seville's guild of carpenters, and contained in all probability live figures.[53]

At what point in time the Corpus Christi *representacions* in Spain acquired dialogue is uncertain, but a handful of references suggests that by 1500—10 spoken plays as well as simply tableaux on floats were in existence. At Salamanca in 1501 the Corpus Christi *juegos* (entertainments) included a play featuring shepherds and a hut; two years later Lucas Fernandez was paid for a 'shepherds' play' for the same festival.[54] From a list of eleven *representacions y entremesos* given at Valencia in 1517, some employing floats, others using figures walking on foot (*de peu*), Professor Shergold concludes that some at least required dialogue, spoken or sung, although Spanish processions continued to include static dumb-shows. But there is little doubt that by the early decades of the sixteenth century true drama had emerged from parades associated with the Feast of Corpus Christi, written 'for a pageantry that was already in existence'.

Whether a similar genesis can be postulated for the much earlier emergence of the English mystery cycles, not all of which were played at Corpus Christi, is a matter for conjecture: the most sustained and best-documented case for the plays having their origin in processional tableaux has been made out by Martin Stevens and by Alan H. Nelson.[55] Certainly many medieval English towns and cities mounted processions at Corpus Christi and other feast days akin to those in Spain; Hereford possesses a list of twenty-seven guilds and their dumb-shows from 1503 which includes Adam and Eve, 'Noye ship', the Nativity, 'The iii kings of Colen', 'The good Lord ridyng on an asse', '*Jesus pendens in cruce*' (Jesus hanging on the cross), Burial and Resurrection episodes, 'Knyghtes in harnes', and 'Seynt Keterina with tres (?) tormentors'.[56] Another list from Dublin dated 1498[57] indicates a parade sequence of figures walking in procession rather than a dramatic presentation with dialogue; its participants include 'Adam and Eve, with an angill following berrying a swerde'; 'Noe, with his shipp, apparalid acordyng'; 'The three kynges of Collynn, ridyng worshupfully, with the offerance, with a sterr afor them'. There is no evidence that Hereford or Dublin possessed cycle plays linked to the processions, although Beverley's street procession of the Purification did terminate in a mime; however, Nelson contends that it is from similar types of display that the Corpus Christi plays developed by the provision of dialogue for the figures riding on the processing vehicles, walking beside them, or simply parading by themselves.

Processional origins have also been advanced for a number of Corpus Christi plays in German, including those from Innsbruck, Freiburg, Künzelsau, and Ingolstadt:[58] that linked with Innsbruck, the earliest *Fronleichnamsspiel*, its manuscript dated 1391, contains only 756 lines in a sequence of monologues by Adam, Eve, the apostles and prophets, the three Magi, and the pope;[59] and this relatively brief play with its thirty set-speeches, many illustrating prophecies of Christ's coming and the clauses of the Apostles' Creed, appears ideally suited to processional delivery at one or more stations on the processional route through Innsbruck, for performances of such a short text would certainly not delay the onward movement of floats unduly. Significant here is a document of 1558 from Draguignan in southern France, concerning a Corpus Christi procession, which reads:

The said play [i.e. pageant with speeches] shall be performed with the procession as in times past, with as many and as brief episodes as possible, and it shall be declaimed while the procession proceeds without anyone in the play coming to a halt, so that undue length and confusion in both procession and play are avoided, and so that visitors can watch the proceedings without inconvenience.

Le dit jeu jora avec la procession comme auparadvant et le plus d'istoeres et plus brieves que puront estre seront et se dira tout en cheminant sans ce que personne du jeu s'areste pour eviter prolixité et confusion tant de ladite prosession que jeu, et que les estrangiers le voient aisement.[60]

This reference suggests that in some areas of Europe mobile performances of short plays with dialogue *were* given as an integral part of Corpus Christi processions, but that the speeches had to be kept brief to avoid holding up the rest of the parade, and it is at least feasible that in Britain short dramatic dialogues recited from moving floats supplied the earliest acorns from which the great oaks of cycle sequences grew.

It was undoubtedly in the British Isles that the Corpus Christi plays enjoyed their chief popularity and underwent their most extensive artistic development, even giving their name to plays performed at other seasons. Elsewhere in Europe Corpus Christi drama is the exception, for Passion plays dominated the field of religious theatre, and Whitsun presentations were also popular (as indeed they were in parts of Britain), while processional performances were unusual, at least where lengthy spoken drama was involved.[61] While processional presentation even in Britain may not have been as common as was once thought, this method of staging plays was employed here more often than on the Continent. Theo Stemmler has argued[62] that the reason for the vogue and expansion of the Corpus Christi procession in Britain lies in a national predilection for the joyous procession celebrated on Palm Sunday at the beginning of Holy Week in which the copious use of symbolism reached its zenith in the bearing of the Eucharist enclosed in a shrine. This well-established liturgical tradition, in Stemmler's view, inevitably suggested the originally processional mode of presentation as appropriate to English plays celebrating the Eucharist; and certainly the importance attached to the Palm Sunday processional tradition cannot be overlooked.

Unfortunately pictorial and verbal descriptions of the English pageant-waggons are late in origin, and do not carry the authority of undisputed personal testimony: the two most famous (or notorious) documentary testimonials are those of Archdeacon Robert Rogers of Chester (d. 1596–6), as rendered by his son David in about 1609, and of Sir William Dugdale in his *Antiquities of Warwickshire* (1656). Both retain interest despite their lack of complete reliability. Dugdale's description of the Coventry plays is very imprecise, and no doubt quite mistaken about the involvement of friars: it runs

Before the suppression of the Monasteries, this City was very famous for the *Pageants* that were play'd therein, upon *Corpus-Christi-day*; which occasioning very great confluence of people thither from far and near, was of no small benefit thereto; which *Pageants* being acted with mighty state and reverence by the Friers of this House, had Theaters for the severall Scenes, very large and high, placed upon wheels, and drawn to all the eminent parts of the City, for the better advantage of Spectators.[63]

David Rogers, a partisan opponent of the plays, compiled from materials collected by his father a longer and more precise account of the Chester performances, of which the following is the core:

the manner of which playes was thus: They weare devided into 24 pagiantes or partes, acordinge to the number of ye Companyes of ye Cittie, and every Company brought forthe their pagiente which was ye cariage or place [plays?] which they played in: And yerelye before these were played there was a man fitted for ye purpose which did ride as I take it upon St George's daye throughe ye Cittie and there published the tyme and the matter of ye playes in breife which was called ye readinge of the banes. They weare played upon Monday, Tuseday and Wenseday in Witson weeke. And they first beganne at ye Abbay gates & when the firste pagiente was played at ye Abbaye gates then it was wheeled from thence to the Pentice at ye highe crosse before ye Mayor, and before yt was donne the seconde came, and ye firste wente into the Watergate streete, & from thence unto ye Bridge streete, and soe all one after an other tell all ye pagaintes weare played appoynted for ye firste daye, and so likewise for the seconde & the thirde daye: these pagaintes or cariage was a highe place made like a howse with ij rowmes beinge open on ye tope: the lower rowme they apparrelled & dressed them selves and in the higher roume they played, and they stoode upon 6 wheeles. And when they had done with one carriage in one place they wheeled the same from one streete to an other, first from ye Abbaye gate to ye Pentise, then to the Watergate streete, then to ye Bridge streete, throughe the lanes & so to the Estgate streete. And thus they came from one streete to an other, keapeinge a direct order in every streete, for before ye first cariage was gone, ye seconde came, and so the thirde, and so orderly till ye laste was donne, all in order, without any stayeinge in any place; for, worde beinge broughte how every place was neere done, they came, and made no place to tarye, tell ye last was played.[64]

Can earlier information supplement, modify, or correct that provided by Dugdale and Rogers? Records in fact do not always make it clear that pageant-waggons are in use:[65] the 1376 reference to the provision of accommodation for three *pagine* at York probably alludes to effigies or tableaux capable of being carried around bodily, but another allusion in the succeeding year from Beverley, in connection with the Tailors' Company's expenses on 'a pageant of the play of Corpus Christi [*pagine ludi Corporis Christi*], suggests that a mobile float or some other structure capable of bearing wooden or human figures in a 'play' may be meant. An order of 1390, also from Beverley, emphasises the distinction between the pageant itself and 'the play' staged upon it, in commanding all the craftsmen of the thirty-eight town-guilds to have their

plays and pageants ready henceforward every Corpus Christi day, in manner and form according to the ancient custom of the town of Beverley, in order to play them in honour of Corpus Christi.
ludos et pagentes paratos amodo qualibet die in festo Corporis Christi, modo et forma secundum antiquam consuetudinem ville Beverlaci, ad ludendum in honore Corporis Christi.

Confirmation that 'plays' and 'pagentes' originally referred to sepa-

rate entities comes in an order of 1411 which arranges for 'worship-
ful men of the worthier sort', although not guildsmen, to present a play
at the feast, these men agreeing that they would 'have a fitting and
worthy pageant constructed, and a suitable play performed on the same
[*honestam et honorabilem pagendam fabricari faciant, et honestum ludum ludi
in eadem*]'. Here the 'pageant' is plainly a vehicle or stage of some kind,
built to accommodate a *ludus*. However, as Stanley Kahrl points out, the
verbal distinction is not always maintained, and by a natural semantic
extension, the term 'pageant' comes to be equated with *ludus* or 'play':
thus in 1493 the Beverley Drapers were called on to 'play or cause to be
played at the feast of Corpus Christi a certain pageant called Demyng
Pylate [*ludant vel ludi faciant in Festo Corporis Christi quamdam pagendam
vacatum Demying Pylate*]'. Care is therefore needed in distinguishing a
reference to a simple effigy or static tableau from one to a wheeled
vehicle, and to a vehicle from one to an acted play. The term is used
with similar ambivalence in Rogers's description.

Even where a mobile vehicle is definitely referred to, very few contemporary references to 'pageants' tell us a great deal about their
appearance and use. The fullest set of details may be found among the
inventory of the Norwich Grocers' Company who presented the Fall,
made in 1565[66] which includes the following entries:

A Pageant, that is to saye, a Howse of Waynskott paynted and buylded on a
Carte with fowre whelys.
A square topp to sett over ye sayde Howse.
A Gryffon, gylte, with a *fane* to sette on ye sayde toppe.
A bygger Iron fane to sett on ye ende of ye Pageante.
3 paynted clothes to hang abowte ye Pageant.
6 Horsse Clothes, stayned, with †knopps† and tassells.

*pennant   †knobs

A recently discovered indenture made in 1433 between the York
Mercers and the masters of the pageant of Doomsday[67] also mentions 'a
Pagent with iiij wheles' as well as a 'helle mouthe', and lists

A grete *coster* of rede damaske payntid for the bakke syde of the pagent; ij
other lesse costers for ij sydes of the Pagent; iij other costers †of lewent brede†.
for the sides of the Pagent; A litel coster iiij squared to hang at the bakke of
God; iiij Irens to bere uppe Heven; iiij finale ‡coterelles‡ and a Iren pynne;
A §brandreth§ of Iren that God sall sitte uppon when he sall fly uppe to Heven,
with iiij ‖rapes‖ at iiij corners ... ij shorte rolles of ¶tre¶ to putte forthe
the pagent.

*hanging,   curtain   †of   an   eleventh's   breadth   ‡cotter-pins   §grid-framework
‖ropes   ¶wood

A number of permissible inferences can be drawn from the two documents. The York Mercers' pageant-waggon at least was dismantled each year and stored, being brought out of the pageant-house on rollers after reassembly by labourers paid to carry out the operation and mount the pageant on its four-wheeled base. Its Heaven seems to have been a flat platform elevated on four iron poles braced at the corners of the waggon, forming a solid enough structure to support the weight of God the Son, who apparently ascended to Heaven on a Judgement-seat of iron suspended from the upper level of the cart and was no doubt raised on a system of pulleys by hidden stagehands. The Norwich Grocers' pageant was built of oak planking, in the form of a house set on a horse-drawn cart with four wheels, surmounted by a square flat (?) roof supported on posts at the corners, decorated with devices and banners and hung about with draperies. These '3 paynted clothes' like the York 'costers' create problems: one might assume that they were needed to mask the underside of the waggon from the front and the sides, as may have been the case with the 'cloth to lap abowt the pajent' recorded by the Coventry Smiths in 1440: in an agreement made in 1452/3 with Thomas Colclow, the Smiths also laid down as one of the conditions that Colclow was to 'find clothys that gon abowte the pajant and find russhes therto' for the floor.[68] But the York Mercers' indenture clearly states that the main curtains enclosed the stage on 'the bakke syde' and 'ij sydes', leaving 'iij other costers' for the undersides of the waggon, to mask the space below. This seems undeniable but visibility must have been considerably impaired by the side curtaining. Hardin Craig asserts that the Norwich hangings were required to conceal the stage only when Adam and Eve were naked, but Rosemary Woolf rightly rejoins that four cloths rather than three would be required to preserve modesty if such were the aim, besides which, the characters would surely have worn the 'cote and hosen' alluded to in the inventory.[69] Glynne Wickham's conjectural reconstruction suggests that two cloths simply masked the front and rear of the pageant stage, leaving its ends exposed, but that the third served to divide the pageant floor into a rear tiring-house area for the actors, and a forward area where the scenic devices (*loca*) might be set up on the lines of a booth-stage.[70] Wickham's surmise concerning dressing-room facilities makes him sceptical of Rogers's testimony that the actors changed in a lower room and per-formed in a higher one, and F. M. Salter expresses doubts that the weight of a stage and its structures could be supported above a 'dress-ing-room'. But Wickham's plan wastes precious stage-room: casts could have used the space beneath the cart's sturdy lower framework as a greenroom, safely masked behind 'paynted clothes'; although one may doubt, as Craig points out,[71] the need for dressing accommodation where characters mostly wore modern dress, and especially in processional performance, where there would scarcely be time to remove one's costume between appearances. However, the provision of 'waiting-space' would have offered the players welcome respite from the public gaze, as well as the opportunity for making dramatic exits and entrances (possibly by means of trap-doors).

Wickham is similarly dubious of Rogers's remark that the pageants were 'all open on the tope':[72] not only is a roof clearly essential for sheltering and supporting the technical machinery which many cycle plays require, but the York Mercers' indenture and the Norwich inventory mention one, and several Coventry records allude to it. In 1540, for instance, the Drapers paid 18d. 'for mendyng the bateling [battlement] yn the toppe of the pagent', and in 1567 'carvyng bords and crest for the toppe of the padgen' cost the company 3s.[73] But Rogers may mean not that each Chester pageant was open to the elements, but that its 'higher rowme' was not masked by curtains as at York but open on all sides so that the action taking place could be seen by all, a possible indication that the three cloths at Norwich cloaked the space from the waggon's base to the ground, rather than the stage itself as the York indenture states. Curtaining procedure perhaps varied from city to city.

Pictorial evidence substantiates in part the most likely conjectures concerning the appearance of the English pageant-waggons. Two illustrations record a procession of biblical tableaux held at Louvain (Leuven) in 1594 in honour of the Virgin Mary, while a painted panel by Daniel van Alsloot in the Victoria and Albert Museum in London commemorates the entry of the Archduchess Isabella into Brussels in 1615 (see Illustration 8).[74] The Louvain drawings show tableaux of the Annunciation and of the Nativity simply staged on curtainless open platforms on wheels, surmounted by sloping roofs on pillars, that for the Annunciation being elaborately decorated although the Nativity framework represents the rustic stable, having a roof of open cross-beams on which sits God the Father and from which a star is suspended, while the corner-columns are in rough brickwork. A short pelmet hangs below each platform to hide all but the bases of the four wheels. The Brussels entry also includes amidst a wealth of ingenious Baroque floats an Annunciation scene and one of the Nativity, each mounted on a four-wheeled pageant-waggon. The Brussels pageants appear to be much higher from the ground than the Louvain vehicles: the Nativity apparently stands at a height of at least 2 metres (6 feet) above street-

8   A pageant-waggon depicting the Annunciation, Brussels, 1615: detail
from a painted panel by Daniel van Alsloot

level, and the entire structure must be between $4\frac{1}{2}$ and 6 metres (15 and
20 feet) high. The sloping roof of the Nativity scene certainly seems
capable of concealing technical machinery if need arose, and is well
supported by six sturdy pillars: on both conveyances the space from the
base of the stage to the ground is hidden by a richly patterned cloth
which permits the visible wheels to revolve freely. The Annunciation
has an elaborately decorated flat roof piled with foliage and supported
on four pillars, while the stage area is hung on *two* sides with curtains,
which the holy dove parts to reveal the suggestion of a bed with a bolster
in what is possibly an inner room beyond. The curtained stage appears
to endorse in part the evidence of the York Mercers' indenture, but the
Nativity cart is certainly 'open on ye tope' if we accept that phrase as
meaning 'void of curtains'.

Two horses pull the Louvain Annunciation float, four the Brussels waggon, but whether horses or men drew the English carts is open to argument. The York Mercers' pageant was probably handled by the players themselves, but the Coventry records for 1467 include a payment of 22d. for 'met and drynk on mynstrelles and on men to drawe the pagent'; thirty years later the accounts earmark 12d. 'for the horssyng of the padgeant' and payments to various men 'for dryvyng the pagent' appear after this date.[75] The expenses for the 1504–5 Canterbury 'show' of Thomas à Becket, a parade of effigies still referred to as 'pageants', include a payment 'To iiij men to helpe to cary the Pagent', but horses were presumably introduced soon after this, for in 1514–15 there appears the entry:

Item paied to Jamys Colman & hys hors with a laborer to cary a boute the pagent   xij[d]

and similar payments recur.[76] A reference from Bungay in Suffolk dated 1514, uses the same equivocal phrase for the transportation of a number of pageants damaged in an outbreak of vandalism: 'the whyche wer ever wont tofore to be caryed abowt the seyd Town upon the seyd daye in the honor of the blissyd Sacrement'.[77] Later, in 1562–3, Chelmsford churchwardens' accounts contain a payment 'for tenn men to beare the pagiante', which seems an unequivocal reference to the employment of human musclepower,[78] but this pageant was almost certainly a model, and as far as one can judge, only the simpler and lighter forms of pageant could have been carried on men's shoulders in this fashion.

Both the Norwich Grocers' and York Mercers' accounts mention four-wheeled waggons and one version of Rogers's description states that the Chester waggons had four wheels rather than six. Nelson, who has researched the topic most fully, argues that a six-wheeled vehicle would have created too many problems in manoeuvring, two pivoted axles being needed for proper steering,[79] and it is significant that the Louvain and Brussels vehicles show four-wheeled pageants in operation. Other references are equivocal: the York Cartwrights in 1501 were excused a contribution to the Corpus Christi expenses by providing four new wheels for a pageant waggon,[80] and the Coventry Weavers' account-book lists a payment in 1542 'to the wryght for makynge the ij lytyll whellys', but these might indicate either four or six wheels *in toto*.[81] At all events, many accounts refer to the necessity for 'sope' and 'grece' to ensure that, however many wheels the carts possessed, they at least revolved smoothly without unseemly grinding sounds.

More vital to our understanding of the use of pageants are their dimensions. Calculations have been based on the estimated width of medieval streets, on the likely size of the pageant-houses used to garage the floats when not in use[82] — the earliest Coventry reference dated 1392 speaks of a tenement in Little Park Street being partly employed as a *domum pro le pagent pannarum Coventre* (a house for the Coventry Drapers' pageant) — and on the Louvain and Brussels pictures. F. M. Salter, working from the dimensions of the Coventry Tailors' 'carriage house' (5 virgates long by $3\frac{1}{2}$ virgates wide) reckoned the height of the pageant as $4\frac{1}{2}$–5 metres (15–17 feet), its width 6 metres (20 feet), and its depth $4\frac{1}{2}$ metres (15 feet); Arnold Williams estimates the overall stage as $5\frac{1}{2} \times 2\frac{1}{2}$ metres (18 × 8 feet), while M. James Young suggests 6 × 3 metres (20 × 10 feet) as a maximum for the York pageant-waggons at least.[83] Given that medieval streets were rarely more than $7\frac{1}{2}$–9 metres (25–30 feet) wide, it seems unwise to exceed the figures advanced by Young.

It has been argued that in some places the pageant-waggons were not employed for processional performances at all, but were simply paraded to an open space where they could be used as scenery in a static production (see p. 120 below). However, records make it clear that at Chester and Coventry at least, pageant-waggons were used in the fashion traditionally associated with the cycle plays, namely as mobile platform-stages drawn about the streets and halting for the purpose of performance. Yet considerable difficulties are created by the knowledge that pageant-stages often had to hold an extensive cast of characters and a good deal of scenery. A line spoken by a soldier in the York pageant of *The Dream of Pilate's Wife* (Play 30) hints at this lack of space on a platform estimated to contain two *loca* and six characters (although non-speaking extras may also have been present):

> 'Here, ye gomes, gose a rome, giffe us gate'
> Here, you blokes, make room, clear the way[84]

The Coventry Drapers who presented the Last Judgement would seem to have had a full waggon, for their properties and machinery included 'Hell mouth — a fire kept at it; windlass and three fathom of cord; earthquake, barrell for the same, a pillar for the words of the barrel painted; three worlds painted and a piece that bears them; a link to set the world on fire; pulpits for the angels; cross, rosin, a ladder.'[85] Some of these may not have appeared on one cart, but the characters for this play include God, two demons, six souls, two spirits, four angels, three patriarchs, two worms of conscience, two singers, a Pharisee, and a Prologue. Some of the heavenly figures may have occupied the flat roof, but even if Hellmouth or the three worlds were separately located (possibly in the street as seems to have been the case with the York Doomsday pageant, at least until 1501 when a small wheeled cart supplied a mobile Hell), the stage is still likely to have been crowded. Moreover, the presence at Coventry of the windlass and cord reminds us that ascents to and descents from Heaven were frequently depicted in the cycles, and, unless one assumes the use of some independent structure such as a tower or a special scaffold for miraculous flying effects,[86] at least some of the necessary technical apparatus must have been housed up in the pageant roof. There is also the need to accommodate such items as Mount Calvary or the hill which, as Wickham points out, was used on successive days by the three Chester guilds presenting the Shepherds' play, the Flagellation, and the Resurrection, sharing the use of a single pageant-waggon to do so.[87] The Chester Vintners, Goldsmiths, and Dyers evidently did the same.

The ability of confined pageant-stages to contain the required dramatic action has been variously explained. The pageant may have acted simply as a scenic background to the plays, which were mainly performed down in the street, so that when Christ descended to judge mankind in the York Doomsday play, he came down from the waggon to ground level, returning for the ascent into Heaven. But while stage-directions for the Coventry Shearmen and Taylors' pageant certainly include the celebrated rubrics: 'the iij kyngis speykyth in the strete' and 'Here Erode ragis in the pagond and in the strete also',[88] their very existence does suggest an exceptional extension of the usual acting-area, and it seems unlikely that where space for spectators was at a premium, a large portion of it would be permanently earmarked for performance purposes. An allusion to the normal congestion experienced by a close-packed medieval audience seems to be preserved in the York Satan's cry in *The Temptation* (Play 22):

> Make rome *be-lyve* and late me gang, quickly
> What makis here all this thrang?

Glynne Wickham argues from the Coventry records that a 'scaffold', namely a wooden platform, supplemented the playing-area, indicated by such entries as that in the Mercers' accounts for 1584 referring to a payment of 5s. 4d. 'for drivinge the pagante and skaffolds', and those included in the Smiths' expenses for the same year:

Item payde to Cookeson for makynge of a whele to the skaffolde viij[d]
Item payde for a iron pynne & a cotter for the skaffolde whele iiij[d]

The Coventry Cappers, too, spent 2s. 6d. 'for our partes at the setting &

drivinge of the pagyn and skaffoldes'.[89] Wickham claims that such portable scaffolds or platforms placed in front of the main pageant extended the available area and served as an unencumbered forward acting-area, analogous to the Elizabethan apron-stage or the medieval *platea*.[90] This ingenious reaction to the overloaded pageant-cart is open to serious objections: there is no evidence that a second stage was standard, the 1584 performance at Coventry involving a new play, *The Destruction of Jerusalem*, which possibly received idiosyncratic staging. Secondly, in York at least, where most of the known locations of the performance-places can be identified, the width of the streets would never have allowed a scaffold cart to be placed beside a pageant cart without blocking the road and forcing spectators into the space at the sides of the stage. M. James Young also points out that the word 'scaffold' is used nowhere else to indicate a frontal stage-area, and that the supplementary Coventry scaffold only has a single wheel suggesting a much lighter structure that a platform. Alan Nelson argues further that two such carts placed alongside each other would still be separated by their wheels, the beds of conventional waggons of the time being narrower than their wheel-bases; to build superstructures out beyond the wheel-base would certainly be possible, but they would be dangerously unbalanced.

Great caution must therefore be exercised when making assertions about the way the pageant-waggons were used: M. James Young's thesis,[91] based on the York Mercers' records for 1464, argues the need for two waggons to cope with the demands of the cycle's final spectacle, the Doomsday pageant. But references to 'nayls for both pagyants' and 'havyng of both pagyantes agayn to the pagyant hows' are explained by a previous entry dated 1463 which makes it clear that the 'new pageant' was simply a wheelless structure for 'the sallys [souls] to ryse owt of', possibly a coffin-shaped structure large enough to hold four souls, set down in the *platea* before the play began, and taken up at the end. Once again we are alerted to the variable uses made of the term 'pageant'.

The guild's pageant-waggons were probably first involved in the traditional Corpus Christi or some other religious procession, and originally carried *tableaux vivants* only. These tableaux halted at several sites or stations along the processional route, probably at those points where the Host itself came to rest for a few moments before moving on. Brief mimes and even dialogues were perhaps presented at those moments, but it is unlikely that a play of even five minutes' duration was allowed. The York records give us great insight into the problems

of organising even a few virtually mute pageants processing in sequence through the streets. In 1394 it was laid down on pain of a fine
that 'all the pageants for Corpus Christi shall be played in the places
anciently assigned to them and not in other places',[92] implying that
waggons were stopping at random to enable performances to be given,
and delaying the procession unduly. There is some doubt as to whether
the civic leaders of the community marched in the Corpus Christi
procession before or behind the guild pageants at York, but even if the
mayor and officials went ahead, unauthorised halts would certainly
delay the succeeding pageants. In 1398—9 the question was still vexing
the minds of the commons who complained to the mayor and aldermen

that . . . they incur great expense and costs in connection with the play and
the pageants of Corpus Christi which cannot be played or performed on the
very day on which they should be staged, because the aforesaid pageants
are played in so many places to the great harm and discomfort of the said
commons and to those strangers resorting to the said city on the same day
for the same reason . . .

and requested that ten stations only should be prescribed as lawful
stopping-places for the procession, fines being laid down for ignoring
the ordinance and delaying the pageants. Banners, set up at the approved halts in order to identify them and so regulate abuse of the
system, were also demanded.

Whether or not stricter control over the procession at York was
exercised after 1398—9, the problem remained acute, possibly because
the guilds' histrionic aspirations prevented much increase in speed.
York's famous *ordo paginarum* (arrangement of pageants) drawn up by
the Common Clerk, Roger Burton, in 1415, the year of Agincourt,
describes the pageants briefly, and it is noteworthy that we meet
phrases such as *angelus loquens pastoribus, Pastores loquentes ad invincem*
(sic), and *Herodes interogans eos de puero Jesu* ('the angel speaking to the
shepherds', 'The shepherds speaking among themselves', 'Herod
questioning them [the Magi] about the boy Jesus')[93] which suggest
developed dialogues. In 1421 the Painters, Stainers, Pinners, and
Latoners (sheetmetal workers) proposed to the mayor and council that
since 'the play on Corpus Christi Day in this city . . . is, alas, becoming
more and more hindered on account of the multiplicity of pageants',
they should combine their two pageants into one, 'feeling that the
matter of both pageants could be presented as one pageant, and the
speeches more fittingly delivered to the listening people in a shortened
performance of the play'. No doubt cumulative speeches were to blame
for delays.

However, when in 1426 William Melton, a learned friar of the Order of Minorites, exhorted the York Council to separate the liturgical procession of the Host from the parade of pageants with their brief dramatic offerings, it was not on the grounds of length or inefficiency, but because Melton felt that the pageants diverted the laity from divine worship and thereby caused them to forfeit the benefits of the indulgences granted. He stressed the need for performing the 'plays' on a different day from the religious procession and service, and according to civic records, it was decided that thereafter the performances would take place on the Wednesday preceding the religious procession on the Feast of Corpus Christi itself.[94] Several scholars believe that this scheme was in fact never put into operation, for in 1433 at least the pageants apparently appeared on the feast day as before, and it may be that they still formed part of the religious procession; Alan Nelson thinks that pageants and procession did not separate until about 1468 when the parade with the Host was shifted to the day after Corpus Christi, leaving the plays to occupy the feast day itself. This certainly was the case by 1476.[95] However, Martin Stevens and others strongly believe that Melton's visit of 1426 had a decisive effect on the York plays; freeing them to expand from brief processional dialogue into mature drama; after 1426 the players on the pageant-waggons were under no pressure to deliver their lines as swiftly as possible, and the authors of the texts were able to elaborate their biblical material.

Thus by about the middle of the fifteenth century plays of some duration rather than brief dumb-shows or dialogues were probably being exhibited on the pageant-carts; a reference from Coventry dated 1441 states:

Ordinatum est quod Robertus Eme et omnes alii qui ludunt in festo Corporis Christi bene et suficienter ludant, ita quod nulla impedicio fiat in aliquo ioco.[96]
It is laid down that Robert Eme and all those others who perform in plays at the Feast of Corpus Christi should act skilfully and adequately, and that no hindrance to any play should be allowed to occur.

In 1442 the Coventry fair held on the Friday following Corpus Christi was expanded to occupy the whole of the ensuing week, a possible indication that the annual procession had become transformed into a sequence of plays attracting a large crowd of spectators to the city.[97]

The number of stations at which the carts halted varies from town to town. As we have seen, the authorities at York first laid down a total of ten stations although by 1542 the number had grown to sixteen: it was possible to arrange for a station to be located before one's business premises or one's house, provided one paid for the privilege, as a number of municipal documents make clear.[98] For example, in 1478 Henry Watson and Thomas Diconson, York fishmongers, were leased at an annual cost of eleven shillings *ludum sive lusum Corporis Cristi . . . ludendum in alta strata de Ousegate inter tenementa modo in tenura prefatorum Henrici et Thome* [the Corpus Christi play or game . . . to be performed in the high street of Ousegate between the properties now leased by the aforesaid Henry and Thomas]'. There was gain to be extracted from erecting stands at a station sited on one's door as the York authorities had realised as early as June 1416, when the council decided to lease the lucrative stations in advance to the highest bidders. The erection of stands for spectators at these rented stations in York ties in with Rogers's reference to 'scafoldes and stages made in the streetes in those places where they determined to playe theire pagiantes' at Chester.

York appears to have been unique among British cities in the number of stations the authorities were prepared to permit: Beverley appears to have maintained only seven, according to a record of 1449;[99] at Chester, where the plays took place on the three days following Whitsun (at least by the late sixteenth century),[100] no more than five or six stations can be assumed from Rogers's account. Coventry looks to have earmarked only two or three stopping-places,[101] as the construction of 'iij worldys' for burning in the Drapers' Doomsday play in 1556 and 1558 indicates, one universe presumably being set alight at each station. However, even with a small number of stations and a relatively short sequence of plays to be performed (the Coventry cycle has been estimated as containing a total of ten New Testament episodes), it was not always possible to play the entire cycle. The description of Queen Margaret's visit to Coventry in 1457 has traditionally been thought to confirm that she watched a processional performance presented on pageant-carts pausing at a number of stations distributed through the city, and discontinued because of the onset of darkness:

On Corpus Christi *yeven* at nyght then next †suyng† came the quene from Kelyngworth to Coventre; at which tyme she wold not be met, but came prively to se the play there on the morowe; and she ‡sygh‡ then alle the pagentes pleyde save Domes-day, which myght not be pleyde for lak of day. And she was loged at Richard Wodes the grocer . . . and there all the pleys were furst pleyde.[102]

*eve †following ‡saw

Martin Stevens has questioned whether this account[103] describes a normal presentation of the Coventry plays with the queen witnessing the plays from the first station ('there all the pleys were furst pleyde') on a regular processional route; he believes that either the queen watched a static performance specially staged in her honour which could not be finished in daylight (perhaps because it started late), or that the queen simply lodged at a house which had been the site of the plays when they were 'furst pleyde'. Stevens argues that ambiguities in the Coventry description vitiate it as a reliable guide to the usual method of processional staging in medieval cities and towns.

However, the chief problem for all organisers of processional performances was the shortage of time available for all the plays to be viewed. Clearly ordinances were needed to speed processions on their way and to penalise those who made unauthorised stops and delayed those waggons coming behind. In 1554 the York Girdlers were fined ten shillings 'for that the Girdlars on Corpus Cristi day did not forthwith folowe with their pageant in dewe course accordyng to thordynaunce and proclamacion therof made but taried an wholle hower and more in hyndrans and stoppyng of the rest of the pageantz folowyng and to the disorderyng of the same.'[104] But regardless of the delays, not all the plays of the York cycle could be presented in daylight hours: during 1431–2 the Masons who presented the non-scriptural play of Fergus who tried to interfere with the funeral of the Virgin Mary complained that 'they could seldom or never bring forth and perform their pageant in full daylight as the preceding pageants do'. Since at least three more pageants were performed after that of Fergus, the traditional view is that the York plays must have continued after darkness fell, being played by torchlight in order to complete the sequence.

However, the claim that all forty-eight pageants of the extant York cycle were performed in the streets of the city during the course of a long summer's day, beginning at 4.30 a.m. and continuing until well after midnight, has recently been challenged by scholars who believe that such a performance would have constituted an impossible marathon for casts and spectators alike. Martin Stevens and Alan H. Nelson in particular have demonstrated that to present the complete cycle at even twelve stations on the processional route would occupy a period of over twenty hours, since performances of so many plays of differing lengths would involve lengthy pauses in the smooth flow of carts through the streets.[105] Audiences might be presumed to have grown restive, while they waited for the first pageant to reach the twelfth station, or endured the long gap between one play's departure and the arrival of the next. Obviously when performances take place simultaneously casts are enormous, yet opportunities for the actors to double are limited, since no player can begin to perform in a second episode until he has finished in the first. However, part of a York ordinance of 3 April 1476 has been used to support the notion that doubling was legislated for, provided no player contracted to appear in more than two plays: the relevant section decrees that

no plaier that shall plaie in the saide Corpus Christi plaie be *conducte and Reteyned* to plaie but twise on the day of the saide playe, and that he or thay so plaing plaie not overe twise the saide day upon payne of †xls† to forfet unto the Chaumbre as often tymes as he or thay shall be founden defautie in the same.[106]

*engaged and hired   †forty shillings

Some contend that this sentence simply prohibited an actor from being employed by more than two guilds; others see it as an indication that no player could perform his part in the pageant to which he was committed more than twice, in other words, that the procession was only permitted to halt twice for each play to be performed. This seems a clumsy way of stating that only two actual performances of each play were to be presented along the processional route, but it would certainly help to explain how the York plays might have been staged in the manner traditionally associated with them.

Nelson has demonstrated the unlikelihood of the York cycle's suitability for street presentation by a careful assessment of the time-span involved for a complete performance to take place: he has gone on to argue that, although the pageant-waggons and players processed through the streets, only a single *indoor* performance of the extant text was given every year in York, a private presentation for the mayor, aldermen, civic dignitaries, and their distinguished guests. Nelson contends that the vehicles simply passed along the city streets, bearing tableaux in which live performers presented brief pieces of dramatic action for the common spectators thronging the route; then, after the procession had completed its circuit, the plays of the York cycle were staged 'in the Chambre at the Common Hall gates' for the benefit of a select audience of worthies. Nelson finds evidence for this in the frequent renting of the chamber for the use of the mayor, aldermen, 'and many others of the council' at the time of Corpus Christi, and in allusions to wine and meals being consumed there and to the hanging of the room with tapestries and the use of trestles and forms.[107] The York repertory of religious plays included a Pater Noster play and a Creed play, and these, too, Nelson argues, were presented in the chamber: in an entry of 1558, typical of those he quotes, the council lays down 'that this yere Pater Nostr play beyng playd on Corpus Christi day, dynar with brekfast and supper shalbe provyded by the Chambrelaynes for my sayd Lord Mayour, aldermen, and xxiiij^{or} [twenty-four] as hath ben accustomed at Corpus Christi play in the Chambre at the Commonhall yates.' Another reference held by Nelson to support his theory dates from 1538 and records a payment of 6s. 8d. 'to Thomas Flemyng for the Chambre that my lorde and his bredryn stondyth in of Corpus Cristy day to here the playe accustomyd therfore'; a similar payment to Flemyng in 1535 was also 'for the Chamber that my lorde Mayer and his Bredren stude [stood] in of Corpus Cristi day and the Fryday after to here the play', although on this occasion it was the Creed play that they watched during the two days' performance. The chamber at Common Hall gates in Coney Street, York;[108] was apparently part of one of the city's inns, belonging to the city council but leased out to private tenants, who would then lease it back to the city for special functions. The chamber appears to have been its largest single room, possibly on an upstairs floor and running the length of the building. This 'Inn of the Common Hall' also abutted on the site of the eighth station on the processional route, and we find that several tenants of the chamber also leased this station at the time of Corpus Christi.

If one accepts Nelson's system of timing the duration of the performances (an important proviso), one cannot deny that the extant cycle could never have been staged *in toto* at York without serious inconvenience, in the 'true-processional' manner (that is, as a sequence presented in a set order to a succession of audiences watching the plays in that order).[109] Yet there is evidence that the York plays or something like them were staged in processional form for the general populace: Margaret Dorrell, who has re-examined much of the extant material,[110] argues that not *all* the plays need have been presented in any one year, any more than in any other place where cycle sequences exist: Wakefield for instance possesses two celebrated Shepherds' plays, which would obviously not have been presented as part of the same year's offering. The official 'register' at York is an attempt to create an official record of all the pageants, not a guarantee that every episode was staged on every occasion the Corpus Christi play was presented. Indeed, those theatre producers of recent years who have been compelled through considerations of time or resources to create and direct 'scaled-down' versions of the cycle plays may in fact be following the example of their medieval predecessors.

Margaret Dorrell has also queried Nelson's allocations of performance-time for the plays, maintaining that swift playing and speedy transitions between stations would enable the whole presentation to be completed by torchlight at about half past twelve at night. Admittedly, Dorrell's interpretation of the documentary evidence presupposes that a tremendous pace was maintained throughout the long day, and perhaps her conjectural programme of pageants would require modification if it were to occupy a reasonable watching- and playing-period. What she does make clear is that not all the allusions in the York records to pageants being 'played' or 'heard' at the various stations suggest that terse dialogues alone constituted the commons' experience of the 'play': from 1493—4 comes an ordinance of the Spurriers and Lorimers (Spur-makers and Bit-makers): 'it is ordeyned and ennacted that every maister of the said craftes opon Corpus Cristi day yerely shall attend uppon ther pagiaunt frome [the time when] the mateir of play be bequite at the furst place unto such tyme as the said play be played and funshed [finished] thurgh the toun at the last playse'.[111] The phrase 'the mateir of the play be bequite' sounds as if something fuller than brief speeches were presented at each station, casting doubt on the notion that full processional performances were impossible.

Moreover, Nelson's hypothesis concerning the single indoor performance at York glosses over all the complications of mounting plays with large casts and involving bulky properties and furnishings in even the 'chamber of generous proportions' he proposes. Problems of accommodating forty spectators and securing adequate exits and entrances and off-stage assembly areas for large casts, of providing in a confined space scenic devices for so many different plays, and access to the building for large numbers of performers — all seem insurmountable. The mind is overwhelmed by a confused medley of cloud machines, Noah's Ark, the cross for Calvary, scenic houses, thrones, and Hell-mouths blocking the stairways and passages of the 'Inn of the Common Hall' as players and musicians struggled vainly to reach or leave the chamber. If any kind of presentation resulted, it must have proved quite unworthy of mayoral attention.

Furthermore, it might be argued that the evidence for the use of the chamber in the Common Hall by the heads of temporal government at York does not necessarily mean that the Corpus Christi plays were presented inside the chamber, but that the mayor and his fellows watched outdoor performances at the adjacent eighth station in Coney Street from the comfort of an upstairs room provided with comfortable seating and ample refreshments; after all, the mayor and corporation watched the Chester pageants from the windows and galleries of the townhall. Nelson refutes this notion by arguing from records of 1524, 1527, and 1538 that the mayor's party traditionally watched the parade of Corpus Christi pageants from an earlier station, namely the sixth in front of Common Hall itself, which for him automatically rules out any possibility that they could then have adjourned to the chamber to watch the pageants pass and perform in the street for a second time.[112] But if the procession were of some duration and likely to occupy the greater part of the day (and any conjectural scheme proposed involves a lengthy period of time), the mayor and his party might wish to retire and take their meals while the procession of floats continued to wind on its way: to rent a convenient chamber from which to continue to watch the proceedings while fortifying themselves would surely have been eminently practical.

Stanley Kahrl, who adopts the view that the pageant-waggons did travel through the streets in the traditional manner, suggests that while spectators saw all the waggons pass in turn, they only witnessed the dramatic action in mime form until the procession stopped.[113] Then, with every station occupied by a pageant-waggon, each guild presented the whole of its play to whichever audience occupied the station at which a particular cart had halted. After the play, the waggons moved on to a second agreed point at which the players would once again perform. Arguing that each waggon was only allowed to make two such full-length stops, Kahrl claims that the York document of 3 April 1476 referring to the fact 'that no plaier . . . shall plaie . . . but twise on the day of the saide playe' is an injunction forbidding any guild to delay the procession by presenting their individual portion of the cycle on more than the two occasions stipulated. Speed was still of the essence; hence the York Proclamation of 1415 which states 'that every player that shall play be redy in his pagiaunt at convenyant tyme, that is to say, at the mydhowre betwix iiij[th] and v[th] of the cloke in the mornyng, and then all other pageantz fast folowyng ilkon after other as ther course is, without tarieng.'

Kahrl's view answers some objections to a full-length processional presentation, but it does impose a somewhat unlikely reading on the phrase concerning the embargo on the same actor performing more than twice, while also implying that later pageants must have spent a great deal of time waiting to set off and the early ones been kept waiting for the last cart to finish. The fact that *all* the performers were instructed to be on their pageant-waggons by 4.30 a.m. does not suggest the kind of staggered start or procedure envisaged by Professor Kahrl.

The most convincing compromise is that of Martin Stevens, who also argues that the probable procedure adopted was for the pageants to process in the traditional manner, bearing various tableaux of biblical scenes, but that they finally assembled, after proceding through the streets, at the Pavement, the largest open space York could offer, traditionally the last station on the route, and the only one at which no rental was levied.[114] Here the plays were performed (although even in this setting the whole of the extant cycle might not have been played), and made available to the public at large rather than to a small group of civic notables. Pageant-waggons could be wheeled into the open space to form a half or a full circle or a square; the performers would have used the waggons as *sedes* set up in juxtaposition according to medieval stage convention. Given this form of presentation, there appears to be some purpose in the instruction that 'no plaier . . . shall plaie . . . but twise on the day of the saide playe', since the temptation to accept several parts (and the fees attached) would have been considerable if a stationary performance at the final station were in question. It would also be a great economy to have only a single set depicting, say, Calvary, which could nonetheless be used by several different casts, while for such a performance, far fewer actors would be required. Such a mode of performance, moreover, appears to be attested to in several other medieval towns, notably Aberdeen and Louth in Lincolnshire[115] and it may ultimately be discovered to have been the method employed at many centres.

Stevens's intriguing interpretation of the facts is unlikely to be substantiated at present: his theory like Nelson's is also open to the objection that some York records apparently refer to true performances taking place at the stations. Recent debate warns us that in our current state of knowledge, we simply should not dogmatise. Medieval street theatre involved a wide range of possible methods.

5

OPEN-AIR THEATRE

Amyens: What's that Ducdame?
Jacques: 'Tis a Greeke invocation, to call fools into a circle.

As You Like It, II. 5

When performances of religious plays began to be organised outside as well as inside medieval churches, it was natural that they should at first have found sites close to those edifices, for their dramatic requirements as well as their spiritual associations demanded it. The most notable example of an outdoor play which still relies in large measure on the architectural background of a place of worship is the *Ordo Repraesentacionis Adae*, better known as *Le Mystère* or *Le Jeu d'Adam*, almost certainly staged on the *parvis* or open space outside some church or cathedral in southern England or northern France between 1146 and 1174. Many commentators assume that the staging occurred on the forecourt before the great western façade of some edifice, possibly one possessing a flat-roofed porch suitable for scenes set in the earthly Paradise. In their view, if Paradise could not be conveniently sited above the west door, a raised platform could have been built around the door, with steps or ladders to provide access. However, Grace Frank[1] argues that an audience watching the play from the western front of the building would be unlikely to hear the liturgical *lectio* beginning *Vos, inquam, convenio* (You, I say, I summon) read (according to the stage direction) in the church choir to introduce the prophets of the play's third section, since the choir was, of course, at the east end of the church. She argues that the playing-area was more probably at the entrance to the south transept, many transepts possessing large portals with steps leading up to them, and that this would allow spectators to hear reading or singing within the choir through the open south door without difficulty.

Professor Frank also questions the siting of Paradise on some elevated platform approached by steps or ladders: although Paradise is certainly described as constructed in a 'more conspicuous place' (*Constituatur paradisus loco eminenciori*), reference is never made to characters ascending or descending in order to approach or leave it, and the stage direc-

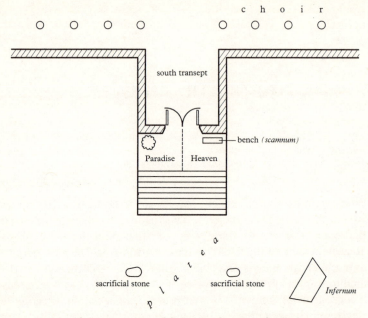

9   A conjectural reconstruction of the setting for *Le Mystère d'Adam, c.* 1146—74

tions suggest easy access to the Paradise area: when we read that the
devils approach 'very near to Paradise' (*juxta Paradisum*) to tempt Eve
to eat the forbidden fruit and that 'God comes wearing a stole and enters
Paradise looking about him', no mention is made of their climbing up to
reach the area. It therefore seems likely that the more prominent stage
level mentioned was simply the wide top step of a flight leading up to a
door in the south transept, this space being divided into two locations,
one on each side of the door. One area formed the earthly Paradise,
hung about with curtains and silk hangings, decorated with flowers,
foliage, and trees, and offering space enough for Adam and Eve to walk
about in (*spatientur*); the other was an elevated but unlocalised area
which, throughout the play, represents the entry to God's heavenly
dwelling-place in the church building, as when we read '*Tunc vadat
Figura ad ecclesiam* [then the Figure of God goes into the church]'. At
some moments this area represented the threshold of Heaven, but
Grace Frank suggests that it was also used for the speeches of the
prophets, for, since many of them sit on a *scamnum* or bench to deliver
their lines, it would seem appropriate that they should be seated in a
position from which they are visible to the spectators; the upper level

122

would have taken on a new identity for this scene, no explanation being needed, as the medieval imagination was infinitely flexible. Since the play is incomplete we have no means of knowing the other ways in which this strategic location might have been employed during the course of the action.

The reason for hanging Paradise round with curtains so that only the head and shoulders of those within are seen seems curiously clumsy, especially as Adam and Eve are in no sense naked. The apparent purpose of the instruction is that Adam's costume change (and possibly Eve's, though it is not mentioned) at the Fall has to be contrived in full view of the audience, since the stage direction informs us that Adam is to bend down so that he cannot be seen by the people, remove his splendid raiment and put on impoverished garments sewn together from fig-leaves. Nevertheless it seems rather drastic to obscure much of the action in Paradise simply to engineer a single change of costume, and the true reason for the hangings is probably that since, to the medieval mind, Paradise was conceived as a literal garden, in art and on stage it had to be provided with an appropriate 'wall'.[2]

The open playing-area at the foot of the church steps, the *platea*, was of course used extensively in the course of *Le Mystère d'Adam*, and the ease with which Diabolus makes frequent sorties through the *platea* (*faciet discursum per plateam*), and on one occasion even among the spectators (*discursum faciet per populum*), suggests that *platea* and audience were on the same level. It is to the *platea* that Adam and Eve are exiled from Paradise to till the soil; here the devils come and 'plant' thorns and thistles where corn was sown (presumably by scattering ready-cut bushes over the area); here Cain and Abel cultivate the ground and make sacrifice at 'two huge stones which have been made ready for this scene', placed so that one is on God's right hand, one on his left, when he appears. Thus the *platea* is associated with both earthly and diabolical activity, and assumes different identities as need arises. The chief constructed scene is Hell-mouth (*infernum*) from which the devils emerge onto the *platea* and to which they retire; what form the structure took we cannot say, but we know that it had doors or gates (*portas*) and was enclosed, since the devils are instructed to make sufficient noise with their shouts and utensils for it to be heard outside. Smoke issues forth in the conventional manner, but since 'Hell' would almost certainly have been a wooden structure at this date, fire does not seem to have featured in the presentation. *Le Mystère d'Adam* reveals other details of staging: to parry Cain's murdering blow Abel is to conceal a pot in his clothing, and some of the instructions concerning gesture and move-

123

ment will be examined in Chapter 7. We might welcome a fuller account of the way by which the 'artfully constructed' serpent arose beside the Tree of Knowledge; Professor Frank argues for a cloth or paper replica manipulated by means of a thread by either Adam or Eve.

Adam appears to form part of a thriving tradition of vernacular plays, and it is safe to assume that by the close of the twelfth century, sacred drama had joined the wide variety of secular entertainments played out of doors in the summer months. Although inside the churches Latin liturgical dramas continued to be presented and room may also have been found there for vernacular plays such as the Toledo *Reyes Magos* (see page 64 above), there is evidence of a movement in the opposite direction in Spain, since the *Siete Partidas* (*c.* 1260) of Alfonso the Wise (1252–84) provide for the clergy to present dramas outside the churches, which suggests the use of vernacular texts. In London popular open-air religious plays (*miracula*) treating of the lives and deaths of saints and martyrs appear as early as 1170–80, according to the commendation bestowed on them by William Fitzstephen in his *Life of St Thomas Becket*, where he compares London favourably with ancient Rome for the piety of its dramatic art: 'London, in place of theatrical spectacles and stage plays, has sacred dramas, representations of the miracles performed by holy confessors, or representations of the sufferings by which the steadfastness of martyrs manifested itself.'[3]

How many presentations of this period can be positively assigned to open-air sites is uncertain: the performance of a St Nicholas's Day play, announced in an English sermon of *c.* 1250 by the statement that its staging is for the benefit of 'Bothe this lewed and this clerkes [both for the common people and the literate]', suggests that vernacular plays for open-air consumption were usual.[4] Two liturgical play-prologues in Anglo-Norman and English survive from the late thirteenth century, but give no indication of what types of play they precede, or where they were to be staged; the tone of one suggests that a pagan emperor or even Herod is about to enter. It was doubtless clerical participation in *miracula* and scriptural plays of this popular and unsanctioned kind that various popes, and clerics such as Robert Grosseteste (see p. 19 above) condemned and sought to outlaw, and we may assume that their continued performance outside church premises never ceased to offend the susceptible.[5]

Two extant French plays of the thirteenth century may have been presented in the open, and a tavern-yard or a market-place seems a likely venue for them both. Composed in and centred on the town of Arras, the anonymous *Courtois d'Arras* (*c.* 1225) and Adam de la Halle's

Le Jeu de la Feuillée (*c.* 1275) are splendid examples of early vernacular drama:[6] in the former, a comic version of the Prodigal Son story, two specific locations are needed, one to represent the prodigal Courtois's country home from which he departs and to which he returns, the other the inn, scene of his discomfiture by Pourette and Manchevaire, two cunning city harlots. Both structures require entrances to the *platea* accessible from the rear, from whence food and drink have to be brought on for the tavern scene, and possibly this sequence took place on the *platea* as if on a terrace or in a courtyard, the inn being either an actual one incorporated into the action, or imagined as lying behind the stage. The remainder of the *platea* would then be free for Courtois's travels and for his herding of the swine prior to his return. His father might then enter his *mansion* from behind to greet Courtois, and perhaps when celebrations are called for, further characters might enter by the same entrance to prepare for festivities occupying the entire *platea*, tables and benches from the tavern being employed once more.

An inn-yard appears the ideal setting for *Le Jeu de la Feuillée* (*The Play of the Leafy Bower*) by Adam de la Halle (or le Bossu) (*c.* 1238 – *c.* 1289), in which only a single locale is involved. A yard or terrace abutting on the door of a tavern near the Petit-Marché at Arras seems perfectly suited to Adam's varied *pot-pourri*, a blend of urban life and airy fantasy, one essential feature of which is the fairy feast arranged on a table in some leaf-covered bower or shrine set apart from the main action. The open space may have been occupied by tables and benches which, if the scene were an actual tavern, would not appear incongruous, especially as the entertainment itself with its linked 'turns' is something like a smoking concert or revue.[7] The staging needs of Adam's other play, *Le Jeu de Robin et Marion* (*c.* 1283) are even simpler. This, the first secular music-drama known in France, virtually demands open-air performance, and may well have been played first at the court of the expatriate Count Robert of Artois, in the type of pastoral landscape described, with meadows backed by woods, some bushes where the boastful but cowardly shepherd Robin can hide from his rival Sire Aubert, and a grassy bank where the shepherds can recline while they sing, play pastoral games (*bergeries*), flirt, and picnic. No definite locations are established by the text, but it is hard to accept that the entire action was imagined as taking place in one spot. Since a generalised country setting is created, no doubt the first spectators accepted the convention later adopted on the Elizabethan stage that, although the scenery had not altered, the presence of fresh characters or a new development in the plot meant that the scene lay in 'another part of the forest'.

An outdoor location was doubtless used by the presenters of *Le Garçon et l'Aveugle* (*The Boy and the Blind Man*) (*c.* 1280), the rather cruel Flemish farce from Tournai, which may have been staged in a market-place or inn-yard or in any spot where two *jongleurs* (entertainers) might ply their trade, although there seems to be a need for a 'practical' house to be available: perhaps a door or archway sufficed. Similarly Rutebeuf's dramatic monologue for a quack-doctor of folk-tradition, *Le Dit de l'Herberie* (*The Herbalist's Tale*), and the bawdy English fragment, the *Interludium de Clerico et Puella* (*The Interlude of the Clerk and the Girl*), a routine for three entertainers and a clever dog, could have been improvised almost anywhere, indoors or out, since they require little or no scenery.[8]

A passage in a saint's life from Beverley in Yorkshire[9] sheds some light on outdoor performance in thirteenth-century Britain: a 'representation of the Lord's Resurrection' (possibly *La Seinte Resureccion*) presented in the parish churchyard on a summer's day in about 1220 became the occasion of a miracle wrought by St John of Beverley on the body of a youthful spectator who entered the church and fell from the *triforium* while trying to gain a better view through the windows. The choice of the churchyard-site is of considerable interest in view of the use made of such locations for ceremonies derived from pagan rites (see pp. 15–18 above), and mention of 'the usual masked players' again hints that this was one of those unauthorised *miracula* at which stricter ecclesiastics might look askance. Also of interest is the fact that the large audience formed itself into a circle or *corona* enclosing the action, for many purpose-built 'place-and-scaffold' stages adopted this shape later. The opening of the passage runs:

It happened that one summertime a representation of the Lord's Resurrection was presented in words and gestures by the usual masked players, between the buttresses on the north side of the Church of the Blessed John. A great crowd, both men and women, flocked together there, drawn by a variety of motives, for example, enjoyment, or because of curiosity, or with the pious intention of arousing themselves to devotion. However, when many people, and especially those short in stature, failed to obtain a satisfactory view because of the closely-packed people standing around in a circle, most of them went into the church.

Little information can be gleaned concerning the staging of a lost play from Regensburg (Ratisbon) in Bavaria performed on 7 February 1194, described as an *ordo* 'showing the creation of the angels and the downfall of Lucifer and his supporters, and the creation of man and his fall, and the prophets', and having apparent links with *Le Mystère d'Adam*.[10] Nor do details survive for the Siena Passion play of *c.* 1200.[11]

But of the Padua Passion and Resurrection drama of 1243 or 1244 we discover that it was staged *'solemniter et ordinate in Prato Vallis* [in a solemn and orderly manner in the Valley Meadow]',[12] and also performed out-of-doors was the play of Christ (*repraesentatio Ludi Christi*) from the north-west Italian town of Cividale del Friuli, recorded in the city's chronicles for 7 May 1298 as having been presented by the city's clergy on Whitsunday and the two subsequent days, 'in the city courtyard of my Lord the Patriarch of Cividale [*in curia domini patriarche Austrie Civitatis*]', the events covered including the Passion, Resurrection, Ascension, and Pentecost, and culminating in the Day of Judgement. In 1304 the same site was selected for a somewhat fuller sequence of Whitsun plays, when the Cividale clergy or cathedral chapter added the Creation and Fall of Man, the Annunciation and Nativity, and the coming of Antichrist to the 1298 episodes.[13] Around the end of the thirteenth century, in 1290 and 1302, plays were presented near the stone cross of the cemetery of St Martial of Limoges, but details are not known.[14] In 1301 the Prioress of Clerkenwell in London complained to King Edward I of damage to crops caused by crowds assembling in Clerkenwell Fields to watch wrestling-matches and miracle plays; indeed the fields were a traditional centre for every type of popular entertainment.[15] But our picture of the use of open-air sites is a fragmentary one, although a pattern of usage emerges in that churchyards, various kinds of courtyard, and public places of resort, all seem to have been favoured.

In considering medieval stage locations after about 1300, we must first examine the emergence of the great vernacular religious dramas of the late Middle Ages, for these were the main dramatic fare offered in city squares, market-places, monastic courtyards, and a variety of other open spaces. The most striking are the famous cyclic sequences of Germany, France, and Britain, and the origins of this impulse towards the creation of cycle dramas have become the subject of scholarly controversy over the last twenty or thirty years.[16]

Many scholars have argued that, despite the cosmic sweep of the Tegernsee *Antichristus* and Hildegard's *Ordo Virtutum*, composers of Latin liturgical drama never felt the urge to encompass the whole of Christian history or the deeds of the Apostles in a comprehensive series of plays. Since each *Ordo* or *Officium* had grown out of church worship for a specific day and depended on that day's liturgy for its incidents, there was never any motive for assimilating this type of play into a cyclic sequence. Glynne Wickham, for example, rejects the earlier view of Chambers and Hardin Craig that vernacular cycles in

Europe descended directly from the Latin liturgical drama through adaptation and translation, preferring to

admit the likelihood of two dramas of single Christian origin but of independent motivation: the drama of the Real Presence within the liturgy and the imitative drama of Christ's Humanity in the world outside. The one is a drama of adoration, praise and thanksgiving: the other is a drama of humour, suffering and violence, of laughter and sorrow. Where the former remains ritualistic, the latter carries with it the germs of tragedy and comedy.[17]

V. A. Kolve has made the point in slightly different terms, emphasising the difference between the word *ludus* or 'play', 'the generic term for the vernacular drama' in England, and terms such as *ordo* used for a drama for which

The church and the liturgy were its natural milieu. It was simple, dignified, ritualistic, limited in its means; it was called *ordo, processio, repraesentatio*. When the drama moved into the streets and the market place, into a milieu already the home of men's playing and games, it was redefined *as* game and allowed to exploit fully its nonearnest, gratuitous nature at the same time as its range of subject and its cast of sacred personae grew.

Both Wickham and Kolve stress the importance of the institution of the Feast of Corpus Christi (see pp. 97–9 above) in stimulating the growth of what they see as a new vernacular cyclic form. They believe that the Feast, with its accent on thanksgiving for salvation symbolised in the Mass, acted as a creative nucleus for the Corpus Christi cycle, and that the nature and purpose of the new festival defined the structure of sequences which thus became dramatic expressions of the significance of Corpus Christi. By illustrating the rôle of Christ's sacrifice in redeeming mankind, the cycle plays represent a radical break with the Latin church music-dramas with their precise liturgical themes: 'To play the whole story . . . is in the deepest sense to *celebrate* the Corpus Christi sacrament, to explain its necessity and power, and to show how that power will be made manifest at the end of the world.'[18]

However, the view that the content of the cycle plays reflects the theme of the Corpus Christi festival is open to some objections.[19] While a fresh stimulus to dramatic composition may have resulted from the celebration of Corpus Christi, it is curious that the institution of the Eucharist at the Last Supper receives little stress in the extant English cycles, while many similar plays of the cycle type are known to have been staged at times other than at the Feast of Corpus Christi, the Whitsun period being chosen for example at Cividale, and the week following Easter elsewhere. Alan Nelson contends that 'the Corpus Christi cycles bear no distinctive relationship to the doctrines celebrated on Corpus Christi' and sees an already established pattern of significant events in scriptural history as determining the choice of subject-matter in the plays, with the pageant-processions discussed in Chapter 4 acting as intermediaries. For Nelson 'the fifteenth-century English dramatic cycles developed out of fourteenth-century festival processions. A corollary of this argument is that the doctrinal relationship of the Corpus Christi dramatic play to the feast of Corpus Christi is almost entirely incidental.'[20]

Moreover, while granting that the vernacular cycle sequences are unlikely to have been composed simply by stringing together a sequence of pre-existing liturgical plays in translation, one cannot deny that some early plays certainly hint at a 'cyclic impulse'. Many works involve several incidents and a variety of scenes: the Klosterneuburg *Ordo Paschalis* requires six different locations, while a number of Passion plays run several episodes together to form one lengthy sequence. Besides, Theo Stemmler and Rosemary Woolf point out[21] that religious plays in the twelfth century had become partly detached from 'liturgical time', in that one sequence might combine several incidents actually celebrated liturgically on different days, as in the cases of the Benediktbeuern and Monte Cassino Easter plays which link Passion and Resurrection episodes, or the Anglo-Norman *Seinte Resureccion* which begins with Joseph of Arimathea's request for Christ's body on Good Friday. Bad weather might also mean that outdoor plays had to be performed — irrespective of their religious theme — on fine summer Sundays rather than on their rightful holy day. The Beverley Resurrection drama provides a graphic example of this, being presented not at the obvious festival of Easter, but in the summer, on a day which Rosemary Woolf considers 'may be safely inferred to be a Sunday'.

The genesis of the cyclic drama is incapable of being pinpointed precisely: Woolf assumes an unproven tradition of twelfth-century vernacular cycles, conjecturing that plays such as *Le Mystère d'Adam* helped to establish a pattern, its performance taking place on Septuagesima Sunday (the third Sunday before Lent). The lost Regensburg *Ordo Creacionis* was admittedly performed on the Monday of Septuagesima 1194,[22] but the contention that Septuagesima cycles may have been known elsewhere receives only partial confirmation from the lost *Ludus Prophetarum* from the Latvian town of Riga which was performed in the winter of 1204. Presentation at Septuagesima is thus feasible; however, although the range of plays included the mock battle between Gideon's forces and those of the Philistines (see pp. 223–4 below), and the 'wars' of Herod, it did not necessarily involve the Massacre of the

Innocents, the Nativity, or other cyclic elements as some have claimed. Even its reference to dramatisation of the teachings of the Old and New Testaments (*doctrina Veteris et Novi Testamenti*) do not automatically render performance of a unified cycle drama certain.[23] Claims have also been made for the cyclic character of some of the Perugian *laude drammatiche* (see pp. 65–6 above), but again the evidence is far from indisputable.[24]

In England the picture remains obscured for a long period. Wickham's arguments for the existence of Latin cycles performed by the monks of St Werburgh's Abbey, Chester, before 1278 must remain conjectural.[25] The Prioress of Clerkenwell's complaint to Edward I concerned miracle plays, which are unlikely to have been cyclic in character, although contemporary with the 1304 Whitsun sequence at Cividale del Friuli. Rosemary Woolf's claim that an English vernacular cycle was in production by 1320–30, largely because lines from an apparent drama in which the devil tempts Eve are quoted in a sermon associated with John Sheppey, Bishop of Rochester (d. 1360), is not irrefutable:[26] the existence of a play on the Fall does not necessarily imply the existence of a full cycle, even though such an episode may be regarded theologically as essential to a complete treatment of Christ's redemption of mankind. Further evidence for an early English cycle is hard to find. F. M. Salter has demolished the tradition that the Chester cycle was first presented in the vernacular in 1327–8.[27] Certainly the payment of half a mark in about 1350 for 'a play of the Children of Israel [*in ludo filiorum Israelis*]' by William de Lenne and his wife on entering the Guild of Corpus Christi in Cambridge may imply that a Latin or vernacular cycle including Moses or the Massacre of the Innocents took place there at about this time, but it is equally likely that the play was an isolated piece, for which the performance fee of a half a mark was standard at this period.[28]

Definite evidence for cyclic performances on the Continent appears somewhat earlier than in Britain. From the late thirteenth century come two fragments from the oldest German religious drama, an Easter Passion play probably staged at Kloster Muri in Switzerland, in which there are animated appearances by the spice-seller of tradition and a swaggering Pilate and his comic servant, not to mention a battle between Christ and Satan at the Harrowing of Hell.[29] More important in establishing the cyclic pattern is the mixed Latin and German *Wiener Passionspiel (Vienna Passion Play)* of *c.* 1300,[30] involving a full theologically integrated sequence beginning with the Fall of Lucifer and that of Man, which would no doubt conclude with Christ's Passion, Crucifixion, and Resurrection, did we possess the complete text. Scenically the play does not require elements not already found in the Latin liturgical dramas, and it is significant that its action and speeches are in some respects very close to those of the Passion play of Benediktbeuern, notably in the presentation of Mary Magdalen. Usually, the vernacular plays and the Latin pieces contrast strongly in tone since the former now aim at a more popular audience. This is emphasised by the most complete Passion play in German, from St Gall in Switzerland (*c.* 1300–50),[31] which contains an extended sequence of Gospel events, and by the *Fronleichnamsspiel* (*Corpus Christi Play*) from Innsbruck (*c.* 1391)[32] which suggests a sequence beginning with the Fall and the inclusion of Gospel events up to the Resurrection, albeit conveyed through a series of dramatic monologues (see p. 101 above).

The other important source of evidence for early cyclic presentations is France, where Passion sequences were popular, the earliest surviving example, *La Passion du Palatinus* (*c.* 1300),[33] probably stemming from Burgundy and drawing on material now lost. The work opens with the Entry into Jerusalem and abounds in humorous contemporary touches, particularly among the low-life characters who torture and crucify Christ (such as the blacksmith's wife who forges the nails for the cross when her husband refuses). At roughly the same time appears the somewhat uninspired compilation of texts known as the *Passion d'Autun*,[34] the shorter version of which contains scenes and characters not found elsewhere, demonstrating that the desire to expand and elaborate on existing materials was felt even among relatively unskilled arrangers. Another early French play which prefigures the fully developed cycle sequences is *Le Jour de Jugement* (*c.* 1330),[35] a music-drama which includes as its main action the legendary exploits of Antichrist, beginning with a conclave of devils in Hell, proceeding to a Harrowing in which all ranks of medieval society are represented, and culminating in the Last Judgement, where light scenery made of painted cloth mounted on wicker framework is engulfed in real flames (cf. pp. 172–4 below). This ambitious play involves 94 rôles and sweeping cosmic transitions which recall the Tegernsee play 170 years previously, and anticipate the wide panoramic scope of the spectacles of the next two centuries of French dramatic history.

Whatever the impulses which led to the development of the cycle form, responsibility for the staging of religious drama now became shared equally between the Church and the cities and towns of western Europe. Churchmen still played a vital rôle in guiding the endeavours of the organisers, performers, and craftsmen of those communities prosperous and ambitious enough to stage drama, ensuring that the basic purpose, theme, and treatment remained Christian, whatever worldly scenes and figures might enter the action: typical is the comment about the Valenciennes Passion of 1547 that 'le tout fut veu, examiné, et approuvé par les Theologiens et autres Deputes de Monseigneur de Combray [the whole enterprise was seen, inspected, and approved by. . . his Grace the Archbishop of Cambrai]'. Clerics might still take responsibility for composing scripts: for the Romans performance of 1509 the text of *Le Mystère des Trois Doms* (*The Mystery Play of the Three Monks*) was written by a Canon Pra who was paid 255 florins for it; they might even appear on stage themselves (see pp. 197–8 below); the degree of control and participation must have varied from place to place. But the main initiative now passed to the citizens and municipal authorities: each community felt free to follow its own system of play presentation, and the staging of the great annual cycle performances or of the occasional drama of epic proportions became a matter of intense civic pride and was the subject of frequent inter-communal rivalry. Particularly important was the rôle of the wealthier trade- and craft-guilds, those unique medieval associations dedicated to charitable works, mutual self-help, and the promotion of their own interests. Some guilds assumed responsibility for contributing their own play to the communal enterprise as only one of their annual obligations. Guilds also seem to have been formed exclusively for the purpose of staging plays, and of these the French *confréries* and the Italian *compagnie* are the best known. Nor should the part played by religious guilds and fraternities such as the frequently encountered Guilds of Corpus Christi be forgotten. All these bodies had large responsibilities to discharge, and their contributions to the development of medieval drama were immense.

This adjustment of sponsorship meant that civic considerations as well as doctrinal ones tended to dictate not only the organisation of the plays but their tone and the choice of sites and personnel too; for, if Glynne Wickham is right

the drama associated with Corpus Christi was directed towards the frivolous rich and the covetous tradesman in an effort to re-dedicate society to Christ and Christ's service in the remembrance that Christ had died to save mankind . . . Market-squares were thus as appropriate a *platea* or acting place for these performances as convent courtyards, laymen more desirable as actors than clerics, and civic wealth as necessary to finance production of these *ludi* as clerical scribes to provide the texts.[36]

Once the opportunity occurred to stage religious plays — were they Passion or Easter plays, Corpus Christi or Whitsun cycles — in the open air, their organisers had a wide range of choice in the matter of potential sites. In and around medieval towns and cities areas for public assemblies of various kinds existed, and these no doubt included places where *miracula* or secular plays were already being presented. It is not impossible that ecclesiastical and civic authorities deliberately chose to site plays of a religious nature in places traditionally associated with profane performances: the Beverley Resurrection play may have been one such attempt to combat the popularity of churchyard presentations.

The mounting of drama in churchyards and cemeteries during the Middle Ages is attested to by a number of sources: the Beverley *Resurrection* and plays in the cemetery of St Martial at Limoges have already been discussed; later we hear of a Passion play from Poitiers (1508) directed by Jean Bouchet, for which the probable site was the cemetery of Saint Cybard, a traditional playing-site where it was customary to enclose the acting-area by ditches, the dug soil from which served as a sloping mound upon which spectators could be accommodated.[37] A production of 1541 in Paris attended by the Duke of Cleves was staged either in the gardens or in the former cemetery of the Augustines, while the Wakefield cycle was possibly performed in Goodybower Close, a field containing a quarry pit, and directly adjacent to the north side of the parish churchyard, which could account for Joseph of Arimathea's suggestion concerning Christ's corpse, 'Bere we hym furth unto the Kyrke'; the Wakefield cycle could supply a partial parallel to the Beverley *Resurrection* staged 'between the buttresses on the north side of the church'[38]; in fact, some suggest that it must have been presented nearer to the church than the Close. However, the quarry pit itself, if disused, may well have been used as its sloping sides and flat base would have provided an excellent amphitheatre for performances. In the sixteenth century a quarry-site at Shrewsbury apparently supplied a setting for drama, for in 1516 there is a reference in the Corporation accounts to a saint play performed '*in quarera post muros* [in the quarry outside the walls]', and in 1570 the grant of 'a certain pasture called "Behind the walls"' excepts 'the Quarrell where the plases [plays] have bine accustomyd to be used'.[39] Thomas Churchyard in *The Worthiness of Wales* (1587) describes the place in admiring terms:

> I had such haste, in hope to be but briefe,
> That monuments, in churches were forgot:
> And somewhat more, behind the walles as chiefe,
> Where playes have bin, which is most worthie note.

There is a ground, newe made theator wise,
Both deepe and hye, in goodly auncient guise:
Where well may sit, ten thousand men at ease,
And yet the one, the other not displease.

A space below, to bayt both bull and beare,
For players too, great roume and place at will.
And in the same, a cocke pit wondrous *feare*,   fair
Besides where men, may wrastle in their fill.
A ground most apt, and they that sits above,
At once in vewe, all this may see for love:
At Astons play, who had beheld this then,
Might well have seene, there twentie thousand men.[40]

A note informs us that 'Maister Aston was a good and godly preacher', but he was also Headmaster of Shrewsbury School from 1561 onwards, and his 'plays' were no doubt staged by his pupils, the last recorded in 1568.

Amphitheatres, natural, ancient, or purpose-built, offered excellent sites for open-air presentations, and performance 'in the round' is now regarded as a significant medieval mode of dramatic staging. When vast crowds had to be arranged in positions from which the stage-action could be seen, the advantages of a circular raked auditorium become obvious, and a number of fortunate continental towns such as Bourges, Saumur, Orange, Nîmes and Arles, possessed the remnants of Roman amphitheatres which offered ideal sites for medieval performances, even if they only served as basic outlines for further construction as at Saumur in 1534 and Bourges in 1536.[41] Elsewhere, more extensive remains relieved organisers of the necessity to construct theatres: there is even a record in 1497 of religious plays being staged in the ruins of the Colosseum at Rome.[42] In Britain the most striking example of the use of circular sites occurs in Cornwall where earthwork amphitheatres, constructed on the bases of prehistoric fortifications or on more mundane cattle-enclosures, encircled a level 'playing-place' (*the plan-an-gwarry*).[43] The only probable surviving example of this form of theatre-site in Cornwall is the Piran Round, near Perranporth, but there is evidence that many others existed, perhaps the most notable situated near the church of St Just on the Penwith peninsula, an amphitheatre which stood until at least the eighteenth century and of which the site itself is still visible today. William Borlase in his *Observations on the Antiquities Historical and Monumental of Cornwall* of 1745 describes it as being an exact circle 126 feet ($38\frac{1}{2}$ metres) in diameter with its embankment 7 feet (2 metres) high and its outer circumference traced by a ditch; 6 tiers of seats were apparently formed from stone slabs, and a rampart 7 feet (2 metres) wide ran around the top of the bank. Later evidence suggests that a stone wall surrounded the enclosure. In his *Natural History of Cornwall* (1758) Borlase describes the 'round' at Piran as consisting of a mound 8 feet (2½ metres) high, with 7 tiers of seats cut out of the turf embankment, and an outer ditch; although highly successful performances are staged there today, we cannot be entirely certain that its rôle as a theatre-site dates back to the Middle Ages. However, the Piran Round is clearly the *kind* of site utilised for drama in Cornwall during the period under discussion.

Very closely related to such structures are the specially built amphitheatres of which several French examples are recorded:[44] at Autun in 1516 a wooden amphitheatre was built around a central playing-space separated from the audience by a water-filled ditch; at Doué-la-Fontaine near Saumur in 1539 the citizens also built an amphitheatre on antique lines, enclosing a central sandy arena 30 metres (99 feet) across and separated from the tiered banks of seating by a low wall. A few years earlier in 1545, Jean Bouchet, who had staged several productions in his home-town of Poitiers, sent directions on staging a *Tragédie du Christ Occis* (*Tragedy of the Slain Christ*) to Issoudun near Bourges, and here too a wooden amphitheatre was specially erected: a contemporary observer informs us that 'they constructed a genuine theatre in wood, such as the Romans built before Pompey's great theatre [*ils construisirent un vrai théâtre en bois, tel que les Romains en ont édifié avant le grand théâtre de Pompée*]'. When Jean Neyron built his 'permanent' theatre at Lyon in 1540 it was built on the circular principle, and when the citizens of Meaux set up a theatre in 1547, it followed a similar pattern.[45] An outdoor theatre erected for a performance of the *Vieux Testament* before the Duke of Cleves at the Hôtel de Flandre at Paris in June 1541 is described thus:

Behind this edifice [the Hôtel itself] a large elegant theatre was set up covered with a high awning of silk, and this theatre was built in a circular form according to the ancient Roman fashion, in such a way that everyone could sit down, one above the other, arranged in twenty tiers, and above three levels extended right round, all conveniently divided into boxes and galleries.[46]

Descriptions of specially built amphitheatres may be supplemented from the manuscript of the English morality play, *The Castel of Perseverance* (*c.* 1400–25), one of the few surviving medieval plays for which a stage-plan is extant. This important sketch has been frequently reproduced (see Illustration 15, p. 157), and exhaustively studied, notably by Richard Southern in *The Medieval Theatre in the Round*.

Southern's interpretation is fully discussed below (pp. 156–9), but here it may be said that the theatre of Southern's conjectural reconstruction bears a striking resemblance to that of the Cornish 'rounds' and of some of the continental stages for whose appearance documentary evidence exists. Here, too, is a central *platea* surrounded by an earth embankment with terraces where spectators may sit and scaffolds to house the actors may be erected if necessary; here, too, is the ditch created by digging out the soil for the mound. While not consciously conceived as an imitation of a classical amphitheatre, as were some of its sixteenth-century successors, the theatre-site for *The Castel of Perseverance* has affinities with it, at least in its provision of a circular auditorium and a central playing-area.

It is perhaps notable that many medieval outdoor playing-places continued to be located close to religious buildings of one sort or another; the use of churchyards has been referred to, but another favoured site was the courtyard of a monastic establishment.[47] Thus in 1466 the children of Compiègne staged three *mystères* in the courtyard of the Abbey of Saint-Cornille; two years later *Le Jeu de Madame Saincte Catherine de Sienne* was played in the courtyard of the order of Grands Proischeurs de Metz, platforms erected around the walls hiding the tombs and inscriptions; a bishop's courtyard served for a Passion play of 1528 at Soissons. Possibly the most ambitious performance in such a setting was at Romans in 1509 when *Le Mystère des Trois Doms* took place in the quadrangle of the local Franciscan monastery, '*la cour des Cordeliers*', scaffolds being set up around the walls as at Metz, but instead of the central area being level, it was raised above the ground, for reasons which will shortly appear.[48] When the townsfolk of nearby Vienne were inspired to emulate the Romans performance in 1510, their site, too, had ecclesiastical associations; their *Passion* was staged 'in the great garden of the Abbey of St Peter'. In the English cathedral city of Lincoln, one possible home of the N-Town cycle, although both Norwich and King's Lynn have also been canvassed, the site now favoured as the likeliest for the dramatic (as opposed to the processional) performance is the Minster Close, a large open space between the west front of the cathedral and Exchequer Gate, a performing-area well-suited to accommodate a horde of spectators and the necessary scenic scaffolds. While there is evidence that plays were also staged just outside the city walls in what was known as Broadgate, Minster Close remains the probable site of the annual St Anne's Day cycle performances, lying close to the cathedral as it did[49] (see p. 160 below).

But any convenient enclosed space was liable to be occupied for theatrical purposes during the Middle Ages: at Nancy in 1532 a *mystère* was enacted within the courtyard of the castle itself. Indeed, the custom became so common that in the sixteenth century some princely dwellings were equipped with an inner courtyard specifically to accommodate dramatic presentations.[50] The Valenciennes Passion play of 1547 was presented in the inner court of the Hôtel d'Arschot, 'the house of the high and mighty prince Philippe de Croy, Duke of Arschot, governor of the said town': approach to this central quadrangle was monitored from a high tower – necessary when possibly 2,800 spectators attended each of the two performances held daily. The grounds of the celebrated Hôtels de Flandre and d'Orléans in Paris also seem to have been used for open-air productions, just as the interiors of these buildings were employed for indoor entertainments and for rehearsals during the inclement winter months.[51]

Another popular medieval playing-place was outside the city walls as at Lincoln's Broadgate, which was the site of the former 'Wardyke' or ditch which lay just east of the city wall. Such locations may have been chosen for the support which the adjacent masonry could offer when scaffolds had to be erected: that this was normally the case is suggested by a document from Lyon dated 1506 permitting the Augustinian Friars to

have a large theatre built on the Terreaux, on the ditches [*fossés*] at the Porte de la Lanterne, to play there the Life of St Nicolas de Tolentin, which the Monastery of the Augustines wished to have performed: but only on condition that they do not tamper with the walls of the town, and that they restore the Terreaux to their former condition.[52]

Performances on the *fossés*, ditches or dykes outside the walls of cities and towns, are also found at Nantes in 1518, at Alençon in 1520–1, and at Montauban in 1522.[53] The carpenter's contract from Alençon has survived, and other documents indicate that the theatre was constructed near the Porte de Sées in a right-angle made by the town walls, some of the scaffolds being placed against the walls to give them added stability. The main playing-place was formed by the floor of the ditch (which may have been virtually filled in with rubble or soil by this time) and on its far side, opposite the walls, was a *boulevart*, an earthwork embankment, which also served to provide support for some of the scaffolds. In March 1522 a comparable setting was utilised at Montauban in south-west France (Alençon is in the north-east) for a performance of *Le Mystère du Genre Humain* (*The Mystery Play of Mankind*); a barrier was then erected at each end of the town ditch to discourage unauthorised spectators from watching the proceedings without paying for the privilege! Here the bed of the disused ditch was dried out, smoothed over with added soil, and then used as the base for a platform 20 metres (66 feet) square which served as the main acting-area. The audience watched from two sides of the stage only, namely the two sloping banks of the ditch, and a low wall or parapet (*creneau*), probably of stakes or brushwood (as shown in Fouquet's miniature of the *Martyrdom of St Apollonia* — see Illustration 10), separated the actors from the audience.

The favourite and natural open-air site for drama in most medieval communities seems traditionally to have been a public place or town square, where theatrical performances were well established as early as 960 as we have already seen from King Edgar's reference to the mimi-performing 'in market-places [*in triviis*]' (see p. 27 above). This practice seems to have been universal: at Metz the Place de la Change was fre-quently used from at least 1409 onwards, having been enlarged two years earlier, possibly with dramatic performances in mind.[54] The Redentin Easter play dated 1464 was staged in the market-square of Wismar, a Baltic city near the monastery where the play originated;[55] *Le Mystère de l'Incarnation et de la Nativité* presented at Rouen in 1474 took place in the Place du Neuf Marchié (the New Market-place), the scenic locations apparently being set up on four sides of the central square.[56] The lower part of the Halles at Angers was used for Jean Michel's *Passion* in 1486, the Old Market at Poitiers in 1534. For the celebrated production at Mons in 1501 the Grand Markiet was taken over, and there is clear evidence that houses overlooking the market-square were incorporated into the action, the *mansion* representing Paradise being located in the Maison d'Allemaigne which was also required to contain the machinery by which the Flood was created (see p. 179 below).[57] Other houses in the market-place held privileged spectators who watched the action from the windows while the general public looked on from the roof-tops or from down in the square on two sides of the raised playing-area, a trapezium-shaped apron stage jutting out from one side of the Grand Markiet (see Illustration 11).

A remarkably similar system seems to have applied in a number of German and Swiss cities: rough plans exist for the open-air staging of plays at Alsfeld in 1501, at Frankfurt and Villingen *c.* 1585, and at Lucerne (Luzern) in 1583, all of which indicate performance within an enclosed rectangular area such as a market-place, with the scenic locations distributed across the open space, and spectators being accommodated on scaffolds set up against the houses forming the square, which are themselves utilised as viewing-places for well-to-do

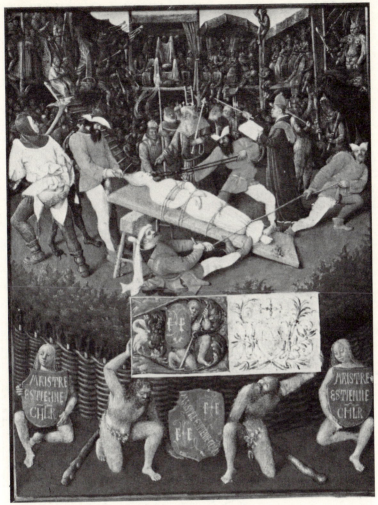

10   *The Martyrdom of St Apollonia*, by Jean Fouquet (*c.* 1460)

and distinguished spectators.[58] In the case of Lucerne, conjecture is
unnecessary for the detailed plans which survive, and the relatively
unaltered condition of the Weinmarkt (wine-market) today, enable
us to reconstruct with a good deal of confidence the staging of the
Passion play there from at least 1560. 'The most important public square
in Lucerne', surrounded by private houses and halls belonging to the
various guilds of the city, was ideal for stage productions, since it was

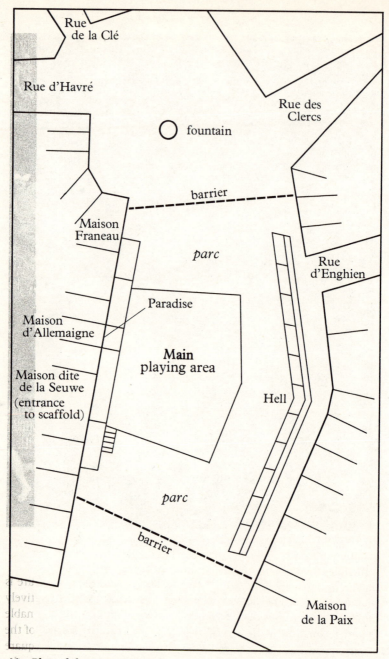

Rue
de la Clé

Rue d'Havré

Rue des
Clercs

○ fountain

barrier

Maison
Franeau

parc

Rue
d'Enghien

Paradise

Maison
d'Allemaigne

Main
playing area

Maison dite
de la Seuwe
(entrance
to scaffold)

Hell

parc

barrier

Maison
de la Paix

11 Plan of the Mons *Passion* in the Grand Markiet, 1501 (after Henri Rey-Flaud)

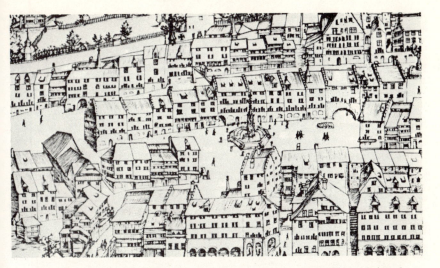

12   Sketch of the Weinmarkt at Lucerne from Martin Martini's *Stadtplan* of 1597

approached by four wide streets and four narrower passages, facilitating arrivals and departures. Together with documents relating to the Mons production of 1501 and to the Valenciennes performance of 1547, the information gathered at Lucerne comprises the most valuable surviving body of material on which to base discussion of staging methods involving open-air sites.[59]

With such a variety of open spaces at their disposal, it might be imagined that those responsible for presenting plays in the Middle Ages would have adopted an equally wide variety of staging methods. But there is, in fact, a striking similarity of approach. It seems useful to begin, then, by treating questions of general staging principle before proceeding to examine the way in which individual productions sometimes adapted principles to suit particular circumstances.

The first general principle of outdoor staging appears to have been that wherever possible some pre-existing location was used, preferably an enclosed or at least a well-defined area. Performances in open country are rare, public places, noble and monastic courtyards, and natural or artificial 'rounds' being preferred, although we do hear in 1437 of certain Carmelites, priests and laymen staging the Life of St Eloi at Dijon, at the Morimont field (*ou champ de Morimont*),[60] while the

13   A platform stage in a rural setting

Clerkenwell Fields were a favoured site for stage-plays (see p. 127 above) and the Valley Meadow was used at Padua (see p. 127 above; also Illustration 13). But generally some kind of specific enclosure was favoured, and even when a theatre-structure had to be specially erected, its designers strove as far as possible to reproduce the conditions provided by a naturally occurring site, such as the Wakefield and Shrewsbury quarries, the market-squares of Mons and Lucerne, or the Minster Close at Lincoln.

The shapes and dimensions of these outdoor theatres obviously varied greatly, but there now seems little doubt that the circle or 'round' very frequently occurred, although the square or rectangle was also used particularly where an available town square or courtyard suggested such a plan.[61] What is seldom found among outdoor theatres of the Middle Ages is the arrangement hallowed by centuries of familiarity with theatres where a rectangular auditorium confronts a proscenium stage occupying its far end. The ability to view a play from the front only would have seemed very restricting to a medieval spectator, and while audience-accommodation on at least two sides of a stage is commonplace, seating in the round is more often recorded.

The size of the theatre-sites is often difficult to gauge: given the vast numbers attending (see p. 232 below) and the large casts often required to appear on stage at one time, we must suppose that quite extensive areas were needed. Thus, of those sites which still remain in something approaching their medieval state, the playing-area of the upper or eastern end of the Weinmarkt at Lucerne employed for the Passion play measures 38 metres (125 feet) in length by 24 metres (80 feet) at its broadest part down to 18 metres (60 feet) at its narrowest.[62] The area available at Lincoln for the staging of the N-Town cycle appears to be approximately 62 × 34 metres (205 × 110 feet), and the Pavement at York, where the York pageants may have formed up for a single static performance of that city's cycle, was probably of comparable dimensions, being one of the largest open spaces in the medieval city, a place of public executions, a bull-baiting arena, as well as one of the two main market-places.[63] The Cornish 'round' at St Just was said to be 38 metres (126 feet) in diameter, and that at Piran runs 44 metres (143 feet) north and south, 41 metres (135 feet) east and west; but these may be exceptional, as Richard Carew in 1602 estimated that 'each eartheen Amphitheatre in some open field' where 'Guary miracles' were staged had 'the Diameter of his enclosed playne some 40. or 50. foot', although the whole of Carew's testimony must be treated with caution.[64] But certainly, given the massive scale of the fifteenth-century Cornish cycle, with its tripartite structure consisting of the *Ordinale de Origine Mundi* (*The Service-Book Containing the Origin of the World*), the *Passio Domini Nostri Jhesu Christi* (*The Passion of Our Lord Jesus Christ*), and the *Ordinale de Resurrexione Domini Nostri Jhesu Christi* (*Our Lord's Resurrection*), each consisting of some 3,000 lines; or of the two-day saint play, *The Life of St Meriasek* (*Beunans Meriasek*) (1504), with its 99 speaking-parts, generous playing-areas were essential.[65] Richard Southern calculates that an arena some 34 metres (110 feet) across would be required for *The Castel of Perseverance*, and Henri Rey-Flaud estimates that, while the *Martyrdom of St Apollonia* depicted in Fouquet's miniature would have been presented in a circular area possibly 20 metres (66 feet) in diameter, the less familiar scene depicted in Fouquet's *Rape of the Sabine Women* in an illustrated manuscript translation of Livy (Bibliothèque Nationale MS Fr. 20071, fol. 9 recto) shows an arena some 40 metres (132 feet) across.[66] The circular pseudo-amphitheatre built at Doué-la-Fontaine probably had a diameter of 30 metres (99 feet).

The dimensions of stages in courtyards and market-squares can rarely be reconstructed with any accuracy.[67] The courtyard of the Hôtel d'Arschot at Valenciennes has been reckoned as between 37 and 35 metres (122 and 115 feet) long by 35 to 32 metres (115 and 105 feet) across, but this of course cannot determine the size of the acting-area or the space occupied by spectators. The *parc* at Alençon for the play of 1521 has been calculated at 35 × 30 metres (115 × 99 feet), but again this does not provide us with the area covered by the stage alone. However, Rey-Flaud estimates that a stage raised on eighty large barrels at Namur in 1460 measures 35 metres (115 feet) by between 15 and 20 metres (50 and 66 feet), the technique devised reminding us of the unique illustration of a performance of the Latin play *Laurentius* on a proscenium-style stage at Cologne in 1581 for which five of the supporting casks can be clearly seen.[68] At Romans the platform erected within the courtyard of the Franciscan monastery for *Le Mystère des Trois Doms* was approximately 36 × 18 metres (119 × 60 feet), a much shallower area than that available at Alençon, but very close in size to that at Namur. However, the relatively confined dimensions of the rectilinear stage prepared in the grounds of the Hôtel d'Orléans, Paris, in 1540 for a *mystère* on the life of St Christopher, suggest a radical departure from the usual practices: only 19.5 metres (64 feet) long by a mere 4.9 metres (16 feet) deep, this platform was set up at one end of the available area, with a scaffold for the audience facing it, as in the modern proscenium theatre; in order to provide for an audience confronting instead of surrounding the stage, the stage itself had to be drastically reduced in size.[69]

The disposition of specific stage-areas must now be considered. Adhering to the *mansion*-principle of staging and tending to recruit large casts and attract large audiences as they did, the chief problem facing the organisers of open-air drama was to accommodate players and scenic structures in such a way as to permit movement on stage and a clear view from the auditorium. Many productions used a central playing-area partly or wholly encircled by spectators because of this primary requirement; obviously far greater numbers of spectators could be ranged within a reasonable distance of the action on stage if they surrounded the *platea*, than if they were formed up in rows one behind the other as in the conventional modern auditorium. Provided a circular auditorium could be raked and tiered, problems of seeing and hearing were virtually solved, and the popularity of round theatres can be well understood. In some cases the main playing-area itself was also elevated as at Romans, at Montauban in

1522, and in the market-square at Lucerne. Reasons for thus improving on the level arena at the players' disposal probably varied: at Montauban it may have been felt that the base of a levelled-off ditch did not guarantee stability, while at Romans the provision of a stage meant that digging the underground passages employed for certain special effects (see pp. 177–8 below) would not disturb the soil of the courtyard to a great depth. In the square at Lucerne a platform enabled vertical structures such as the Cross to be more easily erected, although the difficulties of relying on a wooden platform to bear the weight of *mansions* and actors is suggested by the fact that the solidity of the Romans stage had to be specially checked.[70]

The scenic principles employed differed little from those already encountered with the indoor stage. Indeed, E. K. Chambers suggested that many stage settings devised for outdoor use were based on the methods used in church buildings, printing a tentative arrangement of the *lius, mansions,* and *estals* from *La Seinte Resureccion* and comparing it with a sketch of the Donaueschingen (Villingen) Passion;[71] the conjecture that this division of the playing-area might correspond to the presbytery, choir, and nave of a church or cathedral is incapable of proof. However, the Lucerne sketch also shows a stage-area divided into three parts, and M. Blakemore Evans in his account of the performances there advances the hypothesis that both here and at Donaueschingen the central area was on the ground-level, while the portions flanking it were raised scaffolds: such an arrangement would not only make it easier to erect the Cross, but also to stage Christ's Burial and Resurrection, as well as the appearance of the dead from their tombs, traps in the floor of a raised platform being almost indispensable, for it is unlikely that permission would be given for holes to be dug in an important city square.

The number of terms employed to refer to platforms or built structures of the *mansion* type is confusing, and inevitably introduces an element of speculation into attempts to describe medieval presentations.[72] The *platea* or 'place', sometimes referred to in France as the *parc* or the *champ*, creates few problems, although these terms can sometimes refer to the whole level area of the theatre-site, as well as to the main open acting-area. At Amiens in 1501 spectators could be shut out of the *parc*, but at Metz in 1437 the *parc* included not only the playing-area but also nine rows of seats on the same level, even though they were separated from the *platea* by a low parapet as at Doué in 1539. Partly acting as a crowd-barrier and thus corresponding to the ditch or fence found shielding the acting-area at some sites, the low wall was sometimes formed of masonry so that it could serve to protect the spectators in certain scenes, notably those depicting the Flood, as at Bourges in 1536 when the course of a river was diverted to supply the inundation of the entire *platea*, in a similar manner to that described in the *Mistère du Viel Testament* (see pp. 178–9 below).

More ambiguous is the frequent use of terms such as 'scaffold', '*échafaud*', 'stage', '*étage*', '*hourt*', '*hourdement*', to define a miscellany of raised constructions fulfilling a variety of functions in the medieval theatre. Basically a 'scaffold' was an elevated structure set up in the *platea* or on its periphery, but it could either represent some scenic location which the actors would occupy during some or all of the dramatic action (although it could also be used to refer to a complete stage erected at the roadside for the *mystère mimé* or the royal entry), or it could be a framework of scaffolding on which spectators could be accomodated. Thus we find a number of allusions to independent scaffolds on or around the playing-area being reserved for the actors' use: for instance, a stage direction in *Le Mystère de Saint Louis* tells us:

Lunch is taken, and if any players have to double, they should change on the curtained scaffolds without anyone seeing them in their new state, until the play begins again.

Chascun disnet et s'aucuns personnages en jouent deux, ils se doivent abiller en eschauffaus encourtinez sans c'on les voye, tout en estat, quant on commencera.[73]

Different scaffolds would then be assigned to different groups of players, as the Fouquet miniature of the *Martyrdom of Saint Apollonia* (Illustration 10) makes clear, with its depiction of scaffolds comprising Paradise, a royal throne-room, and a Hell on two levels. But the miniature also makes clear that some scaffolds were occupied by musicians and by spectators, too, and there is documentary evidence for this provision: the arrangements for the Tours *Passion* of 1485 included '*deux eschauffauls*' for the reception of Margaret of Austria and her train, while the performers at Seurre in 1496[74] not only decorated their own scenic scaffolds but those to be occupied by spectators from neighbouring towns. There was little distinction made between stage and spectator scaffolds; a list of sale items given in an Amiens document of 1501 includes with the '*hourds*' occupied by players presenting the Deluge others used by a party of dignitaries.[75] Indeed, Fouquet's miniature suggests that during performances players and spectators might find themselves sharing the same scaffold, for the one which contains the vacated throne holds four seated and eight standing figures, some of whom can only be spectators: one may speculate on the possibility that this method of sharing occurred in the public theatres of Elizabethan London when the tiring-house gallery was required for a certain scene.[76]

Typical of place-and-scaffold staging is a production whose details are found in the Frankfurter *Dirigierrolle* (director's script or scenario), entitled the *Ordo sive Registrum* (*c.* 1350),[77] which supplies the plot of a two-day Passion play, complete with stage-directions and cues. The open *platea* frequently changes its identity, being used for a variety of scenes, including the *Ordo Prophetarum* with which the play opens, the banks of the Jordan, the desert for the Temptation of Christ, the Entry into Jerusalem, the road to Emmaus for the *Peregrinus* sequence, and the scene of the debate between Ecclesia and Synagoga. Unlocalised action on the main *platea* also links together the numerous fixed locations, many of which are permanently associated with particular figures, as the opening rubric makes clear: 'Firstly therefore the characters are solemnly led forth to their places with the music of instruments and the noise of trumpets [*Primo igitur persone ad loca sua cum instrumentis musicalibus et clangore tubarum sollempniter deducantur*].'

Specific locations are assigned to Hell-gates, to God or Majestas, who occupies Paradise elevated on an upper level approached by steps which Christ eventually ascends; Herod has his own palace site; Christ has a specific position; Jerusalem and the *locus Iudeorum*, from which Jews advance and to which they retire, are also permanent features. The figures of Mary Magdalen, Martha, and Lazarus are based on Martha's house (*domum Marthe*) at Bethany, and another built structure was no doubt needed for the home of Simon the Pharisee, unless one *mansion* served both Martha and Simon, a potentially confusing situation since Mary is associated with both. Caiaphas the High Priest may have had his own set position, too, and Pilate certainly must have had a fairly elaborate *locus*, consisting of a *pretorium*, a public hall of justice, and an inner *palatium* or private palace, where he leads Christ to question him more closely (. . . *Pylatus ducat eum in palatium*) before returning to the Jews in the *pretorium*. It is in the *palatium*, too, that Pilate's wife is presumably located. The *Dirigierrolle* suggests that Pilate's *locus* consisted of an area earmarked as the *pretorium* on the main *platea*, and a constructed 'house' into which he retired while still remaining in the spectators' view: simultaneous action was thus easily achieved when required. It was doubtless possible to hide the *palatium* by means of curtains at other times. Certainly in many French *mystères*, each scaffold could be screened off in this way: the 'throne-room' scaffold in Fouquet's miniature possesses a front curtain, while a rubric for *Le*

Mystère de Saint Louis informs us that 'they draw the curtains of the bed and around the scaffolds, in order to have lunch',[78] and stage-directions in the N-Town cycle indicate the presence of curtains to hide or reveal the occupants of several scaffolds

> than shal the place ther Cryst is in shal sodeynly un-close rownd Abowtyn shewyng Cryst syttyng at the table and his dyscypulys eche in ere *degre* ...
> And the †Herowdys† scafald shal un-close shewyng Herowdes in astat ... here shal the devyl gon to Pylatys wyf, the corteyn drawyn as she lyth in bedde.[79]

* place   † Herod's

Some fixed locations at Frankfurt were probably permanently visible and occupied by their inhabitants throughout the action, but others were almost certainly not. The permanent Sepulchre can scarcely have been occupied throughout, being required not only for Christ's Entombment and Resurrection, but for John the Baptist's burial and the Raising of Lazarus. The room for the Last Supper may simply have been suggested by the presence of a table and benches, for we read at one point that the table is carried away (*tollatur mensa*) before Jesus washes the disciples' feet. Mount Olivet seems a fixture and makes its own scenic demands, since the organisers are informed that 'green trees in the manner of a garden should be placed there [*ubi posite sint . . . virides arbores in modum orti*]', thus annexing another area of the total *platea*. Even more essential is a site for Calvary though the three crosses may not necessarily have remained in place on both days. The other important new structure of the second day is the inn at Emmaus, where no doubt a *mansion* (possibly Martha's house of the first day) held a table and benches for the meal eaten by the travellers; later a similar *domus* in Galilee (Simon's house?) is called for, also with eating facilities, though here again furniture alone may have sufficed.

How all these structures and locations were deployed about the available stage area must be a matter for conjecture, but many sites required are very close to those envisaged for *La Seinte Resureccion* (see p. 61 above), or for some of the German Passion plays such as those of Alsfeld and Villingen *c.* 1585, and follow a similar pattern. Petersen has made a tentative arrangement of thirty-eight fixed locations, assuming each to have been permanently allocated to one purpose throughout the performance.[80] But it might be argued that since space was always at a premium, a number of different identities were assigned to a single *mansion* or one area during the two-day performance. A glimpse of one construction-method is gained from a description of Satan's Temptation of Christ. We read that Satan leads Jesus 'on to the top of a cask [*super dolium*], which should be placed in the middle of the playing-area to represent the Temple', while a second barrel in another place symbolises the mountain-top. One assumes that these *dolia* were disguised, though the staging can have had few pretensions to realism. As a result authors and audiences were able to benefit from the dramatic use of simultaneous action — while Christ prays in one part of the Garden of Gethsemane the disciples sleep in another, and Judas is seen conspiring with the Jews in Jerusalem. Curiously, a similar technique is not used during the same incident in the N-Town cycle when Judas moves between the High Priest's house and the Upper Room where the Passover is being celebrated, for action in the latter is hidden by curtains.[81]

Information concerning a similar setting has been extracted from documents relating to the performance in 1583 of the Passion play in the market-place at Lucerne.[82] Here '*Höfe*' or 'houses' were set up on four sides of the irregular quadrangle which constituted the performance-area, where other locations were also established, each allotted to a specific figure or group as at Frankfurt. The Lucerne documents offer the fullest details extant of a medieval production. The director, Renward Cysat, drew a sketch-plan for each day's performance, and provided an explanation of the distribution of the 'houses' and the actors allocated to each, a preliminary sketch (which demonstrates that the staging arrangements at Lucerne were by no means hard and fast, but subject to alteration as circumstances dictated), and a final summary of the relevant dimensions, made on the day after the performance.

The only way by which the extent and diversity of the Lucerne stage-area could be fully appreciated would be to list the many locations on Cysat's plans. From Heaven where God and the angels occupied the Haus zur Sonne, with its four wind-instrumentalists below, to Hellmouth at the opposite end of the square; from Mount Sinai which was shifted slightly on the second day to serve as the Mount of Olives (a structure large enough to conceal the painter instructed to daub the hillside with red paint to simulate Christ's bloody sweat during the Agony), to the stable for the Nativity scenes, and the tree climbed by Zachaeus and later used to hang Judas from, scarcely a Biblical location seems to be omitted. The largest scaffolds are those designed to support the lords of the Temple, Herod and his court, Moses and his attendants, the *Proclamator* (or Prologue) and his company, including musicians, Pilate and his entourage, the Magi and their followers; while the structure representing the Synagogue is intended to contain twenty-five performers. The main *platea* abounds in special features including sacrificial altars, wells, gardens, a prison, places where tables and benches allow meals to be eaten, and a general burial area where Lazarus is interred and from which six dead souls arise at the Crucifixion. Pride of place on the second day is given to the three crosses erected before the Haus zur Sonne, beside the site allocated on the first day to the earthly Paradise which, true to iconographical tradition, is neatly fenced about, and contains the Tree of Knowledge complete with apples (*Der Boum mitt den öpflen . . .*).[83] Here in the 1583 performance Adam and Eve were provided with a trench in which to lie hidden until their creation. On the second day the fence of the earthly Paradise was shifted slightly stage right to enclose the Garden of Gethsemane 'in which the Saviour was taken prisoner'.

Scenes which required water — like Joseph's cistern and the well for the Women of Samaria — were no problem, thanks to the presence of the fountain in the square; and the River Jordan was formed by tapping the fountain water and channelling it across the playing-area where it primarily served John the Baptist in baptising Christ, although it visited other *loca* before passing out of the square under a specially erected bridge. The ambitious range of scenic structures deployed at Lucerne certainly makes one wish one had witnessed the presentation.

Remarkably similar staging methods were employed in France where market-places, town dykes, and courtyards were adapted for dramatic purposes: the Rouen *Mystère de l'Incarnation et de la Nativité de Jésus-Christ* presented in the New Market at Christmas 1474 anticipates the Lucerne scheme by establishing Paradise at or before the Inn of the Crowned Axe, while on the other side of the square Hell ('in the form of a huge mouth closing and opening when need arises') was located in front of the inn 'where the sign of the Angel hangs'; between them on the north side the installations (*establies*) representing the towns of Nazareth, Jerusalem, Bethlehem, and Rome were found. Facing them across the square were places for the prophets foretelling Christ's birth.[84]

In other parts of France the stage-area consisted of the same central open space incorporating or fringed by a number of scenic scaffolds or specific locations of various types — platforms, furnished areas, enclosures, *mansions*, and elevations such as hills. It is clear from numerous references that scaffolds erected for many French *mystères* offered the use of both upper and lower levels, the higher *étages* serving as accomodation for spectators as well as elevating the *mansions* needed for scenes set in Paradise, on mountain-tops, or involving authoritative characters such as kings and emperors. Typical is the contract of 1520 drawn up for the Alençon play, which provides among other things for the construction of 'a scaffold to serve as Paradise which ... shall have three levels [*estaiges*]',[85] and for 'another scaffold to serve as Hell ... made and constructed with one upper level ... in a lean-to style ... On the said lean-to another little elevation shall be made to serve as Limbo.' Other scaffolds are provided for the convenience of the audience, and both uses are clearly revealed in Fouquet's miniature which shows at least two of the scaffolds occupied by important visitors, while Heaven and imperial court take up two corresponding *étages*, although the latter also seems to contain spectators! Hell on the right of Fouquet's picture is the only scaffold with two levels visible, the upper room or *parloir* set above the familiar Hell-mouth *en bas*. Ladders or inclined planes with slats permitted access to and from the *parterre* (ground level) where humbler *mansions* and other scenic *loca* were found, along with the less affluent members of the public.[86] Texts make frequent allusions to characters ascending to their scaffolds from the ground, and descending in the same manner: it is, for example, a common feature of angelic behaviour in both French and English cyclic drama (see pp. 170–1 below).

Strikingly similar to the use made of the Haus zur Sonne at Lucerne is that made of the Maison d'Allemaigne in the Grand Markiet at Mons in 1501, which not only appears to have served as Paradise but also to house the 'machinery' which effected the Flood. The Mons production doubtless followed the general principles of staging discovered elsewhere, but the copious documentation brought to light by Gustave Cohen unfortunately does not permit us to form a very accurate picture of the scaffolds and their locations.[87] Cohen suggested that the scenic devices were distributed along a single *hourt* 40 metres (130 feet) long, extending from the Maison dite de la Seuwe where the entry to the *hourt* was, past the Maison d'Allemaigne to the Maison Franeau, but Henri Rey-Flaud, pointing to the inconsistency with which the terms *hourt* and *parc* are employed at Mons, argues instead that scaffolds were placed all round the square and on the central raised platform which formed the main playing-area. These scaffolds could serve, as elsewhere, either as viewing-places or as parts of the set. Buildings around the square could either contain privileged spectators, or else be incorporated into the action. The whole area was sealed off at each end, and common spectators who could not afford a seat on the raised scaffolding paid an admission-fee to stand beside the central platform in the *parc* thus enclosed (see Illustration 11).

The locations required by the Mons performance conform to the traditional pattern of Frankfurt and Lucerne.[88] The two most important were again the celestial Paradise and Hell, the former being furnished with ladders and cords for the various heavenly ascents and descents called for during the action. God, splendidly costumed, sat on a throne, his presence hidden as need arose by means of curtains: around or behind him turned the familiar device of a wheel adorned with wooden angels, while cloths bearing the sun, the moon, the stars, were unfurled here, and at the Creation birds (*certains oyseaux de toutte sorte*) were released from Paradise. Hell, a magnificent construction in the shape of a huge toad with open jaws, featured Satan and a chained Lucifer surrounded by dragons and serpents. Within the jaws of Hell were seen wheels of torment and a boiling cauldron where the damned writhed, while burning charcoal and gunpowder supplied the expected flames and explosions. It is little wonder that preparing and manning the 'special effects' in Hell occupied Maistre Jehan du Fayt and his seventeen assistants nine days.

Other notable requirements of the Mons production included the Temple at Jerusalem complete with its pinnacle, Mount Tabor which later doubled as the Mount of Olives, a pool large enough to float a small barque, and three crosses sited at Calvary, but Cohen in his account estimated that almost seventy separate locations were needed, Jerusalem, Nazareth, Bethlehem, Egypt, Bethany, and Emmaus among them. A further interesting feature is that most of the scenic *loca* at Mons were apparently labelled, for a priest, Jehan Portier, was paid to write out ninety-eight signs *de grosse lettre*, and nails were bought to attach them to the settings.

Many of the sites called for at Mons in 1501 feature in the celebrated *Passion* staged at nearby Valenciennes in 1547, for which Hubert Cailleau's drawing is almost too well known. It depicts roughly a dozen scenic areas apparently juxtaposed along the length of a single platform, with an elevated Paradise stage right and a two-level Hell stage left, and the traditional Temple, Palace with a prison below, Nazareth and Jerusalem, and has led many commentators to believe that, in order to support the large number of *mansions* and scenic areas demanded by lengthy cyclic texts, stages extending many feet in length were the inevitable answer. The general reliability of Cailleau's depiction of the Valenciennes staging has been upheld by Élie Konigson (who suggests the painting of the set is a 'purified' version omitting subsidiary scaffolds and machinery), and more recently queried by Henri Rey-Flaud.[89] In this debate Rey-Flaud appears to have a stronger case than Konigson. Arguing that Cailleau painted his miniature of the production thirty years afterwards, drawing on another's memories of it, he asserts that not only is Cailleau strongly influenced by Renaissance pictorial tastes and his own earlier work, but that his drawing leaves out some very necessary sites, notably the Palace of Annas, and the Mountain. In conclusion, Rey-Flaud claims that the Valenciennes production followed the theatre-in-the-round convention so often found elsewhere.

However, a compromise can perhaps be reached. While Cailleau's infinitely extended platform may be rejected as extremely unlikely, the general nature of the *mansions* he portrays does not seem totally inconsistent with what we know of such structures elsewhere: the roofed edifices such as the Temple, Palace, and the *Salle* at Valenciennes seem to resemble, for example, descriptions of the 'towers, small turrets, castles, towns' set up on the platform at Romans in 1509, where they were doubtless formed from upright pillars supporting a simple roof, the lack of side-walls enabling spectators easily to witness action within the *mansions*.[90] Cailleau's 'sea', too, consisting of a trap sunk into the stage-floor with a pool of water set into it, seems to resemble comparable constructions elsewhere, while the stone-built Hell (*enfer*) with its ancillary Limbo, its instruments of torture mounted on the upper storey and its grotesque mouth from which devils emerge and within which damned souls boil, might almost be an illustration of the Mons 'Hell' of 1501. Cailleau's Paradise is the usual elevated structure in which God sits in majesty, surrounded by a turning circle of angelic supporters, and while the artist has obviously stylised this location, Élie Konigson makes an interesting case for the practicability of his suggested setting. Thus, while the Valenciennes scaffolds are almost certain to have occupied all four sides of the courtyard at the Hôtel d'Arschot, the scenic devices themselves may not have been so far different from those shown by Cailleau in his miniature, at least in essentials.

The wealth of detail concerning open-air staging which survives from French and German sources is unfortunately absent from British archives in all but a few cases. Some of the most interesting material is, perhaps not surprisingly, Cornish in origin: happily, a manuscript of the Cornish cycle or *Ordinalia* includes plans showing the staging arrangements for each of its performances which lasted for three days.[91] A circular theatre is set round with eight *loca* whose occupants are indicated for each day, and it is likely that many of these locations assumed a form familiar to us from Fouquet's miniature and French accounts — namely that of a rudimentary roofed structure of wood,

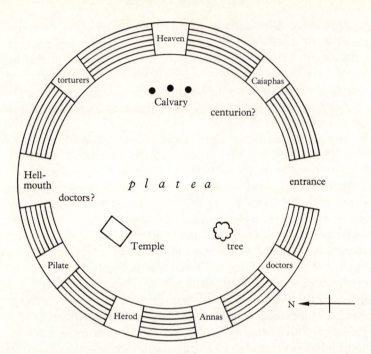

Heaven

torturers

Caiaphas

• • •
Calvary

centurion?

Hell-
mouth

p l a t e a

entrance

doctors?

Temple

tree

Pilate

doctors

Herod

Annas

N ←——

14   A conjectural reconstruction of the staging of the *Passio Domini* from the Cornish Cycle (after Neville Denny)

probably curtained all round to enable its inhabitants to be hidden when necessary. Instead of being mounted on free-standing scaffolds, however, the Cornish *mansions* were in nearly every case built into the circumference of the earthen embankment enclosing the central *platea*, with a fore-stage jutting out from the *mansion* itself, access being provided by steps or ladders. Spectators occupied the terraced seating provided in the spaces between the eight *loca*, the most dominant and elaborate of which was probably the *Coelum* or Heaven (sited to the east) which retained its identity permanently throughout the three days. Also required at each day's performance was the scaffold given over to the torturers (*Tortores*) stage right of the heavenly *mansion*, while the late Neville Denny was inclined to think that *Infernum* or Hell, probably the traditional 'mouth', lying at a gap in the bank to the north and not directly opposite Heaven, also maintained its identity throughout, despite the manuscript's ascription of this position to the doctors on the second day of the play. The north-west location is shared between Pharoah (Day 1), and Pilate (Days 2 and 3), while King David occupies the most westerly scaffold on the first day, being succeeded by Herod, and lastly by the emperor. Next comes the site used successively by Solomon, Annas, and Joseph of Arimathea; the position furthest south is devoted to Abraham, Caiaphas, and Nicodemus, although Denny conjectured that this was the position adopted by the doctors of the second day; the station next to Heaven is shared between the bishop, the centurion of Day 2, and the soldiers, though here again the doctors or Caiaphas may have been included on the second day, since the centurion's rôle is only a minor one. On the grass of the *platea* it is necessary to construct a hill to serve for the Temptation and the Ascension, and as the Mount of Olives and Calvary, in much the same way as at Frankfurt and Lucerne; also required are the Temple at Jerusalem, and a structure to represent the Sepulchre, although Denny again suggested that the space under Heaven's scaffold might have served, just as space beneath the torturers' scaffold could have been used as the Prison. Other locations could have been easily suggested by bringing a few properties or pieces of furniture on to the main *platea*, and it seems at least arguable that several specific areas could have been employed in rotation for those scenes which could not be staged fittingly on the permanent scaffolds on the embankment. In a setting where multiple simultaneous action was often the norm, such a fluid arrangement was entirely satisfactory. Indeed, in such a theatre the principal excitements would be both the constantly changing focus of dramatic interest from area to area, and the awareness of different happenings occurring at same moment.

Analogous in its staging requirements is the Cornish saint play of *The Life of Meriasek*, which needs a circular playing-place; plans in the manuscript allocate points on the raked circumference to scaffolds assigned to appropriate characters for both days of the play.[92] Thirteen individual permanent *loca* on the bank are designated for each day, but (as in the cycle plans) Heaven retains its dominant position to the east, with the torturers to the stage right of it, and *Infernum* to the right of that, on both days. A variant fourteenth permanent feature is the Chapel (*Capella*) which on the plan occupies the centre of the *platea* only on the first day, but which seems to be required to act as the College and perhaps the Temple on the second. Scaffolds are assigned according to the play's demands just as in the Cornish cycle, so that while Constantine, the Bishop of Kernou, and Sylvester appear on both days and retain the same scaffolds, other scaffolds are allocated according to need, so that the station occupied by Meriasek's Father on the first day is given to the Earl of Vannes on Day 2. Although a fair amount of the dialogue takes place on the scaffolds, characters descend to the *platea* to accomplish the dramatic action, returning when their participation is no longer required. It is probable that they could then retire out of sight within their booths since several stage directions refer to 'the tent', presumably allusions to curtained *mansions* of the continental type.

The most remarkable British example of staging in the round is perhaps that postulated for the fifteenth-century morality *The Castel of Perseverance*, the manuscript of which appears to include a rough stage-plan, which must be among the best-known theatre-sketches in the world.[93] It shows a circular arena with a castellated structure at its centre and a rubric written above it: 'this is the Castel of Perseveraunse that stondyth in the myddys of the place; but lete no men sytte ther, for lettynge [hindering] of syt; for ther schal be the best of all'. At the tower's foot is a bed, and written below is 'Mankynde is [Mankind's] bed schal be under the Castel and ther schal the sowle lye under the bed tyl he schal ryse and pleye'. Two concentric circles surround the *platea*, and the legend inscribed between them runs: 'this is the watyr a-bowte the place if any dyche may be mad ther it schal be pleyed; or ellys that it be strongly barryd al a-bowt; and lete nowth [not] over many stytelerys be with-inne the plase'. Outside this ring five scaffolds are described, that to the south assigned to *Caro* (Flesh), that to the west to *Mundus* (The World) and, following the tradition already familiar to us, that to the north to Belial, that to the east to God; a fifth is allotted to Coveytyse (Covetousness) and lies to the north-east. There are other instructions on the plan, but these are those chiefly concerned with the play's staging.

Richard Southern in *The Medieval Theatre in the Round* has carried out a brilliant and exhaustive analysis of the staging of *The Castel of Perseverance*, from which only the main conclusions can be set forth here. Basically, Southern advocates methods of production similar to those employed by continental theatres in the round, in that characters performed both on their individual scaffolds and down in the central *platea*. Thus we read that one group of figures descends 'into the place together', that at one point Mankind ascends to the World's scaffold, and that towards the end the four daughters of God ascend to his throne, bearing with them the Soul of Mankind. Southern imagines that the characters were also free to retire into curtained *mansions* on the scaffolds when not involved in a particular part of the action.

But it is the more unusual and controversial aspects of the play's treatment which give to *The Castel of Perseverance* its particular interest;

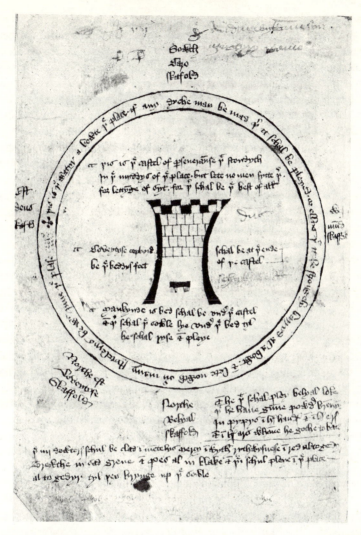

15 Manuscript drawing of the setting for *The Castel of Perseverance* (1400–25)

these include the siting of the ditch or barrier apparently surrounding the playing-place, the rôle of the 'stytelerys', and the arrangements made for spectators. Southern is convinced that the water-filled ditch 'was there to keep people away from the show who had not paid for

157

admission',[94] and that consequently it must have been dug outside both the 'place' *and* the accommodation for spectators on the earthen embankment thrown up when the ditch was excavated. But there is no need to assume that the play was not given free: we know too little of the circumstances of its production to be categorical on this point. Moreover, the rubric inscribed between the concentric circles on the plan clearly states that 'this is the watyr a-bowte *the place*' (my italics): the scaffolds, too, are shown as erected on the *outer* rim of the trench, and nothing in the sketch indicates that a ditch surrounded the theatre-site as a whole. At Autun in 1516 a ditch separated audience and players, and it was certainly the practice in some French open-air theatres to separate the inner *platea* off from spectators by a low wall (*creneau*), a brushwood fence, or wattle hurdles (*claies*) combined with a trench which supplied the soil from which the terraces around the *platea* were fashioned.[95] The hurdles or fencing would be erected at the base of the ditch to hold back the soil of the *platea* while not obscuring it, and the gap prevented over-exuberant members of the audience from over-running the playing-area in the way that modern spectators invade soccer pitches and cricket fields at moments of extreme emotion.

The presence of the mysterious stytelerys in the 'place' is also important. Southern's lexicographical researches lead him to conclude that the stytelerys were marshals whose function was to control the crowds attending the performance — 'front-of-house staff' whose rôle can be perhaps paralleled by the five or six *sergents* in a northern French production of 1499 posted at the entrance to the *parc* to 'remove those who make a nuisance of themselves [*widier ceux qui empescheroient*]'.[96] However, the rubric suggests that the stytelerys were active in the 'place' and as a result Southern regards them as responsible for keeping order particularly among those spectators who, in his view, were permitted to watch the play *from inside the circular arena itself*.

This is certainly Southern's most controversial suggestion regarding the staging of the play. Briefly, he argues his case on the basis of the rubric running 'this is the Castel of Perseveraunse that stondyth in the myddys of the place; but lete no men sytte ther, for lettynge of syt; for ther schal be the best of all', interpreting this as meaning that watching from other sections of the 'place' *was* allowed. Grammatically the sentence is vague, but 'ther' could equally well imply that no one was to view the play from the 'place' *at all*, or even that nobody was to climb the castle-structure and watch from there. It does seem improbable that spectators would have been allowed to occupy the *platea*; however well the stytelerys controlled them, as Southern believes, they would surely impede the action disastrously, as well as interfering with the view of the play enjoyed by spectators on the lower terraces of the embankment, especially if they remained standing in the way Southern suggests in his sketch of the play in progress. In the present writer's view, the stytelerys simply supervised the occupation of the earthen 'mound' before the performance and kept order during it; they were consigned to the 'place' merely because it was the only possible area from which they could perform their duties satisfactorily. The insistence that there should be 'nowth over many' of them is intended to ensure that their presence in the playing-area remained as unobtrusive as possible.

Southern's entire thesis concerning staging in the round has been challenged by Nathalie Crohn Schmitt in a well-known essay[97] which attempts to show that the imagined plan of a theatre is in fact a set-design, in which no 'mound' is drawn since it was irrelevant to the set, and the ditch is simply the moat of the castle, both of them being drawn in greater detail than the rest of the sketch. Whether the ditch lay between the castle and the rest of the *platea*, or between the total *platea* and audience, bridges would be required to enable the characters to cross it safely, and certainly no such structures are shown on the drawing, but as Nathalie Schmitt points out, Southern's bridges over his *external* ditch are not depicted either! If the ditch separated *platea* and scaffolds, one solution might have been to place the ladders or slatted inclined planes leading down from the scaffolds at such angle that they carried the players over the ditch directly on to the *platea*. Indeed, Fouquet's illustration of *St Apollonia* suggests that the inclined plane from Heaven crosses the brushwood fence in this manner. At all events, whether the trench depicted in the *Castel* sketch forms the castle-moat or the perimeter of the 'place', the burden of the evidence does not seem to support Southern's theory of an outer ditch; nevertheless his account provides the most thorough examination of evidence for the staging of the most ambitious of British morality dramas.

There remain for discussion the cyclic sequences of Wakefield and N-Town, the Digby plays of *The Conversion of St Paul* and *Mary Magdalene*, and the Scots presentation of *Ane Satyre of the Thrie Estaitis* by Sir David Lyndsay. We have already seen it suggested that the Wakefield cycle was presented at one fixed site (see p. 133 above), possibly as an addition to an earlier procession through the streets of the town during which some speeches might have been delivered; the total performance, however, was probably only given as the culmination of the procession, as Martin Stevens has suggested was the case at York (see pp. 119–20 above), or took place on a different day, as he claims occurred at Wakefield.[98] Martial Rose, who has studied and staged the Wakefield cycle extensively, and Alan H. Nelson postulate a place-and-scaffold presentation very much on the lines described at Frankfurt, Lucerne, and elsewhere: certainly there are textual references to 'this greyn', 'this playn', and 'this place' all suggesting a conventional *platea*, while the torturers mention that they have brought Christ from 'sir pilate . . . into oure ryng', which sounds like a movement down from Pilate's scaffold into the circular arena.

Far more fully documented is the staging of the N-Town cycle, and Martial Rose, Stanley Kahrl, and Kenneth Cameron are among those who have explored the evidence most thoroughly.[99] A basic problem with this cycle is that, while evidence regarding the Old Testament plays suggests processional staging, the later Passion sequence in particular is clearly intended for production on the ground, so there may have been a late attempt to adapt processional plays to a fixed place-and-scaffold mode. The likeliest place for static performance, as has been indicated, was the space within the Minster Close at Lincoln, which offered a convenient enclosure for performers and spectators. Here permanent scaffolds could be erected on lines now familiar, although as Kahrl and Cameron have shown, the only single permanent location required for the early plays of the sequence would be a Heaven (but a Hell might also have been used if New Testament episodes were to follow); possibly movable pageant-waggons such as a wheeled Noah's Ark supplied the other Old Testament settings, being brought into the Minster Close and then dragged out again when the action demanding their presence was completed. Later plays require both fixed *loca* of the traditional kind – temples, private houses, the Golden Gate, the mountain – but also room for movable pageants such as the Cordwainers' Bethlehem to be introduced, possibly drawn up against a fixed platform. However, the most elaborate portion of the cycle, the Passion sequence, demands the usual permanent scaffolds for Annas, Caiaphas, and Herod, a curtained Council house and a house for Simon, Mount Olivet, a Heaven and a Hell, Calvary, the Temple, and the Sepulchre; the last part of the cycle required a 'castel of Emmaus', and sundry other areas including graves from which the dead arise. The similarities between the N-Town plays, and *La Seinte Resureccion* or Alsfeld, Villinger, and Lucerne performances could scarcely be more strikingly conveyed, although the sequential pageant-waggon style of performance may have recommenced at Lincoln after the Resurrection sequence. Rose, however, argues for *mansion* staging throughout.

The Digby plays of *St Paul* and *Mary Magdalene* create a number of difficulties for theatre historians anxious to reconstruct the conditions of their performance:[100] some commentators believe that the three parts of *The Conversion of St Paul* were staged at three separate sites within one town, the audience following the players from one 'station' to another if they wished to witness the whole presentation. This hypothesis has been based on the words of the *Poeta* who acts as Prologue, Epilogue, and as Expositor twice during the action, and who remarks after two episodes in a speech headed '*Poeta, si placet* [Poet, if so desired]':

> ffynally of this stacon thus we mak a conclusyon
> besechyng thys audyens to folow and succede
> with all your delygens this general processyon ...

But it has been pointed out that the Latin rubric which follows the speech and reads '*ffinis istius stacionis, et altera sequitur* [The end of that station, and the other follows]' makes it clear that 'stacon' is sometimes the term used for each episode of the play, and that the audience is not being asked to follow the action in a physical sense at all, for 'processyon' probably means 'process, procedure' and hence the play's argument. Later the *Poeta* requests the audience to pay attention to 'thys pagent at thys lytyll stacion', and from this Glynne Wickham has argued that the performance was a static one but with the sets representing Jerusalem and Heaven wheeled on to the site on pageant-waggons and the *platea* used for the other locations. Mary del Villar, however, canvasses the likelihood of place-and-scaffold staging, with five scaffolds employed about the *platea* to represent the necessary locations, including those Wickham places on pageant-carts. More recently John Coldewey has argued in support of the earliest interpretation of 'processyon' and visualises an audience following the *Poeta* out of the 'place' to another site and returning for the third section of the play. The exact method of staging *The Conversion of St Paul* is unlikely to be determined very readily at present.

Mary Magdalene, a much more lengthy and spectacular play, offers fewer problems of staging, for despite its heavy scenic demands, there is little in the action which could not be met by the usual place-and-scaffold arrangement. David Bevington[101] has advanced a possible stage-design based on analogy with *The Castel of Perseverance*, with the Castle of Magdalene in the centre of the *platea*, and eleven scaffolds including Heaven in the east and Hell in the north, and those of World and Flesh to the west and north, on its perimeter; while obviously only conjectural, this plan demonstrates how the play could have employed traditional methods to create its highly ambitious dramatic effects. Hell seems to have been on two levels, for at one point we read 'Here shal entyr the Prinse of Dylles [Devils] in a stage, and helle ondyrneth that stage', and no doubt the Devil's scaffold was built over the traditional Hell-mouth as in the Valenciennes illustration. At another point one of the scaffolds is set on fire by devils; later 'a ship comes into the place', and here we must assume that if this structure were not the familiar wheeled ship of street pageant and *entremet*, a stretch of water or a stream was present in the *platea* as at Lucerne. When *Ane Satyre of the Thrie Estaitis* was staged on the Castle Hill at Cupar in Fife on Whit Tuesday 1552, such a stream was available for use, for the Ladyburn, crossed by a bridge, flanked the area chosen as the *platea* or 'green' and indeed separated spectators and players in a way rejected by Richard Southern when siting the ditch for *The Castel of Perseverance*.[102] Dramatic use was also made of the stream, characters wading through it or undergoing mock baptism in it, and the Pardoner's relics being thrown into it, a possible clue to the dramatic relevance of an *internal* ditch in *The Castel* when *Garcio* (the Boy) threatens to throw *Humanum Genus* 'into a lake' (line 2927).[103] A fence breached by the Bonygate marked the boundary with the main playing-area, a 'Palyeoun' (pavilion) serving as a tiring-house for the actors to which they retired by way of the gate; here, too, were the stocks in which Veritie and Chastitie were confined, and the gallows on which the Vices were ultimately hanged. Within the main area a number of scaffolds were arranged, possibly in a circle, the chief and most imposing of which is that assigned to King Humanitie and his attendants: it doubtless bore some resemblance to the 'throne-room' scaffold of the Fouquet miniature, and was approached by the usual ladder, for during the play 'the Carle' climbs up and sits in the king's seat, and being deprived of the ladder by the herald Diligence is forced to 'loup aff [leap off] the scaffald' to the ground. Other scenic requirements include a raised platform or pulpit for the preaching of Veritie, Folly, and the doctor, seating for the Estates Spiritual and Temporal, and a table at which a good deal of drinking takes place. Wickham also allots a pavilion within the *platea* to the king, but this must remain conjectural, although Humanitie certainly retires at one point to make love to Sensualitie, but the notion may have been conveyed by having the couple withdraw to the general 'Palyeoun' outside the gate.

The important matter of entrances and exits remains for consideration. That processional entries as indicated by the opening rubric of the Frankfurt *Dirigierrolle* were common is apparent from other references to such parades. At Seurre in 1496 the performers 'were placed in order by the said Master Andrieu according to the register, and marched to the sounds of trumpets, bugles, *bucinae* [horns], organs, harps, tabors, and other low- and high-pitched instruments, playing far and wide right up to the said *parc*, then making a circuit as is required in such circumstances . . .'[104] Such entries would doubtless be made through the main gates in the theatre enclosure, or through a gap in the embankment-wall if an amphitheatrical setting such as the Cornish 'round' was employed. At Lucerne, where gates appear to have been erected to control access to the Weinmarkt, the players' entries and departures from the square were part of an elaborate procession from and to the *Petri Kapelle* where the performers dressed and prepared for a long day on their scaffolds and in the *platea*.[105] The entrance procession was arranged by groups and followed as far as possible the order of the play's episodes, although not every character paraded. The splendour and variety of such processions reminds one of the impressive *monstres* of some French presentations, which consisted of a parade to the playing-site of all the scenic waggons and characters in costume for a final dress-rehearsal (see p. 207 below).[106]

In many instances players were forced to remain 'on the set' for the whole of the day's performance, although arrangements obviously had to be made for them to eat and to answer the calls of nature: at Romans, for instance, an actors' 'retraict' was provided beneath the stage-platform. But at several sites at least, a system of trap-doors and underground passages not only permitted performers to leave their assigned places when not required, but enabled a number of striking theatrical effects to be created with a minimum of contrivance. Thus for the Mons performance the presence of traps in the stage-floor is evidently envisaged, since a stage-direction reads '*Et s'endoivent aller par les secrez de terre ceulx qui ne doivent plus parler pour ce jour* [And those who do not have further lines to speak that day should depart by the underground devices]'.[107] At Romans erecting a central platform enabled the organisers to reduce the depth of the excavated passages which connected with the space beneath the stage: ladders enabled actors to make appearances through various trap-doors set into the surface of the platform, while doors in the side of the stage allowed them to depart when not needed. The traps at both Mons and Romans were hidden with foliage which was strewn across the whole playing area. In the amphitheatre at Doué-la-Fontaine underground corridors 1.2 metres (4 feet) wide and 1.8 metres (5½ feet) high formed an irregular cross in the centre of its sandy arena, giving access to at least three possible points of emergence. A similar system was in operation at Bourges in 1536 for *Les Actes des Apôtres*, permitting such miraculous effects as that described in *Le Mystère de la Résurrection*: 'And Jesus dressed in white, accompanied by three angels... should suddenly and with precision [*subtilement*] spring forth from below the ground beside his tomb, by a little wooden trap, covered with earth, which closes again without anyone perceiving it.' Such an effect possibly explains the presence of the shallow tunnel known as 'the Devil's Spoon' in the Cornish 'round' at Perranporth (see pp. 177–8 below).

Our final concern must be with the provisions made for spectators in the open-air theatres of the Middle Ages, and here again questions of nomenclature make it difficult to maintain too many assertions. A frequently encountered problem is to decide if an allusion to a 'scaffold' refers to a structure intended to contain actors or audience: at times, we know it may well have held both, as Fouquet's miniature reveals. Like some of the actors' scaffolds, those intended purely for spectators also seem to have been constructed on several levels (*étages*) so that the well-to-do might sit at a higher level than the *plebs*: this is particularly so in the circular theatres of France;[108] thus at Vienne in 1510 we read that the *escharfaux* consisted of two storeys (*éstages*) in addition to '*le bas pour le commun peuple*', and that the upper levels were formed of two circuits each of 48 *chambres*, each capable of being locked. At Autun in 1516 the *chambres* totalled 240; at Romans in 1509 100. These separated *chambres*, more usually referred to as '*loges*' (although the term could also include the actors' booths on the scaffolds), were akin to the modern theatre-box, and it was here that the more affluent and privileged spectators were able to rent more commodious and exclusive accommodation than that offered to the general populace. None the less, in many French theatres such as those at Romans, Vienne, and Valenciennes the commons enjoyed the luxury of seating, wooden benches being provided for their convenience at Valenciennes: these seats were known as *degrés* and appear to have been arranged in raked tiers or level rows, both apparently referred to as *pantes*, around or on two sides of the playing-sites, with the players' scaffolds set among them if the need arose. However, as the Fouquet miniature and other evidence make clear, seating was not an inevitable feature, and the humbler spectators must often have had to stand, especially if they were well to the rear of an unraked auditorium, or if there were no provision made for sitting on the terraces. At Lucerne the practice appears to have been for stands to be set up in the Weinmarkt by the City Fathers, a large stand at the fountain-end of the square and others before the houses on each side of the playing-area. Some of these stands seem to have been made available for honoured guests of the city, and no doubt for wealthy and privileged citizens too, but possibly others were kept free for the commons, who probably stood to watch the performance.[109]

Certainly at Lucerne it was the custom for some spectators to watch the play from the windows of houses overlooking the square, and the same procedure took place at Mons, where the nobility and important visitors occupied these vantage-points. For the ordinary citizen attendance at the play involved rising early, queueing at the gate to gain access to the *parc* or *champ*, and once admitted, making his way to the best viewing-position he could find consistent with his means, height, weight, and physical stamina. He would doubtless be competing for a favourable position with audiences running into thousands at some sites, possibly as many as 9,000 at Romans,[110] and he would sometimes have to decide whether his purse was sufficiently long to justify a payment adequate to take the weight off his legs or reduce the strain on his temper. At many theatre-sites the comfort and convenience of the spectators was clearly a major consideration; thus at Bourges in 1536 a brightly painted awning was stretched across the amphitheatre 'to protect the spectators both from bad weather and from the heat of the sun', and a 'lofty tent of silk' sheltered the outdoor theatre erected at the Hôtel de Flandre in June 1541.[111] But for members of the general public in the Middle Ages watching dramatic performances out of doors might be attended by elements of discomfort undreamt of even by those who make a habit of enduring the dubious delights of 'open-air theatre' in Britain today.

6

RESOURCES AND EFFECTS

Signes are taken for wonders: (*Master wee would faine see a Signe*, that is, a miracle.)
And, in this sense, it is a *Signe*, to wonder at.

Lancelot Andrewes, Sermon, Christmas Day, 1618

Most playgoers, however sophisticated and urbane they may consider
themselves, enjoy those moments when the theatre asserts its privilege and transforms the rational, predictable world by some piece of
breathtaking legerdemain, some spectacular or mystifying effect.
The child in us all responds to the flying ballet, the transformation
scene, the apparent death-fall, the cleverly simulated execution. In a
pre-electronic era such as the Middle Ages, similar wonders and
marvels were a staple ingredient of stage production, and instead of
being suppressed or played down in the interests of cerebration, they
were the subject of a great deal of devoted effort and technical expertise.

The liturgical plays in their customary settings did not offer many
opportunities for arresting scenic devices, however. In addition, although monastic or cathedral communities, with their large bands of
craftsmen and artisans, did not lack the necessary technical knowledge or facilities, church-drama, in its major phase at least, did not
encourage the use of elaborate equipment within a cathedral precinct,
say — drama was still intimately linked with acts of worship. Moreover,
the medieval mind readily appreciated the use of symbols and did not
demand realistic scenic devices, so only in a handful of instances do
the plays exploit opportunities for special effects.

Some interesting effects obtained in liturgical plays result from the
use of fire and light, which have always played an important rôle in
Christian worship. It is a simple step from providing for candles or
tapers to be carried in an ecclesiastical ceremony to arranging to have
them borne by participants in a liturgical drama, and candles or
tapers were in fact carried by the three Marys in some of the *Visitationes
Sepulchri*. In the Fleury *Visitatio* the angel at Christ's tomb holds a
branched candelabrum in his right hand (*ramum candelarum plenum*

tenens in manu dextera), while at Coutances the angels carry hollow rods packed with ten blazing candles, to represent the lightning which strikes down the soldiers guarding the sepulchre.[1] More elaborate was the use of lighting in plays featuring the Magi, to represent the star guiding the three sages to Christ's birthplace at Bethlehem. In the Limoges *Magi* we read of a *stella* hanging on a wire or thread (*pendentem in filo*) going before the three wise men as they journey, but a later text from Rouen gives instructions that a crown light or *corona* is to be lit where it hangs before the altar of the Holy Cross which symbolises the manger, 'in the manner of the star [*pendens in modum Stelle accendatur*]', and that the Magi are to move down the nave towards it. An earlier text from Montpellier and others from Laon, Fleury and Benedikt-beuern suggest that the star 'appears' or 'rises' rather than being placed in position in advance, presupposing some mechanism to produce a sudden appearance.[2] The *corona* of the later Rouen version was one of the usual forms of supplementary lighting available in medieval church buildings, and consisted of a central glass bowl surrounded by ancillary ones, all containing fuel and a floating cotton wick, the whole being encircled by a piece of ornamental metal which gave the lamp its name.[3] Medieval illustrations often show the *corona* suspended on a chain from a high archway, although three chains appear to have been more common; the *corona* could be kindled into instant brilliance, and in ceremonies connected with the *Quem Quaeritis* trope at Monza in Italy it is ignited just as the procession of clergy and choristers enters the choir, to produce a sudden blaze of light suggestive of the rising sun on Easter morning.

The precise means by which the *corona* was utilised to suggest the moving star in the Magi plays is unclear; Gustave Cohen advances the view that the light was suspended by a string from an upper gallery of the church and that someone simply walked along with it, keeping the star a little ahead of the pursuing Magi.[4] Fletcher Collins's theory is that the crown light was threaded by means of its triple chain through a taut wire stretched across the building, and its movement controlled by pulleys at each end of the nave. Pulleys are not strictly necessary, as a light string could have drawn the lamp to and fro, but whatever the answer, the *corona* appears to have been one of the earliest 'special devices' in medieval drama, of whose use we have positive evidence.

Lighting continued to be an important feature in later plays: it was occasionally suggested by non-naturalistic devices such as the drawing of a curtain painted half white and half black to symbolise the division of night from day (as in the creation scene of the *Mistère du Viel*

Testament) or of one decorated with pictures of a sun or a moon or the stars, several of which were sold after the Mons *Passion* of 1501, or the suspension of a shining golden sun at Lucerne, which was reversed at Christ's death on the cross to reveal a blood-coloured face,[5] but natural light sources were preferred. Since many of the plays under discussion were performed outside, any intensification of light could only be relative, but many of the cycle dramas require the traditional star of Bethlehem to appear, and machinery of the kind employed in the church-dramas was doubtless used to make the star rise, 'go before' the three kings, and sink out of sight. At Mons several operators were required to manage this technical device or *'secret'*, while at Lucerne in 1583 the technician who directed the devices of the star and the Holy Ghost was stationed in the Haus zur Sonne at as high a level as could be arranged.[6] At Valenciennes in 1547 the obscuring of the star while the kings spoke with Herod was effected by means of a cloud suspended from the Heavens, and this method may have been used elsewhere. In plays of the Chester cycle, however, an angel carried the star (*Angelus portans Stellam*), possibly in the form of a burning torch or a framework set with candles, a simple and effective device very much in keeping with the character of these plays.[7] This technique is also found at Erlau, when this performer sometimes bore the title of *Stellafer* or *Sterntrager* (Star-bearer).

Light also added vital splendour to the scenic region assigned to Heaven: this was frequently accomplished by the use of gold paint which could be applied to God's throne or to the great sun which in many cases seems to have backed the *mansion* of Heaven: gold foil also seems to have been a stock commodity in achieving this effect in medieval productions, as accounts from New Romney in Kent for 1560 make clear. At Bourges in 1536 a more elaborate Heaven was constructed, with a rainbow-like throne at its centre, behind which two golden suns revolved ceaselessly, in opposite directions, and the Valenciennes production of 1547 had a similar sun-wheel revolving continuously: no doubt these bore some relationship to devices employed at Saragossa in 1414 and at Barcelona in 1481, in which wheels bearing images or human figures dressed as angels revolved to music, in opposite directions if more than one wheel were involved (see pp. 93–4 above).[8] At Barcelona use was made of artificial lights, and in Italy the *sacre rappresentazioni* exploited the dramatic use of lighting. Of the *Annunciation* devised by Brunelleschi (1377–1446) for performance at the church of San Felice in the Piazza in Florence we learn from Giorgio Vasari that

On high was a Heaven full of living and moving figures, and a quantity of lights which flashed in and out ... For this effect Filippo had arranged a half-globe between two rafters of the roof of the church, like a hollow porringer or a barber's basin turned upside down. It was formed of thin laths secured to an iron star which revolved round a great iron ring upon which it was poised ... children, twelve in all, being arranged, as I have said, on pedestals and clad like angels with gilt wings and caps of gold lace, took one another's hands when the time came, and extending their arms, they appeared to be dancing, especially as the basin was always turning and moving. Inside this and above the heads of the angels were three circles or garlands of lights arranged like some tiny lanterns which could not turn over. These lights looked like stars from the ground.[9]

In 1439 when the Russian bishop, Abraham of Souzdal, attended a performance of the Annunciation play in the church of the Annunziata at Florence, he wrote of the throne of God surrounded by seven globes in which small oil lamps burnt and whose diameter increased successively in size, the smallest being two feet across: these represented the planets.[10] Some years later, further marvels of illumination were wrought by Francesco d'Angelo (1447–88), known as La Cecca, whose *Annunciation* at the Church of the Carmine won the praise of Vasari;

the heaven was somewhat larger than that of San Felice in Piazza, though with almost the same apparatus. As the Church of the Carmine where this was enacted, is considerably broader and loftier than San Felice, another heaven, besides the one which received Christ, was arranged over the principal tribune [gallery], in which large wheels like windlasses moved ten circles representing the ten heavens, from the centre to the circumference, full of lights representing the stars, arranged in copper lanterns and so fixed that when the wheel turned they always remained in position.[11]

Heaven was an essential location and materials chosen for its decoration were usually as expensive as could be procured or afforded; they were intended to give this area of the stage qualities of radiance and unearthly splendour, '*grande clarté*' or '*grand lumière*' being terms used to describe it in the rubrics of French *mystère* texts. Whether candles or torches or reflective surfaces were employed to produce such effects is uncertain, but there is clear evidence that gilded clothing, weapons, and make-up contributed to the heavenly glow frequently demanded by writers for moments of high dramatic significance such as the Annunciation, Nativity, or Resurrection. Gilded faces for Christ or an angelic figure are common (see Illustration 16 for contemporary application of the device): striking instances occur in scenes of Christ's Transfiguration, where a gilded mask was sometimes used in conjunction with a snow-white robe and golden gloves to create the desired

16 Scene from the author's production of *The Play Called Corpus Christi* at Bangor Cathedral, March 1972

dazzling effect. The Mons documents include references to the archangel Raphael having his face painted: one reads 'Note here to warn a painter to go into Paradise to paint the face of Raphael red [i.e. red-gold] [*Nota d'ycy advertir ung paintre de aller en Paradis pour poindre rouge la face de Raphael*]'.[12]

Another method used to give Heaven status was to set it on a higher level than the remainder of the scenic *mansions*: as early as the liturgical plays angels often transmitted their messages from a 'high place' as in the Beauvais *Daniel* (see p. 56 above). As machinery came to be introduced, movement between earth and heaven began to be attempted, the suggestion in the Fleury *Conversion* play (see p. 58 above) that St Paul should be lowered in a basket from an upper level indicating an awareness of the theatrical possibilities of such a vertical descent, even if it proved impracticable. In simpler or less affluent presentations, ladders or ramps were the only means by which heavenly beings could reach the *platea* from a height, and for these Fouquet's

170

miniature gives us clear evidence; but in more elaborate productions, technical machinery allowed for spectacular flights to be made between heaven and earth in both directions. These *voleries* formed a very important element of such productions as the *Passions* at Mons in 1501 and Valenciennes in 1547, and the *Actes des Apôtres* at Bourges in 1536.

The basic scenic unit in creating such effects was the fabricated cloud found universally among late medieval dramatic records: the 1564 inventory of the Lincoln Corpus Christi Guild includes 'a fyrmament with a fierye clowde & a Duble Clowde',[13] while the churchwardens' accounts from Chelmsford in Essex for 1562–3 include a payment 'for fyftie fadam of lyne for the cloudes'. The Cornish *Gwreans an Bys* (*The Creation of the World*) begins with a reference which may cast light on the Lincoln 'duble clowde': 'The father must be in a clowde and when he speakethe of [i.e. out of] heaven let ye levys open.' Here no doubt Heaven was provided with folding panels (levys) or perhaps sliding curtains fashioned to resemble clouds, and these were parted by the actor playing God at the commencement of the action. Parallel cases of the heavens opening can be found elsewhere in Europe where artificial cloud-forms may also have been used to surround Heaven with a fleecy nimbus on occasions.[14]

Contributing more to the spectators' sense of the marvellous was the employment of clouds to mask the machinery necessary for ascents and descents simulating flight or translation from one sphere to another. It seems to have been common for scenic clouds to be suspended on wires or strings from some suitable high point, and then lowered to very effective purpose by means of a pulley at certain important junctures in the action, as in the Transfiguration staged at Valenciennes where Christ is hidden long enough to exchange his robe for a white one and for his face and hands to be rendered gold with make-up or a mask, or at Bourges in 1536 where clouds masked various miraculous movements by the apostles. The same kind of technology seems to have been employed to lower and raise humans wearing some kind of safety-harness, the two most striking instances occuring in the Chester and Wakefield Ascensions[15] in which Christ appears to rise above the playing-area without the aid of any supporting mechanism, although a suspended cloud may have helped to give the impression of height. This is the impression given by the Chester stage-direction that Jesus *'stabit in medio quasi supra nubes* [pauses in mid-air, as if standing upon the clouds]'. The character was thus presumably winched aloft by means of a harness beneath his robes (cf.

pp. 73, 93 above); in both plays stage-directions indicate that Christ goes to the 'place of ascension' and stands there for a sufficient length of time to allow the necessary attachments to be made.

Having evolved apparatus for raising and lowering human actors or clouds of cloth and canvas, it was a relatively small step to develop a method for raising and lowering a platform or some other vehicle whose outline could be obscured with a cloudy camouflage. Properly balanced and counterweighted to ensure the safety of its passengers, the cloud-chariot is a well-attested feature of both secular and sacred medieval dramatics, as in various royal entertainments where angels and other figures descend to pay homage to a princely spectator (see pp. 93—above). In religious plays the cloud-vehicle is particularly associated with scenes depicting the Annunciation, Nativity, Transfiguration, and Ascension. Such a device could be used to convey a single figure to Earth or to Heaven, as in the York Transfiguration where we read simply that '*Hic descendunt nubes, Pater in nube* [Here the clouds descend, God the Father in a cloud]', or at the Ascension where Christ calls down a cloud to bear him to the Father.[16] More ambitious structures could be devised to 'fly' as many as five or six figures at a time, as some of the elaborately staged French *mystères* indicate. A favourite effect appears to have been the rapid ascent of Christ and Satan to the pinnacle of the Temple at Jerusalem during the Temptation scene, legislated for in the Mons arrangements of 1501; from the text of Jean Michel's *Passion* we learn that Jesus mounted on Satan's shoulders and 'by means of a sudden counterweight [*par ung soudain contrepoid*]' they were hoisted together to the topmost point of the pinnacle, a somewhat perilous journey for the performers.[17] More gradual ascents and descents were less alarming, and information from Angers, Mons, Bourges, and Valenciennes supplies a picture of cloud machines travelling to and from Heaven bearing angels, dead souls, allegorical figures, as well as Christ. The method of securing figures to the machines is made clear in the Romans accounts which mention three belts (*santures*) with catches (*clavetes*) for the angels '*pour desandre de paradis*', and the needful windlass or 'wynd', for controlling such descents and ascents appears several times in the accounts for repairs kept by the Drapers' Company at Coventry.[18] Presumably similar winching equipment helped to achieve such staggering effects as those recorded at Valenciennes where, for example, the prison-tower in which Joseph of Arimathea was incarcerated was miraculously lifted into the air to enable him to escape.[19]

We shall now examine the use made of fire in the medieval theatre.

Here again the Church developed the rôle of this element in liturgical drama by a natural extension of its traditional place in Christian worship. In the Tours *Ludus Paschalis*, for example, the soldiers guarding the sepulchre are felled to the ground by means of *fulgura* (lightning, thunderbolts) thrown by the angel to simulate lightning,[20] and these *fulgura* were doubtless some kind of early fire-crackers or squibs which exploded in a shower of sparks. This effect retained its dramatic appeal, for one of the stage effects or *feintes* created at Bourges in 1536 showed a number of Jews seeking to prevent the burial of the Virgin Mary blinded by artificial fire in the likeness of lightning (*force feu en maniere de fouldre*);[21] in the Digby play depicting St Paul struck down on the road to Damascus, we read that 'Here commith a fervent with gret tempest',[22] 'fervent' being assumed to mean a thunderbolt or lighting-flash. Fireworks also played an essential part in the depiction of hellish creatures; although the angels at the Nativity in the Valenciennes production held Roman candles in their hands as they flew and sang, more usually it was devils who carried fireworks or had them secreted about their persons, in their diabolic masks and elsewhere; the Bourges descriptions speak of two devils belching fire from their mouths and horns, and holding sparkling brands in their hooves.[23] Lucifer in the Cornish *Gwreans an Bys* is described at one point as 'apareled fowle with fyre', and his counterpart in *The Castel of Perseverance* is of course the subject of one of the most famous instructions in medieval drama: 'he that schal pleye Belyal loke that he have gunne powder brennynge In pypys in his hands & in his eris & in his ars whanne he gothe to battel'.[24] It is little wonder that accidents such as that at Seurre in 1496 (see p. 214 below) befell actors playing the part of Satan.

Not only human performers ejected flames from various parts of their anatomies: serpents and dragons belched forth fire from nose, mouth, and eyes as did the traditional Hell-mouth, where a fire was often kept burning and stirred into life when needed; in 1557 the Coventry Drapers paid someone fourpence 'for kepyng of fyer at hell-mothe'.[25] Religious plays gave ample opportunity for other incandescent effects: the flaming swords of angels, the burning bush from which God speaks to Moses, the destruction of houses, shrines, and idols, even the burnt offerings made by Cain and Abel (contrived at Lucerne by soaking Cain's sacrificial grain in water and filling Abel's lamb with wood-shavings to produce contrasting results when lit),[26] all gratified the medieval desire to see realistic dramatic effects. For the Last Judgement as performed at Coventry by the Drapers three worlds were constructed (in 1556 at a cost of 2s., in 1558 3s. 8d.) only to be set alight for an additional 5d.; in the French *Miracles de Nostre Dame* a hermit burns down his hut, and the city gates at Burgos are consumed by fire; in the Digby *Mary Magdalene* the devils set light to the 'howse' and 'make a sowth [soot]' and later in the same play 'a clowd from heven' sets the heathen temple on fire, a spectacular device possibly achieved by the same means as at Valenciennes where idols, 'which broke and fell of their own accord' when Joseph and Mary fled to Egypt with Jesus, were triggered off by 'lightning or rockets' flying through the air.[27] These were no doubt connected to a wire running to the tops of the columns where the idols stood, and closely resemble the Florentine device commented on by Bishop Abraham of Souzdal in 1439 when he attended the Annunciation play, in which a fire came down from heaven and ignited all the lamps in the church: W. D. Young suggests that the fire ran down gunpowder-coated wires to the wicks of the lamps or that fuses of already burning *aqua vitae* were devised.[28] Fire from Heaven was also a popular feature of scenes involving the Pentecostal flame, where burning fragments of tow or flax were dropped from some upper region, although a dove was sometimes substituted: both devices can be traced back to Christian ritual usage. In the Alsfeld *Passionsspiel* (1501) is found the rubric 'And the angels send fire from heaven accompanied by thunder', although this symbolises only the gift of tongues, the descent of the Holy Spirit being represented by a dove; at Bourges in 1536 the Holy Spirit descends in fire to St Denis.[29]

The Hell-mouth is traditionally deemed a major feature of medieval staging, but it is not as omnipresent as we might assume from its prevalence in graphic art, possibly because of its complex structure. Hell might well be located off-stage or represented by a conventional *mansion* (with an iron door and a grating), or by a tower-like structure, rather than as a dragon or toad's head with gaping jaws: the Latin-Provençal *Sponsus* may have utilised the church crypt,[30] and there is no evidence that *Le Mystère d'Adam* employed such a structure (see p. 123 above). When a set-piece *was* built, one of its most arresting properties was that it could open and shut its jaws, as in the Metz *Passion* of 1437.

La bouche et entree de l'enfer de icelluy jeu estoit très bien faicte; car par ung engin, elle se ouvroit et reclooit seule quand les diables y voulloient entrer ou issir.
(The mouth and entrance to the Hell in this play were very well constructed; for through machinery it opened and closed by itself when the devils wished to go in or come out.)[31]

Some kind of hinged device was required for such an orifice; however, at Romans for *Le Mystère des Trois Doms*, several openings were provided in the head for a mass exit of devils takes place through various *troux* (holes), which may have included nostrils, eyes, and ears.[32]

The devils of the medieval stage were frequently dressed as animals, and animals live and fake played a considerable part in theatrical presentations: we have already detected the presence of men or boys clad in skins as lions in the two liturgical dramas of *Daniel*; lions feature too in the miracle of St Ignatius, and at various points in the Bourges *Actes des Apôtres* where tigers, a leopard, a wild boar, a camel and a dromedary, serpents, dragons, and a monster with a goat's head, a hare's head, and an ox's body, are also called for. Clearly all these were either portrayed by men in skins or by static models containing machinery like that which enabled the 'large and well-made' dromedary in the Bourges parade or *monstre* to move its head, open its mouth, and stick its tongue in and out, or the twelve-foot-long dragon to move its head, eyes, tail, and fiery tongue.[33] Mechanical serpents can be traced back at least as far as *Le Mystère d'Adam*, although we have no means of knowing how complicated a device was necessary for that presentation.

In some productions no attempt was made at the realistic depiction of animals. The Chester cycle version of *The Deluge* or *Noes Fludde* suggests a simple solution to the problem of representing the birds and beasts in the Ark: the Ark is to be 'borded rownde aboute. And one the bordes all the beastes and fowles ... paynted'; the 1607 manuscript describes them as painted on cards which Noah's family hand into the Ark.[34] However, living animals were also employed on a variety of occasions: in *Les Miracles de Nostre Dame* horses, donkeys, and dogs appear, and horses are made extensive use of in the Cornish *Life of St Meriasek*; these, along with live birds, seem to have been the most commonly requisitioned creatures in medieval drama generally. Doves or pigeons, required in scenes where the Holy Spirit had to be portrayed, were a feature of church ceremonial already; such a bird was often required in plays featuring Noah, to be dispatched from the Ark along with a raven, although the return of the dove bearing the olive spray was no doubt not left to chance but arranged by means of a dummy bird on a line, or by attaching a line to the real bird. Certainly at Mons a line was tied to the dove who returns to the Ark with nothing in its beak, and *'ung futif* [an image]' is sent back from Paradise bearing the branch.[35] Birds were also used to symbolise souls: at Alsfeld a white dove was released at Christ's death on the cross, and in the Donaueschingen Passion play a black bird represented the black soul of Judas after his hanging.[36] At Bourges in 1536 an owl appeared, trained by a falconer to fly and sit on the shoulder of Herod Agrippus prior to his departure for Hell, although there is no evidence that the dog in the same performance which sang at the command of Simon Magus could actually perform the feat himself.[37] Certainly the celebrated figure of Balaam's Ass who appears in the early *Ordines Prophetarum* from Laon and Rouen required human aid in addressing his remarks to his master; either a player dressed up as a donkey, as the Chester Cappers' play indicates: 'for this there should be somebody disguised as the ass [*hic oportet aliquis transformiari in speciem asinae*]'[38] or a model on wheels was constructed, with a boy hidden in the body to supply the voice.

Dummy performers were not confined to the animal kingdom; images of the Virgin and Child featured in liturgical performances, as in the *Pastores* at Rouen where they were hidden behind a curtain drawn later by the Midwives,[39] and an artificially contrived angel was flown in a Canterbury pageant early in the sixteenth century.[40] But the chief use of dummy figures was to enable violent or horrific forms of death or torture to be inflicted on human bodies without harming the performers themselves.

In some cases where the torments of martyrdom or the pangs of death required representation, an actor could be protected, either by the use of dummy weapons such as 'soft' truncheons, staves, and stones, or knives with retractable blades, or by the performer wearing some form of protective device or costume, as when Abel in *Le Mystère d'Adam* conceals a pot beneath his clothing, or Christ wears a leather body-suit to spare the actor from the worst effects of beatings and other injuries inflicted in the course of the Passion (see p. 212 below).[41] Techniques were devised for a flow of blood to be simulated: a bladder of blood could be secreted about the actor's person; or whips or scourges could be dipped in red paint or animal blood to leave marks on the actor's body or fleshings; specially prepared weapons could be used as at Lucerne where Cain's axe concealed a container of blood which split open and Longinus's spearhead was full of blood which ran down over the actor's hands.[42] Apparatus was evolved to enable Judas to hang himself without causing himself serious injury, and no doubt the payment of fourpence to a certain Fawston at Coventry in 1573 'for hangyng Judas'[43] was made for some *feinte* in the form of a harness which suspended the actor's body safely but convincingly on the gallows. Even with such precautions, accidents could occur, for in 1437 at Metz, the cleric playing Judas was left hanging too long, and nearly lost his life as a result.[44]

On numerous occasions, where beheadings, mutilations, burnings, drownings, and other bodily sufferings were to be put on view, human lives plainly could not be put at risk: dummies were fashioned to be thrown through the air, tossed into the flames of Hell, decapitated, burnt in ovens, torn limb from limb, or carved up. Only thus could St Denis, for example, in the long French saint play be whipped, racked, tormented on a red-hot grill, assaulted by wild animals, steeped in a furnace, crucified, and beheaded, his bones broken and his bowels exposed through his split belly. Only thus could the naked St Barbara be shown bound to a stake, beaten, burnt, and deprived of her breasts, rolled in a nail-studded barrel, and dragged over a mountain by the hair before final execution.[45] The figure of the tormented St Apollonia in Fouquet's miniature is no doubt such a substitute. These substitutions were ingeniously achieved. At Valenciennes the beheading of John the Baptist was accomplished by the use of a fake head and a table with a hole cut in it, into which the performer placed his head, the dummy one lying beside his; the table receiving the impact of the blow from the executioner, the dummy head was held up, doubtless streaming with blood while the actor feigned death, his own head hidden by the table. At Bourges in 1536 the severed head of St Paul was required to make three jumps across the stage floor.[46] One of the cleverest pieces of equipment for replacing an actor by a dummy figure is found at both Romans and Bourges: it consists of a turntable known as the *trébuchet* on which the character about to die was placed and presumably secured, while underneath, on the reverse side of the table, a dummy was fastened; at some point in the action the table is turned over, and the dummy revealed, while the actor is released from below the *trébuchet*.[47] At some locations the human actor apparently so butchered could escape by one of the underground passages already described; elsewhere his living presence could be masked by the crowd, by those engaged in tormenting him, or by draperies.

Underground passages where they existed and trap-doors which led beneath the stage maintained the atmosphere of mystery and wonder which surrounded many of the tricks perpetrated on the audiences at medieval performances. As early as the *Peregrinus* plays Christ was required to appear and disappear without difficulty, and later plays made even more extensive demands of this kind. *Mansions* could probably be curtained off, so that exits and costume-changes might be effected without being visible to spectators, but when a dead character's corpse was apparently burnt in his coffin, as in *Le Mystère des Trois Doms* in 1509, a simple curtain was inadequate. Then a specially prepared coffin was needed from which the actor could escape through a trap in the stage-floor, and so away to rejoin his fellows while his coffin went up in smoke.[48] By means of traps or underground trenches burials could be carried out on stage and the dead could arise from their graves as at Valenciennes. For the Bourges presentation of 1536 the stage staff were informed that 'there should be a coffin to place St Mathias in, and he should be placed over a trap leading to a passage (*une trappe coulouere*) so that he can escape from it underground'.[49] In the Mons *Passion* of 1501 the devil Fergalus is told to proceed by the passage to a trap above which stands a girl possessed by a demon: on the expulsion of the demon, Fergalus comes out from beneath the girl, masked by smoke and the firing of a cannon from below.[50]

A trap-door or a basin below the level of the playing-area helped in the creation of effects involving water, which the plays use a good deal. One of the most important Old Testament scenes in the mystery plays was the Flood, and this was handled in a number of ways, depending on the kind of resources available, although it is often impossible to tell whether the waters were real or feigned. The *Mistère du Viel Testament* in describing the flood gives us no clue to its realisation:

Icy surmonteront les eaues tout le lieu, la ou l'on joue le mistere, et y pourra avoir plusieurs hommes et femmes qui feront semblant d'eulx noyer, qui ne parleront point. (Here the waters shall rise above the entire area where the mystery play is performed, and there might be several men and women who shall pretend to drown, and they shall not speak.)[51]

An earlier rubric describing the creation of the sea points to the probability that a painted cloth sufficed for the ocean; it speaks of '*Adonques se doit monstrer comme une mer, qui par avant ayt este couverte, et des poissons dedans icelle mer* [Then something resembling a sea should be shown, which had been covered over before, and some fish in this same sea]': perhaps the fish were simply cut-out shapes manipulated by stage-hands. The probability that the waters were artificially created becomes virtually certain when we read that when the Children of Israel seek to cross the Red Sea, Moses lifts his rod and the sea parts (*le mer se depart*), an effect surely scarcely feasible with real water.[52]

Other productions solved the problems of controlling quantities of water. Where arenas were supplied with an enclosing parapet, the whole *platea* could be inundated as at Bourges, where an underground aqueduct enabled water from a nearby river to be conveyed to and from the stage area.[53] Elsewhere a specially constructed basin was used for marine effects: several of the *Miracles de Nostre Dame* demand a pool of water for scenes involving baptism or boats, and the method lingered on at least as late as the Valenciennes production of 1547. The *Resurrection* attributed to Jean Michel suggests the presence of such a basin when speaking of St Peter walking on the water, a feat accomplished by the use of a board beneath the surface of the pool, unnecessary if the water were not really there.[54] A similar facility may have been provided at Mons where one Jehan Bracquet was paid to go to Jemapes, a riverside town, and fetch a 'little wooden boat' to be used in the play.[55] The 'sea' served both for the Ark to float on, and as the Sea of Galilee, but the most sensational aquatic effect at Mons was undoubtedly the Flood for which special equipment was lodged in the *mansion* of Heaven situated in the Maison d'Allemaigne: wine barrels filled with water, outlet pipes, hempen ropes attached to pulleys which upended the barrels, were prepared to 'let the water come [*laissier venir les eaues*]' when the cue was given.[56]

For the flood episodes the Ark was necessary to the salvation of Noah and his family, and boats in general played some part in medieval performances. They were of three main types: practical vessels like Jehan Bracquet's which could actually be floated on the water; stage-boats with wheels intended to move about the stage but not float; and pre-fabricated Arks which could be assembled on stage in plays centred on Noah but remained static. Practicable vessels were rarely required to do more than glide across the surface of the water: the Bourges account refers to 'a pulley at the masthead and a peg in the ground, and a rope passed through the said pulley to steer the said ship'; thus the ship's progress could be controlled from off-stage by a stage-hand pulling on the rope.[57] A similar device was used at Valenciennes where Satan steered a boat on the sea 'without touching it'.

Wheeled ships were a feature of both popular processions and royal entertainments, so their appearance in public religious dramas is not surprising. The vessel employed in the Digby play of *Mary Magdalene* was no doubt of this type, for we read at one point 'Her goth the shep owt of the place' and at another '*Et tunc navis venit in plateam* [And then the ship comes into the place]'.[58] Stage-directions found in the N-Town cycle suggests that a wheeled vehicle was used here, too; Noah and his family leave the stage to fetch their ship, and return in it later.[59] Elsewhere in England the Ark appears to have been present throughout the episode, either on the pageant-waggon as at Chester, or on stage as in the Wakefield, where it seems likely that *Noah* actors mimed the building of the vessel, although in the Cornish *Gwreans an Bys* the mention of tools and timber, planks, ropes, mast, pitch and tar, 'to make the arcke'[60] suggest that practical building operations were actually carried out on stage, and this may have been so elsewhere.

The provision of water and ships often meant that manifestations of storm and tempest were required, and medieval drama took full advantage of opportunities for sound effects, many produced by means still employed even in the days of tape-machines and specially arranged recordings. At Mons, for example, Pierart Viscave, a brass-worker, was paid to supply two large copper sheets in Hell to make thunder; two large casks filled with stones were rotated to supplement the sheeting:[61] their operators were particularly warned to follow their cue-sheets, and not to forget to stop when God bade the thunder cease. Thunder and allied effects were always in demand, notably for moments of divine intervention or occasions when the denizens of Hell took a hand in the action. Thus, the conversion of St Paul or the miraculous release of an apostle from prison could be accompanied by lightning and earth-quake, and the descent of the Holy Spirit by thunder, while the *Passion de Semur* calls on the devils to make 'a great thundering and smoke and noise',[62] just as in the earlier *Mystère d'Adam* they strike pots and kettles and shout loudly. Their efforts were often supplemented by igniting gunpowder, a commodity which features frequently in expense accounts,[63] by cannon-fire, and by fireworks, whose usefulness has already been examined.

Although neither marvel nor machine, it is appropriate to add here a few words on that most important of medieval dramatic sounds, namely music. It must be firmly stressed that, despite their severance from the liturgical music-drama of the church, outdoor plays, cyclic or isolated, sacred or secular, still made full use of musical effects. Audiences clearly expected performances to be embellished and punctuated with music, and items from instrumental overtures and *entr'actes* to choral numbers and solos, were a well-tried and well-exploited feature of most medieval presentations. Musicians formed an important section of medieval dramatic companies, amateur and professional, and actors themselves had to be prepared to cope competently with stage-directions reading 'Here they sing'.

The primary importance of music in liturgical drama scarcely requires further emphasis: it was, after all, the very fabric of the performance, and the full musical resources of medieval ecclesiastical establishments were available for its satisfactory realisation. Just as the natural medium of the plays was sung Latin, so their musical basis rested on the traditional melodies of the liturgy — antiphons, sequences, hymns — performed by clerics and choristers, augmented chiefly by the use of organ, drums, finger cymbals, and a range of bells from the great *campanae* in abbey and cathedral towers to handbells and chimes. Other instruments such as harps or a horn may have been used for special effects as in *The Play of Daniel* or the *Sponsus*, but concrete evidence for the extensive use of instruments is slight: the sung texts are no doubt effective enough without embellishment, despite the impact they make in modern realisations involving generous instrumental supplementation.[64]

An integral part of the liturgical plays, music might also have been employed in a supporting rôle in plays involving transitions from place to place, processional entries and exits, or moments of stillness, but it is only with the development of vernacular religious drama outside the church that truly 'incidental music' evolves. The opportunities offered for music make a valuable contribution to the dramatic impact of the *mystères* and *miracles*, Corpus Christi plays and moralities, and seem to have been taken full advantage of, for well-chosen music could serve to deepen an audience's appreciation of the stage situation just as a film score does in the present-day cinema. Extensive references to payments to musicians and singers in municipal accounts and elsewhere indicate the value set on their services by those responsible for ensuring that the plays were worthily and inspiringly set forth.[65]

Vocal music plays a large part in both the sacred and secular plays of the period: Latin liturgical hymns such as the *Veni creator spiritus* or the *Salvator mundi Domine* survive in the Chester cycle, while the *Te Deum laudamus* almost invariably concluded the performance of a French *mystère*: the *Passion* of Arnoul Greban included the *Kyrie* and *Gloria* of the Mass, and a great deal was made in the English cycles of the angelic performance of the *Gloria in excelsis Deo* which is immediately followed by the shepherds' attempt to emulate the heavenly messengers with their own more bucolic rendering. It is the traditionally music-loving shepherds, too, who often supply a vernacular song, probably with pipe accompaniment, as they step out on the road to Bethlehem, and in the N-Town sequence they sing to the Christ child in the manger. They sing and dance in the Mons *Passion* of 1501 and perform some quite elaborate musical numbers in the Rouen *Incarnation* of 1474. Indeed, as Howard Brown remarks, 'A shepherd almost never appears on any kind of fifteenth- or sixteenth-century stage without at least talking about music'.[66]

Angels traditionally are singers in medieval drama, although all the performers might be required to join in ensemble numbers. But the heavenly choir of singers often recruited from the local church supplied much of the music for the mystery plays, often accompanied by musicians, whose traditional position was alongside God and the angels in the *mansion* designed as Heaven, and depicted with a fair degree of accuracy in Fouquet's miniature, where an organ, some trumpets and drums, and a few wind instruments form a typical medieval ensemble. The musicians would have been called on to accompany the singers or dancers, to provide appropriate fanfares for important entries and exits, to offer such sound-effects as heavenly thunder or diabolic cacophany, and to supply interlude music for the *pauses* and *siletes*.[67] For these stereotyped fanfares were probably used but longer and more elaborate pieces were required, too: the *pause* seems to have been primarily an instrumental flourish punctuating the action, often dividing it into scenes and episodes, although it could be more lengthy. The *silete*, which might be sung, seems to indicate in the religious drama at least a piece of music intended to ensure silence from the spectators as the actors crossed the wide stage or made time-consuming ascents and descents from their scaffolds; the Mons *Passion* of 1501, describing one of God's descents from Paradise, suggests '*S'il est trop loing, silete* [if he takes too long, play a silete]',[68] and the heavenly platform in the Valenciennes sketch by Cailleau is labelled '*Lieu pour jouer silete*'.

Music also played a large part in the secular theatre: it was the invariable accompaniment of royal entries, of street tableaux, of *entremets* and processions, and small groups of musicians are required for many late medieval interludes and moralities, although actors were themselves often expected to double as minstrels, to pipe a dance-tune or beat a drum as the occasion demanded. Thus a number of French *moralités* and *farces* call for the performance of *chansons, rondeaux* and the like, while many Tudor interludes make provision for songs to be inserted at the discretion of the performers: this is particularly true where boy-players form the cast.[69] When such plays were staged at court or in great houses, accomplished musicians would also be available, and scripts acknowledge that such help would be forthcoming: in *Fulgens and Lucres* and *The Nature of the Four Elements* music and dancing almost intrude into the action, while in *Patient Grissell* and *Damon and Pithias* music is casually requested; in Redford's *Wyt and Science* four of the players must have needed to be skilled performers on the viol, and T. W. Craik has demonstrated that the interlude has partly been composed as a showcase for the musicians' talents. Throughout the Middle Ages, music and drama frequently work in unison.

Such then were some of the more notable features of that aspect of the medieval stage referred to today as 'stage-management': many devices relied on techniques little different from those employed in the contemporary theatre, although the energy to deploy them is now less likely to be provided by musclepower. As we read of the details of construction and execution of *feintes* and devices used on the stage in the Middle Ages, the greatest wonder is that so many modern effects seem to have been within the competence of stage directors almost five hundred years ago. Perhaps even today some of their achievements might give a stage manager food for thought:

There water was seen changed into wine, but so skilfully that it was unbelievable, and more than a hundred people in the audience wanted to taste this wine; similarly, the five loaves and the two fishes were there multiplied and distributed among more than a thousand persons; notwithstanding that, there were twelve baskets of them left over.[70]

Small wonder if medieval audiences regarded themselves more as participants in the action than as mere passive spectators.

7

THE PERFORMERS

Hippolyta: I love not to see wretchednesse orecharged;
             And duty in his service perishing.
Theseus: Why gentle sweet, you shall see no such thing.

A Midsummer Night's Dream. V. 1.

Occasional modern experiments notwithstanding, without performers there cannot be dramatic performances. Stage, scenery, costume, lighting, even a script, may be dispensed with, but the player is the basic component without whom theatrical activity is surely meaningless. Despite recent misgivings that actors run a poor second to expensive sets and costumes when productions are budgeted for, it is still true that theatre audiences will pay to see actors and actresses without insisting on elaborate trappings, but there is little evidence to suggest that the converse applies.

Insuperable problems confront us if we attempt to distinguish legitimate actors from other breeds of performer active during the early Middle Ages. St Eusebius, who was briefly pope in about 310, differentiated between *histriones*, buffoons, and acrobats before banning them indiscriminately from the dinner tables of his bishops, and Firmicus Maternus in the middle of the fourth century distinguished three types of actors: *histriones*, *pantomimi*, and *scaenici ioculatores*, which might be rendered as 'actors', 'pantomime performers', and 'stage entertainers', but when the Council of Africa in 408 offered baptism to those *scenicis atque histrionibus* willing to renounce their professions, one doubts if any clear distinction between two sets of specialists were really intended.[1]

It has been common in the past to attach importance to definitions of actors propounded by the theologian and historian, Archbishop Isidore of Seville (*c.* 560–636), who for his early seventh-century encyclopaedia *Originum sive etymologiarum* drew on a wide variety of earlier sources, but it is significant that nearly all of what he says about the stage and its occupants is firmly couched in the past tense.[2] Tragedians he defines as those who 'sang in chorus the ancient deeds and crimes of wicked kings in mournful song while the people looked on';

comedians as those who 'sang in chorus the doings of private individuals using words and gesture [*dictis atque gestu*], and expressed [imitated? — *exprimebant*] the seduction of virgins and the love of prostitutes in their plots'. Isidore also makes a distinction between *histriones* and *mimi*:

Histriones are those men who, dressed in female garb, mimicked the demeanour of loose women; indeed these men also acted out stories and famous achievements by dancing ... *Mimi* are called by a Greek name, because they would be imitators of human affairs [*quod rerum humanarum sint imitatores*]. For they had their leader [writer? — *auctorem*] who before they played their mime, would recite the story. For the stories were written in such a way by the poets that they would be most suitable for interpretation by movements of the body.

Isidore regards tragedy as epic narrative recited or sung by a chorus, and comedy as a similar representation of everyday events, chiefly amorous, almost certainly in recitation form only, although there is some ambiguity in the Latin verb *exprimebant* which may imply physical portrayal. Only with the *histriones* and the *mimi* does Isidore speak unequivocally of actual physical imitation of human behaviour, which suggests that comedy proper was thought of as merely a *recital* of 'the doings of private individuals'. What interpretation we should place on Isidore's *auctorem* is not clear: is he an 'author' and hence one of the poets referred to later, or is he simply a narrator who recites the text for the miming actors, much as the chorus supplied the narration for a Roman pantomime performer? The several possible meanings of the term *auctor* do not permit us to learn Isidore's view of the matter.[3]

It is far from certain whether we can maintain Isidore's once-for-all division between the respective rôles of *histrio* and *mimus*. The English scholar Alcuin separates *histriones et mimos et saltatores* in a letter of 791, but R. M. Ogilvy maintains that this is a quotation from St Augustine, and may not reflect a later distinction at all.[4] In another letter of *c*. 800 Alcuin remarks that 'it is better to please God than the players [*histrionibus*], to care for the poor rather than for the *mimi*', but he is probably employing two generic terms for the same evil, rather than making a meaningful discrimination. Agobard of Lyon, writing in about 823—4, condemns those clergymen who lavish hospitality on 'actors, mime-players, and the most depraved and empty-headed jesters [*histriones, mymmos, turpissimosque et vanissimos joculares*]': how a *histrio* differed from a *mimus*, or a *mimus* from a *joculator* is never revealed. When Liudprand of Cremona visited Constantinople in 950 and reported that the emperor's appearance resembled that of an actor or *mimus* (*histrionum mimorumve more*), he obviously associated the two terms with each other, and this seems to have been the general tendency by about 1000.[5]

One of the most interesting references to a stage performer during this period is contained in a Latin elegy of the early ninth century,[6] said to be the epitaph of the *mimus* Vitalis, whose art appears to have rested in his ability to mimic the physical characteristics of members of his audience:

> *Fingebam vultus, habitus ac verba loquentum,*
> *Ut plures uno crederes ore loqui.*
> *Ipse etiam, quem nostra oculis geminabat imago,*
> *Horruit in vultus se magis isse meos.*

I assumed the looks, behaviour, and words of those speaking, so that you would believe that many individuals spoke out of one mouth. Indeed, the victim himself, whom my likeness visibly duplicated, shuddered to see himself exist more truly in my features.

Here we have a vivid description of an actual mime player in performance, stressing his skill at 'taking-off' his auditors in a semi-extemporised manner, and it might be argued that it was this gift that distinguished the *mimus* from the *histrio*. It does seem as if the *mimus* were more often associated with domestic entertainments, at least if we judge from a tenth-century sermon by Bishop Attone of Vercelli[7] in which he depicts the faithful: 'They do not delight in theatres, as do the players [*scenici*]; nor in wedding-songs and foolish ballads as do the mime-players [*mimi*], nor in dancers and the circus, as do actors [*histriones*] or worshippers of idols, whom, alas, certain Christians still imitate in many places.' But if the association of the *mimus* with weddings and foolery is helpful, linking the *histrio* with dancing and the circus is certainly confusing!

Papias in his eleventh-century *Vocabularium* certainly associates the *mimus* with the *joculator* or jester, but though he goes on to say that his speciality was as an 'imitator of human affairs [*rerum humanarum imitator*]' as Isidore does, he assigns *mimi* the task of providing the mimed performances which accompanied 'the recitation of comedies'.[8] Nicholas Trevet (see p. 48 above) in his commentary on Seneca's *Hercules Furens* continues this notion in describing the classical theatre, with its arena and 'house': 'In it was a platform on which the poet stood to recite his poems. Outside it were the mimes, who accompanied the reciting of the poems by physical action, adapting their gestures to whatsoever character the poet was interpreting.'[9]

Honorius of Autun in his *Gemma Animae* (*c.* 1100) implies that tragedy was arranged differently. According to his account, the narrators themselves imitated what they were describing: 'it is known therefore that those who recited tragedies in the theatre, represented the actions of fighting men to the people by means of gestures [*sciendum quod hi qui tragoedias in theatris recitabant, actus pugnantium gestibus populo repraesentabant*]'[10]

That men of the Middle Ages may have used the term *histriones* more usually to define 'straight' acting appears to receive some support when we consider the testimony of John of Salisbury (*c.* 1115–80), pupil of Peter Abelard and secretary to Thomas à Becket, in his *Polycraticus* (*c.* 1159), where he reveals a sounder understanding of the usual classical theatrical practice than those who viewed it as based on recitation-and-mime presentations. John says:[11] And there were certain actors [*histriones*], who by bodily movement, by the art of words and by vocal modulations represented to public view true and fictional stories. You find them in Plautus and Menander, and through them the art of our Terence became known.' John of Salisbury's actors of the ancient theatre are described as *histriones*: the *mimi* to him are a later phenomenon, which he includes as part of the 'general stage of the jesters [*tota ioculatorum scena*]', along with acrobats, clowns, gladiators, wrestlers, and jugglers, to be unreservedly condemned.

But if any such division was intended by John of Salisbury, its validity was not maintained for long: although the Lateran Council of 1215 distinguishes between '*mimis, joculatoribus, et histrionibus*',[12] Hugutius (Uguccione) of Pisa, in his dictionary *Magnae Derivationes* (1197–1201) not only identifies the *histrio* with the *joculator*, but he assigns to the *histrio* those miming rôles in comic representations which Isidore and Papias allocated to the *mimus*![13] In the same way the *Penitential* of Thomas de Cabham or Chabham, sub-dean of Salisbury Cathedral in the early fourteenth century, leaves no doubt that in one medieval mind at least the term *histrio* covered a multitude of theatrical sins:[14]

There are three types of *histriones*. Some transform and transfigure their bodies with lewd dancing and postures, either by stripping off their clothing, or by putting on dreadful masks, and all such are doomed to damnation, unless they leave their occupation. There are others besides who have no profession, but act in a reprehensible way, having no fixed abode; they follow after the courts of great ones and say scandalous and disgraceful things about those who are not there, in order to please the others. And indeed such man are damned, because the Apostle forbids us to eat food with such people, and such buffoons [*scurrae*] are called vagrants [*vagi*], since they are good for nothing, except gobbling up food and abusing people. There is still a third type of *histriones*, those who have musical instruments to delight mankind, and of these there are two classes. Some frequent public drinking-sessions and licentious gatherings, and there they sing diverse songs to urge men to wantonness, and such are damned just like the rest. There are also others, who are called *joculatores*, who sing of the heroic deeds of princes and the lives of saints, and they bring comfort to men both in sickness and in poverty, and these do not create numberless evils as do the male and female dancers, and others who act in shameless representations.

However, while Thomas de Cabham enrols *pantomimi, mimi, scurrae,* and *joculatores* under the banner of *histriones*, which now seems a loose term for 'entertainers', what does seem quite explicit in his testimony is that all his remarks are set in the present tense, as if he had some personal knowledge of what he describes, and if so, his testimony is of great value. Similarly Adam of Bremen writing his *Gesta* in the late eleventh century, uses the present tense to describe how Archbishop Adalbert of Hamburg debarred from his presence 'pantomime players.... who tend to amuse most people by their obscene movements'.[15]

Whatever rôles we assign to *histrio, mimus, scurra, scenicus* and *joculator*, obviously some medieval entertainers were regarded as 'imitators of human actions', or character-impersonators who assumed the 'looks, behaviour, and words' of members of their audience. However, if we accept Thomas de Cabham's account as first-hand evidence, he does not seem to wish to isolate a class of *histriones* who simply performed in plays, although he does mention as an afterthought 'others who act in shameless representations [*alii qui ludunt in imaginibus inhonestis*]'. It appears as if acting was just one of the talents a versatile medieval entertainer might boast: in a French fabliau *Du Vilain au buffet*,[16] we hear how among a band of *jongleurs* dancing and performing acrobatics and juggling tricks,

> L'uns fait l'ivre, l'autre le sot,
> Lis uns chante, li autres note,
> Et li autres dit la Riote,
> Et li autres la Jonglerie.   (142—5)

One plays the drunkard, one the fool, some sing and others play, and some recite 'The Riot', and others 'The Jongleur'.

Allardyce Nicoll finds an intriguing reference in Bretel's poem *Le Tournoi de Chauvency* (c. 1285) already alluded to (p. 15 above) where, in a description of post-joust entertainments, we hear how 'they made each other's acquaintance and found out who could dance the Hypocrite (?), the Hermit, the Pilgrim, the Provençal, the Shepherd and his Sweetheart, the *Berangier*, or the Garland [*Chapelet*]', but these appear to be mimed dances performed by dinner-guests 'after the wine' rather than a professional presentation.[17] Nicoll also alludes to a description of an entertainer in Jean de Hauteseille's twelfth-century Latin translation of the Book of Sinibâd known as the *Dolopathos*,[18] which relates how the man 'tries to imitate what he has seen and heard; he performs comic gestures and breaks up his words(?) [*gestus comicos repraesentat, frangit verba*]', but there is no evidence that this has reference to contemporary practice. In fact incontrovertible allusions to the actual content of early dramatic performances are not quite so easily come by as Nicoll asserts.

Rosemary Woolf suggests that evidence for a mimetic tradition based on stage imitations of human character or mood is contained in two early thirteenth-century works, 'The Vision of Thurkill', and the *Ancrene Wisse*.[19] We have already cited the anecdote of an Essex peasant who goes to Hell where in a large circular theatre the damned were treated to performances by some of their number (see p. 47 above): one of the proud imitated the expressions, gestures, and words of a haughty man; a crooked lawyer mimed receiving bribes, playing all the parts himself like the *pantomimus*; a pair of adulterers re-enacted their sin on stage. The *Ancrene Wisse* portrays several of the Seven Deadly Sins as the devil's entertainers, trumpeters, *joculatores*, and jugglers, and Envy the *joculator* with his screwed-up face may well be a portrait of a contemporary comedian. The extravagant and stylised postures and gestures of figures which feature in scenes on misericords, roof-bosses, bench-ends, corbels, or in the margins of medieval manuscripts may also preserve for us the eloquent acting style of the medieval *mimus*.[20]

It is now time to consider Benjamin Hunningher's claim that the *mimi* were responsible for introducing the dramatic element into the liturgical tropes. Nicoll in *Masks, Mimes and Miracles* draws attention to St John Chrysostom's accusation that fourth-century supporters of the Arian heresy had introduced the habits of the *mimi* and the dancers into church worship, in an attempt to make their services popular, countering the popularity of the mime stage by adopting some of its techniques.[21] Hunningher's contention is that in the ninth and tenth centuries the official Church, still feeling the need to combat the appeal of popular pagan rituals, formed an alliance with the *mimi*, to import dramatic impersonation into the rendition of the *Quem Quaeritis* trope of Easter, transforming it from symbolic liturgy to primitive theatrical performance. The *mimi* became respectable servants of the Church; the Church had the satisfaction of seeing its drama professionally staged.[22]

Mimi did visit monastic communities, a practice condemned by King Edgar *c*. 960, but one objection to their involvement in church performances is that the Church, with its past history marked by outright condemnations of professional entertainers, surely could not have imported *mimi* to perform in the liturgical sequences even on an official basis without some voice somewhere being raised in protest. As far as we know no such voice was heard.[23] Aelred of Rievaulx in his *Speculum Charitatis* accused English priests of using wild theatrical gestures, vocal and facial distortions, dramatic pauses and other practices more suited to the theatre than the church, but he says nothing suggesting the introduction of professional *mimi*.[24]

There is also the indisputable evidence of the *Regularis Concordia* that the *Visitatio Sepulchri* sequence was to be performed by four members of the brotherhood, suggesting that other dramatic inci-dents could be enacted by clerics quite satisfactorily without profes-sional help. Furthermore Hunningher partly bases his conclusions on illustrations from a tenth-century book of tropes from the abbey of St Martial (Bibliothèque Nationale MS Lat 1118), in which he claims *mimi* are depicted and that the illustrator had seen them performing in church dramas. But as Helena M. Gamer has demonstrated,[25] these figures are court entertainers traditionally belonging to King David, who also appears surrounded by dancers and musicians in a manu-script illumination in the early tenth-century *Psalterium Aureum* from the monastery of St Gall.[26] Perhaps we should accept that only rarely were clergy and *mimi* prepared to accommodate each other's presence, and that the importation of professional performers into liturgical as well as vernacular religious dramas is unlikely though not impossible. But it is fairly clear that the *mimi* were not a major force in the genesis of medieval church-drama.

The kind of acting liturgical performers were called on to supply involved few opportunities for individual characterisations; indeed, such expressions would have been frowned on had they been attempted by those appearing as the three Marys, disciples, or as Christ himself. What was required was doubtless an iconographical representation of the scriptural figure, not a naturalistic portrayal of a human being. The acting of liturgical drama was conceived of in formal, stylised terms and governed by considerations of liturgical propriety. Restraint and decorum are the keynotes; although the communication of deep feeling is often indicated, its physical expression as defined by rubrics is invariably restricted to a number of conventional, semi-hieratic gestures. Some actions may have been presented in a freer manner: the *Regularis Concordia's* text of the *Visitatio*, for example, instructs the Marys to come to the site of the sepulchre 'hesitantly, like people seeking something'. We can be fairly sure that no attempt was made to maintain a convincing illusion of actuality for, since there was never any possibility that priests and choristers might be mistaken for women and angels, the acting style employed had no pretensions to naturalism. Only in a handful of cases, such as certain portrayals of Herod, was characterisation of a less constricted kind possibly attempted.

What inferences can be safely drawn from the texts of liturgical plays are not extensive:[27] indications of the manner in which sung lines are to be delivered are sparing, chiefly involving matters of pitch and volume. Emotions of sorrow and joy are conveyed in the Fleury *Visitatio* where Mary Magdalen behaves *'quasi tristis'*, and in the Barking *Visitatio* where the Marys sing first *'flebili voce et submissa* [in low and tearful voices]' and Mary Magdalen later responds to Christ's resurrection *'voce letabunda* [with joyful voice]'. The Coutances text requires the Marys to ask 'Who shall roll away the stone?' *'voce lacrimabili'*, and at Bamberg they put the same question with a more naturalistic touch, *'querula voce* [with complaining voice]'. Vocal interpretation of liturgical drama does not appear to have been ambitious according to the principal aims modestly set forth in the introduction to *Le Mystère d'Adam*:

And this Adam should be well instructed as to when he ought to respond, lest he be too hasty or too slow in answering. Let not only he but all the characters be rehearsed in this way so that they speak in the right places, and make gestures in keeping with what they are saying, and in speaking the verses, neither add nor take away a syllable, but pronounce them all boldly, and let them say whatever has to be said in the right order.

The 'gestures in keeping with what they are saying' are also far from taxing: physical action in the *Visitatio* includes the displaying of the crucifix, the grave-clothes or the napkin (*sudarium*) to the choir or congregation, kneeling or genuflecting, the censing of the altar or the specially constructed sepulchre, lifting a cloth or raising a curtain, the kissing of altars or the *sudarium*, and the collection of vessels from a side-altar or from a cleric representing the seller of ointments, which may have involved a brief dumb-show. Instructions to turn to the choir, the congregation, or another character often occur, and indicating or pointing to various objects or persons on stage is a favourite method of drawing attention to them, indeed it can become a virtually automatic gesture as in the remarkable *Planctus Mariae* from Cividale del Friuli where thirty-one of the seventy-nine stage-directions involve pointing to figures or objects. The introduction to *Adam* suggests something of the same technique: 'Whoever mentions the name of Paradise, let him look towards it and point it out with his hand.' Thus the Figure of God indicates to Adam the Paradise, its trees, the forbidden tree and its fruit, to which Adam and the Devil also point. At the end of the Tours *Ludus Paschalis* Mary Magdalen shows the disciples the sepulchre, the angels, the *sudarium,* and the cross in sequence.

In the more developed plays there is more elaborate physical action: Peter and John in the *Visitatio* race to the sepulchre, and in several texts Peter is described as limping (*claudicante*); Pilate's soldiers who guard the tomb at Coutances 'speak in character [*dicant personagia sua*],' which may have involved improvised dialogue or mime. In the same text the soldiers are struck down 'as if dead', by two angels bearing hollow rods set with candles to represent lightning, and the Klosterneuburg *Ordo Paschalis* has an angel strike one guard with a sword, precipitating the fall of the rest; the Tours play has the angel hurl a thunderbolt among the soldiery. The Klosterneuburg text includes a Harrowing in which Christ breaks down the doors of Hell, and a scene where the chief priests (*Pontiffices*) bribe the guards with gifts. Such plays anticipate the Passion plays of the *Carmina Burana* manuscript in which a high degree of elaboration is involved: in both Christ is crucified and his side pierced, and the shorter play ends with the enigmatic stage-direction '*Et Joseph honorifice sepaliat eum* [And Joseph honourably buries him]', which is intriguing if only for its lack of practical details. The longer version calls for many lively pieces of stage direction: boys strew fronds and garments in Christ's way as he enters Jerusalem; Mary Magdalen apparently goes to bed with her lover; a crowd of Jews follows Judas to Gethsemane to take Jesus with swords, cudgels, and lanterns; the Jews give Christ a slap round the face (*dent ei alapas*); the Devil leads Judas to the gallows where he is hanged. A subtler touch is provided by the kiss exchanged between Pilate and Herod as they meet together during Christ's trial, a purely theatrical moment conveying their evil affinity much more effectively than any dialogue.

The plays of Christmas describe physical action in greatest detail, for Herod is often provided with colourful gestures which enhance his rôle as belligerent tyrant. At Compiègne and Rouen he greets the Magi with a kiss, and at Rouen invites them to sit on thrones beside his own; at Freising, Rouen, and in the Fleury *Herod* he angrily throws the book of prophecies to the ground, having perused it. At Rouen he brandishes his sword all around, while at Bilsen, 'swelling with anger', he scatters swords everywhere, and menaces the Magi with his club. In the Fleury *Herod* the king and his son threaten the star with their swords, a neat dramatic image, while in the *Ordo Rachelis* from Fleury Herod as if deranged turns his anger on himself and attempts suicide on hearing of the Magi's escape, being only prevented and gradually pacified by his court. In the Christmas play from Benediktbeuern Herod is consumed by worms (we are not told how this effect was staged!) and finally received by devils. The Archisynagogus from the Benediktbeuern play is left free to make a great deal of noise and disturbance, laughing raucously and excessively, bawling and shouting, writhing his head and body about, stamping on the ground with his foot, and 'with his stick imitating the behaviour of the Jews in every way'.

It is generally the evil and theologically disreputable figures in the plays who have the greatest opportunities for physical activity. In *Le Mystère d'Adam* the devils run about the acting area, making suitably demonic gestures, and carrying out wild sorties possibly into the audience. Their greatest moment comes when they carry Adam and Eve to Hell:

Then shall come the Devil and three or four devils with him, bearing in their hands fetters and iron chains which they place on the necks of Adam and Eve. And some will push and others pull them to Hell; further devils still will be close by waiting for them as they come, and they will make a great dance of triumph over their ruin; and each of these other devils will point them out as they arrive, and will receive them and send them off to Hell. And they will make a great cloud of smoke to arise from within, and shout one to another in Hell, rejoicing, and crash their pots and cauldrons together, so that they can be heard outside.

Later in the play the devils drag Cain away to Hell beating him, and with superb arrogance they carry off even the prophets of the third section as they complete their utterances.

Indications of feelings and emotions are less often encountered than suggestions for actions. The Fleury *Visitatio* instructs the Marys to walk haltingly (*pedetemtim*) and suggests that Christ should draw back from Mary Magdalen as if avoiding her touch. Eloquent, too, is the Fleury *Peregrinus* direction that the disciples should approach Christ on his appearance to them and 'touch his hands and feet gently'. *Adam* is richer in this respect than most of the strictly liturgical plays: the Devil veers from mirth and hilarity to sadness, and appears to Eve 'fawning and with joyful features'. For speaking to Satan Adam rebukes Eve *'moleste ferens* [in great annoyance]', and he and his wife express their guilt after eating the fruit by adopting the stance so often depicted in medieval art: 'standing before the Figure of God, yet not fully upright, but on account of their shame at their sin somewhat bowed down and full of grief'. Even more poignant is the stage direction describing how the fallen Adam and Eve return to their agricultural labours to find that the Devil has planted thorns and thistles in their field: 'When Adam and Eve come to their field and see thorns and thistles sprung up, stricken with violent sorrow they throw themselves to the ground, and lying there they beat their breasts and thighs, making their grief known by their actions.' Cain, a combination of mockery and defiance, expresses his opinion of Abel at one point by making a savage face (*torvum vultum*), rushing on Abel to kill him 'like a madman [*quasi furibundus*]' and *Adam* contains one of the few small details of production technique recoverable from the liturgical plays: we learn that Abel is to have an earthenware pot (*ollam*) concealed in his clothes, and it is this which Cain strikes violently 'as if he was killing Abel'. Another graphic detail comes from the Besançon Magi play in which the kings are attended by pages in Persian clothing, one blacked-up to resemble a Moor: the pages carry cups which their masters later present to the Christ child, but the nicest touch comes with the remark that the kings are to have 'a little book [*liburet*] where what they ought to do and chant is noted and written down'. Many medieval cleric-actors probably relied on such *petits libures* to guide them through the perils and dangers of liturgical performance.

Costume in these dramas was not based exclusively on ecclesiastical garb; Fletcher Collins argues that references to standard vestments were included to satisfy official requirements and considerable liberty was exercised in clothing the characters, especially the women − Mary Magdalen being described in the Fleury *Resuscitatio Lazari* as being '*habitu meretrico* [dressed like a whore]'.[28] However, it may be felt that Collins over emphasises both the permitted freedom from liturgical restraint, and the desire for accurate representation. The most commonly mentioned vestments are the alb (a white under-tunic reaching to the feet with narrow sleeves), the dalmatic (a long loose upper-tunic with wide sleeves), and the cope (a long cloak made of a semi-circular piece of material often bearing elaborate designs). Although generally speaking different groups of characters wear different types of garments, no attempt seems to have been made to reserve a certain class of vestment for certain characters: angels, Marys, Christ, shepherds, Magi, and prophets all wear the alb, one Mont-St-Michel text specifying that Christ's must be 'stained as if with blood'. The most common vestment worn by the Marys is the cope, white again being the predominant colour, though purple is selected at Trier. Copes are also the usual wear for the disciples in the *Peregrinus*, and they clothe the Magi at Besançon and Rouen. Stoles are mainly worn by angels, violet featuring at Narbonne, and red at Besançon. In *Adam* the stole is used as a sign of authority when the Figure of God dons one before entering Paradise to judge Adam and Eve, just as a medieval priest would have done when expelling sinners from church on Ash Wednesday.

The amice, a piece of white linen worn around the neck and shoulders, is chiefly found on the angels and Marys, drawn up over the head, in several instances, to conceal the sex of the performer. This mild concession to realism is also discovered in the half-covered faces of the Marys at Sainte-Chapelle, Paris, and the use of veils at an unidentified French monastery, and at Dublin and Barking; in the Rouen *Peregrinus* Mary Magdalen wears 'a binding wound around his head in feminine style [*vinctus in modum mulieris caput circumligatus*]'. Eve in *Le Mystère d'Adam* supplements her woman's white garments with a white silk wimple. Other small realistic details are the frequently bare feet of Christ, wings for the angels at Narbonne, Besançon, and Padua, and crowns for the Magi and kings among the prophets. Most of the hand-properties are once again ecclesiastical in origin: they include thuribles, candles, 'silver vessels', pyxes, ampullae for the Marys, Christ's crown of thorns, gifts for the Magi, palms, staves, swords, books, mitres, and a variety of objects associated with the prophets of the *Ordo Prophetarum* by which they might be easily identified.

The purely theatrical possibilities latent in costume are rarely grasped in the liturgical plays, but a few instances stand out. In the Fleury *Visitatio* Christ first appears humbly clad as a gardener and then returns in the splendour of a white dalmatic, a white fillet, and a costly phylactery on his head, carrying a golden garment in his left hand and a cross with a standard in his right. A similar change has to be much more swiftly accomplished at Coutances, where Christ returns in a silk cope or cloak (*pallium*) which presumably hides his gardener's costume. In the Fleury play of the *Peregrinus* Christ first appears clad like the disciples, in pilgrim's attire carrying a wallet and a long palm branch, with a pointed hat on his head, wearing a furry cloak, and barefooted, but on his reappearance he is transformed by a white tunic, a red cope, a white fillet tinged with gold (*aurifrisia*), and the addition of a gold cross in his hand. More dramatic perhaps is Mary Magdalen's laying aside of her 'wordly garments' for a black *pallium* after her conversion in the Benediktbeuern Passion play, and the scene in which Adam in *Le Mystère d'Adam* removes his red tunic and substitutes poor clothes sewn together out of fig-leaves. In two other instances a change of fortune is marked by a change of dress, a theatrical device made good use of in a number of English morality plays and interludes: in the Laon *Joseph*, the hero, first stripped and placed in the cistern by his brothers, is later taken out and dressed in splendid clothing; in the Beauvais *Play of Daniel* the reverse process takes place when the envious counsellors of King Darius are divested of their robes before being thrown into the pit to be consumed by lions.

It must be generally accepted that the participants in Latin liturgical drama were almost exclusively amateurs — the various ranks of clergy, choristers, nuns in convents, even the occasional bishop. But one does wonder if clergy sought help when rôles such as devils or soldiers or the lions in the Beauvais *Daniel* (if they were visible) were required, although here again we must not rush to assume that nineteenth-century attitudes to clerical dignity applied, or that clerical dignity was quite such a precariously balanced commodity as it sometimes seems today.

In parts of sixteenth-century Spain it was the custom for teams of professional actors to be employed to supply the needful play-performances to grace Corpus Christi celebrations, as at Seville in 1538 and at Toledo in 1542, while Lope de Rueda's troupe was engaged by the civic authorities at the former in 1543 and 1559, and at the latter in 1561. But the extent to which the organisers of the great religious dramas of the Middle Ages drew on professional assistance to strengthen their casts is unknown. Musicians and technicians were often professionals, and some players were professionals at least in so far as they were paid for their services in several places, particularly in England, where the wealthier guilds at least could afford to hire players to perform the cycle plays, and where the leading guildsmen might also be civic dignitaries who were required for official duties on important occasions such as Corpus Christi Day. But it is doubtful whether many hired players were full-time professionals dependent on their acting talent alone to earn them a living, and it may still be claimed that the casts of the medieval religious dramas were predominantly amateur.

All through the Middle Ages clerics and clerks continued to play an important part in the staging of dramas. The *Siete Partidas* (*c.* 1260) of Alfonso the Wise recognises that while clerics are forbidden to participate in *juegos de escarnios*, they may play in liturgical pieces of a devotional nature, so long as these are performed in large cities, seats of archbishops or bishops, not in small towns and villages, and without thought of financial gain.[29] Later clerics seem to have taken part in public performances quite freely.[30] At Metz in 1437 clerics not only played the parts of St John, Jesus, Judas, and Titus, but a priest was even prepared to play the part of Christ's executioner (*le bourreau de Dieu*). At Troyes in 1490 a Dominican Nicole Molu confessed to neglecting his religious duties for seven years in order to study and enact the rôle of Christ, but it was perhaps just these very exacting demands made by the part which led to its being assigned to a cleric at Mons in 1501, and at Lucerne in 1583 and 1597 where it was played on both occasions by Johann Müller, *'luttpriester im Hof* [priest in the Court]'. The clergy did not always receive the leading sacred rôles. At Mons clerics not only took the parts of the Prologue, Mary Magdalen, Cain, Herod, St Peter and other Apostles, but also Beelzebub, and in 1508 we find a *cantor* playing the part of Satan! Some plays were entirely cast from clerics: at Laval in 1507 the clergy of Ste-Thugal presented 'Abraham's Sacrifice' in the main square, and in the same year ecclesiastics at Amboise received permission to grow beards in order to play their rôles in a local *mystère*. The 'Early Banns' of Chester refer to a play 'sett forth' by the local clergy in honour of the Corpus Christi feast, although there is no indication whether this was merely a tableau or a full dramatic presentation. In a list of *c.* 1520 priests at Beverley are actually assigned one of the plays in the Corpus Christi cycle itself, that of the 'Coronacion of Our Lady'. Clerics were also in demand as directors. In Romans in 1436 two *curés* received five florins for staging a play, while at Mons in 1501 several of those appointed as *superintendants du Jeu* were ecclesiastics who also played important parts: Godeffroy curé of Bertaymont played Cain and St Phillip, and Maistre Estievene de Ponceau who played Satan may have been a priest. At Valencia in 1517 several payments to clerics are recorded: Mossen Jordi Mas received 9s. for a 'representacio' of St Sebastian, in which he instructed the actors as well as playing one of the parts himself. Mossen Miguel Juhan, 'cantor of the Cathedral', directed a performance of Christ's descent from the cross, while Mossen Miguel Pineda produced a 'misterio y representacio' of the 'holy Fathers'. At Lucerne in 1583 clerics chiefly played small parts, with the exception of the priest playing Christ, and Herr Probst Volrich Herman who played the aged Isaac, Joseph 'the consort of Mary', Aman one of the Jews, and Cleophas the disciple.

It is difficult to make any broad generalisations about the social class of the actors in the vernacular dramas of the Middle Ages: such vast numbers were required that almost everyone with any talent at all would appear to have been needed to fill the 494 roles in the *Actes des Apôtres* or the 350 parts in the Mons *Passion* of 1501. What is probably de Mézières's *Estoire de Griseldis* (1395), which was doubtless acted by courtiers and retainers, is essentially a private piece, and the Constable of Castile who in 1462 played the part of one of the Magi at an Epiphany banquet in Jaén was also among friends, but a nobleman played the part of Brisebarre, '*premier tyran*', at Romans in *Le Mystère des Trois Doms* in 1509, and the cast also included the Town Treasurer, the Town Justice, the Canon, and the representative of the Archbishop of Vienne.[31] At Grenoble in 1535 a doctor at law was set down for the part of Jesus which he attempted to relinquish after five months of rehearsals,[32] while the law clerks of the famous Basochiens were prominent in staging every kind of play including religious ones. In England, too, the parish clerks seem to have been active in performing plays, as the famous performances at the Skinners Well, or Clerkenwell, in London in the last decades of the fourteenth century indicate.[33] Here in August 1384 'the clerks of London' staged 'a certain highly sumptuous play [*quendam ludum valde sumptuosum*]' which lasted five days. The clerks played again in 1390 and 1391, Richard II on the first occasion commanding that they be paid £10 in recompense. In 1393 they staged 'the pley of seynt Katerine' but we hear nothing further until 1409 when a great seven-day cycle from Creation to Doomsday was featured, and witnessed by a large concourse of nobles and gentry. Alan Nelson suggests that some of these productions influenced Chaucer's *Miller's Tale*, and certainly his dapper would-be seducer Absalon is both parish-clerk and actor:

> Somtyme, to shewe his lightnesse and maistrye,
> He pleyeth Herodes upon a scaffold hye.
>
> (*The Canterbury Tales*, A 3383–4)

However, the bourgeoisie and commons also found their histrionic talents appreciated. Admittedly there were those critics whose opinions of amateur players echo those expressed by Philostrate in *A Midsummer Night's Dream*, most notorious among them being a procurator-general at the Parlement de Paris who gave his view of the actors of the Confrérie de la Passion in 1542 as 'unlettered fellows unskilled in such matters, of low rank, such as a joiner, a tipstaff, a tapestry-maker, a fishmonger'.[34] But talent among the humble was not always despised. We learn from the Mons accounts that some of the cast were recompensed for the loss of wages while performing: that a saddler acted several parts, a joiner played Noah, while one farmer's rôles included Flesh, a Jew, Herodias, and Mary Salome! However, at Lucerne later in the century, guild members and servants were confined to minor rôles with only a few exceptions; the major parts were very much sought after by state and city officials and by members of the leading city families. Indeed some rôles became regarded as almost hereditary, while individual families might supply several members of the cast: thus the Schytterberg family provided four actors in 1545 and six in 1571. On the other hand, the payment of twelve schillings to 'the little table-maker' who played Zacheus in 1531 suggests that less prosperous members of the cast were given financial assistance to enable them to participate in the plays.[35]

Women did not play a large part in the vernacular religious drama, probably because they lacked the vocal resources or training to project their lines; furthermore, the organisations responsible for the presentations were male, and drew on male resources.[36] Yet it is not true to say that women never acted in these productions. The 'daughter of Dediet the glazier' at Metz in 1468 delighted everyone with her performance in the role of St Catherine, a part which involved committing some 2,300 lines to memory, which she accomplished perfectly, speaking 'with such feeling and so piteously that she provoked several people to tears'; her crowning reward was to make a rich marriage with a nobleman.[37] However, the citizens of Metz did not accept the inevitability of actresses for all time: in 1485 Lyonnard, a barber's son, played St Barbara 'so discreetly and devoutly that several people cried with compassion'; we are told that he was 'a very good-looking boy and resembled a beautiful young girl'.[38] The Chester 'Early Banns' certainly includes among its list of companies and their plays the entry

> The wurshipffull wyffys of this towne
> Ffynd of our lady thassumpcon

(folio 88)

but it seems unlikely that an all-female cast could have presented a play containing male characters even by about 1500; at Mons in 1501 even the parts of Eve, Noah's wife, Herodias, and Mary Magdalen (the latter taken by a priest and canon of St-Germain) were all played by men; girls appeared in minor rôles, the most important parts being taken by 'Wandru, daughter of Jorge de le Nerle', who played the Virgin Mary aged fourteen, the wife of John the Evangelist, and Salome, daughter of Herodias![39] At Romans for *Le Mystère des Trois Doms* all the female rôles were taken by women, and the same applies at Bozen (Bolzano) in 1514. In 1535 Grenoble witnessed the performance of Francoise Buatier, who gained attention 'by her gestures, her voice, her articulation, her delivery; she knew how to charm all the spectators, to the point of arousing universal admiration; grace and beauty in her were added to good speaking'.[40] In the London Lord Mayor's Shows of 1523 and 1534 a number of girls appeared, and in the Coventry *Destruction of Jerusalem* in 1584 the part of 'Solome' may have been played by a woman, although 'Frauncys Coccks' who received 12d. for playing it could presumably be of either sex.[41] At Valenciennes in 1547 the parts of Mary Magdalen, St Anne, Wisdom, Justice, and Truth were undertaken by men, but a young girl Jeannette Caraheu played the Virgin Mary, and four other girls had minor rôles.[42] The burghers of Lucerne did not admit women to the cast of their Passion play: in fact, the city clerk Renward Cysat, director (*Regent*) of the play in 1583 and 1597, served his dramatic apprenticeship by taking the important rôle of *Maria Virgo* in 1571.[43] Young boys also participated in the plays as pages, or as angels where choirboys were particularly valuable for the singing rôles, and in Italy the *sacre rappresentazioni* were often presented entirely by boys.

Before we go on to consider the way in which plays were cast, rehearsed, and performed, something further must be said of the organisers of the productions. Sharing the responsibility for the artistic and financial success of the presentation with the authorities of the medieval Church were a number of lay associations, among which the most prominent are the craft and trade guilds of the towns of Britain and Germany, and charitable societies of roughly the same type known as *cofradías* in Spain. When the *sacre rappresentazioni* came to their full magnificence in great Italian cities such as Urbino and Florence in the fifteenth century, their organisation was undertaken by specially founded guilds called *compagnie*, to which even the aristocracy gave their support. These committees of management supervised the theatrical, technical, administrative, and commercial progress of the production, acted as hirers and firers of directors, players, technicians and labourers, and brought the whole project to fruition. In France amateur players were apt to band themselves into guilds or societies for mutual support and congenial companionship.[44] The custom seems to have begun with the *trouvères*, and Jean Bodel (see p. 67 above) was a member of the Confrérie de la Ste Chandelle at Arras, a society formed of *jongleurs* and bourgeois citizens from Arras, a blend of writers' guild and friendly society dedicated to act as custodians of a candle which had miraculously appeared to one of their number. Arras also possessed a Confrérie des Ardents de Notre-Dame, a guild of local poets and *jongleurs*, to which the bourgeoisie were also admitted, and Adam de la Halle's *Jeu de la Feuillée* (*c.* 1275) may have been written for an Arras *confrérie* at their annual summer festival. At the same time as the *confréries* flourished, patrician families seem to have formed their own literary societies or *puys*, organising feasts, tournaments, and literary competitions, electing a prince of poets every year. It was under the auspices of the *confréries* and the *puys* that amateur dramatics developed in France, and although they had very different purposes — charitable, literary, recreational, devotional — and often contained both lay and clerical members, these organisations accepted responsibility for stage productions and recruited actors from among their numbers. The earliest record of a *confrérie* pledged to stage plays comes from Nantes in 1371, but the most famous group is the Parisian Confrérie de la Passion et Résurrection which was active in the capital by at least 1380, and in 1402 received letters patent from Charles VI giving the society the right without further permission to '*jouer quelque Misterre que ce soit, soit la dicte Passion, et Résurreccion, ou autre quelconque tant de saincts comme de sainctes* [to play any *mystère* whatsoever, be it the said Passion and Resurrection, or any other matter such as plays of male and female saints]'; they were also granted permission to stage performances in Paris and its suburbs or anywhere else they pleased, and to wear their costumes where they chose to go, without molestation. The *confrérie* continued to perform religious plays until forbidden to do so by the Parlement de Paris in 1548 (see p. 240 above).

Other guilds of amateur actors appear in late medieval France: apart from the various *confréries* in Chartres, Rouen, Amiens, Limoges, and other places, there is evidence of drama-playing *puys* in Paris, Rouen, Caen, and Dieppe. More light hearted and ribald was the fare offered by the *sociétés joyeuses*, in which students and law clerks played a prominent part. In Paris the two most famous groups were the Basochiens, and the Enfants-sans-souci, the latter probably an off-shoot of the former; each high court of justice in France had its own division of a society of law clerks known as the Basoche, and the Basochiens were perhaps originally affiliated to the Basoche du Palais in Paris. Other groups are found outside the capital. Their repertoire included farces and moralities, while the Enfants-sans-souci were probably a separate group of Basochiens specialising in performances of *sotties* (plays featuring *sots* or fools), although each group allowed the other to use its repertoire of plays. The urge to band together is not confined to organised societies, however. At Mons in 1501 the actors appearing in certain sequences formed themselves into separate companies, a requirement largely dictated by the need to rehearse and take refreshment together: thus the accounts record payments to '*Lucifer et sa compaignie*' and '*la compaignie infernalle*', and Gustave Cohen notes with amusement that while God the Father and his associates preferred to take supper after the show at L'Auberge du Griffon, Lucifer and the devils frequented À le Clef; one wonders if limited accommodation or mutual antipathy were the principal consideration.[45]

The methods of selecting casts are full of interest: often huge companies of actors were required, and in some districts proclamations invited potential players to audition for parts.[46] For the 1541 representation of the *Actes des Apôtres* by the Confrérie de la Passion in Paris, a 'cry' was made at every cross-road inviting all men of goodwill to attend at the '*salle de la Passion*' of the Hôtel de Flandre at 8 a.m. on St Stephen's Day 1540, in order to be tried out for the rôles in the play. In England the individual guilds accepted the task of finding players either recruited from their own members or hired for the purpose, as a document from Coventry in 1453 indicates: 'Thomas Colclow, skynner, fro this day forth shull have the rewle of the pajaunt unto the end of xij yers next folowing, he for to find the pleyers and all that longeth therto all the seide terme.' The York Mercers, too, appear to have hired players for their pageant of Doomsday in which many guildsmen would have been prevented from appearing by their duties as civic officials. At Lucerne, as soon as the production date had been decided, announcements were made from the city's pulpits, that all those who wished to participate should register their names at the city clerk's office, together with details of any rôle preferred. Evidently there was great eagerness to take part, and aspirants sometimes applied for the same rôle, Pilate and the Prologue being particularly sought after in 1597. Certain rôles had become almost hereditary perquisites of influential families, and there were also the inevitable rivalries over the plum parts:

J. Hans Ruodolff Sonnenberg desires the part of the Saviour in case the Reverend Priest [Müller] should not appear in it again

J. Hans Ruodolff Sonnenberg begert den Salvator stand im faal. H. Lüttpriester inne nit wider versahen sollte.

All these matters had to be settled by the Lucerne *Verordneten*, a production committee consisting of representatives of the Brotherhood of the Crown of Thorns and of the city council. At Seurre casting was assigned to the mayor himself and three assessors; York followed something of the same practice, as the city council's ordinance of 3 April 1476 makes clear:

That yerely in the tyme of lentyn there shall be called afore the Maire for the tyme beyng iiij of the most Conyng discrete and able playeres within this Citie to serche, here and examen all the plaiers and plaies and pagentes thrughoute all the artificeres belonging to Corpus Christi plaie; And all suche as thay shall fynde sufficant in persoune and Conyng to the honor of the Citie and worship of the saide Craftes for to admitte and able, and all other insufficant persounes either in connyng, voice or persoune to discharge, ammove and avoide.

And that no plaier that shall plaie in the saide Corpus Christi plaie be conducte and Reteyned to plaie but twise on the day of the saide playe, and that he or thay so plaing plaie not overe twise the saide day upon payne of xls to forfet unto the Chaumbre as often tymes as he or thay shall be founden defautie in the same.[47]

The criteria at York seem to have been 'cunning', 'voice' and 'person', which equate no doubt to 'acting ability', 'vocal range and delivery', and 'physical presence': the director of the Lucerne Passion play laid down similar guidelines for his successors in 1592.

The Lucerne documents make it clear that some effort was expended to choose suitable casts, moral probity as well as stature, physique, voice and appearance being taken into account! The Valenciennes contract of 1547 enjoins the *ordonnateur* to cast the parts with care, and Jean Bouchet who produced the Poitiers *Passion* in 1508 lays stress on choosing actors who speak well, and on assigning rôles to those players who fit them best:[48]

> *Je vous supply que tous vos personnages,*
> *Vous assignez à gens selon leurs aages*
> *Et que n'usez tant d'habits empruntés*
> *(Fussent-ils d'or) qu'ils ne soient adjustez*
> *Commondément aux gens selon leur roolles.*

I beseech you to assign all your parts to people according to their ages, and not to use borrowed stage costumes (even if they are gold ones) that are not happily suited to the rôles people are playing.

Nevertheless indications of bad feeling over casting and accusations of partiality and favouritism are found in the Lucerne records, and were no doubt common elsewhere too.

The York ordinance of 1476 quoted above raises the interesting question of doubling, which has already been discussed (see p. 116 above): multiplying of rôles taken by individual players is certainly known in other European cities. At Mons several actors played three parts or more; two actors were required for the part of Lucifer, one to assume the form of the serpent in the temptation scene, 'since Lucifer certainly would not have enough time to put on the serpent's disguise'. At Lucerne taking multiple rôles was a regular tradition, Peter Leeman in 1597 playing nine minor parts; occasionally impossible combinations were discovered at rehearsals, and adjustments were needed: thus lines spoken by Longinus were reassigned in 1597 to allow Hauptmann Batt am Ryn to play both Longinus and Lucifer.[49]

At Lucerne the actors were nominally allowed only fourteen days to accept or refuse the rôles assigned to them by the committee, and in 1597 every actor accepting his part or parts had to pay a fee to production expenses according to the importance of his rôle. Thus the sum of forty schillings each was exacted from the *Proclamator* (Prologue), God the Father, Christ, Lucifer, and thirty-four others; Adam, Eve, the Virgin Mary, Magdalen, Beelzebub, and thirty-five others paid thirty schillings.

In most places the casts of the plays were bound by an agreement which seems to have been seriously treated as a binding contract between actors and organisers. An undertaking from Beverley, dated 1391, depicts one man assuming overall responsibility for a particular play:

John of Arras, *hairer* [came] in the Gild Hall before the twelve keepers of the town of Beverley, and undertook for himself and his fellows of the same craft to play a play called Paradise adequately, viz, every year on Corpus Christi day when the other craftsmen of the same town play, during the life of the said John Arras at his own proper cost, willing and granting that he will pay to the community of the town of Beverley for every default in the aforesaid play, 10s, Nicholas Falconer being his surety.[50]

*maker of hair-cloth?

Elsewhere the individual actors entered into private recognisances, as at New Romney in 1555 where three groups of cast members on pledging £5 each, received official assurance that

The Condycon of this recognysaunce is suche that where the Above bounden parties have taken upon them to be players in ye stage playe At New Romney aforeseyd to be played (by the grace of god) At the feaste of pentecost next comyng And have receyvyd players Speachys or partes in the seyd playe . . . Yf they & every of them do learne before the seyd feaste of pentecost theire partes before lymytted & be redye then to playe the same / And further do at every tyme of the rehearse of theseyd playe com to Romney aforeseyd & Rehearse theire seyd partes (Reasonable cause not lettyng) That then this present Recognysance shalbe voyde & of none effect or elles shall abyde in all his full strength & vertue /[51]

Injunctions at York and Wakefield state that the plays should be staged at authorised places only and at nowhere else on pain of a fine, that every player should be 'redy in his pagiaunt' by 4.30 a.m. (York) or 5 a.m. (Wakefield), and that at York if 'all maner of craftmen that bringeth furthe ther pageantez in order and course by good players well arayed and openly spekyng' shall fail to do so, 100 s. should be 'paide to the chambre without any pardon'.[52] A ruling by the Coventry city council in 1443–4 made it an offence for a member of one guild to appear in another guild's production, without prior permission from the mayor.[53] At Lucerne an actor was fined for going to the tavern or drinking while his rehearsal was still in progress, and this did not include other penalties for infringing Lenten observances. The fullest account of the pressures on players comes from *l'obligation* or contract drawn up to govern procedure at the Valenciennes production of 1547:[54] an actor was bound by oath to appear, only illness being accepted as a valid excuse; to accept any rôle allocated to him and not to throw a part up once he had agreed to play it; to attend rehearsals at prescribed times; and to be at the theatre by seven in the morning, ready to begin the play at midday. Actors were forbidden to interfere with the running of the play by the organisers or to complain about their decisions; to leave the wings without directorial permission; to handle the takings; to visit any illicit social gathering or hostelry before, during, or after the performance, but to be satisfied with the refreshments offered them where they were playing. They were to pay a gold *écu* (crown piece) out of which to meet expenses or fines; they were to submit possible disputes to the supervisors and not go to law with them. In short, the Valenciennes contract includes conditions which every present-day director must have wished for at some time or other: medieval performers must have been truly dedicated to have accepted them.

All the same it is clear that many of these rules were sometimes breached, and physical violence was clearly involved on several occasions.[55] At Chester in 1399 the Corpus Christi procession led to a battle between the Weavers and the Fullers; and at York in 1419 members of the Carpenters' and Cordwainers' Guilds attacked the Skinners with clubs and axes. At Bungay in Suffolk in 1514 the town bailiff and others broke up five of the pageants after a procession; and competition between guilds over the Corpus Christi celebrations occasioned the issue of an ordinance of *c.* 1536 from Newcastle-upon-Tyne which speaks of 'avoideing [doing away with] of dissencion and discord that hath been amongst the Crafts of the saide Towne as of man slaughter and murder and other mischiefs in time comeing which hath been lately attempted amongst the fellowshipp of the said crafts of the Tailor of the same Towne.'

Fines for incompetence are found, too.[56] At Beverley in 1392 several guilds were punished for the inadequacy of their offering, and in 1520 Richard Trollopp, alderman of the Painters, was fined because 'their play of *lez iij Kynges of culleyn* [Cologne] was badly and confusedly played, in contempt of the whole community, before many strangers' and Richard Gaynstant of the Tailors was penalised 'because his play of *slepyng pylate* was badly played', as was that of the Drapers, who were also fined. The Websters of Aberdeen were fined because 'thai did nocht it that accordit thame to do' in a Candlemas presentation, and the Baxters were summoned before the civic authorities in 1532 'for the wanting of their pagane in Corpus Christi processioun tha usit afore'. Fines were imposed at Beverley in 1423 on Roger Penykoke for failing to present his pageant at North Bar, and on John Sutton 'for impeding the play of diverse pageants'; in 1450 five fishers were penalised for not having their play ready on time, and the same fate befell the Butchers who arrived late with their piece in 1459. In 1452 Henry Couper, a webster, had to pay 6s. 8d. because he did not know his part, and this may also have been the reason for the Coventry authorities fining 'Crystover Dale playing Jhu [Jesus]' and 'Hew Heyns pleynge Anne' in 1450. Lucerne officials were equally strict, and the players were cautioned in 1597: 'Everyone is warned once more that each man must diligently pay heed to his position, be it in respect of speech, equipment, gesture or other matters pertaining thereto, for our gracious lords will have a close watch kept and will punish those guilty of infringements and disobedience'.[57]

Rehearsals seem to have varied in frequency and intensity from place to place:[58] in England individual rehearsals could be organised under the auspices of the several guilds and so reduce the period of time required for full-cast rehearsals. Thus the 1574 records of the Coventry Coopers, when three rehearsals and one 'generall rehearse' represent all the practice the players seem to have received, may be taken as typical. The Smiths' records for 1490 list a 'furste reherse of our players in ester weke' and a 'Second Reherse in Whyttsonweke', suggesting that only two rehearsals of the *Trial and Crucifixion* were held with everybody present that year. How much advance notice the actors received of their parts varied: the New Romney players were evidently assigned their rôles for Whitsun 1556 by 27 December 1555 when they signed recognisances, yet the York council did not decide that the Creed play should be staged at Corpus Christi 1568 until 13 February, when they decreed that 'after expert and mete players found owte for the conyng handlyng of the sayd playe, than every of theym to have their partes fair wrytten and delyvered theym in tyme soo that they may have leysure to kunne every one his part'. By contrast the Mons *Passion* of 1501 required at least forty-eight rehearsals at the Hôtel de Ville, not excessive when one considers that a text of some 35,000 lines was presented; on the other hand rehearsals for the three-day *Mystère des Trois Doms* at Romans in late May 1509 only began on 18 March; these were also held at the townhall, and there seem to have been seven held, roughly one a week till 29 April. At Lucerne the Passion play was split into twelve small units which could be rehearsed separately: players were urged to practise their episodes in small private groups, and there were special rehearsals for those most in need of them. Rehearsal sessions began a month before Lent and were held in the city's Schützenhaus, but at Lincoln around 1479 a private house was used, and at New Romney in 1560 the parish church. Rehearsals in France culminated in many places with the grand procession known as *le monstre*, mentioned earlier (p. 163 above) and a 'general rehearse', approximating to the 'public dress-rehearsal' of the present day, at which the production committee and local dignitaries were allowed to see the final fruits of their efforts and of the financial nourishment they had provided.

Organising rehearsals was only one of the many tasks which devolved upon the director and his assistants: they had to supervise every aspect of the production, including the properties, costumes, staging, music, and so forth, and the chief organiser was no doubt responsible for his own script in some cases. At Mons four of the cast seem to have directed the play, with the assistance of four other members; at Romans the *commissaires* appointed M. Sanche of Dijon *maître du jeu*; Jean Bouchet, rhetorician and attorney, staged the *Passion* at Poitiers in 1508; while the mayor of Bourges and a rich seed-merchant are among the directors of the Bourges *Actes des Apôtres* of

1536. Noblemen and ecclesiastics are also found as directors of continental religious drama during this period. The citizens of New Romney in 1560 selected one Gover Martyn as their 'Devyser', and he not only appears to have directed the piece, but also to have written or at least adapted the script: we find him purchasing 'stuff' in London, being granted 3s. 2d. for supper and drink for himself and his men (plus 2d. for bow strings), and being paid £4 'for his servyce at our play' supplemented by further payments of 26s. 8d. and 20s.[59] At Chelmsford in 1562 one Burles, 'a propertie player' was imported, probably from London, to direct the first two plays staged: he oversaw the construction of the scaffolds, kept accounts, designed scenery, and ordered properties. He was boarded in the district for about nine weeks, and received a total of £4 15s. 4d. in payment.[60] It would be interesting to discover whether there were others like Martyn and Burles active at this period.

One of the chief administrative worries with amateur drama is to offer sufficient inducement to the actors to ensure their attendance. In the Middle Ages one of the chief attractions was no doubt the free food and drink offered, not only during and after the performances, but also at rehearsals, often in the form of a breakfast since rehearsals were frequently held early in the morning before a day's work. In 1554 the Chester Smiths apportioned 2s. 8d. to 'flesh at the breckfast and bacon'.[61] Other records list payments made for refreshments, either at rehearsals as at New Romney[62] in 1560:

Item payd to Lawrance Ffan for *bere* fett to ye church when the play was rehersed the xxxj^th of marche   vjd

*beer

or during the performance, as at Coventry[63] in 1494:

Item in expence on the pleares for makyng them to drynke and hete at every reste   iij^d

or York in 1462 when 6d. was allocated for 'drynk upon Corpus Christi Day be the way'. Such practices were widespread on the Continent too; at Romans in 1509, for instance, the players received cakes, fruit, and wine after the show. At Besançon in 1421 the metropolitan chapter laid down that cantors performing the *Actes des Apôtres* should receive a quarter of mutton, a *setier* (virtually a gallon) of wine, and six loaves of white bread, but it was forbidden for these provisions to be brought to them while they were still in their stalls for fear of spoiling their copes.[64]

But of course payment in hard cash was also a feature of some productions,[65] for at Valenciennes in 1547 the total sum shared between organisers and players was over 1,230 livres. At Hull in 1483 Robert Brown received 6d. for playing God but Thomas Sawyr received 10d. in the same part eleven years later; on both occasions Noah's payment was 1s. Adam and Eve both got 6d. at Perth in 1518, but the devil and St Erasmus obtained 8d. each, while the tormenters who presumably were those responsible for winding the saint's intestines out on to a drum, were paid 1s. each for their labours. The fullest records come from Coventry where payments to participants in the Smiths' pageant of Christ's Trial and Crucifixion in 1490 include 2s. to Christ and to Pilate's wife, but 3s. 4d. to 'Heroude' and 4s. to Pilate; those receiving the highest payments may, of course, have been professionals attached to some lord or magnate. Pilate in the Cappers' *Resurrection and Descent to Hell* in 1565 also got 4s., while Christ had to be content with 20d., 'the demon' with 16d.; in 1538 the Drapers' God received 3s. 4d., a payment also made in 1556 and in 1560 when Robert Croo took the part. In the Smiths' 'New Play' of 1573 God also accepted 3s. 4d., this being the celebrated production in which one Fawston is set down to receive 4d. 'for hangyng Judas', and another 4d. 'for Coc croyng' presumably in the scene where Peter denies Christ. In the following year the Chester Coopers' accounts record the sum of 2d. 'spend apon Thomas Marler to get him to pleay', suggesting that a popular actor may have been exploiting his ability to draw the crowds. Some of the payments may seen arbitrary and illogical, but even the lowest-paid English player might have been consoled had he known that at Mons and Lucerne the casts received no pecuniary reward at all for their services, which were given freely for the greater glory of God and the wider renown of the city and its inhabitants.

Indeed, in several places it even appears to have been customary for the players, in addition to decorating their own scaffolds (see p. 146 above), to supply their own costumes and the less expensive properties.[66] At Romans only certain of the more unusual characters such as Lucifer and Proserpine were provided with costumes, and at Lucerne only the dress and properties for Judas were supplied at the city's expense, Judas being an unpopular part, although occasional 'grants towards expenses' were made to less affluent actors. Various methods of obtaining costumes were devised: the organisers were fortunate in that contemporary clothing was usually worn by the majority of characters. The Coventry Smiths' accounts for 1487 include a 'reward to Maisturres Grymesby for lendyng off her geir for Pylatt's wyfe'; in 1579 the Smiths

hired or borrowed a gown of the Tailors and Shearmen's Guild, and the
Mercers' accounts for 1584 record a payment of 32s. 'for hieringe
apparell for the playeres'. For *Le Mystère de l'Incarnation et de la Nativité* at
Rouen in 1474 the church authorities lent an archbishop's cross,
ornaments, and tunics for the angels; at Lincoln in 1515 the city council
announced

> That wher divers garmentes & other *heriormentes* is yerly Boroyd in the
> †Cuntrey† for the Arryeyng of the pagentes of Scaynt Anne gyld, now the
> knyghtes & gentylmen be ‡Freyd with‡ the plage So that the §graceman§ Can
> Borowght none Sutch garmentes, wherfore every Alderman Schall prepare &
> Setfoorth in the Seid Arrey ij good gownes And every ‖ Scheryff pere ‖ A
> gowne And every Chaumberlen pere A gowne & the persons with Theym To
> weyre the Same

*Ornaments   †district   ‡scared of   §chief guild officer   ‖ former sheriff

which, although probably referring to a procession rather than a play,
indicates clearly the necessity for obtaining clothing of sufficient quality
to grace the shows of the late Middle Ages. In 1521 the same problem
arose, and the council agreed to borrow 'A gowne of my Lady Powes
for one of the Maryes & thother Mary To be Arayed in the cremysyng
[crimson] gowne of velvet that longith to the Same gyld'.[67]

Some guilds may have been bequeathed clothes for their actors, if the
will of William Pisford of Coventry is typical, for in 1517 he left the
Tanners' Company a scarlet and a crimson gown 'to make use of at
the time of their plays',[68] and in this way organisations were able to
build up theatrical wardrobes for their own needs, and to hire out to
others. An inventory of church goods made by the churchwardens of
Chelmsford in 1563 includes such a collection of costumes mostly made
from old vestments, and over the next twelve years hiring fees brought
in about £29, this versatile collection being eventually sold off in 1574
when it fetched almost £7.[69] When Worcester Cathedral sold its 'players
gere' in 1576 the inventory included 'A Ks [king's] cloke of Tysshew',
'a lyttil cloke of tysshew', 'A gowne of silk', 'A Jerkyn of greene, 2
cappes, and the devils apparell'. The Brotherhood of the Crown of
Thorns at Lucerne evidently had such a store of costumes and properties, but as is so often the case, control was insufficient, and garments
and other items were loaned out and not returned, so that stern rules
had to be laid down for their safety.[70]

It would be impossible to cite every available detail of costumes
worn in the vernacular religious dramas. In many cases vestments that
had served the liturgical drama so well continued to form the staple
of a large number of costumes, but a greater freedom was probably

possible. We do not know, for example, how the diabolical characters were clad in the few liturgical plays in which they feature, but in the vernacular pieces we hear of 'the devill in his featheres all ragged and rente' (Coventry 'Late Banns'), of 'ij pound of heare [hair] for the demons cotts & hose' (Coventry Drapers 1572), or of the devil Enguignart in *Le Jour de Jugement* dressed as a young dandy of the day in a blue surcoat with long ermine-lined sleeves falling almost to the floor, and a red hood: attendant devils on this occasion were painted red or black, with wiggling tails, and gaudily coloured shields which they beat with their pitchforks. Rabelais describes, probably from life, a parade of devils in which the demons are 'decked out in the skins of wolves, calves, and rams, topped with the heads of sheep and the horns of bulls, and huge kitchen hooks, with strong leather belts round their waists from which great cow-bells and mule-bells hung, making a horrific din'.[71]

In many places masks were an important feature of devilish costume, and they also feature among the details of Herod's equipment; allusions to 'the fauchon and Herod's face' or 'peyntyng and mendyng of Herodes heed' are found several times in the Coventry list of expenses, and his other accoutrements from time to time include a 'crest' or helmet, which was probably embellished in some way to show his kingship. One ingenious use for a mask occurs in *The Life of St Meriasek* when the Emperor Constantine's leprosy is graphically indicated by means of 'a vysour'. Herod doubtless was provided with a sword, just as at Coventry Pilate was celebrated for wielding his 'malle' or 'cloobe' which features so often in the accounts of the Cappers' Company. Satan is often provided with a weapon of some kind too. Herod's costume at Lucerne was to be the 'most costly and splendid' that could be obtained, with a Jewish and heathen feeling about it; Pilate was to be dressed 'as a provincial bailiff or governor, rich, rough, with a draped pointed hat, heathen and imposing, in a burgher's coat with sleeves reaching below the knee, sabre and high boots. A sceptre or staff in his hand.' Colour was an important element: the N-Town text describes Annas as 'be-seyn after [arrayed like] a busshop [bishop] of the hoold lawe, in a skarlet gowne, and over that a blew tabbard furryd with whyte and a mytere on his hed after the hoold lawe'.

God at Lucerne wore the traditional alb and magnificent cope of earlier days with a diadem, long grey hair and a beard, but elsewhere there was less reliance on ecclesiastical vestments:[72] for the Coventry play of Doomsday and elsewhere a large number of skins were purchased for his 'coat'; at Coventry in 1565 three yards of 'redde sendall' were bought 'for God', and at New Romney the relatively large sum of 4s. 8d. was 'payd to Burton for skynes for the ij^d godheddes Coote & for makyng'. At Norwich 'a face and heare for the Father' indicate that there at least God was masked and wore a wig. (Fake hair seems to have been a favourite method of disguise for many characters: in the Chelmsford inventory of 1563 we read that the church possessed twenty-three fake beards and as many wigs.) Christ, too, was often an expensive figure to clothe, even in a play such as the Coventry *Trial and Crucifixion* where we might expect only a simple white garment to suffice: in 1451 the Smiths paid 18d. for 'vj skynnys of whit leder to Godds garment', and in 1553 five 'schepskens' were needed, 3s. being spent on their purchase and having them made up, and it has been suggested that this was in fact a protective garment to resemble a naked torso in the flagellation scene (see pp. 176–7 above). The York Mercers made provision in 1433 for Christ's tunic to display the marks of his Passion, and we read of 'a sirke [shirt] wounded'. In 1490 the Coventry Christ seems to have worn a gilded wig (cheverel); in Jean Michel's *Passion* of roughly the same period, at the Transfiguration Christ re-appears to the disciples in 'the whitest robe that can be obtained with his face and hands all burnished gold. And behind him a great sun with rays streaming from it'. The Mons accounts also place great stress on the garments to be furnished for Christ, and there are three separate references to the Transfiguration costume, where he wears 'a robe of white sackcloth and white hose' and his hands and face are burnished. This reflects the relative artistic integrity of the Mons production, in contrast to the Bourges presentation of *Les Actes des Apôtres* in 1536 where all the resources of a prosperous textile industry could be deployed: where the Mons apostles were dressed *en leur habis mecanicques* (as artisans), those at Bourges wore velvet, satin and damask robes, St Andrew's robes being of gold brocade and his cloak embroidered with pearls; those playing queens displayed a plethora of expensive jewellery, Herod's wife wearing a velvet dress of crimson-violet, its sleeves slashed to reveal their cloth-of-gold linings and a purple satin mantle lined with silver; her black-velvet headdress was set with pearls, and a sapphire was set into the point of each shoe. But even the poorer characters were costumed in rich silk.

By contrast with such excess, various accounts describe what characters intended to appear naked actually wore on stage: the total nudity of Adam and Eve before the Fall is not impossible, since we know that naked women sometimes posed in street pageants during the fifteenth and sixteenth centuries and appeared in Italian court entertainments[73] (see p. 94 above), but given that Eve was usually played by a man, some kind of basic garment to conceal the fact was no doubt needed, even for audiences not preoccupied with strict verisimilitude. When in *Le Mystère de saint Vincent* the saint is told that he will be stripped completely naked (*Despouilles serez tres tout nu*) the stage direction tells us that 'they strip him down to a loin-cloth [*jusques aux petits draps*]', and one takes '*jusques aux*' to mean 'thus far and no farther'.[74] Probably the same basic garment was worn in many productions by Adam and Eve, by Marcellus, the young man divested of his cloak in the Garden of Gethsemane in the Donaueschingen Passion play, and by the adult souls released from Hell later in the same play, who are said to be '*nackent*' in contrast to the many small children '*Gantz nackent*';[75] presumably Christ crucified on the cross was similarly dressed in a loin-cloth.

In several instances Adam and Eve were clad in the medieval equivalent of the modern body-stocking or leotard and tights:[76] the 1565 inventory of the Norwich Grocers' Guild who presented the Creation includes '2 costes and a payre hosen for Eve, stayned [dyed]' and 'A cote and hosen for Adam, steyned', although these may be post-lapsarian garments only, as in the Mons play of 1501 where two *plichons* (fur-cloaks) are given the characters to hide their nakedness. However, some confirmation that the Norwich costumes were worn throughout is found in the Lucerne accounts, where in 1538 Adam and Eve are simply listed as '*nackend*' but in a later list we are informed that they are '*in lybkleider, alls nacket* [in body-clothing, as if naked]', and a 1583 entry confirms that they wore '*Lybkleidern über den blossen lyb* [body-clothing over the bare skin]': Adam should have long hair (not grey or black) and a short beard; Eve's 'beautiful long feminine hair' was, one assumes, a wig. The English stage-directions to the Cornish *Creation of the World* also confirm the idea; Adam and Eve are to be 'aparlet in whytt lether', but they act as if naked, for there are to be 'fig leaves redy to cover ther members', and (as at Mons) there are 'garmentis of skynnes to be geven to Adam and Eva by the angell'.

Of the quality of the acting performances themselves very little can now be gleaned; hardly any direct accounts of late medieval acting have come down to us. Again one must assume that convention and tradition governed much of what was seen on the medieval stage, although there were no doubt individuals who stood out for their willingness to play a part to tear a cat in, or for their incompetence (a young girl at Dijon in 1511 who mocked a feeble actor was beaten by his wife as a result!)[77] but there is no valid reason to assume that medieval Europe suffered from a dearth of creditable amateur actors: the sheer actability of many of the rôles in medieval drama does not suggest players unable to take advantage of the histrionic opportunities offered them. Of course, there are attacks on performers' acting abilities, the most savage that mounted by a procurator-general against the Confrérie de la Passion in 1542 where he described the players thus:

Both the organisers and the players are ignorant fellows, labourers and mechanics, not knowing A from B, who have never been taught or trained to perform such plays in theatres and public places, and moreover they lack fluency of speech, propriety of diction, correctly accented pronunciation, and any notion of what they are saying, so much so that .... derision and public clamour often arise in the theatre itself, to such an extent that instead of producing enlightenment, their performance results in uproar and mockery.[78]

Against this we may set the compliment paid to the actors who presented *Les Actes des Apôtres* at Bourges in 1536,[79] by an eye-witness who described the plays as 'well and excellently performed by earnest men who knew so well how to depict the characters which they represented by signs and gestures, that the majority of the onlookers considered the business to be the truth and not pretence'.

That the actors needed to be dedicated men in many cases is made clear by a variety of anecdotes — for example, those narrow escapes from death by characters such as Christ and Judas, or an unfortunate Satan in the *mystère* of St Martin at Seurre in 1496, whose costume caught alight as he was about to emerge from the trapdoor of Hell, and who was badly burnt on the buttocks; 'but he was so speedily rescued, undressed, and re-costumed, that without betraying any sign that something was wrong, he went out and played his part'.[80] Such stoical indifference may be felt to be within the very best traditions of the amateur theatre! Familiar also are the strictures expressed here and there about unauthorised additions being made to the official text. A French manuscript of a play staged in 1456 includes the acid comment: 'Rejected and not included in this manuscript are any unusual additions which some of the players of this *mystère* thought fit to add at will [*cuidèrent. adjouster à leur plaisance*], in that they were irrelevant to the subject and were censured by masters of theology'.[81]

From several accounts and pictures of medieval productions it is clear that the *maître du jeu* actually appeared on the stage himself during the play to prevent mishaps and to give the players what aid he could; his likeness appears in the famous illustrations by Hubert Cailleau for the Valenciennes play of 1547, a script in one hand and a short staff in the other, but portrayed off-stage, as a lone figure. In Jean Fouquet's illumination of the staging of *The Martyrdom of St Apollonia* (see Illustration 10), however, he is a much more forceful presence, standing boldly forth among his actors, vigorously gesturing with his stick, and with the prompt-copy open in his other hand. Richard Carew in his account of the Cornish cycle supports this pictorial evidence when he writes that 'the players conne not their parts without booke, but are prompted by one called the Ordinary, who followeth at their back with the book in his hand, and telleth them softly what they must pronounce aloud',[82] which presumably means that the Ordinary cued the players and generally supervised the performance from on stage. As we have seen, actors were in fact supposed to know their lines, or most of them.

As to the acting style employed, we may again assume that psychological realism was neither expected nor sought after; it is unlikely that the technique of acting differed greatly from those employed in the Latin church-drama, except that perhaps greater scope was offered for uninhibited and expansive performances in some of the more virtuoso rôles such as Lucifer, Herod, and Pilate, while the comic vignettes of Cain, Mrs Noah, Joseph, and the individual devils could be more fully developed outside a liturgical framework. But there is little to suggest that the more devotional rôles such as God, Christ, the Virgin Mary, angels and apostles, were played in a more naturalistic style as a result of being featured in public vernacular dramas. Indeed, in such parts, striving for the realism encountered in everyday life would have been considered indecorous; these characters were still deemed to represent the Creator of the Universe, the Son of God, the Mother of Christ, and any attempt to stress their humanity by making their impersonation on stage conform too closely to actual beings of the mundane world would have been deplored. Iconographical tradition, too, would have controlled the conventions here, as in so many other aspects of the pre-Renaissance stage, and spectators would not expect to witness an 'individual interpretation' of figures already familiar to them from stained-glass window or sculpted façade. In processional performance, where several actors would be required to present God or Christ or Mary, a certain agreed convention of playing would perforce prevail.

Before we leave the amateur theatre, mention must be made of the countless 'dramatic societies' recruited from the inhabitants of English towns and villages who staged plays in their own community and visited other towns to perform there.[83] In towns these groups, like the professionals, seem to have attended on the mayor of the community or the lord of the manor, and then, having performed to official satisfaction, were allowed to play for the benefit of the populace; at court and in monastic institutions, one command performance might be all that could be hoped for. What seems to be an early reference to such a troupe occurs in the records of Winchester College for 1400 when a gift was made to '*lusoribus civitatis Wynton*' (players of the city of Winchester), and a similar troupe were paid 2s. at Epiphany 1466 for presenting four interludes. Between 1422 and 1461 Maxstoke Priory paid various sums to players from 'Eton' Coventry, Daventry, and nearby Coleshill, and Henry VI was generous to some '*jeweis* [Jews] *de Abyndon*' who played interludes before him at Christmas 1427. Obviously such amateur companies could not afford to play far from their place of origin: the household accounts of the Howard family of Stoke-by-Nayland in Suffolk cite payments to players from Stoke itself in January 1466, from Thorington Street, Coggeshall, and Hadleigh in 1481, from 'Esterforde' (which I cannot identify) in 1482, from Sudbury (1483), Chelmsford (1490), and 'Lanam' (1472) which Chambers identifies with Lavenham, but.which might be read as 'Langham', a village a few miles from Stoke. At all events all these places (even Lavenham) lie within a thirty-kilometre (twenty-mile) radius of the Howard home. It was performances by such groups that the king enjoyed or endured as he travelled the country on his royal progresses; when players came to the court in London to appear before royalty and the nobility, it does not appear that they were recruited from much further away than East Anglia, although 'Frenche Pleyers' were received in 1494 and again in 1495.

Amateur players appear to have visited each other's towns fairly often during the second half of the fifteenth century, if the Kentish records are typical of the country as a whole. Such exchanges are well documented for Kentish east coast towns: thus, between August 1450 and July 1452 Lydd gave hospitality at the home of Richard Glover to the '*lusoribus de Romene* [the players of New Romney]' and the wording of the entry suggests their play was also presented in the house; at Christmas 1452 'the men of Herne' played before the mayor of Dover; on 7 July 1454 the people of Lydd entertained players from Ham Street some ten miles off, the play presented possibly having some connection with the Translation of St Thomas of Canterbury celebrated that day. On 1 November of the same year the players of New Romney staged a play at Lydd to commemorate the dedication of the church there, and they did the same in November 1462; they appeared at Lydd again on Whit Monday 1466, and again in 1476—7. New Romney entertained the Lydd troupe in 1456—7, and again in 1467—8; actors from Hythe appeared there in 1465–7. In 1462–3 the citizens of Sandwich enjoyed something of a festival of amateur drama, for during this period they entertained players from Herne, nearby Ash, Deal and Canterbury, and even found 8d. to reward two performers from their own town. By 1489–90 the mayor was witnessing a play brought from as far away as Reading. But it was perhaps Dover which witnessed the widest range of amateur dramatics: in addition to local companies like those from Herne, Thanet, Hythe, Boughton, Sandwich, and Canterbury, as well as many anonymous *'homines ludentes'*, the town also entertained as early as 1475–6 'a pleyar of Pykardy' and 'iiij Playeres of london' in 1484–5 (who may be identified with those receiving 10s. at court in July 1498); in 1486–7 a company from Calais performed in Dover, receiving 5s. and helping to consume 18d. worth of wine, 2d. more than the Canterbury players drank earlier in the same year. Besides local and visiting presentations collaborative productions between towns and villages were not unknown: on 20 July 1511 twenty-seven East Anglian villages combined to stage a play on St George at Bassingbourn, near Cambridge.[84]

There remain the activities of the semi-professional players, forerunners of those ambitious troupes who by the end of the sixteenth century had established Europe's first public theatres in England and Spain. Records suggest that the only players who may be described as true professionals are members of those troupes attached to noble households, who also performed other tasks but who as itinerant companies often played in the private houses of the nobility, in monasteries and similar foundations, and to the common people. The emergence of professional acting in the West cannot be charted with any accuracy, but we may assume that the stage-player gradually separated himself from his minstrel associates during the late fourteenth and fifteenth centuries, to become eventually the professional actor of the Elizabethan playhouses and the Spanish courtyard theatres known as *corrales*. In seeking a more precise picture, we immediately come up against the familiar problem of terminology: Giles Dawson has recently claimed[85] from Kentish records that in the period before 1550 *mimi* and *ministrelli* (minstrels) are two names for the same type of performer, and that *histriones* is a term for minstrels: whether 'minstrels' included drama in their repertoire is not known. However, a reference from Selby Abbey in Yorkshire[86] warns us against interpreting *histriones* as being exclusively used to mean 'play-actors': it reads:

In rewardo dato histrionibus domini Principis videlicet tumblers hoc anno   ijs.

In reward given to the entertainers of the Lord Prince, that is to say tumblers, this year 2s.

The terms Kentish scribes employ for 'players' include *lusores*, *ludatores* and *homines ludentes*, but the attempt to differentiate between the kinds of entertainment offered by 'minstrels' and their kind, and 'players' and theirs, must await further evidence. A minstrel doubtless offered more than music and song and, as Stanley Kahrl points out,[87] English actors continued to be known for their acrobatic, dancing and musical prowess well into the reign of Elizabeth, while the singing clown was an essential member of the London dramatic companies. Demarcation disputes do not seem to have troubled the minds of late medieval or Elizabethan entertainers, and perhaps they do not need to trouble us.

The exact moment at which we may unequivocally state that acting performances as distinct from songs and foolery formed part of an evening's entertainment by professionals is also hard to pinpoint. Where payments to wandering minstrels and *ludentes* are recorded, the earliest evidence of their professing separate skills appears to come from the town accounts of King's Lynn for 1370–1,[88] where two individual payments are set down:

Item de ijs datis menestrallis primo die maij [Item: 2s given to the minstrels on the 1st of May]
Item de iijs iiijd datis Ludentibus eodem die [Item: 3s. 4d. given to the players on the same day]

— a fairly clear indication that the *'menestralles'* and the *'ludentes'* offered different types of diversion to the folk of King's Lynn. In 1384—5 the accounts record two payments for stage-plays:

Et de iijs iiijd solutis quibusdam ludentibus interludium die Corporis Christi de dono [And 3s. 4d. given as a gift to certain players for an interlude on Corpus Christi Day]
Et de iijs iiijd solutis ludentibus interludium Sanci Thome Martiris de dono Maioris [And 3s. 4d. given to players for an interlude of St Thomas the Martyr as a gift from the Mayor]

and the account rolls of Selby Abbey for 1431–2 record a payment to *ludentibus* who played 'before the Lord Abbot at the feast of the Nativity of the Lord'. It would seem as if these performances were staged by troupes of travelling players, paid to entertain their audiences on important feast-days with suitable items from their stock repertoire. A list of expenses incurred at the English court over Christmas 1427,[89] includes the payment of £4 to '*Jakke Travail et ses compaignons feisans*

diverses jeuues et entreludes dedeins le feste de Noell devant notre dit sire le roi
[Jack Travail and his companions putting on various plays and interludes during the feast of Christmas before our aforesaid lord the King]';
this is accompanied by the note of the payment of '20 sol' to the Jews of
Abingdon who staged other interludes during the same period. These
presumably were a local amateur group yet it is interesting to note
both they and Jack Travail's men offered 'entreludes' for the royal delectation. Twenty years later an account book from York gives a glimpse of
another group when it records that in 1447 a payment of 2d. was made
to two players, 'Joly Wat and Malkyn'.[90]

The growing number of allusions to *'ludentes'* and *'lusores'* after
about 1450, and the fact that 'players in their enterludes' are recognised as an individual group in the Act of Apparel of 1464, suggests
that stage-plays were a popular form of entertainment by the middle
of the century, and that professional actors were beginning to establish a meaningful if modest identity. Like the various troupes of
minstrels attached to noble households, the companies of players
appear to have attached themselves to members of the nobility and
the royal family, the earliest indisputable indication coming on 24
January 1478 when Dover corporation paid 5s. to 'playares of my
lord of Arundell', and did so again in Dover in 1478–9; in the following year the townsfolk of Lydd paid 12d to *'lusoribus domini de
Arundell'*, the Earl being Lord Warden of the Cinque Ports at the time.[91]
In 1482 the household of Lord John Howard, later Duke of Norfolk,
records among other payments (including several to amateur players):

9 Jan. 1482, Item, to Senclowe, that he paid to my Lord of Essex men, plaiers,
xx[d].
25 Dec. 1482. Item, on Crystemas day, my Lord gaff to iiij pleyers of my lord
of Gloucestres, iij[s] iiij[d].[92]

Within a year 'my lord of Gloucestre' would be Richard III of England,
and he doubtless retained his players as part of the royal household.

Not only princes and nobles set store by having a troupe of players
under their protection to supply them with dramatic fare when the
need arose, but even relatively modestly placed gentry such as Sir John
Paston kept among their retainers amateur actors such as 'W. Woode'
whose untimely departure has already been alluded to (p. 20 above),
together with Paston's rueful complaint that he had'kepyd hym thys
iij yere to pleye Seynt Jorge *and* Robynhod *and* Shryff off Notyngham'.[93]
The aristocratic custom of maintaining players in one's household is
alluded to by Samuel Cox in a letter of 1591,[94] in which he regrets that

actors no longer 'exercise their interludes' during the season of Christmas, describing the player-retainers of the past as 'such as pertained
to noblemen, and were ordinary servants in their house, and only
for Christmas times used such plays, without making profession
to be players to go abroad for gain.' These men, protected by the
badge of some great lord or important dignitary, were the forerunners
of the Lord Chamberlain's Men or the Lord Admiral's Men of the latter
part of the sixteenth century. At what stage they received their patron's
permission to travel the country in search of audiences is uncertain, but
since the right to entertain outside their lord's household was granted
to minstrels and *histriones* at a fairly early date, it is unlikely to have
been withheld from players. As early as 1465–5 one of the rooms at
Durham Priory was being identified as 'le Playerchambre', and the Winchester college accounts for 1467 contain a payment of 2s to 'John
Pontisbery and his companion' *'ludentibus in aula in die circumcisionis*
[for playing in the hall at the Feast of the Circumcision]' which may
refer to a professional performance, although no patron is named.[95]
It must be remembered that it was not until the Act of 1572 that 'Comon
Players in Enterludes' were obliged to seek the patronage of a noble
protector and even after that date, there was still some dissatisfaction
with the scheme of authorisation, notably from Puritan polemicists
such as Stephen Gosson: 'Such like men, under the title of their maisters
or as reteiners, are priviledged to roave abroad, and permitted to pub-
lish their mametree [idolatry] in everie Temple of God, and that
through England, unto the horrible contempt of praier. So that now the
Sanctuarie is become a plaiers stage, and a den of theeves and adulterers.'[96]

A more temperate picture of the players' proceedings is provided by
Robert Willis in his *Mount Tabor* (1639) where he describes the performance of a moral interlude at Gloucester during his youth (1570–80),
observing

In the city of Gloucester the manner is (as I think it is in other like corporations)
that when Players of Enterludes come to towne, they first attend the Mayor
to enforme him what noble-mans servants they are, and so to get licence for
their publike playing: and if the Mayor like the Actors, or would show respect
to their Lord and Master, he appoints them to play their first play before him-
selfe and the Aldermen and Common Counsell of the City; and that is called
the Mayor's play, where every one that will comes in without money, the
Mayor giving the players a reward as hee thinks fit to shew respect unto them.
At such a play my father tooke me with him, and made mee stand betweene his
leggs as he sate upon one of the benches, where we saw and heard very
well.[97]

Professional players were thus established in Britain by the end of the fifteenth century:[98] although there is no evidence of a regular company of actors at the Scottish court, payments to 'Patrick Johnson and his fallowis' in 1488 and 1489 take on significance in the light of Johnson's tenure of a court position, possibly as a minstrel. By 1494 Henry VII of England certainly had in his household four *'lusores regis, alias in lingua Anglicana*, les pleyars of the Kyngs enterluds' who received five marks as their yearly wage, and special amounts for playing before the king himself. In 1503 they were sent to perform in Scotland under their appropriately named leader John English, during the celebrations at Margaret Tudor's marriage with James IV in Edinburgh. Also performing at the English court during the 1490s were 'my Lorde of Oxon players', and 'my Lorde of Northumberlande Pleyers', and on 1 January 1506 'my lorde Princes players' played in the hall, no doubt under the eye of their youthful patron, later Henry VIII, who was to increase the number of royal interluders to eight. During 1496 the corporation of Shrewsbury entertained, along with the King's and Queen's minstrels, players under the auspices of the Prince, the Earl of Derby, and the Earl of Shrewsbury; a few years earlier (1490–2) the young Thomas More had served in Cardinal Morton's household and stepped in among the players at Christmas, improvising himself a part. A little later, Henry Percy, Earl of Northumberland, was estimating expenditure of 33s. 4d. 'for rewardes to Players for Playes playd in Christynmas by Stranegers in my house' for the year 1511–12, which presumably excluded performances by the Earl's own troupe; in 1514–15 the total sum had risen to 72s. By about 1522–3 the players could be assured of an even more liberal welcome, for a list of Al maner of Rewardis' notes that 'My Lorde usith and accustometh to gif yerely when his Lordshipp is at home to every Erlis Players that comes to his Lordshipe betwixt Christynmas ande Candlemas If he be his speciall Lorde and Frende ande Kynsman xxˢ .... to every Lordis Players, xˢ.' Given sixteenth-century monetary values, a winter expedition might well have been worth the long journey northwards.

8

FINANCING THE PLAYS

The Show is not the Show
But they that go —

Emily Dickinson, Complete Poems.

Up to this point all too little attention has been focussed on the financial support necessary for medieval stage-productions and on the drama's patrons who, according to Dr Johnson, give the drama's laws. As the staging of plays grew more ambitious and complex, so greater resources had to be mobilised in order to cope with production costs. The processes of development often involved going one step further than on previous occasions, and playwrights, players, and organisers, faced with the task of improving on their own previous best, or of competing with a similar enterprise in an adjacent town, soon found that more elaborate facilities or attractive effects required a correspondingly larger outlay, and expense rapidly became a significant factor when arranging for presentations to take place. This short chapter is therefore devoted to the financing of medieval drama, and to the character and conduct of the medieval audience.

The strain of increasing production costs was felt primarily by those organisations responsible for mounting ambitious public performances in the open-air. The companies of semi-professional interluders in the employ of a great lord for much of the year and only occasionally travelling to perform elsewhere, dependent for their livelihood on the bounty of their patron and their various audiences, were probably less affected, since their costs were unlikely to be very high, given the semi-improvised nature of their shows. Hence our main interest must again lie within the sphere of the vernacular religious drama.

It will be as well to reaffirm from the outset that the medieval church's approach to the dramatic spectator was not as discouraging or disinterested as some writers of the past maintained. Even the strictest divines seem to have smiled on audiences reverently congregated to witness devout plays designed to commemorate and further the faith, even though they condemned their presence at unseemly or mirthful *ludi*.[1] Even if the staging of early liturgical drama were not precisely motivated by the same instinct as that of the N-Town cycle, whose Banns proclaim:

> For we purpose us *pertly* stille in this †prese†   openly   crowd
> The pepyl to plese with pleys ful glad,

none the less the presence of an audience was not treated casually, to judge from recorded allusions to the function of church-drama. Thus the introductory rubric to the *Depositio Crucis* contained in the *Regularis Concordia* (see p. 35 above) suggests that it may be thought desirable to observe its ceremonial 'for strengthening the faith of the unlearned masses and of neophytes [*ad fidem indocti vulgi ac neophytorum corroborandam*]';[2] no doubt Katherine of Sutton, Abbess of Barking from 1363–76, created her ceremony of the Elevation of the Host at the close of Easter Matins in much the same mood:[3]

since the assembly of people seemed to grow cold in their devotion at this time, with human apathy greatly increasing, the venerable Lady Katherine of Sutton, being then in her post of pastoral care, desiring to root out the said apathy entirely, and to stimulate more the devotion of the faithful towards such an honoured ceremony of celebration, laid down with the unanimous agreement of the sisterhood that immediately after the third Respond of Matins on Easter Day a celebration of the Lord's Resurrection should be performed.

A *Visitatio* from St Lambrecht in Austria arranges for the lay congregation to join in the singing of two vernacular hymns, the slightly unusual nature of the practice being stressed by the wording of one of the rubrics: *Tunc incipiat ipsa plebs istum clamorem* [Then let the common people themselves begin this hymn loudly],[4] and the Fleury *Herod* also refers to the presence of the *plebs* when its shepherds invite the people to worship at the manger in the rubric running '*invitent populus circumstantem adorandum infantem* [let them invite the people standing around to adore the child]'. That the same traditions of participation and proselytisation continued beyond the strictly liturgical arena is testified by the 1204 record of the *Ludus Prophetarum* from Riga (see p. 129 above), when indeed, the pagan spectators seem to have misunderstood the exact nature of the participation required of them!

That winter a most well-organised *Play of the Prophets* was performed ... in the centre of Riga, in order that those of the heathen persuasion might learn the rudiments of the Christian faith through the evidence of their own eyes. The content of this play or comedy was carefully explained to the neophytes and the pagans who were present, through an expositor [*interpres*].

However, when Gideon's force fought against the Philistines, the pagans, frightened that they themselves were about to be slaughtered, began to run away, but they were brought back again although very wary.[5]

The same kind of motivation lies behind the earliest German *Fronleichnamsspiel* of 1391 from Innsbruck, which begins with the rubric:

Here begins a play about the Catholic faith, beneficial to the devotion of the simple people, to be performed on Corpus Christi Day, or during the octave [i.e. the festival and the seven days afterwards].
Incipit ludus utilis pro devotione simplicium intimandus et peragendus die corporis Christi, vel infra octavas, de fide katholica.[6]

Striking evidence that the Corpus Christi plays often actually fulfilled their didactic purposes is contained in a well-known anecdote from the Lake District recorded by a Puritan parson of the seventeenth century, who had asked an old man of Cartmel if he had ever heard of salvation through Christ:

Oh sir, said he, I think I heard of that man you speak of, once in a play at Kendal called Corpus Christi play, where there was a man on a tree and blood ran down, &c. And after, he professed that though he was a good Churchman ... yet he could not remember that ever he heard of salvation by Jesus Christ, but in that play.[7]

Thus the spectator's importance in the medieval theatre and the desirability of his watching religious drama is well attested to. Less well documented is the rôle played by the audience in secular performances, but the tone of such pieces as *Le Garçon et l'Aveugle, De Clerico et Puella*, the farce of *Maître Pathelin*, or the Tudor interludes of John Heywood, indicates that audience response and involvement were primary considerations with devisers of profane as well as sacred entertainments. In each case, to stage a presentation as worthily and satisfyingly as possible was essential, for inadequate productions meant in the religious sphere an obscuring of the Christian message and disgrace in the eyes of the community, while in the secular sector failure would certainly mean the withdrawal of patronal largesse or popular liberality. In both instances, spectators form an integral element of the performance, and some financial outlay was a preliminary requisite for eventual success.

Unfortunately almost all monetary details of medieval productions occur late in the period, and deductions based on such evidence are unlikely to possess general validity for preceding centuries. Local practices differ one from another too, and while resemblances are occasionally remarkable, even typical financial procedures merely demonstrate once again that the medieval stage exploited a wide *variety* of methods in attaining its ends.

Thus the great civic spectacles of the fifteenth and sixteenth centuries were sponsored in a number of different ways. The fact that these productions were communal affairs, supported by both the church and the city authorities acting through both the religious fraternities and craft guilds or through organisations specially established to stage and control the presentations, meant that financial support was not hard to seek or difficult to arrange, at least in theory. Considerable resources were available, especially if the city were prosperous and its citizens jealous of its reputation. Occasionally the nobility and even royalty are found making a contribution to expenses, as in 1456 when René of Anjou (see pp. 88—9 above) paid eighteen gold *écus* for a command performance of a Resurrection play at Metz:[8] no doubt when his daughter Margaret visited Coventry for the plays in the following year (see pp. 114—15 above), an appropriate sum found its way into the city's coffers. Certainly in 1462 René remitted 600 livres in taxes at Saumur because a *mystère* of the Passion there incurred heavy expenditure. But such windfalls were not regular payments which could be relied on: sounder methods of financing the plays had to be found, and these included the soliciting of monetary gifts, loans, or guarantees from private individuals, the levy of a tax on the community as a whole, on sponsoring bodies such as the guilds, or on the actors themselves, and the raising of funds by means which included the time-honoured *quête* (street or house-to-house collecting), sales of produce, 'church-ales', and earmarking rents and tithes for dramatic purposes. The wisdom of securing such funds in advance is demonstrated in a payment made by the municipal authorities at Rouen in 1454 to four *confréries* who had staged a *mystère* on the life of St Catherine, allocated as a gesture of sympathy because the play had been 'celebrated and presented in a most distinguished way, with very high expenses and costs, greater indeed by a good deal than what they managed to collect [*célébré et démonstré moult notablement à très grands frais et coustaiges et plus grands de beaucoup que l'on ne cudoit*]'.[9]

The most obvious method of financing medieval civic dramatics was from municipal funds, and this appears to have been the practice adopted most widely on the Continent, the treasury being replenished from any income subsequently received. Occasionally this arrangement worked to the benefit of the town, but often it was far from satisfactory: expenses for the staging of *Le Mystère des Trois Doms* at Romans in 1509 totalled 1,737 florins, and the takings and sale of materials only realised just over 738 florins, leaving the town and the Chapter of St Bernard to find almost 1,000 florins to cover the deficit. Similarly, the 1501 production at Mons lost money: expenses came to 2,281 livres, 18 sols, 6 deniers, and receipts to only 1,338 livres, 4 sols, 4 deniers, the deficit again having to be made up, presumably out of civic funds.[10] Later in the century at Lucerne, the city bore the main share of the total production costs, that share for the 1571 presentation amounting to over 1,233 Gulden, excluding the cost of erecting stands for spectators and stations for the actors. In addition, the Brotherhood of the Crown of Thorns and private individuals made some contribution, but no details of these survive. The high expenditure at Lucerne does not seem to have been offset by entrance fees or other receipts, but no doubt the incidental advantages accruing to the town in the form of increased commercial benefits compensated for the financial burdens: however, in 1571 the city council certainly refused to meet exorbitant debts incurred by extravagant groups of actors and then claimed as legitimate expenses for subsistence. At Valenciennes, by contrast, the organisers and performers themselves financed the production and shared the profits: expenditure totalled over 4,179 livres, but receipts came to over 4,680 livres; when the proceeds from the sale of materials after the performance were added, the grand profit was 1,230 livres, 2 sols, 3 deniers, which was divided among the 'sharers', something of a triumph for private enterprise.[11]

In Britain a variety of methods was employed to support drama: the means most often referred to is the tax variously known as 'Pageant-pence' or 'Pageant-silver' levied on all the members of a guild partici-pating in the performances or processions of Corpus Christi or some other feast day. The records of the York Glovers of about 1476 state that native-born guildsmen paid 2d. annually towards the guild's pageant, while 'straungers' were assessed at 4d. In 1525 the Coventry Weavers received 'of the masters for the pagynt money xvj s iiij d', while the Smiths in '6 Edw VI [1552–3] reseyved of the craft for pagent pencys iij s iiij d', and the Cappers in 1562 accepted 'of the fellowship for pageant xxxij s iiij d'. On 18 June 1519 the Lincoln Common Council recorded that 'it is Agreid that every man And woman within this Citie beyng Able Schall be Broder & Syster in Scaynt Anne gyld & to pay yerely iiij[d] Man & wyf at the lest.' At Chester the Smiths' Company in 1554 was levying 2s. 4d. annually from each of its guildsmen and about 1d. from each of its journeymen, and in 1575 one Arthur Tailer, a dyer, went to prison rather than contribute to the pageant-money.[12]

Such levies doubtless went some of the way towards meeting the necessary expenses of performance, bearing in mind that pageant-carts, stages, properties and costumes could often be preserved and used again in subsequent years, although sometimes it was a matter of pride that fresh apparel and furnishings should appear each year. The aldermen and sheriffs of Lincoln made their contribution to the St Anne's Guild parade in costume form, as an ordinance of the council dated 28 May 1523 makes plain:

Also it is Agreid that every Alderman of this Citie Schall Acordyng to An olde Acte Afore made have A gowne for preparyng of the kynges in Scaynt Anne Gyld *Awther* of hys Awne As it is Afore ordynyd or els To borow one gowne for that dey uppon payn of xl^s To be Forfyt of every person that dooth the Contrary & payd And every †Scheryfpere† To Have Won person Arayed in An honest Gowne of Cloth goyng Among the profytes in procession of the Same Gyld uppon payn of xx^s.[13]
*either †a minor dignitary.

But in many places a claim on the city's budget obviously did not offer sufficient security, either because resources were non-existent, limited, or suspect, or because the authorities were not concerned to take responsibility for dramatic ventures. In some cases, communal assets were pooled, as at Bassingbourn, Cambridgeshire, in July 1511 (see p. 217 above); recent research has revealed similar practices taking place at Blighborough in Suffolk and Dunmow in Essex, large parishes which acted as centres of dramatic activity for a much wider area. Entries in the New Romney records for 1560, where we read 'recd of the gifte of the parishe of Ivechurch towardes our playe iij^s iij^d ... recd of the gyfte of the towne of Lydd towardes our playe x^s', may refer to similarly organised payments although, since Lydd was quite wealthy and sizeable enough to have its own plays, it is doubtful if the payment of ten shillings were anything more than a gesture of good will or a *quid pro quo*.[14]

The New Romney production of 1560 was partly floated on private loans, and this seems to have been the case elsewhere: in 1491 three or four hundred private citizens of Rouen contributed to the costs of mounting a *mystère* for Charles VIII, presumably in the belief that they would see their money back when the show was staged.[15] At Louth in Lincolnshire in 1556–7 it was Mr Goodall, the local schoolmaster, who financed the staging of plays, one of the two relevant records reading: 'paid to Mr Goodall for certeyn mony by him laid furth for the furnishing of the play played in the Markit stede [place] on Corpus Christi Day'.[16] At Chelmsford in 1562 the 'summer dramatic festival' of four plays in the town and its environs was supported by loans from nine prominent townsmen who invested a total of almost £21 between them; the plays were a financial disaster, losing over £11, and one contributor's personal investment of £4 was apparently never returned. The rest were repaid from other sources of church income, which (as we have already seen) included hiring fees for its extensive wardrobe of costumes: by 1574 the hiring charges had brought in almost £29 for the church, and the sale of the costumes fetched almost £7.[17] Sales of clothing and materials immediately after the production were also common, and helped greatly in defraying any loss: at Mons in 1501 sales of cloth raised 18 livres, materials at Romans in 1509 realised 58 florins, and 728 livres at Valenciennes. Selling the New Romney wardrobe in 1560 brought in £10, and 40s. resulted from selling the 'hole stage of the play' at Canterbury in 1542–3.[18]

Individual investment and municipal generosity were often supplemented with fund-raising ventures:[19] doubtless typical was a 'church-ale' held after a play performed at Bishop's Stortford around 1490 at which a collection was made, while at the church of St Mary Hill, London, an annual 'Hocking' (see p. 8 above) raised enough money for a dinner for the collectors as well as providing funds for drama. At Holbeach, Lincolnshire, in 1539 16d. 'Gaderett in ye chyrches upon Corpus Christy day' was probably applied to defray the costs of a pageant there.[20] At Heybridge in Essex farm produce was collected together by the churchwardens and afterwards sold to benefit future play-performances, while at Ipswich[21] in 1445 40s. a year raised in grazing rights 'from the farmers of the Common Marshe and the Portmen's medow' was allocated to the maintenance of the Corpus Christi pageant and its stages. It is also reported (though uncorroborated) that at Lincoln in 1420 tithes amounting to 8s. 8d. were assigned to Thomas Chamberlayne for a spectacle or pageant;[22] there seems little doubt that the fee paid for the right to the rents of Lincoln's St Anne's Guild, whose collection was reorganised in 1515, was partly used to finance annual pageants in the city. Such fees complemented the 4d. required of each brother and sister of the guild and noted above. Civic corporations also raised considerable sums from renting to the guilds pageant-houses where waggons and gear were stored:[23] at York these rents ranged from 4d. to 1s., and at Chester from 4d. to 8d.

Actors too were frequently compelled to contribute to the cost of mounting plays in which they appeared; at Valenciennes, as we have seen (page 205 above) the terms of their contract provided for each performer to pay a gold *écu* from which his fines were to be deducted, and which acted as his 'membership fee', enabling him to share in any final profit or loss on the production. In the same way, at Lucerne late in the century, a general fund to assist the city council with production expenses was created, to which actors paid a tax consistent with the importance of the rôle undertaken, thirty-eight parts being assessed at the top rate of forty schillings, and forty more at thirty schillings. But it seems unlikely that everyone's fee was duly paid.[24]

Not so casually enforced was the elaborate system of fines and forfeits imposed collectively and individually, on those pageant-masters, guilds, or fraternities who failed to 'bring forth' their pageant or who performed their appointed play inadequately, and on those players who forgot their lines, arrived late or were absent without cause, disputed the superintendents' decisions, or drank during rehearsals or performances. These sums too were in all likelihood ploughed back into the subsidies allotted to the plays on future occasions: the authorities were not seeking to profit from the weaknesses of the organisers or their casts, but to uphold a high standard of presentation, and to assert their right to see money well spent.

Many medieval performances were presented without a charge being made to spectators, a notion which our more commercially minded age may find incredible; we may attribute such apparent liberality to a desire not to sully the doctrinal purity of the plays' impact, or to the difficulties of collecting donations or enforcing a charge in congested areas. However, it remains true that records from dramatic centres such as Chester and Coventry contain no mention of monies received, while it is unlikely that even at Lucerne, where more copious documentation exists, any entrance charges were exacted, at least by the city fathers. Windows in buildings overlooking the marketplace were certainly rented out for private profit, and it is just possible that seats in the specially erected stands had to be reserved in advance and a hiring-fee paid, but the fact is not recorded. More lucrative at Lucerne was the practice of supplying lodgings for visiting spectators who also spent their cash liberally in the city's shops and hostelries: similar customs noted elsewhere formed a regular feature of medieval theatrical attendance. Thus at Issoudun in 1535, we are informed, *'tout le jeu dura un mois, et presque tous les bourgeois d'Issoudun logeaient des etrangers tout comme aux foires de Francfort* [the play in its entirety lasted a month, and almost all the citizens of Issoudun put up visitors exactly as they do for the fairs at Frankfurt].[25]

However, admission fees were known, and if the play were satisfactorily performed and the box-office efficiently organised, this was probably the most reliable method of ensuring a satisfactory return on capital investment, given good weather and a judicious budget which permitted dignity but curbed opulence. Spectator-accommodation and admission procedure obviously varied from place to place, but in most cases a hierarchical arrangement was maintained, on the principle that privilege and comfort had to be paid for at a higher rate than the mere opportunity to spectate. Such a segregated system may have derived from the world of medieval tournaments where privileged officials and dignitaries and the court ladies in whose honour the jousts and tilts were staged occupied raised stands or scaffolds sheltered from the elements with roofs and hangings, the women's accommodation separated from the men's, while the common people often had an area of the tiltyard or even special stands designated for their own use.[26] Segregation by rank is a similar feature of medieval front-of-house management: typical is what we read of the *Passion* staged at Vienne in 1510 in the 'great garden of St Peter's Abbey' where 'the most gorgeous scaffolds were constructed, consisting of two storeys, in addition to the ground level for the common people [*furent faicts les plus beaux escharfaux questoyent a deux estages oultre le bas pour le commun peuple*]'. At Tours on 30 July 1485 a sum of over fifteen livres was provided to furnish two scaffolds for Margaret of Austria's ladies-in-waiting, gentlemen, and court officials to watch a Passion play; at Montferrand in 1477 the spectators' scaffolds had to be hastily enlarged to accommodate the well-to-do, and the burghers of Lucerne for their 1583 performance were particularly concerned to reserve certain stands for visiting clergy and distinguished guests. Elsewhere rooms in private houses overlooking the playing-place or processional route were hired or commandeered for the use of royal or noble spectators. Thus Margaret of Anjou probably watched the Coventry plays from the house of 'Richard Wodes the grocer' in 1457, and Henry VII saw the London pageants for Katherine of Aragon in 1501 from the home of a haberdasher, William Geffrey; the mayor and his brethren witnessed the procession at Chester from the galleries and windows of the townhall, and I have suggested that this may have been partially the practice at York (see pp. 118–19 above).[27]

When admission charges were levied, affluence rather than eminence was the chief factor in determining a spectator's location: at Mons in 1501 entry to the arena or *parc* cost twelve deniers, while admission to the raised seating cost three sous, which may even have been an additional rather than an alternative charge. At the Valenciennes performance of 1547 the entrance fee was six deniers but it cost twice that amount to view the play from seating mounted on the scaffolds, and at Romans in 1509, while a seat on the scaffold could be purchased for one sol on each of the first two days and only ½ a sol on the third, it cost three florins a day to rent a *loge* or private box, 36 times the price of a seat in the stands. At Valence-sur-Rhône in 1526 the privileged places were not rated uniformly: *loges* on two different levels were leased at two different prices, the lower *chambres* being rated at fifteen sous, the higher at only twelve, possibly because they were less accessible or less well shielded from the sunlight: a sliding scale of reductions applied to those occupying the *loges* closest to the infernal *mansion*, since pleasure or concentration might be impaired by the diabolic din emanating from that region! Accommodation for the commons was obviously not as sumptuous or comfortable as that provided for the better-off, whose *loges* or *chambres* were often handsomely carpeted and adorned with hangings, but even the ordinary spectator's convenience was consulted, so that the provision of seats was often though not invariably a feature of even the cheapest areas of the auditorium, in France at least. When Jean Neyron erected his theatre at Lyon in 1540, basing it on the accustomed pattern, it was observed that 'the galleries had three storeys one above the other, and there was a large and spacious area below with benches for the humbler folk', while the Valenciennes records mention the provision of wood for scaffolds and benches 'on the lower level [*d'en bas*]'. At Meaux in 1547 we are told that there were tiered wooden seats (*degrés de planche*) all round the playing-area. On the other hand, in some situations such as the more modest stage arrangement depicted in Fouquet's miniature, some spectators (probably those at the rear) had to stand in order to see the action; those nearer the front probably sat on the ground or knelt.[28]

Unfortunately, it is more difficult to build up a clear picture of British as opposed to French practice, far less data concerning admission and seating arrangements having survived. It may be inferred from what information exists in Britain, that if any charge was made to spectators, the organisers of plays relied on 'passing the hat round' among the audience, and trusted their 'gatherers' to deliver up all that they had been able to collect. Substantial sums might be realised by this means, especially if indoor performance made evasion ineffective: three church presentations of saints' plays at Braintree in Essex during 1523, 1525, and 1534 grossed £6 14s. 11½d., £8 9s. 6d., and £14 17s. 6½d. respectively; the total takings for the four open-air performances at New Romney in 1560 came to over £26, if one includes the 'giftes' from Ivychurch and Lydd. However, when at Sutterton in Lincolnshire in 1525–6 3s. 6½d. was 'Resavyd of Gateryng' on the occasion that players of Frampton and Kirton performed, their reward of 6s. 8d. presumably had to be supplemented out of parish funds.[29]

The financial background to the major cycle sequences in Britain is far from clear: we know that at York the stations on the processional route, leased out after 1416 by the civic authorities to the highest bidder who would pay for the privilege, were furnished with scaffolds containing seating for which spectators were charged a fee. Thus on 11 May 1554 the city council decreed 'that suche as woll have pageantz played before ther doores shall come in and aggree for theym before Trynytie Sonday next or elles to have none and the places to be appoynted by discrecion of my Lord Maior accustomed.'[30] However, during the sixteenth century revenues from the lease of stations declined, partly the result of lower rentals, partly through the establishment of several lease-free stations for civic notables: it is unclear whether stands for paying spectators were erected at these sites, or whether the public could watch there for nothing. The documents referring to rentals on the stations at York are among the few we possess which shed any light on the levying of admission fees for watching drama in Britain during the period under discussion. The likeliest inference is that on most occasions and at most centres the cycle plays and pageants could be viewed free of charge, although comfort and a superior prospect might have to be paid for.

The size, behaviour, and control of medieval audiences remain for analysis, but here again wide variations render generalisation impossible. To discover the true number of spectators attending representations in the Middle Ages is difficult, and contemporary estimates must be approached with caution, for medieval chroniclers have a dubious record for accuracy especially where large totals of any kind are involved. Henri Rey-Flaud has estimated that roughly 5,000 spectators a day would have attended the *mystères* staged at Romans in 1509, at Vienne in the following year, and at Valenciennes in 1547, and that this figure was probably surpassed only in exceptional circumstances, as at Reims in 1490 (*c.* 5,600), Autun in 1516, and Bourges in 1536.[31] How far these numbers correspond to those witnessing an English cycle performance is a matter for speculation, especially when the actual method of performance itself is often so uncertain. Most of the figures from the Continent derive from records of (or calculations based on) single-site presentations: processional performance complicates the assessment of audience size to an impossible extent. But we can use the extant information as a rough guide to the typical number of spectators attending public performances in the Middle Ages.

Such extensive audiences created problems of crowd-control for those responsible for good order at the plays: in several places strict rules were laid down concerning even eligibility as a spectator, for at Beauvais in 1452 the commons were expressly forbidden to occupy the better seats without a ticket.[32] At Mons in 1501 no children under ten were admitted, no frail elderly people, and no pregnant women; no children were allowed to attend at Valence in 1526, although at Romans in 1509 the carpenters were specifically instructed to add a cross-beam to the barriers before the *chambres 'à cause des petis enfans* [on account of the tiny children]'. Solicitude for the well-being of the clientèle at Romans is notable: here four *'lieux d'aisance'* occupied the corners of the theatre and each *chambre* was provided with a key so that valuables could be left in the box overnight. At Vienne too lavatories or *'retraits'* were available in 1510, and during lengthy performances any lack of such facilities must have been sorely felt.[33] Food and drink were certainly a prerequisite for attendance at most medieval performances, whether bought in the playing-place itself, imported from home, or supplied gratis; thus at Amiens in 1445 it was agreed that 'the mayor and the magistrates will dine on their scaffold'.[34]

No doubt such vast crowds as attended medieval plays in holiday mood produced a considerable volume of noise, since texts and accounts abound in references to the necessity for silence during the performance.[35] At Angers in 1486 the organisers decreed that the Prologue, a priest, should celebrate Mass before the play began, 'both to make a better start and to ensure silence [*pour mieux commancer et avoir sillence*]', while on the third day children were to 'sing sweetly until perfect silence shall prevail [*chantans melodieusement jusques ad ce que bonne silence soit faite*]'. St Peter in *Le Mystère de saint Étienne* makes a typical request for silence at the play's opening:

> *Doulces gens, un pou escouter*
> *Pesiblement, sans noise faire*

Gentle people, listen peacefully for a little while without making a trouble.

and at Autun in 1516 it is recorded as worthy of mention that 'God granted that on this occasion no whistlings, common uproar, mockery, or barracking were let forth'. But such a peaceful atmosphere could rarely be guaranteed, and it appears to have been the general custom, as it was in northern France in 1449, to have five or six officials to 'throw out those who make a nuisance of themselves [*widier ceux qui empescheroient*]', a possible function of the 'stytelerys' of *The Castel of Perseverance*: 'controllers' certainly feature at Romans and Valenciennes. Brawls and quarrels both on stage and in the auditorium did mar the proceedings occasionally: at Romans in 1509 one of those playing the devils attacked a woman in the audience who owed him money, while at Sainte-Honorine in 1516 a fight broke out among the spectators, bringing the play to a halt.[36] In 1419 the York Skinners were set upon by the Cordwainers and Carpenters as they processed with their torches on Corpus Christi Day.[37] Nor was such violence always extraneous to the dramatic offering: when in 1502 a Terentian comedy in Latin was presented at the episcopal palace at Metz before an audience of clerics and townsfolk, the commons, realising that they were not going to understand the play, attacked the performers and so compelled the actors to desist.[38]

However, such incidents, though serious, must be kept in proportion, and even when the Reformation and its doctrinal controversy sparked off a number of partisan demonstrations and outbreaks of violence at performances of plays,[39] such affrays were still sufficiently unusual to be chronicled for posterity. In general medieval playgoers were probably no better or worse in their behaviour than any similar body of publicly assembled spectators at any period of history, and one may imagine that, their principal object in assembling to watch plays being their own enjoyment, they themselves in their corporate identity as an audience usually acted as the most effective guardians of good order and public morality.

EPILOGUE

That swich a noble theatre it was,
I dar wel seyen in this world ther nas.

Geoffrey Chaucer, *The Knyghtes Tale*.

The impact of the western European Renaissance of the fifteenth and
sixteenth centuries did not sweep away medieval artistic forms and
practices overnight. Men continued to present plays in the medieval
manner late into the sixteenth century, and even the co-existence of
newer modes of staging did not divert them from long-familiar techniques and conventions.

The historian of theater must regard the sixteenth century as an age of
transition when he notices the existence, side by side, of the most diverse
stage forms — the old medieval and the new Renaissance. And we cannot
even say that, as the century progressed, the medieval multiple stage with
mansions in juxtaposition was replaced by the Renaissance stage with its
unity of impression ... Some sixteenth-century stages were frankly medieval,
others had a definite Renaissance character, still others were what I would
like to call hybrid stage forms, incorporating stylistically heterogeneous elements in contrast to the other stylistically pure stages.[1]

Nevertheless the main initiative in matters of dramatic composition
and presentation rested very much with advocates of those neo-classical
modes whose vogue accompanied the scholarly and artistic recovery of
the spirit of the Greek and Roman cultures. In the field of drama, a
recent commentator assures us that 'perhaps no other genre, not even
the epic, shows such a direct and overwhelming influence from Graeco-
Roman example',[2] and the predominantly Italian fashion for translating and performing classical drama was not only matched by a spate of
literary imitations of Plautus and Seneca, but by a growing interest in
rediscovering the practical details of theatrical performance in classical
times. Even before the discovery, and publication in 1486, of Vitruvius's
ten books *De Architectura*, with its fifth book devoted to theatre-
planning, a number of eminent Italian artists and designers, stimulated
by the recovery of the scientific principles of perspective, had begun to
revolutionise the basic aesthetic notions which had lain behind
medieval stage-presentation.[3]

The results of their work can be observed transforming the visual arts before they become apparent in the theatre, and George Kernodle has shown convincingly how the new principles of the Renaissance stage were manifested most markedly in an artistic quest for a more mature and complex kind of unity:

Where the Middle Ages had been content with many disparate units or details which were only loosely bound together, the new age felt that these units or details must be organized into some kind of unity ... While a time art had to present each point of reference, each scenic element, separately, a space art could achieve unity by organizing all the separate elements into one picture or one architectural structure.[4]

Kernodle argues that it was in new principles expressed through architecture, painting, and the plastic arts that neo-classical scenic design had its origin rather than in the rediscovery of the classical stage, but it still seems probable that Vitruvius's treatise, with its description of the *scenae frons* at the rear of the stage platform pierced by its exit and entrance doors, helped to condition men's minds to an alternative method of staging from one which employed multiple settings consisting of a number of separated locations in juxtaposition. Those anxious to follow the precedents of antiquity would in particular be swift to adopt methods of presentation governed by the notion that only a single location be portrayed on stage, and while we should not assume that the aim behind such designs was to create a photographically accurate reproduction of an actual street or landscape, since conventional, symbolic, two-dimensional devices did still appear, the Renaissance stage-picture had as its main objective a much greater degree of realism and illusion than the medieval stage had ever striven for: 'the convention of an open street scene organized by perspective enabled [men] to represent space and depth with an illusion of reality that had not been possible before'.[5]

Evidence for the establishment of this principle in stage practice is not easily found: the new desire for unity did not manifest itself in new techniques all at once. In 1513, when Plautus's *Poenulus* was presented in Rome for the Medici festival there, Tommaso Inghirami who had directed earlier performances of Plautus in the 1490s mounted the piece on a temporary wooden stage, 27 metres (90 feet) long by 6 metres (20 feet) deep, backed by a scenic façade divided by means of columns into five compartments, each screened off by a gold curtain across the front, apparently conforming to the 1493 woodcuts and the 1502 description in Badius Ascensius's editions of Terence.[6] Each 'hiding place' represented a citizen's house, and two further means of access were provided on each side of the stage, but all that seems to differ from medieval convention is that the houses are now deemed to be part of a single location. Similar settings may have been used by Konrad Celtus in the hall of Vienna University where he presented plays by Terence and Plautus with student casts from 1502–3 onwards; certainly at Leipzig in the 1530s, when one Muschler produced a German translation of Terence's *Hecyra* in the city-hall, three scenic houses were arranged along the proscenium to suggest a residential street between the harbour and the market of a Greek city. Yet although the multiple setting of the typical medieval production was gradually being eroded (even outside Italy) by the pure Renaissance single setting on illusionistic principles, demonstrating a new feeling for the unity of place, for a time the two principles of staging lived side by side in many European countries, each content to mingle its scenic forms and conventions with those derived from the other.

In Italy, however, the introduction of the illusion of perspective into stage scenery, and the affluence of those princely sponsors who could command the services of inventive designers and technicians, meant that the trend towards verisimilitude was much more marked there than in countries where symbolic convention still ruled virtually unchallenged. As early as 1513, when Bibbiena's *La Calandria*, staged at the court of Urbino, enjoyed the advantages of perspective scenery by Girolamo Genga, Baldassare Castiglione, author of the celebrated *Book of the Courtier*, described the occasion thus:

The stage represented a very beautiful city, with streets, palaces, churches, and towers. The streets looked as if they were real, and everything was done in relief, and made even more striking through the art of painting and well-conceived perspective. Among other things there was an octagonal temple in low relief ... done in stucco and decorated with the most beautiful historical pictures. The windows seemed to be made of alabaster, while all the architraves and cornices gave the impression of having been made of fine gold and ultramarine blue. At certain points were pieces of glass used in imitation of jewels, which looked like genuine gems. Round the temple were carved pillars and statues that simulated marble.[7]

Such admiring emphasis on isolated marvels of visual illusion and deception also occurs in accounts of medieval plays, as we have seen, but that the entire stage-setting should now deceive the eye as to its actuality is a departure of some importance. When *La Calandria* was revived at Rome in 1514, the perspective scenery by Baldassare Peruzzi won this significant comment from Giorgio Vasari in his *Lives of the Painters*: 'It is wonderful how, in the narrow space, he depicted his streets, palaces and curious temples, loggias and cornices, *all made to make them appear to be what they represent* [my italics].'[8] Critical comments like these become commonplace as the century proceeds, and perspective scenery received encouraging endorsement with the publication in 1545 of the second book of Sebastiano Serlio's *Regole generali di architectura.* Serlio was a pupil of Peruzzi, and had himself constructed a theatre on Vitruvian principles in the courtyard of the Academy at Vicenza during the 1530s: in his book he offers advice on building perspective stage-sets after the models described by Vitruvius as characteristic of the Greek theatre. For comedies, a street scene is appropriate, with 'a brawthell or bawdy house', an inn, a church, and various domestic dwellings 'for Citizens'; for tragedies, a similar street is necessary but containing 'none but stately houses' ('for that actions of love, strange adventures, and cruell murthers ... happen always in the houses of great Lords, Dukes, Princes, and Kings'); a rustic scene with woodland and cottages is recommended for satyr plays. However, Serlio emphasises the scenic delights to be achieved through skilful artifice backed by conspicuous expenditure, rather than the desirability of verisimilitude:

you must make these things of Silke, which will be more commendable then the naturall things themselves: and as in other Scenes for Comedies or Tragedies, the houses or other artificiall things are painted, so you must make Trees, Hearbs, and other things in these; the more such things cost, the more they are esteemed, for they are things which stately and great persons doe, which are enemies to nigardlinesse. This have I seene in some Scenes made by Ieronimo Genga, for the pleasure and delight of his lord and patron Francisco Maria, Duke of Urbin: wherein I saw so great liberalitie used by the Prince, and so good a conceit in the workman, and so good Art and proportion in things therein represented, as ever I saw in all my life before. Oh good Lord, what magnificence was there to be seene.[9]

The Italians might differ as to the relative values to be placed on magnificence and realism, but their attitude to stage illusion contrasted greatly with that of those who still worked within purely medieval stage conventions. Comments on the alleged incongruities and inadequacies of medieval staging methods were heard from humanist writers such as the Dutch playwright Cornelius Crocus in the preface to his *Joseph* in 1535: 'It is impossible to tolerate that places which are widely separated are suddenly forced together on one stage, a thing which by itself is most absurd and has no precedent in antiquity.'[10] A similar gibe at the medieval principle of geographically disparate but simultaneously visible scenic structures placed in juxtaposition on the playing-area is found in the *Poetices* (1561) of Julius Caesar Scaliger, where the Frenchman remarks: 'Nowadays they act plays in France in such a fashion that everything remains in full view of the audience. The whole scenic apparatus is set up on a high place. The characters in the play never leave the stage. Those who do not speak are presumed to be absent. It is highly ridiculous.'[11] Sir Philip Sidney in *An Apology for Poetrie* (written *c.* 1581–3) complains in equivalent terms of English stage-plays,

where you shal have *Asia* of the one side, and *Affrick* of the other, and so many other under-kingdoms, that the Player, when he commeth in, must ever begin with telling where he is, or els the tale wil not be conceived. Now ye shal have three Ladies walke to gather flowers, and then we must beleeve the stage to be a Garden. By and by, we heare newes of shipwracke in the same place, and then wee are to blame if we accept it not for a Rock. Upon the backe of that, comes out a hidious Monster, with fire and smoke . . . two Armies flye in, re-presented with foure swords and bucklers, and then what harde heart will not receive it for a pitched fielde?[12]

A more marked example of a fundamental lack of sympathy with medieval staging-methods could scarcely be imagined.

Other forces at work during the sixteenth century sought to outlaw medieval dramatic performances, not on aesthetic but doctrinal grounds. It was inevitable that, since so much medieval drama origin-ated in and centred on the beliefs and practices of the Roman Catholic Church, Reformist zeal should demand its suppression in those countries where Protestantism was to establish itself as the national faith. Harold C. Gardiner has perceptively observed:

The very nature of the doctrinal content of Protestantism carried within itself the seed that was to spring later into open hostility to any dramatic representa-tions of sacred history such as Catholic Europe had known. The subjectivism of Protestantism, which called for an ever-increasing rejection of the mediation of creatures between the soul and God, particularly when these creatures, in representing the saints and holy things, could be misunderstood as incentives to idolatry, would see in the religious stage but another horrible example of how Rome was content with the outward symbol, leaving the reality it re-presented untouched, uncared for. The individualism which rejected any authoritative interpretation of the Scriptures would scarcely tolerate the traditional meanings of Bible phrase and incident, such as the religious stage propagated. A theology which overemphasized to distortion the severer aspects of Christian revelation would have little patience with the literature which owed its origin in great part to the surge of Christian sensibility and tenderness, which had its first stirrings in the twelfth century and swept over Europe in the thirteenth and fourteenth, bringing with it a new concept of art and poetry.[13]

These are admittedly the words of a Jesuit scholar unsympathetic to Protestantism, but Father Gardiner amply demonstrates how, particularly in England, the religious stage did not disappear.

because ecclesiastical authority simply made vocal and effective a traditional Catholic mistrust of the religious drama or because the people were only too glad to shake off the economic burdens of the plays, which a declining guild system and new forms of poverty rendered them unable to support longer. The plays did not die out through distaste but remained extremely popular until their last days, which came, not from any internal decay, but from an external force, the hostility of the Reformation.[14]

It is clear that in Protestant countries performances of the traditional religious plays, far from falling gradually into abeyance, were deliberately extinguished by those who regarded such representations as idolatrous relics of a superstitious past; with them went many of the theatrical forms and conventions discussed in this book.

Instances of such suppressions can be multiplied from countries subject to the infiltration of Protestant ideas during the sixteenth century: after its performance in 1523 the Freiburg Whitsun play was abandoned, and in the same year the Nuremberg Good Friday play met with the same fate. The most celebrated prohibition is contained in a decree of the Paris Parlement of 17 November 1548, which forbade the Confrérie de la Passion to present sacred *mystères*, and began a movement which soon spread to the French provinces, being followed by similar measures in the Parlements of Bordeaux and Rouen in 1556, and at Rennes before 1565.[15] In the Paris edict the Parlement

restrains and forbids the said petitioners to perform the mystery play of our Saviour's Passion, or to play other sacred *mystères* on pain of a discretionary fine, permitting them nevertheless the freedom to present other worthy and lawful secular *mystères* without offending or harming anyone; and the said court forbids all others to perform or stage henceforth any plays or *mystères*, in the city or its suburbs as well as in the outskirts of Paris, except under the name of the said *confrérie* and for the benefit of the same.[16]

In the year that the Parisian ban was promulgated, it was agreed at a law day held on 10 December 1548 in Hereford to spend the money contributed by 'dyvers corporacions of artiffycers, craftes, and occupacions in the sayd cytey, who were bound by the grauntes of their corporacions yerely to bring forthe and set forward dyvers pageauntes of ancyentt historyes in the processyons in the sayd cytey upon the day and feast of Corpus Christi, which now ys and are omitted and surceased'[17] on repairs to the 'ruinous and decayed' causeways, pavements, streets, and walls, or on cleaning the town ditch. It may be that the Hereford 'plays' were simply a procession of religious tableaux, but their discontinuance by 1548 seems definite enough. In the same year plays featuring the Death, Assumption, and Coronation of the Blessed Virgin Mary were excised from the annual performance of the York cycle,[18] and when in 1561 plans were laid for a revival of performances in that city, it was agreed 'that Corpus Christi play shalbe played this yere with good players as hath ben accustomed Except onely the pagiantes of the dyenge, assumption, and Coronacion of our Lady.'[19]

But religious drama in York was not allowed to continue unrestrictedly: in 1568, the year in which the New Romney Whitsun play scheduled for production was cancelled probably because of its papist associations, the city corporation of York, after deciding to present the York Creed play rather than the Corpus Christi cycle, encountered the opposition of Matthew Hutton, Dean of York Minster and a member of the Commission for Ecclesiastical Causes in the North. Hutton's advice to the mayor and city fathers is highly significant:

as I find so manie things that I muche like because of th'antiquities, so I see manie things that I cannot allow because they be disagreeinge from the sinceritie of the gospell, the which things, yf they should either be altogether cancelled or altered into other matters, the whole drift of the play should be altered, and therefore I dare not put my pen unto it, thoghe in good will I assure you yf I were worthie to geve your lordshipp and your right worshipfull counsel, suerlie mine advise shuld be that it shuld not be plaied, for thoghe it was plawsible to [ten? twenty?] years agoe, and would now also of the ignorant sort be well liked, yet now in the happie time of the gospell [Reformation], I knowe the learned will mislike it, and how the state will beare it, I know not.[20]

The play was withdrawn, and never heard of again, while the following year saw the final performance of the Corpus Christi cycle in York until the twentieth century.

Nor was York the only city in northern England to feel the censor's hand: in the summer of 1575 the Chester cycle was given its final performance for several hundred years.[21] The plays had already come under the ban of Edmund Grindal, Archbishop of York, in 1571, but his prohibition had arrived too late to prevent the performances, although the mayor for that year, John Hankey, had been summoned before the Privy Council to account for his evident disrespect for higher authority. In 1575 Sir John Savage was mayor, and could hardly claim ignorance of the official attitude, for both the archbishop and the Lord President of the North had written forbidding the production, which nevertheless went ahead. Savage, too, was summoned to appear before the Privy Council, and his letter of 10 November 1575 requests support from the corporation in certifying that he had not acted on his personal authority alone: his mayoral successor, Henry Hardware, wrote defending Savage on 21 November, stressing that his predecessor had acted

only accordinge to an order concluded & agried upon for dyvers good & great consideracons redoundinge to the comon wealthe & benefite & profitte of the saide citie in assemblie there holden accordinge to the auncient and laudable usages & customes there hadd & used fur above mans remembrance by & with the assente, consente & agreament of his saide then brethrene the aldermen of the saide citie & of the comen counsell of the same.²²

But many ancient and laudable usages and customs were now under suspicion: in the same year that the Chester plays were staged for the last time, the General Assembly of the Church of Scotland ruled in the following terms:

Forasmuche as it is considered that the playing of clerk-plays, comedies or tragedies, upon the canonicall parts of the Scriptures, induceth & bringeth with it a contempt and profanation of the same, it is thought meete and concluded, that no clerk-plays, comedies or tragedies, be made upon canonicall Scriptures, *other* New or Old, in time coming, other upon the Lord's Day or upon a worke day: that the contraveeners, if they be ministers, be secluded from their functions, and that others be corrected by the discipline of the kirk.²³
*either

Such threats were not idle ones: the Kirk Session of Perth in 1577 threatened to refuse baptism to the children of those who persisted in performing the Corpus Christi pageants there;

becaws certane inhabitantis of yis town alsweill aganis ye expres commandment of ye civill magistratts in cownsall as aganis ye Ministeris prohibitoun in pulpitt hes playit Corpus Christeis play upon Thursday ye vj of Junij last, quhilk day wes wount to be callit Corpus Christeis Day to ye great sklander of ye kirk of God and dishonour to yis haill town. And becaws ye said play is idolatrous, superstitiows, and also sclanderows alsweill be resoun of ye Idell day . . . ²⁴

they felt justified in taking action to prevent any recurrence of such a disgrace.

The previous year the proposed staging of the Wakefield Corpus Christi plays came under the interdict of the Diocesan Court of High Commission which included Matthew Hutton: on 27 May 1576 the Court expressed its views:

This daie upon intelligence geven to the saide Commission that it is meant and purposed that in the towne of Wakefeld shalbe plaid this yere in Whitsonweke next or thereaboutes a plaie commonlie called Corpus Christi plaie which hath bene heretofore used there, wherein they are done t'understand that there be many thinges used which tende to the derogation of the Majestie and glorie of God, the prophanation of the sacramentes and the maunteynaunce of superstition and idolatrie, the said Commissioners decreed a lettre to be written and sent to the baylyffe, burgesses and other the inhabitantes of the said towne of Wakefeld that in the said playe no pageant be used or set furthe wherin the Majestye of God the Father, God the Sonne, or God the Holie Ghoste or the administration of either the Sacramentes of baptisme or of the Lordes Supper be counterfeyted or represented, or anythinge plaied which tende to the maintenaunce of superstition and idolatrie or which be contrarie to the lawes of God or of the realme.[25]

The inhabitants of Wakefield can have had little doubt that the plays' days were numbered.

Even in those continental countries which remained staunchly Roman Catholic, the leaders of the Counter-Reformation, while not as hostile to religious drama as were their Protestant opponents, became much more cautious in their attitude to Christian drama, and subjected it to a far closer control than in the Middle Ages, when the chief matters for concern were clerical participation in *ludi* and undue excess in such celebrations as the Feast of Fools. The Church modified its traditional policy towards the stage, and while Harold C. Gardiner may be forgetting the antagonism of individual clerics, he is probably right when he asserts that 'such a modification was not a congenial one, not one which sprang from any constitutional bias against the religious stage, but simply a step that was forced upon the Church by the stress of the times and by that awakening introspection which was directly caused by the attacks of the Reformation'.[26] While records of the Council of Trent (1545–63) do not contain any overt allusions to religious drama, the spirit of the Council, with its concern for purification and uniformity in liturgical matters and clarification and definition in doctrinal ones, alerted the Church to possible abuses and excesses in religious plays, even those performed within the precincts of ecclesiastical buildings.[27] A new severity towards the religious stage may be detected in the writings of such clerics as Archbishop Charles Borromeo of Milan, John Molanus of Louvain University, and the Spanish Jesuit Juan Mariana, and in the decrees of Synods such as those held at Haarlem in 1564, and at Saint-Omer in 1583, which dictated that plays had to be examined in advance for heretical tendencies, and only performed exactly as permitted.[28] An ecclesiastical council which met at Salamanca in 1565 was troubled by the unsuitability of material employed in the vernacular Nativity plays, decreeing that they should be submitted to the bishop or his deputy for approval and adding that anything which might divert the congregation from their devotions was to be deferred; a total prohibition on plays and *danzas* attempted by the Council of Toledo in 1582 led to performances being discontinued at times of Divine Office. But the fact that even the Church of Rome felt some regulation of previous practice was needful suggests that a more defensive attitude towards religious drama now prevailed.[29]

By this time, too, professional players realised the advantages of establishing permanent playing-places for themselves; dependent on public and private favour as they were, often forced by financial need to travel long distances to earn a precarious living, lacking the means to expand their activities, or to control access to their performances, compelled to seek their audiences rather than have their audiences seek them, unable to build up any kind of regular clientèle, it is little wonder that in England and Spain at least actors sought to acquire suitable and less temporary accommodation.

In Spain the professional actor of the sixteenth century was a relatively new phenomenon, and it is to the playwright, Lope de Rueda, that the establishment of the profession there is due.[30] Forming his company to perform in his own plays, he and his troupe were active from about 1540 until Lope's death in 1565, staging performances of *autos* for the Corpus Christi celebrations as well as secular plays in inn-yards and public squares, and on the patios of houses for the common people; his company entertained the nobility, staged entertainments for royal entries, and even appeared in the new cathedral at Segovia on a stage between the two choirs in 1558. In the same year he may even have established a permanent theatre or a playing-place in Valladolid. If so, Lope anticipated by roughly ten years the setting up of stages in the rented yards or *corrales* at the centre of housing blocks in various Spanish towns, so creating permanent theatre sites. The earliest firm record dates from May 1568 when Alonso Velázquez's company performed in a yard belonging to the Cofradía de la Pasión y Sangre de Jesucristo, one of the several charitable organisations which sponsored dramatic performances in Madrid in order to benefit hospitals run under their auspices.[31] In 1574 a second *cofradía* was also seeking to sponsor performances, and after some legal sparring with the Cofradía de la Pasión, a compromise enabled both groups to benefit from the proceeds derived from productions in the *corrales*, where stages, platforms for seating, and awnings transformed courtyards into virtual theatre buildings.

In England open spaces enclosed between walls were also being exploited for theatrical purposes: in London and the provinces the rectangular courtyards of inns particularly suggested themselves as suitable playing-areas, since here the traditional booth stage on trestles or barrels might be set up against one of the four walls, and the performance given to spectators standing on three sides of the platform, or watching from the windows and galleries which overlooked the yard. A gated entrance meant that access to the yard and the collection of the price of admission could be efficiently controlled.[32] Recent scholarship, however, has demonstrated that some of the inn-yard theatres of Elizabethan London involved more than temporary installations, and that permanent stages together with stands for the accommodation of spectators were erected at the Red Lion and Boar's Head Inns at Whitechapel at least, the Red Lion construction being recorded in the Court-Book of the Carpenters' Company for 1567. But dramatic performances at London inns date back at least ten years before this, the earliest records alluding to plays at the Boar's Head and the Saracen's Head in Islington in 1557.[33]

Doubt must remain as to the precise rôle of the expanding commercial theatre in contributing to the demise of the medieval stage, since there is little evidence that the cycle plays declined in popularity as a result of the increasing supply of secular plays, and permanent or semi-permanent sites to house them. Yet in offering an alternative style of drama to meet playgoers' needs, professional troupes did largely replace the predominantly amateur communal theatre of the Middle Ages, especially in Spain where they took over the presentation of religious drama, even performing in churches, much to the distaste of Juan Mariana in his *Tractatus VII Historici et Theologici* (1609).[34] In England it may be assumed that the professional companies, both static and peripatetic, by rapidly capturing the public's affection, diverted its attention from the loss of one of its richest and more rewarding corporate assets: a thriving traditional and popular theatre created over several centuries and genuinely belonging to the whole community. In April 1576, James Burbage leased from one Giles Allen a plot of land north of Bishopsgate in London, in order to erect on it a purpose-built theatre, but well before this a new relationship between players and public had begun to evolve. As commercial considerations came to dominate, no longer did hard labour and varied skills, time, talent, and monetary levy, weld together people and presentation; no longer was a public dramatic performance the result of widespread communal activity but something to be purchased like any other commodity; no longer could spectators identify with local performers whose personal habits and usual daily pursuits they recognised and acknowledged. The new theatres might inherit some conventions and customs from an earlier age but now an invisible wall had sprung up between the paid actor on his apron stage and the paying audience in pit and galleries. It has still to be demolished.

CHRONOLOGICAL TABLE
800—1576

800	Charlemagne crowned Holy Roman Emperor
c. 840–912	Notker Balbulus
850	Death of Amalarius, Bishop of Metz
c. 920—930	*Quem Quaeritis* composed, St Martial, Limoges
c. 930–950	*Quem Quaeritis* composed, St Gall
c. 935–1002	Hrotswitha of Gandersheim
c. 953	Twelfth Night diversion at Byzantine Court
c. 965–975	*Regularis Concordia* compiled
c. 1000—1100	Earliest liturgical dramas composed
c. 1100	*Sponsus* (Latin-Provençal)
c. 1110	Play on St Katherine performed at Dunstable
1120–30	Hilarius's *Historia de Daniel*
1146–74	*Le Mystère d'Adam* (Anglo-Norman)
c. 1147–1223	Giraldus Cambrensis
c. 1150	Monte Cassino Passion play
c. 1155	*Ordo Virtutum* (Hildegard of Bingen); *Reyes Magos* (Toledo)
c. 1159	*Polycraticus* (John of Salisbury)
c. 1160	Tegernsee *Ludus de Antichristo*
1162	*De Investigatione Antichristi* (Gerhoh von Reichersberg)
c. 1175	*La Seinte Resureccion* (Anglo-Norman)
c. 1180	Beauvais *Ludus Danielis*
1194	Regensburg *Ordo Creacionis*
c. 1200	*Le Jeu de St Nicolas* (Jean Bodel); Siena Passion play
1204	*Ludus Prophetarum* staged at Riga
c. 1220	Beverley Resurrection play mentioned
c. 1225	*Courtois d'Arras*
1234	Pope Gregory IX's decretal regarding religious plays
1243–4	Padua Passion and Resurrection play
1250–1300	Kloster Muri Passion play; Benediktbeuern Passion plays
c. 1260	*Siete Partidas* of Alfonso X of Castile
c. 1261	*Théophile* (Rutebeuf)
c. 1275	*Le Jeu de la Feuillée* (Adam de la Halle)
c. 1280	*Le Garçon et l'Aveugle*
c. 1283	*Le Jeu de Robin et Marion* (Adam de la Halle)
c. 1284	Origny-Saint-Benoîte *Ludus Paschalis*
c. 1285	*Le Tournoi de Chauvency* (Jacques Bretel)
1298	Parade of trade guilds in London to mark English victory at Falkirk; Cividale Pentecost cycle (also in 1304)

c. 1300	*La Passion du Palatinus; La Passion d'Autun; Vienna Passion Play; Dux Moraud; De Clerico et Puella*
1300–50	St Gall Passion play
1311	Observation of the Feast of Corpus Christi ratified
1313	Edward II enters Paris
c. 1330	*Le Jour de Jugement*
c. 1339–82	*Les Miracles de Nostre Dame* written and staged
1350–75	Cornish *Ordinalia* composed
1350–1400	Frankfurt *Dirigierrolle* drawn up
1363–76	Barking *Visitatio* (Katherine of Sutton)
1371	Earliest known *confrérie* set up at Nantes
c. 1372	De Mézières's *Presentation of the Virgin Mary*, Avignon
1376	First mention of the York 'pagine'
1377	Coronation celebrations for Richard II; mumming at Kennington, London; Beverley 'pagine' first mentioned
1378	*Entremet* of the Conquest of Jerusalem at Paris banquet
1389	The *Pas Saladin* staged in the streets of Paris
1391	Manuscript of the Innsbruck *Fronleichnamsspiel (Corpus Christi Play)* dated
1392	First mention of the Coventry 'pagent'
1393	Performers burnt to death in Paris *mommerie*
c. 1395	*L'Estoire de Griseldis*
1399	Coronation celebrations of Martin I, Saragossa
c. 1400	*The Pride of Life*
1400–25	*The Castel of Perseverance*
1400–40	*La Passion d'Arras* (Mercadé)
1400–50	N-Town cycle first staged
1402	Charles VI recognises the Confrérie de la Passion et Resurrection
1409	London clerks appear in a cycle play
1415	York *Ordo Paginarum* drawn up
1426	William Melton visits York and advises on pageants
c. 1430	Momeries by John Lydgate written and performed at court
1439	Abraham of Souzdal attends Florentine *Annunciation* spectacle
c. 1450–70	*Le Mystère de la Passion* (Gerban) composed
1452–78	*Les Actes des Apôtres* (Greban brothers?) composed
1457	Margaret of Anjou visits Coventry for the cycle plays
1462	First mention of the Chester plays
1464	The Redentin Easter play
c. 1465–70	*Mankind*
1474	*Le Mystère de l'Incarnation et de la Nativité de Jésus-Christ* played at Rouen
c. 1480	Jean Michel's *Passion* composed
c. 1480–1520	*Mary Magdalene* and *The Conversion of St Paul* (Digby manuscript) written
1484	Plautus's *Aulularia* performed at Rome
1486	Vitruvius's *De Architectura* published
1493	Badius Ascensius's edition of Terence published at Lyon
c. 1495	*Elkerlyck/Everyman; Nature* (Henry Medwall)

1496	*Le Mystère de St Martin* staged at Seurre
c. 1497	*Fulgens and Lucres* (Medwall)
1501	Passion play at Mons; Alsfeld Passion play; wedding celebrations for Prince Arthur, London
1502	Plautus's *Menaechmi* staged before the pope
1504	*Beunans Meriasek (The Life of St Meriasek)*
1509	*Le Mystère des Trois Doms* performed at Romans
1510	Vienne Passion play
1512	The masque introduced into England
1513	Plautus's *Poenulus* staged at Rome; Bibbiena's *La Calandria* staged at Urbino (1514 in Rome)
c. 1515	*Magnyfycence* (John Skelton)
1522	Pageants to greet Charles V in London; *Le Mystère du Genre Humain* staged at Montauban
c. 1527	*The Play of the Wether* (John Heywood) ·
1536	*Les Actes des Apôtres* staged at Bourges (1540 in Paris)
c. 1537	*Thersytes*
1539	Confrérie de la Passion at the Hôtel de Flandre, Paris
1542	Procurator-general reports adversely on the Confrérie de la Passion
1545	Serlio's *Regole generali di architectura* (Book II) published
1547	Valenciennes Passion play staged
1548	Paris Parlement forbids performances of *mystères sacrés*
1550	Confrérie de la Passion buys Hôtel de Bourgogne
1550–60	Hans Sachs's main *Fastnachtspiele* written
1552	*Ane Satyre of the Thrie Estaitis* performed, Cupar, Fifeshire
c. 1553	*Respublica; Ralph Roister Doister; Gammer Gurton's Nedle*
1557	Earliest records of performances at London inn-theatres
1560	New Romney Whitsun plays performed
1560–70	First *corrales* opened for performance in Madrid
1561–2	*Gorboduc* (Sackville and Norton)
1565	Lope de Rueda died
1567–8	*Horestes*
1568	Papal reform of the Breviary; first recorded performance in Madrid *corrales*
1569	*Susanna* (Thomas Garter); final performance of York cycle.
1575	*Princely Pleasures* at Kenilworth; final performance of the Chester cycle
1576	Wakefield cycle condemned by Diocesan Court; death of Hans Sachs; The Theatre built in London

NOTES

For reasons of space and convenience the following abbreviations for books and periodicals frequently referred to in the notes have been used. Place of publication is London unless otherwise stated. Full titles will be found in the Select Bibliography.

CM	Henri Rey-Flaud, *Le Cercle magique*, Paris, 1973.
DMC	Karl Young, *The Drama of the Medieval Church*, 2 vols, Oxford, 1933.
EDEMA	Richard Axton, *European Drama of the Early Middle Ages*, 1974
EES	Glynne Wickham, *Early English Stages, 1300–1660*, 2 vols, 1959–72.
EETS (OS)	Early English Text Society (Ordinary Series).
EETS (ES)	Early English Text Society (Extra Series).
EETS (SS)	Early English Text Society (Supplementary Series).
EMP	Rosemary Woolf, *The English Mystery Plays*, 1972.
ERD	Hardin Craig, *English Religious Drama of the Middle Ages*, Oxford, 1955.
HSS	N. D. Shergold, *A History of the Spanish Stage*, Oxford, 1967.
JEGP	*Journal of English and Germanic Philology*.
LPP	Sandro Sticca, *The Latin Passion Play*, Albany, 1970.
MD	David Bevington (ed.), *Medieval Drama*, Boston, 1975.
MED	Jerome Taylor and Alan H. Nelson (eds.), *Medieval English Drama*, Chicago and London, 1972.
MES	Alan H. Nelson, *The Medieval English Stage*, Chicago and London, 1974.
MeS	Gustave Cohen, *Histoire de la mise en scène …*, Paris, 1906; 2nd edn, 1925.
MFD	Grace Frank, *The Medieval French Drama*, Oxford, 1954.
MLR	*Modern Language Review*.
MMM	Allardyce Nicoll, *Masks, Mimes and Miracles*, 1931.
Mons	Gustave Cohen (ed.), *Le Livre de conduite du régisseur …*, Paris, 1925.
MS	E. K. Chambers, *The Mediaeval Stage*, 2 vols, Oxford, 1903.
MT	Glynne Wickham, *The Medieval Theatre*, 1974.
MTR	Richard Southern, *The Medieval Theatre in the Round*, 1957; 2nd rev. edn, 1975.
Ogilvy	J. D. A. Ogilvy, 'Mimi, scurrae, histriones …. *Speculum* 38 (1963), 603–19.
PMLA	*Proceedings of the Modern Language Association of America*.

PPL   M. Blakemore Evans, *The Passion Play of Lucerne*, New York, 1943.
RORD   *Research Opportunities in Renaissance Drama.*
SP   *Studies in Philology.*
TN   *Theatre Notebook.*

1   Ritual survivals

MS, MT, and *EDEMA* all devote space to survivals of pagan rituals, and there are interesting pages in A. P. Rossiter, *English Drama from Early Times to the Elizabethans*, 1950; Benjamin Hunningher, *The Origin of the Theater*, Amsterdam and the Hague, 1955; New York, 1961; and Richard Southern, *The Seven Ages of the Theatre*, 1962. The great seminal work is of course Sir James G. Frazer, *The Golden Bough* (3rd edn, 12 vols, 1907–15; abridged edn, 1922), and also relevant are Jane E. Harrison, *Ancient Art and Ritual*, 1913; and Theodor H. Gaster, *Thespis. Ritual, Myth and Drama in the Ancient Near East*, New York, 1950; 2nd rev. edn, New York, 1961 (paperback reprint, Harper Torchbook, 1966 –all references are to this edition).

1   Foreword to Gaster, *Thespis*, p. 9.
2   Jacques Soustelle, *The Daily Life of the Aztecs*, Paris, 1961; Penguin edn, 1964, p. 155.
3   For full details, see Gaster, *Thespis* pp. 23, 26–49.
4   W. E. Harney, *Brimming Billabongs*, Sydney and London, 1947; London, 1963, pp. 43–4.
5   See Maximilian J. Rudwin, *The Origin of the German Carnival Comedy*, New York, 1920, pp. 29–36; Paolo Toschi, *Le origini del teatro italiano*, Turin, 1955, pp. 166–227.
6   Gaster, *Thespis* p. 83; see also pp. 24–5, 77.
7   *Ibid.*, pp. 399–405.
8   See Alan Brody, *The English Mummers and their Plays*, 1970; E. K. Chambers, *The English Folk Play*, Oxford, 1933; R. J. E. Tiddy, *The Mummer's Play*, Oxford, 1923. Also Gaster, *Thespis* pp. 84–5, 436–9; *MT* pp. 145–50.
9   For discussion, see *EDEMA* pp. 33–4.
10   *MFD* p. 16.
11   For the Riga *ludus*, see *DMC* II. 542; for comments, see *ERD* p. 100; *EMP* p. 37; *EDEMA* p. 44.
12   See *MS* I. 154; II. 264–6.
13   Tacitus, *Germania* 24, cited in *MS* I. 191 note 1.
14   For Olaus Magnus, see *MS* II. 270–1.
15   See Rudwin, *German Carnival Comedy* pp. 15–18.
16   *MS* I. 110–15, 228–42.
17   Recorded on Topic Records 12 T 136.
18   For a fuller account of the Padstow 'Oss, see Southern, *Seven Ages* (2nd edn, 1964), pp. 40–4. The song is recorded on Topic Records 12 T 197.
19   On ritual survivals in Shakespearean comedy, see C. L. Barber, *Shakespeare's Festive Comedy: A Study of Dramatic Form and its Relation to Social Custom*, Princeton, 1969.

20 *MS* I. 176.

21 Ronald Blythe, *Akenfield. Portrait of an English Village*, 1969; Penguin edn, 1972, pp. 62−3.

22 See Trefor M. Owen, *Welsh Folk Customs*, Cardiff, 1959; 3rd edn, 1974, pp. 49−58.

23 See Toschi, *teatro italiano*, for Italian rituals involving the figure of Carnival.

24 Bede, *Historia ecclesiastica gentis Anglorum* II. 15, transl. L. Sherley-Price, Penguin Classics, 1955, p. 128.

25 *Ibid.*, I. 30; Sherley-Price, pp. 86−7.

26 Rudwin, *German Carnival Comedy*, pp. 10, 4, 11.

27 See, for example, C. R. Baskervill, 'Dramatic aspects of medieval folk festivals in England', *SP* 17 (1920), 19−87.

28 For example, those cited by Peter Dronke, *The Medieval Lyric*, 1968, pp. 186−206.

29 *Ibid.* p. 190.

30 A more detailed account in given in *EDEMA* pp. 48−9.

31 *Robert of Brunne's 'Handlyng Synne'*, ed. Frederick J. Furnivall, EETS (OS) 119 (1901), 283−90.

32 Giraldus Cambrensis, *Opera* II. 120. For the Breconshire anecdote, see *The Itinerary through Wales ...*, transl. Sir Richard Colt Hoare, Everyman Library, 1908, pp. 29−30.

33 *MS* I. 161−2 and notes.

34 H. Maxwell (ed.), *The Chronicle of Lanercost*, 1913, p. 29. See also E. K. Chambers, *English Literature at the close of the Middle Ages*, Oxford 1945, p. 71.

35 For discussions of the Feast of Fools and the Boy Bishop, see *MS* I. 274−371 and *DMC* I. 104−11.

36 For the citations which follow, see *MS* I. 90−3, 162−3.

37 See *ed. cit.* p. 283.

38 Cited in *MS* I. 181, from *Grindal's Remains*, Parker Society 175, 1843.

39 H. C. Porter (ed.), *Puritanism in Tudor England*, 1970, p. 76.

40 Quoted by G. L. Brook, *The Harley Lyrics*, Manchester, 1948; 2nd edn, 1956, p. 5, from *Anglia* 42 (1934), 152−4.

41 For Grosseteste's and other prohibitions see *MS* I. 91−3, 179−81.

42 *MT* p. 141.

43 *MES* p. 123; *MS* I. 262.

44 *Records of Early English Drama Newsletter*, Toronto, 1976, I. 3−10. See also *MS* I. 261 note, and *MES* p. 50.

45 Norman Davis (ed.), *The Paston Letters*, Oxford, 1971, I. 461 (Letter 275).

46 *Hall's Chronicle*, ed. Sir H. Ellis, 1809, p. 513. See also *MS* I. 399.

47 From British Museum manuscript Royal 18 A 1. Cited by G. R. Elton, *Politics and Police*, 1972, p. 185.

48 Hugh Latimer, *Seven Sermons Preached before Edward VI*, ed. Edward Arber, Birmingham, 1869, pp. 173−4.

49 *DMC* II. 538.

50 For example, Robert Stumpfl, *Kultspiele des Germanen als Ursprung des mittelalterlichen Dramas*, Berlin, 1936, and Hunningher, *Origin of the Theater*. See also Timothy Fry, 'The alleged influence of pagan ritual on

the formation of the English mystery plays', *American Benedictine Review* 9 (1958—9), 187—201.

2 Classic and christian

For the Latin theatre, W. Beare, *The Roman Stage*, 1950; revised edn, 1964, is invaluable, while *MMM*, is useful, although not always accurate, on the history of the mime players following the fall of Rome. For liturgical drama, the texts and commentary in *DMC* are essential, and Bevington's introductory material to plays printed in *MD* is admirably lucid. Also helpful are the discussions in *EDEMA*, *EMP*, and *MT*, and the account of recent publications provided by C. Clifford Flanigan, 'The liturgical drama and its tradition: a review of scholarship 1965—75', *RORD* 18 (1975), 81—102. Essential further reading must include O. B. Hardison Jr, *Christian Rite and Christian Drama in the Middle Ages*, Baltimore, 1965, and for those who read German, Helmut de Boor, *Die Textgeschichte der lateinischen Osterfeiern*, Tübingen, 1967, and Theo Stemmler, *Liturgische Feiern und geistliche Spiele*, Tübingen, 1970.

1 Pliny, *Nat. Hist.* XXXVI. 24. Quoted in A. M. Nagler (ed.), *A Source Book in Theatrical History*, New York, 1959, pp. 20—2. Beare, *Roman Stage* p. 172, is inclined to reject Pliny's testimony.
2 *Cicero's Letters to his Friends*, transl. W. Glynne Williams, Cambridge, Mass., 1928, quoted in Nagler, *Source Book* pp. 27—8.
3 Quoted *ibid.* p. 29.
4 *MMM* p. 123.
5 See Suetonius, *Life of Nero* 21; see Loeb edn, II. 119.
6 See *MMM* p. 130; *MS* I. 10 and note 3.
7 *MMM* pp. 121—2, 17-18; *MS* I. 10 and note 4.
8 Tertullian, *De Spectaculis* 23; for a stimulating discussion of this issue, see William Nelson, *Fact or Fiction: The Dilemma of the Renaissance Storyteller*, Cambridge, Mass., 1973.
9 *MMM* pp. 136—50; see also Ogilvy for evidence of survivals.
10 *MS* I. 24.
11 *MS* I. 34—5, notes 1 and 3. For subsequent evidence, see Ogilvy.
12 On Hrotswitha, see *EDEMA* pp. 26—9; Sister Mary Marguerite Butler, *Hrotswita: The Theatricality of her Plays*, New York, 1960; E. Zeydel, 'Were Hrotsvitha's dramas performed in her lifetime?' *Speculum* 20 (1945), 443—56. English translations include H. J. W. Tillyard, *The Plays of Rotswitha*, 1923.
13 For text, see *MS* II. 326—8; see also *MMM* p. 171; *EDEMA* pp. 24—5.
14 See *EDEMA* p. 26; *EMP* pp. 28—9; Peter Dronke, *Poetic Individuality in the Middle Ages*, Oxford, 1970, pp. 84—7.
15 For example, Gaster, *Thespis* pp. 401—5.
16 *MFD* p. 13. On these comedies, see also *DMC* I. 7—8.
17 See *EDEMA* pp. 29—30; *MFD* pp. 12—13.
18 Benjamin Hunningher, *The Origin of the Theater*, Amsterdam and the Hague, 1955; New York, 1961.
19 Tertullian, *De Spectaculis* 29.
20 See, among others, *EDEMA*, *EMP*, *HSS*, *LPP*, *MD*, *MT*.

21 *MMM* pp. 212—13.
22 See David N. Dumville, 'Liturgical drama and panegyric responsory from the eighth century', *Journal of Theological Studies (NS)* 23 (1972), 374—406.
23 See *DMC* II. 133—8.
24 For the Byzantine theatre, see Joseph S. Tunnison, *Dramatic Traditions of the Dark Ages*, Chicago, 1907, and George La Piana, 'The Byzantine theatre', *Speculum* 11 (1936), 171—211. See also *MMM* pp. 209—13; *MFD* pp. 3—4.
25 *EMP* p. 5.
26 On Etheria, see *DMC* I. 86—7; Hardison, *Christian Rite* p. 112. For translated extracts from her *Peregrinatio*, see L. Duchesne, *Christian Worship: Its Origin and Evolution*, 1903; 5th edn, 1919, pp. 541—71.
27 See EMP pp. 6—7; for the *Adoratio, Depositio,* and *Elevatio* ceremonies, see *DMC* I. 112—48, together with Karl Young, *The Dramatic Associations of the Easter Sepulchre*, Madison, 1920.
28 For an admirably non-technical but brief discussion of troping, see *MD* pp. 31—3. More sophisticated are Egon Wellesz. *Eastern Elements in Western Chant. Studies in the Early History of Ecclesiastical Music*, Boston, 1947, pp. 153—74 ('The origin of sequences and tropes'); Rembert Weakland OSB, 'The beginning of troping', *Musical Quarterly* 44 (1958), 477—88; Paul Evans, 'Some reflections on the origins of the trope', *Journal of the American Musicological Society* 14 (1961), 119—31; William Smoldon, 'The origins of the *Quem Quaeritis* trope and the Easter Sepulchre music-dramas, as demonstrated by their musical settings', in Sandro Sticca (ed.), *The Medieval Drama*, Albany, 1972.
29 See *DMC* I. 183—5; for Notker, see also *Two Lives of Charlemagne*, transl. Lewis Thorpe, Penguin Classics, 1969, pp. 21—7.
30 For a brief discussion of this highly complex issue, see *EMP* pp. 342—3 (note 24).
31 See Peter Hunter Blair, *An Introduction to Anglo-Saxon England*, Cambridge, 1956, pp. 173—8.
32 See Wolfgang Michael, 'Tradition and Originality in the Medieval Drama in Germany', in Sandro Sticca (ed.), *Medieval Drama* pp. 23—5.
33 Text translated from *DMC* I. 249—50 with some expansion.
34 Smoldon, 'Origins of the *Quem Quaeritis* trope' *passim*.
35 See Richard B. Donovan, *The Liturgical Drama in Medieval Spain*, Toronto, 1958, for an excellent discussion of developments in the Spanish peninsula.
36 In particular, see F. M. Salter, *Mediaeval Drama in Chester*, Toronto, 1955; *EES* I. 314—18.
37 *DMC* I. 678—81.
38 *DMC* I. 477—80.
39 *DMC* I. 451—83.
40 *DMC* I. 310—11.
41 *DMC* I. 411—50.
42 See de Boor, *Textgeschichte*.
43 *DMC* I. 507—12.
44 *DMC* I. 514—16, 518—33.

45 See *EDEMA* pp. 58–60, and Wilfried Werner, *Studien zu den Passions-und Osterspielen des deutschen Mittelalters in ihrem Übergang vom Latein zur Volksprache*, Berlin, 1963, for a discussion of the use of Latin and the vernacular.
46 For the Monte Cassino play, see *LPP passim*.
47 For the Sulmona fragment, see *DMC* I. 701–8.
48 *DMC* I. 697–8.
49 *DMC* II. 8.
50 *DMC* II. 9–20.
51 *HSS* p. 2; see also Donovan, *Liturgical Drama* p. 49.
52 See *DMC* II. 29–171 for examples and discussion of these plays.
53 *DMC* II. 93–7.
54 *DMC* II. 84–9; transl. in *MD* pp. 57–66.
55 *DMC* II. 172–90; transl. in *MD* pp. 180–201.
56 *DMC* II. 423; for the more recent view, see Werner, *Studien*.
57 *DMC* II. 362–4; for an excellent discussion, see *EMP* pp. 45–7.
58 For conflicting views, see *DMC* II. 367–8; *MFD* p. 62; *ERD* p. 75.
59 See A. E. Zucker (transl.) *The Redentin Easter Play*, New York, 1941, p. 130 (note to line 1984).
60 See *EDEMA* p. 104.
61 *DMC* II. 514–20.
62 *DMC* II. 423.
63 See *ERD* pp. 318–19.

3 Indoor theatre

While no single work is exclusively devoted to medieval indoor presentation, a good deal of information is contained in *EDEMA*, *EES*, *HSS*, *MeS*, *MFD*, *MS*, and *MT*; *DMC* is essential for the liturgical drama. I owe a particular debt to Fletcher Collins Jr, *The Production of Medieval Church Music Drama*, Charlottesville, 1972. *EES* and *HSS* offer the fullest accounts of court entertainments in England and Spain respectively, and Enid Welsford, *The Court Masque*, Cambridge, 1927, is still a useful study; Sydney Anglo, *Spectacle, Pageantry and Early Tudor Policy*, Oxford, 1969, may be recommended. Richard Southern, *The Staging of Plays before Shakespeare*, 1973, is exhaustive on 'Tudor interludes' from *Mankind* onwards.

1 Mary H. Marshall, '*Theatre* in the Middle Ages: evidence from dictionaries and glosses', *Symposium* IV (1950), 1–39, 366–89, is a most helpful survey of terminology, on which I have drawn extensively.
2 See Roger S. Loomis, 'Were there theatres in the twelfth and thirteenth centuries?' *Speculum* 20 (1945), 92–8; 'Some evidence for secular theatres in the twelfth and thirteenth centuries', *Theatre Annual* 1945, 33–43; for a refutation, see Dino Bigongiari, 'Were there theatres in the twelfth and thirteenth centuries? '*Romanic Review* 37 (1946), 201–24; see also Marshall, *Symposium* IV and 'Boethius' definition of *persona* and medieval understanding of Roman theater', *Speculum* 25 (1950), 471–82. I have also derived information from Ogilvy.
3 Bigongiari, 'Were there theatres?' p. 222.

4   *The Works of Geoffrey Chaucer*, ed. F. N. Robinson, Boston, 1933; 2nd edn, 1968, p. 321.
5   Marshall, *Symposium* IV, 15; Ogilvy, p. 610.
6   Marshall, *Symposium* IV, 369—70.
7   Roger de Wendover, *Liber qui dicitur flores historiarum* (Rolls series 1887), II. 24—30. See Bigongiari, 'Were there theatres?' p. 215; *CM* 36—8; *EMP* 31—3.
8   *MS* I. 383; II. 190. See Marshall, *Symposium* IV. 381.
9   See Ogilvy, pp. 607, 608, 613—14, etc.
10 For what follows, see Marshall, *Symposium* IV. 8—11, 16—17, 25, 27, etc.
11 *Ibid.* 16—20; *EMP* p. 27.
12 Both are reproduced on adjacent pages of *MMM* pp. 154—5.
13 John Lydgate, *Troy Book*, ed. H. Bergen, EETS (ES) 97, I (1906), 169—70.
14 The following general works may be recommended: A. W. Clapham, *Romanesque Architecture in Western Europe*, Oxford, 1936; Kenneth John Conant, *Carolingian and Romanesque Architecture 800 to 1200*, Pelican History of Art, Harmondsworth, 1959; Paul Frankl, *Gothic Architecture*, Pelican History of Art, Harmondsworth, 1962. For England, see H. M. and Joan Taylor, *Anglo-Saxon Architecture*, 2 vols, Cambridge, 1965.
15 *Encyclopaedia Britannica*, 1962, V. 672.
16 This and the following paragraph are based on A. W. Clapham, *English Romanesque Architecture before the Conquest*, Oxford, 1930, and *English Romanesque Architecture after the Conquest*, Oxford, 1934, supplemented by appropriate entries from *The Oxford Dictionary of the Christian Church*, 1957; 2nd edn, 1974; *The Oxford Companion to Art*, 1970; *The Larousse Encyclopedia of Byzantine and Medieval Art*, Paris, 1958; London, 1963. See also *MT* pp. 15—18.
17 See Collins, *Medieval Church Music-Drama*, *passim*. A conjectural reconstruction of a nave setting for *La Seinte Resureccion* is found in Richard Leacroft, *The Development of the Playhouse in England*, 1973, p. 3.
18 See *DMC* I. 218—20.
19 *DMC* I. 133; *MD* p. 16.
20 On the Easter sepulchre, see *DMC* II. 507—13.
21 For staging in churches, see Collins, *Medieval Church Music-Drama*.
22 The Fleury *Visitatio* is printed in *DMC* I. 393—7 (transl. in *MD* pp. 39—44).
23 The Rouen *Peregrinus* is printed in *DMC* I. 461—2, the Saintes and Sicily versions in *DMC* I. 453—60.
24 *DMC* II. 84—9, 110—13 (transl. in *MD* pp. 57—72).
25 *DMC* II. 290—301 (transl. in *MD* pp. 138—54).
26 *DMC* I. 467—9 (transl. in *MD* pp. 45—9).
27 *DMC* I. 471—5.
28 *DMC* II. 351—7 (transl. in *MD* 170—77).
29 *DMC* I. 507—12.
30 *DMC* II. 16—19.
31 *DMC* II. 219—22 (transl. in *MD* pp. 165—8).
32 *DMC* II. 199—208.

33 *DMC* II. 276–86. For Beauvais, see *ibid*, II. 290–301.
34 Collins, *Medieval Church Music-Drama* pp. 28–9. On the Fleury *Lazarus* and *St Paul* see pp. 155–81.
35 *DMC* II. 325–7.
36 *DMC* II. 330–2.
37 *DMC* II. 338–41; for the Fleury text see *DMC* II. 344–8.
38 On staging the *Filius Getronis*, see *MD* p. 170, and Collins, *Medieval Church Music-Drama* pp. 8–9.
39 The four most developed forms of the so-called *Ludus Paschalis* are given in *DMC* I. 411–50.
40 *LPP* pp. 66–78.
41 The two Benediktbeuern Passion plays are given in *DMC* I. 514–16, 518–33, the latter translated in *MD* pp. 203–23.
42 Text in *DMC* II. 371–87; for a valuable discussion, see *EDEMA* pp. 88–94.
43 See *DMC* II, 392–3.
44 For text and translation, see *MD* pp. 123–36. For some discussion of staging, see Leacroft, *Playhouse in England* pp. 1–3; *MS* II. 83–4; *MFD* pp. 89–91; *CM* pp. 31–2, 44–5; Hardison, *Christian Rite* pp. 262–74.
45 For text, see *DMC* II. 227–42. William E. Colman is preparing a new edition in the Toronto Mediaeval Latin Texts series.
46 See *DMC* II. 522, 484, 451, 543; I. 347–50. There is some evidence that the Dublin text may originally have belonged to Salisbury.
47 *DMC* I. 381–4.
48 See *HSS* and Richard Donovan, *The Liturgical Drama in Medieval Spain*, Toronto, 1958.
49 For the Mallorcan codex, see *HSS* pp. 60–6.
50 *MS* II. 366; *ERD* p. 89; *MFD* p. 94 note 2.
51 For the possibility of performances at St Albans, see Otto Pächt, *The Rise of Pictorial Narrative in England in the Twelfth Century*, Oxford, 1962.
52 *DMC* II. 411.
53 *DMC* II. 412–14.
54 Text in Dronke, *Poetic Individuality* pp. 150–92; for commentary, see *EDEMA* pp. 94–9.
55 Ed. R. Menendez Pidal, 'Auto de los Reyes Magos', *Revista de Archivos* 4 (1900), 453–62. For discussion, see *HSS* pp. 5–6; *EMP* pp. 47–9; *EDEMA* pp. 105–8; Donovan, *Liturgical Drama* pp. 70–2, although the fullest treatment is in Winifred Sturdevant, *El Misterio de los Reyes Magos*, Baltimore and Paris, 1927.
56 Both texts with parallel translations are conveniently located in *MD* pp. 80–136.
57 *DMC* II. 416–17; see comments in Collins, *Medieval Church Music-Drama* p. 6.
58 Apart from Joseph Kennard, *The Italian Theatre*, 2 vols, New York, 1932, which is somewhat imprecise, there is no reliable survey of Italian stage conditions in English at present; the qualified reader should consult the works by Apollonio, D'Ancona, Garrone, and Molinari cited in the Select Bibliography.

59 See Cesare Molinari, *Spettacoli fiorentini del Quattrocento*, Venice, 1961, pp. 35–54; Orville K. Larson, 'Bishop Abraham of Souzdal's description of *Sacre Rappresentazioni*', *Education Theatre Journal* 9 (1957), 208–13.

60 See *MFD* pp. 136–53, and Donald C. Stuart, *Stage Decoration in France in the Middle Ages*, New York, 1910, pp. 85–105. *Les Miracles de Nostre Dame* have been edited by Gaston Paris and Ulysse Robert, 8 vols, Paris, 1876–93, in the Société des Anciens Textes Français series. On staging, see *MFD*; Dorothy Penn, *The Staging of the 'Miracles de Nostre Dame Par Personnages' of MS Cangé*, New York, 1933; Nigel Wilkins, *Two Miracles (La Nonne qui Laissa son abbaie & Saint Valentin)*, Edinburgh, 1972, pp. 6–7.

61 See *MFD* pp. 120–1.

62 Ed. F. J. Warne, Oxford, 1951. For discussion, see *MFD* pp. 93–105, 211–16; *EDEMA* pp. 131–7. There is an English translation in Richard Axton and John Stevens, *Medieval French Plays*, Oxford, 1971.

63 Ed. Grace Frank, Paris, 1925; 2nd edn, 1949. See *MFD* pp. 106–12.

64 See Penn, '*Nostre Dame*' p. 14. For plays of the Ste Geneviève manuscript and other Parisian performances, see Stuart, *Stage Decoration* pp. 85–105, 202–23.

65 Johan Huizinga, *The Waning of the Middle Ages*, 1924; Penguin edn, 1955, p. 252.

66 *HSS* p. 114, note 4.

67 See Laura Hibbard Loomis, 'Secular dramatics in the royal palace, Paris, 1378, 1389, and Chaucer's "Tregetoures"', *Speculum* 33 (1958), 242–55, reprinted in *MED* pp. 98–115. For the Paris *entremet* of 1389, see also *HSS* pp. 121–2; *EES* I. 213–15; *MT* p. 164. For a modern English translation of Froissart's account, see Geoffrey Brereton, *Chronicles*, Penguin Classics, Harmondsworth, 1968, pp. 357–8.

68 *Ed. cit.* p. 139.

69 For what follows, see *HSS* pp. 115–21.

70 Cited by Lee Simonson, *The Stage is Set*, New York, 1932; rev. edn, 1963, p. 197; for the ensuing information, cf. Huizinga, *Waning* pp. 92, 138, 254; *HSS* pp. 128–9.

71 *MS* I. 394.

72 *EES* I. 188–9.

73 See *MS* I. 395, 394, 396; *EES* I. 203.

74 *EES* I. 202–3.

75 For a discussion of Lydgate's momeries, see *EES* I. 191–206. The texts are printed in H. N. MacCracken (ed.), *The Minor Poems of John Lydgate, II Secular Poems*, EETS (OS) 192 (1934), pp. 668–701.

76 *EES* I. 195.

77 Quoted from *The Chronicle of Froissart*, translated by Sir John Bourchier, Lord Berners, 6 vols, 1901–3. The Tudor Translations, vols 27–32, VI. 97–8.

78 For this and subsequent references to Spain, see *HSS* pp. 124–33.

79 See Gordon Kipling, 'The early Tudor disguising: new research opportunities', *RORD* 17 (1974), 3–8. For the 1501 celebrations, see *EES* I. 208–9, 221, 280–1; for those of 1511, see *EES* I. 217–18. Also Anglo, *Spectacle* pp. 98–103, 111–12.

80   *EES* I. 218—19; *MS* I. 401.
81   See *EES* I. 219—21, 244—5; *MT* pp. 166—7; Anglo, *Spectacle* pp. 209—24.
82   *Hall's Chronicle*, ed. Sir H. Ellis, 1809, p. 722.
83   For the staging of interludes, see Southern, *Staging of plays, passim*; T. W. Craik, *The Tudor Interlude*, Leicester, 1958; Leacroft, *Playhouse in England* pp. 9—12. I have adopted Craik's provisional datings (pp. 140—1) throughout.
84   T. E. Lawrenson and Helen Purkis, 'Les Éditions illustrées de Térence dans l'histoire du théâtre' in Jean Jacquot *et al.* (ed.), *Le Lieu Théâtral à la Renaissance*, Paris, 1964, pp. 1—23 and plates; see also *CM* pp. 87—110.
85   Craik, *Tudor Interlude* pp. 10—11; Southern, *Staging of plays* pp. 200—1.
86   Southern, *Staging of plays* pp. 48—55.
87   See Craik, *Tudor Interlude* pp. 11—19, 120—8; Southern, *Staging of plays* pp. 146—67.
88   Southern, *Staging of plays* pp. 413—23.
89   On *Susanna*, see *ibid.*, pp. 443—5, 519—32.
90   Craik, *Tudor Interlude* pp. 19—20.
91   Giles E. Dawson (ed.), *Records of Plays and Players in Kent, 1450—1642*, Malone Society *Collections* VII, Oxford, 1965, pp. xvi—xvii.
92   For details of staging in civic halls, see Southern, *Staging of plays* pp. 329—48.

4   Street theatre

Discussions of dramatic pageantry and aristocratic entertainments are found in *EES*, *HSS*, *MS*, and *MT*; these may be supplemented from more specialised studies including Robert Withington, *English Pageantry: An Historical Outline*, 2 vols, Cambridge, Mass., 1918—20, and George R. Kernodle, *From Art to Theatre*, Chicago, 1944, the latter being especially valuable on the street theatres of the fifteenth and sixteenth centuries. For religious processions and their inclusion of Corpus Christi pageants, see *MES* for England and *HSS* for Spain; on the pageant-waggons, see particularly Stanley Kahrl, *Traditions of Medieval English Drama*, 1974, Chapters 1 and 2; *MD* pp. 234—9; Alan H. Nelson, 'Some configurations of staging in medieval English drama', in *MED*, pp. 116—47; *EES*.

1   Johan Huizinga, *The Waning of the Middle Ages*, 1924; Penguin edn., 1955, p. 9.
2   For the tournament, see *EES* I. 13—50; *MT* pp. 152—7.
3   Sydney Anglo, *Spectacle, Pageantry and Early Tudor Policy*, Oxford, 1969, p. 110.
4   See *EES* I. 17; R. S. Loomis, 'Were there theatres in the twelfth and thirteenth centuries?' *Speculum* 20 (1945), 9.
5   *EES* I. 35.
6   For the Smithfield jousts of 1343, see *MS* I. 392, and those of 1374, *EES* I. 20—1. See also John Stow, *The Survey of London*, Everyman Library edn., 1912; rev. edn, 1956, pp. 240, 339.
7   *HSS* pp. 123—4.

8   *EES* I. 22–4, 43.
9   Huizinga, *Waning* p. 137.
10 *Ibid.* p. 84.
11 *EES* I. 24–5.
12 For similar structures, see *EES* I. 43, and note 73 (p. 366).
13 *HSS* pp. 129–30.
14 See *EES* I. 43–5, 28, 217; Anglo, *Spectacle* pp. 111–12.
15 See *Hall's Chronicle*, ed. Sir H. Ellis, 1809, pp. 517–19 for the full account.
16 Kernodle, *From Art to Theatre* p. 69; plates of the 1515 tableaux are found in Roy Strong, *Splendour at Court*, 1973, pp. 22–4.
17 For examples, see *DMC* I. 431; *HSS* pp. 136–7; *MD* p. 237; *MES* pp. 53, 77; *MS* II. 380.
18 *CM* p. 16.
19 *MS* II. 166–7, note 5.
20 *MS* II. 167, note 1.
21 *HSS* p. 113.
22 *HSS* pp. 113–14.
23 *MFD* pp. 165–6; *MES* p. 35.
24 For this and subsequent references to French entries, see *CM* pp. 17, 23, 16.
25 *CM* pp. 27–32, 19–21.
26 *DMC* II. 542.
27 For a German Corpus Christi expositor, see *Das Künzelsauer Fronleichnamsspiel*, ed. Peter K. Liebenow, Berlin, 1969.
28 *MFD* p. 165; for a fuller account, see Donald C. Stuart, *Stage Decoration in France in the Middle Ages*, New York, 1910, pp. 44–8.
29 *EES* I. 53–4; *MS* II. 167. For Stow's account, see *ed. cit.* p. 88.
30 *EES* I. 54; *MS* II. 167.
31 *EES* I. 54–5.
32 See Froissart, *Chronicles*, transl. Geoffrey Brereton, Penguin Classics, Harmondsworth, 1968, pp. 351–60.
33 See Laura Hibbard Loomis, 'Secular dramatics in the royal palace, Paris, 1378, 1389, and Chaucer's "Tregetoures"', *Speculum* 33 (1958), 242–55, reprinted in *MED*, pp. 98–115.
34 *HSS* p. 116; *EES* I. 349.
35 *HSS* pp. 116–17.
36 *HSS* pp. 137–8.
37 Huizinga, *Waning* pp. 314–15. Kernodle, *From Art to Theatre* p. 66; for this and other examples.
38 See *EES* I and Kernodle, *From Art to Theatre*, for examples. Descriptions and illustrations of later spectacles may be found in Roy Strong, *Splendour*, and A. M. Nagler, *Theatre Festivals of the Medici, 1539–1637*, New Haven and London, 1964.
39 Quoted by Anglo, *Spectacle*, p. 197, from Corpus Christi College, Cambridge, MS 298, No 8.
40 For some of the basic points at issue, see *MD* pp. 234–9; *MES*; F. M. Salter, *Mediaeval Drama in Chester*, Toronto, 1955; Kahrl, *Traditions*.
41 Maximilian J. Rudwin, *The Origin of the German Carnival Comedy*, New

York and London, 1920, pp. 32—5; for ship processions, see pp. 4—6, 8—12.

42 On the ridings, see *EES* I. 53, 66—7, 123—5, 147—9, 168, and *MES*.

43 *EES* I. 64—70. Quoted from Bodleian Library MS E. Museo 94.

44 Translated from *EES* I. 67.

45 *MES* p. 128 for Norwich; p. 141 for Coventry; p. 165 for Chester.

46 *MES* p. 88, quoted from Lucy Toulmin Smith, *English Gilds*, EETS (OS) 40 (1870) pp. 149—50.

47 *EES* I. 147.

48 *MES* p. 42.

49 On the Spanish processions, see *HSS* pp. 52—8, 80—6, 97—112.

50 *HSS* p. 55 discusses these terms.

51 *HSS* pp. 56—7.

52 *HSS* pp. 57—8.

53 *HSS* p. 98.

54 *HSS* p. 85. For the 1517 performance at Valencia, see pp. 73—4.

55 See Martin Stevens, 'The York cycle: from procession to play', *Leeds Studies in English* (NS) VI (1972), 37—61; Alan H. Nelson, *MES*.

56 *MS* II. 368—9; *MES* pp. 182—3.

57 *MS* II. 363—4; *MES* pp. 185—6. For the Beverley procession, see *ibid.*, p. 88.

58 See N. C. Brooks, 'Processional Drama and Dramatic Procession in Germany in the Late Middle Ages', *JEGP* 32 (1933), 141—71.

59 See *ibid.*; *EMP* p. 72; *MES* pp. 36—7. Brooks, *JEGP* 32, p. 167, and Theo Stemmler, *Liturgische Feiern und geistliche Spiele*, Tübingen, 1970, pp. 188—9 claim that a stationary site was employed. The Innsbruck text is printed in F. J. Mone (ed.), *Altteutsche Schauspiele*, Quedlinburg and Leipzig, 1841, pp. 145—64.

60 Quoted in *MES* pp. 35—6 from L. Petit de Julleville, *Les Mystères*, Paris, 1880, II. 209.

61 Stemmler, *Liturgische Feiern* pp. 188—90.

62 *Ibid.* pp. 193—9.

63 Quoted in *MES* p. 139; see also *ERD* pp. 239—40.

64 Quoted in W. W. Greg and F. M. Salter (ed.), *The Trial and Flagellation, with Other Studies in the Chester Cycle*, Malone Society, Oxford, 1935, pp. 146—7, from Harleian MS 1944 of *A breavarye or some fewe Collectiones of the Cittie of Chester . . .* by David Rogers, dated July 1609. Another version with minor variants is contained in Harleian MS 1948 and given in Greg and Salter, pp. 165—6; it states that the waggons had four wheels rather than six.

65 For information in this and the next paragraph, see *MES* pp. 91—3, and Kahrl, *Traditions* pp. 31—2.

66 See *MS* II. 388.

67 See Alexandra F. Johnston and Margaret Dorrell, 'The Doomsday pageant of the York Mercers, 1433', *Leeds Studies in English* (NS) V (1971), pp. 29—34.

68 See Hardin Craig (ed.), *Two Coventry Corpus Christi Plays*, EETS (ES) 87 (1902); 2nd edn, 1957, pp. 83, 84.

69 *ERD* p. 125; *EMP* p. 369, note 87.
70 *EES* I. 173. For other reservations, see Salter, *Mediaeval Drama* pp. 68–9.
71 *ERD* pp. 123–4; Craig thinks that Rogers was misled by the existence of tiring-rooms in the Elizabethan public theatres.
72 *EES* I. 170, 173.
73 Craig, *Corpus Christi Plays* p. 99.
74 The Louvain and Brussels illustrations are reproduced on pp. 119–21 of Nelson, 'Some Configurations' in *MED*.
75 For York, see Alexandra F. Johnston and Margaret Dorrell, 'The York Mercers and their pageant of Doomsday, 1433–1526', *Leeds Studies in English* (NS) VI (1972), 10–35; for Coventry, Craig, *Corpus Christi Plays* pp. 89, 85, 89–108.
76 *MS* II. 345; Giles E. Dawson (ed.), *Records of Plays and Players in Kent, 1450–1642*, Malone Society *Collections* VII, Oxford, 1965, p. 192.
77 *MES* p. 183.
78 *MS* II. 346, and John Coldewey, 'The Digby plays and the Chelmsford records, *RORD* 18 (1975), 105.
79 *MED* p. 118, and Alan H. Nelson, 'Six-wheeled carts: an underview', *Technology and Culture* 13 (1972), 391–416.
80 See *MS* II. 403.
81 Craig, *Corpus Christi Plays* p. 107.
82 See *ibid.* pp. 98–9, and Salter, *Mediaeval Drama* p. 62. The virgate is roughly equivalent to the modern yard (0.91 metres).
83 Arnold Williams, *The Drama of Medieval England*, East Lansing, 1961, pp. 97–8; M. James Young, 'The York pageant wagon', *Speech Monographs* 34 (1967) 1–20, esp. p. 13.
84 Text in Peter Happé (ed.), *English Mystery Plays*, Penguin English Library, Harmondsworth, 1975, p. 494; see Young, 'York pageant wagon' p. 12.
85 Craig, *Corpus Christi Plays* p. 99.
86 For an attempt to reconstruct one such practice, see Harry N. Langdon, 'Staging of the Ascension in the Chester cycle', *TN* 36 (1971–2), 53–60.
87 *EES* I. 170; Salter, *Mediaeval Drama* p. 58.
88 Craig, *Corpus Christi Plays* pp. 19, 27.
89 *Ibid.*, pp. 103, 91, 98.
90 Wickham's main treatment of the pageant-carts and their ancillary scaffolds is found in *EES* I. 168–74; for opposing views, see Kahrl, *Traditions* pp. 17–18; *MES* p. 151–2; Young, 'York pageant wagon' pp. 10–12. For Nelson's view, see also 'Six-wheeled carts'.
91 Young, 'York pageant wagon' pp. 15–16; in fact Young follows the erroneous date of 1472 given by Maud Sellers in *The York Mercers and Merchant Adventurers, 1356–1917*, Surtees Society 129, Durham, 1918, p. 72. For the correct interpretation, see Johnston and Dorrell, *Leeds Studies in English* (NS) VI (1972).
92 See Margaret Dorrell, 'Two studies of the York Corpus Christi play', *Leeds Studies in English* (NS) VI (1972), 63–111, p. 86. On the question of the nature of street-performances at York, see Stevens 'The York

cycle'. For the complaint of 1398–9, see Dorrell, 'Two studies' pp. 66–8.

93 On the 1415 *ordo paginarum* and its interpretation, see the articles by Dorrell and Stevens cited in the previous note. The 1421 proposal is found in Dorrell p. 85.

94 On the significance of Melton's visit and its effect on the York arrangements, see Dorrell, 'Two studies' and Stevens, 'The York cycle'; *MES* pp. 38–47; Kahrl, *Traditions* pp. 45–7, and note 68 (pp. 142–3).

95 *MES* pp. 45–7.

96 Craig, *Corpus Christi Plays* p. 73.

97 *MES* p. 144.

98 See Dorrell, 'Two studies' pp. 88–94.

99 *MES* p. 96.

100 H. Deimling and Dr Matthews (ed.), *The Chester Plays*, EETS (ES) 62 (1892), p. 3.

101 *MES* p. 149.

102 Quoted in *MES* p. 148.

103 Stevens, 'The York cycle' pp. 42–3.

104 See Dorrell, 'Two studies' p. 87.

105 See *MES* pp. 15–37, an expanded version of Nelson's 'Principles of processional staging: York cycle', *Modern Philology* 67 (1970), 303–20. See also Martial Rose, *The Wakefield Mystery Plays*, 1961, pp. 23–4, and Stevens, 'The York cycle'.

106 Quoted in *MES* p. 48.

107 See *MES* pp. 65–9, 72–8; for references to the hire of the Common Hall chamber, see especially pp. 66–8.

108 For this history of the chamber up to its demolition in 1724–5, see *MES* pp. 72–8.

109 Some scholars prefer to speak of this mode of presentation as 'station-to-station' or 'stop-to-stop' staging; see Kahrl, *Traditions* p. 143, note 69; Richard Hosley, 'Three Kinds of Outdoor Theatre before Shakespeare', *American Journal of Theatre History* 12 (1971), 1–33.

110 Dorrell, 'Two studies', esp. pp. 96–101; see also Kahrl, *Traditions* pp. 45–6.

111 Dorrell, 'Two studies' p. 79.

112 *MES* p. 73.

113 See Kahrl, *Traditions* pp. 45–6; for the 1415 Proclamation, see *MES* p. 43.

114 Stevens, 'The York cycle' pp. 52–7.

115 See *MES* pp. 191–4; Anna J. Mill, *Medieval Plays in Scotland*, Edinburgh and London, 1927, p. 63; Stanley Kahrl, 'Medieval Drama in Louth', *RORD* 10 (1967), 129–33.

5 Open-air theatre

The most valuable works on outdoor drama in the Middle Ages include *EES*, *HSS*, *MFD*, *MT* and *MTR*, but indispensable is *CM* with its detailed discussions of French open-air stages; also full of interest are the materials contained in *Mons, PPL,* and other similar collections. See also Alan H. Nelson, 'Some configurations of staging in medieval English drama' in *MED,* pp. 116—47.

1 Grace Frank, 'The Genesis and Staging of the *Jeu d'Adam'*, *PMLA* 54 (1944), 7-17.

2 See, for example, the low wall to the Garden on folios 3v and 4 of W. O. Hassall's facsimile edn of *The Holkham Bible Picture Book,* 1954, and the fence demarcating the Lucerne Paradise in the sketch-plan of 1583 (*PPL,* opp. p. 140). See also Robert Hughes, *Heaven and Hell in Western Art,* 1968.

3 Quoted in *MS* II. 379—80.

4 Carleton Brown, 'An early mention of a St Nicholas play in England', *SP* 28 (1931), 594—601.

5 For assessment of this lost drama, see *EDEMA* pp. 163—6.

6 *Courtois d'Arras* is edited by Edmond Faral (Les Classiques Français du Moyen Âge), Paris, 1911; 2nd rev. edn, 1922. Adam de la Halle's *Le Jeu de la Feuillée* is edited by Ernest Langlois in the same series, Paris, 1923; the other play by Adam, *Le Jeu de Robin et Marion* is edited by Langlois, Paris, 1924, and by Kenneth Varty, 1960. All three plays are translated in Richard Axton and John Stevens, *Medieval French Plays,* Oxford, 1971.

7 See *MFD* p. 229, 231.

8 For these plays, see Mario Roques' edition of *Le Garçon et l'Aveugle* (Les Classiques Français du Moyen Âge), Paris, 1911; 2nd rev. edn, 1921; Edmond Faral (ed.), *Mimes français du xiiie siècle,* Paris, 1910; *MS* II. 324—6.

9 The relevant passage is printed in *DMC* II. 539—40; for comment see *ERD* p. 99; *EMP* pp. 51, 55, 80; *EDEMA* p. 162—3.

10 *DMC* II. 542.

11 *DMC* I. 697—8.

12 *MS* II. 75.

13 The Cividale records are given in *DMC* II. 540—1, and translated (with inaccuracies) in *ERD* pp. 100—1.

14 *MFD* p. 75, note 1.

15 Translated (with Edward's reply) from Public Record Office Ancient Petition 4858 in W. O. Hassall, *They Saw It Happen . . . 55 B.C. — A.D. 1485,* Oxford, 1957, pp. 139—40, see also W. O. Hassall, 'Plays at Clerkenwell', *MLR* 33 (1938), 564—7.

16 See, for example, *ERD, EES, MES,* and V. A. Kolve, *The Play Called Corpus Christi,* 1966; also Stanley J. Kahrl, 'The civic religious drama of medieval England: a review of recent scholarship', *Renaissance Drama* (NS) 6 (1973), 237—48, a useful summary of the position at that date.

17 *EES* I. 314. For Kolve's views, see *Corpus Christi* pp. 8—32, esp.18—19.

18 Kolve, *Corpus Christi* p. 48.

19 See especially *MES,* pp. 1—10.

20 *MES* p. 9.

21 Theo Stemmler, *Liturgische Feiern und Geistliche Spiele,* Tübingen, 1970, pp. 167—72; *EMP* pp. 54—6.

22 *DMC* II. 542.

23 Stemmler, *Liturgische Feiern* p. 171; *ERD* p. 100.
24 For examples of the type, see Vincenzo de Bartholomeis (ed.), *Laude drammatiche e rappresentazioni sacre*, 3 vols, Florence, 1943.
25 *EES* I. 133–42.
26 *EMP* p. 58.
27 F. M. Salter, *Mediaeval Drama in Chester*, Toronto, 1955, pp. 33–42.
28 See *MS* II. 109, 344; *ERD* p. 130. For the latter view, see Salter, *Mediaeval Drama* p. 119; Stanley Kahrl, *Traditions of Medieval English Drama*, 1974, pp. 138–9.
29 Text in Richard Froning (ed.), *Das Drama des Mittelalters*, 3 vols, Stuttgart, 1891–2, I. 228–44.
30 Text in *ibid*. I. 305–24.
31 Text in F. J. Mone (ed.), *Schauspiele des Mittelalters*, 2 vols, Karlsruhe, 1848, I. 72–128.
32 Text in F. J. Mone (ed.), *Altteutsche Schauspiele*, Quedlinburg and Leipzig, 1841, pp. 145–64.
33 Text ed. Grace Frank (Les Classiques Français du Moyen Âge), Paris, 1922. For comment, see *MFD* pp. 126–9; *LPP* pp. 154–6.
34 Text ed. Grace Frank (Société des Anciens Textes Français), Paris, 1934. See *MFD* pp. 129–30.
35 Text ed. Émile Roy, Paris, 1902. See *MFD* pp. 131–5; *MeS* p. 157.
36 *MT* p. 65.
37 See *CM* pp. 138, 233.
38 See Martin Stevens, 'The staging of the Wakefield plays', *RORD* 11 (1968), 115–128.
39 For the Shrewsbury reference for 1516, see *MS* II. 251; see also Arthur Freeman, 'A round outside Cornwall', *TN* 16 (1961), 10–11; Nathalie Crohn Schmitt, 'Was there a medieval theatre in the round?' *TN* 23 (1968–9), 130–42; *TN* 24 (1969–70), 18–25; reprinted in *MED* pp. 292–315.
40 Thomas Churchyard, *The Worthiness of Wales*, 1587; reprinted 1776, p. 97.
41 See *CM* pp. 140, 54, 141.
42 *CM* p. 50 and note 1; *MMM* p. 200.
43 See *CM* p. 50; Neville Denny, 'The Cornish Passion play', in Neville Denny (ed.), *Medieval Drama*, Stratford-on-Avon Studies 16, 1973, pp. 129–30; *MTR* 60–9.
44 *CM* pp. 179–80, 143–6, 140.
45 *CM* pp. 182, 76.
46 *CM* pp. 230–5; *MeS* p. xv.
47 See *CM* pp. 55, 185.
48 See *CM* 161–73; for Vienne, see pp. 67, 173–6.
49 Kenneth Cameron and Stanley J. Kahrl, 'Staging the N-Town cycle', *TN* 21 (1967), 122–38, 152–65, esp. pp. 134–8.
50 See André Chastel, 'Cortile et Théâtre' in Jean Jacquot et al. (ed.), *Le Lieu Théâtral à la Renaissance*, Paris, 1964, pp. 41–7, and *CM* pp. 218–20.
51 *CM* pp. 223–44, esp. pp. 225–7, 233, 242.
52 *CM* p. 181.
53 For Alençon see *CM* pp. 150–9; for Montauban pp. 159–60, note 2.

54 *CM* pp. 184—5, note 2.
55 A. E. Zucker (transl.), *The Redentin Easter Play*, New York, 1941.
56 *CM* pp. 185—7.
57 *CM* pp. 189—98; see also *Mons, passim*.
58 See M. Blakemore Evans, 'The staging of the Donaueschingen Passion play', *MLR* 15 (1920), 65—76, 279—97; see also *CM* pp. 44—9.
59 See *PPL, passim*.
60 *CM* p. 69; p. 65 note 1.
61 See *CM, passim*.
62 See *PPL* p. 139, and the plan opposite p. 140.
63 See Cameron and Kahrl, 'N-Town cycle' p. 137; also Martin Stevens, 'The York cycle: from procession to play', *Leeds Studies in English* (N.S.) VI (1972), 37—61, pp. 52—3.
64 See *MTR* pp. 58—60; *CM* p. 50.
65 On the Cornish cycle, see Denny, 'Cornish Passion play'; Edwin Norris (ed.), *The Ancient Cornish Drama*, 2 vols, Oxford, 1859; Robert Longsworth, *The Cornish Ordinalia: Religion and Dramaturgy*, Cambridge, Mass., 1967; for a modern prose version see Markham Harris (transl.), *The Cornish Ordinalia*, Washington D.C., 1969.
66 *MTR* pp. 68—9; *CM* pp. 135 (and Plate 17), and 146.
67 See *CM* pp. 220, 156, 26.
68 See Carl Niessen, 'La scène du "Laurentius" à Cologne', in Jean Jacquot *et al.* (ed.), *Le Lieu Théâtral* pp. 191—214 and Plate I.
69 *CM* pp. 168 for Romans, 240 for Paris.
70 See *CM* pp. 161—73 for the Romans stage; *PPL* for Lucerne.
71 *MS* II. 82—4; see also Evans, 'Donauecschingen Passion play' pp. 70—1.
72 For a list of terms and well-documented definitions based on French practices see *CM* pp. 61—86, from which much of the succeeding information is taken.
73 *CM* p. 64.
74 *CM* p. 65.
75 *CM* p. 68.
76 See Andrew Gurr, *The Shakespearean Stage 1574—1642*, Cambridge, 1970, pp. 96—8; Richard Hosley, 'The gallery over the stage in the public playhouse of Shakespeare's time', *Shakespeare Quarterly* (1957), 15—31, and 'Shakespeare's use of a gallery over the stage', *Shakespeare Survey* 10 (1957), 77—89.
77 Richard Froning (ed.), *Das Drama* II. 340—73.
78 *CM* p. 59.
79 K. S. Block (ed.), *Ludus Coventriae or The Plaie called Corpus Christi*, EETS (ES) 120 (1922), 254, 283, 289.
80 J. Petersen, 'Aufführung und Bühnenplan des älteren Frankfurter Passionsspiels', *Zeitschrift für deutsches Altertum* 47 (1922), 83—126.
81 *MT* p. 79; Block (ed.), *Ludus Coventriae* p. 254, indicates that action at the Last Supper has been hidden from view until Judas's exchanges with the 'Buschopys' are completed.
82 The ensuing information is taken from *PPL* pp. 138—75.

83 *PPL* p. 143. For Adam and Eve, see pp. 170, 220.
84 *CM* pp. 185–7.
85 The lowest level would doubtless be on the top of the raised embankment, see *CM* pp. 156–8.
86 *CM* pp. 71–6.
87 See *Mons* pp. xliv–xlvii; *CM* pp. 189–98.
88 *Mons* pp. lii–lx.
89 See Élie Konigson, *La Représentation d'un Mystère de la Passion à Valenciennes en 1547*, Paris, 1969, *passim*, but esp. pp. 31–2. For an opposing view, see *CM passim*, but esp. pp. 55, 198–222.
90 *CM* p. 165.
91 See Denny, 'Cornish Passion play' pp. 125–53; the illustrations are also given in *CM* p. 51, etc.
92 For the staging of *St Meriasek*, see Glynne Wickham, 'The staging of saint plays in England', in Sandro Sticca (ed.), *The Medieval Drama*, Albany, 1972, pp. 99–119.
93 On the staging of *The Castel of Perseverance*, see *MTR*; Schmitt, 'Was there a medieval theatre in the round?'.
94 *MTR* p. 50.
95 *CM* pp. 118–22.
96 *CM* p. 282.
97 Schmitt, 'Was there a medieval theatre in the round?'.
98 Stevens, 'The staging of the Wakefield plays'; see also Martial Rose, *The Wakefield Mystery Plays*, 1961; *MES* pp. 86–7.
99 See Martial Rose, 'The staging of the Hegge plays' in Denny (ed.), *Medieval Drama*, pp. 197–221; Cameron and Kahrl, 'N-Town cycle' pp. 122–65.
100 For the staging of the Digby plays, see Wickham, in Sticca (ed.), *The Medieval Drama*, pp. 106–12; Mary del Vilar, 'The Staging of *The Conversion of St Paul*', *TN* 25 (1970–1), 64–8; David L. Jeffrey, 'English saints' plays' in Denny (ed.), *Medieval Drama*, pp. 75–86; John Coldewey, 'The Digby Plays at Chelmsford', *RORD* 18 (1975), 103–21, esp. pp. 112–13.
101 *MD* p. 688.
102 For text, see James Kinsley's edn of 1954; for discussion of staging, see Robert Potter, *The English Morality Play*, 1975, pp. 81–8; Wickham in Sticca (ed.), *The Medieval Drama*, pp. 114–15; John MacQueen, '*Ane Satyre of Thrie Estaitis*', *Studies in Scottish Literature* 3 (1966), 139–43; T. W. Craik, *The Tudor Interlude*, 1958, *passim*.
103 Text in Edgar T. Schell and J. D. Shuchter (ed.), *English Morality Plays and Moral Interludes*, New York, 1969, pp. 5–110; p. 88.
104 *CM* p. 82.
105 *PPL*, pp. 215–20.
106 For the sumptuous *monstre* at Bourges in which more than 700 players took part, see Raymond Lebègue, *Le Mystère des Actes des Apôtres*, Paris, 1929, pp. 90–4.
107 For traps and underground passages, see *CM* p. 193–4 (Mons); 162–6 (Romans); 144–5 (Doué); 84–5 (Bourges).
108 See *CM passim* esp. pp. 67 (Vienne); 77 (Autun); 162 (Romans).

109 See *PPL* pp. 171—5.
110 See *CM* p. 180.
111 *CM* pp. 142, 233.

6 Resources and effects

The only work exclusively devoted to this aspect of medieval staging is William Donald Young's excellent dissertation, 'Devices and *feintes* of the medieval religious theatre in England and France', Stanford University, 1959, which gathers together much information on which I have gratefully drawn; since Young often draws from materials not readily available, I have given his page numbers on occasion. Also of value are Fletcher Collins Jr, *The Production of Medieval Church Music-Drama*, Charlottesville, 1972; *MeS*; *HSS*; but the indispensable aids are the collections of material from Bourges, Coventry, Lucerne, Mons, Romans, and Valenciennes cited below.

1 See *DMC* I. 393—7, 408—10.
2 For plays featuring the star, see *DMC* II. 34—5, 43—5, 68—72, 84—9, 103—6, 172—90.
3 Collins, *Medieval Church Music-Drama* pp. 38—41. For the Monza text, see *DMC* I. 228—9.
4 *MeS* p. 30; for Collins's theory, see *Medieval Church Music-Drama* pp. 40, 315.
5 *Mons* pp. 471—2; *PPL* p. 149. See also Young, 'Devices' pp. 89—92. It is noteworthy that the Elizabethan impressario, Philip Henslowe, in his Inventory of 1598, included a 'clothe of the Sone and Mone'.
6 *Mons* p. 74; *PPL* p. 147.
7 R. M. Lumiansky and David Mills (ed.), *The Chester Mystery Cycle*, EETS (SS) 3 (1974). I. 159. For the Erlau play of the Magi, see Richard Froning (ed.), *Das Drama des Mittelalters*, 3 vols, Stuttgart, 1891—2, III. 939—52.
8 See *HSS* pp. 116—17, 137—8.
9 The complete version is given in Giorgio Vasari, *The Lives of the Painters, Sculptors, and Architects*, transl. A. B. Hinds, Everyman Library, 4 vols. 1927, I. 295—7.
10 See Orville K. Larson, 'Bishop Abraham of Souzdal's description of *Sacre Rappresentazioni*', *Education Theatre Journal* 9 (1957), 208—13.
11 For the full account, see Vasari, *Lives* II. 56—7.
12 *Mons* pp. 410—11.
13 For Lincoln, see Stanley J. Kahrl (ed.), *Records of Plays and Players in Lincolnshire, 1300—1585*, Malone Society *Collections* VIII, Oxford, 1969 (1974), p. 68. For Chelmsford, see *MS* II. 346; for the *Gwreans an Bys*, see Whitley Stokes (ed.), 1864, p. 18. On clouds in general, see Young, 'Devices', pp. 93—103.
14 See, for example, Élie Konigson, *La Répresentation d'un Mystère de la Passion à Valenciennes en 1547*, Paris, 1969, although he places too much reliance on the evidence of Hubert Cailleau's miniatures in determining the actual form of the décor. (See *CM* pp. 198—218.)
15 For Chester, see Lumlansky and Mills, *Chester Mystery Cycle* I. 373; for

Wakefield, see G. England and A. W. Pollard (ed.), *The Towneley Plays*, EETS (ES) 71 (1897), p. 361. See also F. M. Salter, *Mediaeval Drama in Chester*, Toronto, 1955, p. 70; Harry N. Langdon, 'Staging of the Ascension in the Chester cycle', *TN* 26 (1971–2), 53–60.

16 Lucy Toulmin Smith (ed.), *The York Plays*, Oxford, 1885, pp. 190, 461.

17 Quoted by Young, 'Devices', from Louis Paris, *Toiles peintes et tapisseries de la Ville de Reims ou la mise en scène du théâtre des Confréries de la Passion*, Paris, 1843, I. 30.

18 For Romans, see Paul-Emile Giraud and Ulysse Chevalier, (ed.), *Le Mystère des Trois Doms*, Lyon, 1887, p. 615. For Coventry, see Hardin Craig (ed.), *Two Coventry Corpus Christi Plays*, EETS (ES) 87 (1902); 2nd edn, 1957, p. 101.

19 For this and subsequent references to the Valenciennes Passion of 1547, see James de Rothschild, *Catalogue des livres composant la bibliothèque de feu M. le Baron James de Rothschild*, Paris, 1912, Vol. IV. See also Konigson, *Répresentation*.

20 *DMC* I. 439.

21 See Young, 'Devices' pp. 69, 223.

22 *MD* p. 671.

23 For Valenciennes, see Rothschild, *Catalogue* IV. 369; for Bourges, see Raymond Lebègue, *Le Mystère des Actes des Apôtres*, Paris, 1929, pp. 98–9.

24 Mark Eccles (ed.), *The Macro Plays*, EETS (OS) 262 (1969), p. 1.

25 Craig, *Corpus Christi Plays* p. 101.

26 *PPL* p. 182.

27 For Coventry, see Craig, *Corpus Christi Plays* p. 102; for *Les Miracles de Nostre Dame*, see Dorothy Penn, *The Staging of the 'Miracles de Nostre Dame Par Personnages' du MS Cangé*, New York, 1933; for *Mary Magdalene*, see *MD* pp. 713, 736; for Valenciennes, see Rothschild, *Catalogue*.

28 Young, 'Devices' pp. 75–6.

29 For the Alsfeld text, see Froning, *Das Drama* III. 853. For Bourges, see Lebègue, *Actes des Apôtres* pp. 98–9.

30 Donald C. Stuart, *Stage Decoration in France in the Middle Ages*, New York, 1910, p. 30.

31 L. Petit de Julleville, *Les Mystères*, 2 vols, Paris, 1880, II. 13.

32 See Giraud and Chevalier, *Trois Doms* pp. 316 etc.

33 See Lebègue, *Actes des Apôtres* pp. 90–4.

34 See Lumiansky and Mills, *Chester Mystery Cycle* I. 48 and footnote.

35 *Mons* pp. 28–9.

36 For Alsfeld, see Froning, *Das Drama* III. 793; for Donaueschingen, see Eduard Hartl (ed.), *Das Donaueschinger Passionsspiel*, Leipzig, 1942.

37 See Young, 'Devices' pp. 220–1.

38 See Lumiansky and Mills, *Chester Mystery Cycle* I. 88.

39 *DMC* II. 43–5.

40 Giles E. Dawson (ed.), *Records of Plays and Players in Kent, 1450–1642*, Malone Society *Collections* VII, Oxford, 1965, p. 192 (1513–14, 1514–15).

41 See *HSS* pp. 63–4 for the use of 'soft' staves and dummy figures in Spanish *consuetas*.

42 See *PPL* pp. 194, 211.
43 Craig, *Corpus Christi Plays* p. 90.
44 *CM* p. 283.
45 *MFD* pp. 150, 200.
46 Young, 'Devices' p. 179.
47 *Ibid.* pp. 181–7.
48 *Ibid.* p. 81.
49 *Ibid.* p. 128.
50 *Mons*, pp. 180, 184.
51 James de Rothschild (ed.), *Le Mistère du Viel Testament* (Société des Anciens Textes Francais), 6 vols, Paris, 1878–91, I. 228.
52 *Ibid.* I. 24; III. 304.
53 *CM* p. 142.
54 Petit de Julleville, *Les Mystères* I. 400.
55 *Mons*, p. 533.
56 *Ibid.* pp. xlv, lv, 27, 510–11, 514.
57 See the list of *feintes* at Bourges supplied by Young, 'Devices'. (Play VIII. Feinte 8.)
58 See *MD* pp. 733, 740.
59 See K. S. Block (ed.), *Ludus Coventriae or The Plaie called Corpus Christi*, EETS (ES) 120 (1922), pp. 39, 41.
60 See Stokes, *Gwreans an Bys* p. 174.
61 *Mons*, pp. 583, 514.
62 Emile Roy, *Le Mystère de la Passion en France du XIVe au XVIe Siècle*, Paris and Dijon, 1905, p. 106.
63 See examples in *MS* II. 345, 375, 394.
64 See Collins, *Medieval Church Music-Drama* pp. 8, 41–4.
65 For references to English practice, see Fletcher Collins Jr, 'Music in the craft cycles', *PMLA* 47 (1932), 613–21; R. W. Ingram, 'The use of music in English miracle plays', *Anglia* 75 (1957), 55–76; for France, see Howard Meyer Brown, *Music in the French Secular Theater, 1400–1550*, Cambridge, Mass., 1963.
66 Brown, *Music* p. 45.
67 *Ibid.* pp. 46–7, 140–7, for a fuller discussion of these terms.
68 *Mons*, pp. xcv, 9.
69 T. W. Craik, *The Tudor Interlude*, Leicester, 1958, pp. 45–8.
70 Konigson, *La Répresentation* p. 23.

7 The performers

All too little has been written on the medieval player: Edwin J. Duerr, *The Length and Breadth of Acting*, New York, 1962, pp. 63–102, offers a general survey, but I have mainly relied on *DMC, EDEMA, EMP, MeS, MMM, MS, MT,* and Ogilvy, while invaluable for the early period is Fletcher Collins Jr, *The Production of Medieval Church Music-Drama*, Charlottesville, 1972, as are *Mons* and *PPL* later.

1 *MMM* pp. 151. 136. 140.
2 J.-P. Migne (ed.), *Patrologiae cursus completus, series Latina*, lxxxii (1850), pp. 658–9.

3 Isidore's notion that mime players imitate human behaviour is also found in Choricius of Gaza's defence of the Byzantine stage; see *MMM* pp. 99, 120, 124, 142.
4 See *MMM* p. 147; Ogilvy, p. 609.
5 Ogilvy, pp. 611, 613.
6 *EDEMA* pp. 17–18.
7 Quoted in *LPP*, p. 11.
8 For Papias, see Mary H. Marshall, 'Theatre in the Middle Ages: evidence from dictionaries and glosses,' *Symposium* IV (1950), 1–39, 366–89, pp. 19–22.
9 *MMM* p. 208.
10 *MFD* p. 16.
11 J.-P. Migne (ed.), *Patrologiae cursus completus, series Latina*, cxcix (1855), p. 406.
12 *MMM* p. 151.
13 See Marshall, *Symposium* IV, 23–5.
14 *MS* II. 262–3.
15 Quoted by Peter Dronke, *The Medieval Lyric*, 1968, pp. 27–8.
16 *MFD* p. 112 note 1.
17 Maurice Delbouille (ed.), *Le Tournoi de Chauvency*, Paris and Liège, 1932, lines 4181–9. Nicoll's translation (*MMM* p. 158) is very free.
18 *MMM* p. 158.
19 *EMP* pp. 31–4.
20 See M. D. Anderson, *Drama and Imagery in English Medieval Churches*, Cambridge, 1963.
21 *MMM* pp. 139–40.
22 Benjamin Hunningher, *The Origin of the Theater*, Amsterdam and the Hague, 1955; New York, 1961.
23 For attacks on church drama, see *DMC* II. 411–14. See also *EDEMA* pp. 31, 44; *EMP* p. 78.
24 See *DMC* I. 548; *EDEMA* p. 31.
25 Helena M. Gamer, 'Mimes, musicians and the origins of the mediaeval religious play', *Deutsche Beiträge zur Geistigen Überlieferung* 5 (1965), 9–28; see also Ogilvy, p. 616.
26 Reproduced *MT*, Plate 16.
27 Nearly all the ensuing information on liturgical performers is from *DMC*; a convenient text of *Le Mystère d'Adam* with parallel translation is found in *MD* pp. 80–121.
28 Collins, *Medieval Church Music-Drama* pp. 19–22.
29 *HSS* p. 5; *EMP* p. 364, note 19.
30 See *MeS* pp. 197–8; *Mons*, pp. lxxi, civ–cv; *PPL* p. 118; *MS* II. 340–1; *HSS* pp. 73–4.
31 *MeS* p. 197.
32 *MeS* pp. 201, 217. On the Basochiens, see Howard G. Harvey, *The Theatre of the Basoche*, Harvard Studies in Romance Languages XVII, Cambridge, Mass., 1941.
33 See W. O. Hassall, 'Plays at Clerkenwell', *MLR* 33 (1938), 564–7.
34 *MeS* p. 203.
35 *PPL* pp. 116, 115, 19.

36 See *EES* I. 271–2; *MT* pp. 92–3.
37 *MeS* p. 206.
38 *MeS* p. 206. The appropriate tortures were presumably performed on a dummy figure (see p. 177 above).
39 *Mons* pp. c, cii–ciii.
40 *MeS* p. 207.
41 See Hardin Craig (ed.), *Two Coventry Corpus Christi Plays*, EETS (ES) 87 (1902); 2nd edn, 1957, p. 91.
42 *MeS* p. 207.
43 *PPL* p. 1.
44 For the *confréries*, see *EDEMA* pp. 132, 144–5; *MFD* pp. 96–7, 146–7, 167–8.
45 See *Mons*, pp. ciii–civ, lxxv.
46 See Raymond Lebègue, *Le Mystère des Actes des Apôtres*, Paris, 1929, pp. 188–9; Craig, *Corpus Christi Plays* p. 83; *PPL* pp. 82–4, 112.
47 *MES* pp. 47–8.
48 *MeS* p. 172.
49 *PPL* p. 88.
50 *MES* p. 92.
51 Giles E. Dawson (ed.), *Records of Plays and Players in Kent, 1450–1642*, Malone Society *Collections* VII, Oxford, 1965, pp. 203–4.
52 See *MES* pp. 43, 84.
53 *MES* p. 143.
54 *MeS* pp. 215–17.
55 See *MES* pp. 154, 183, 13.
56 See *MES* pp. 92, 98–9, 193; *MS* II. 331.
57 *PPL* p. 100.
58 See *MT* pp. 78–9, 81; Craig, *Corpus Christi Plays* p. 83; Dawson, *Records* pp. 202–4; *MES* p. 61; *MeS* p. 61; *Mons* p. lxxvii; *EES* I. 304; *PPL* pp. 97–100, 113.
59 See Dawson, *Records* pp. 207–11.
60 See John Coldewey, 'The Digby Plays and the Chelmsford Records', *RORD* 18 (1975), 103–21.
61 *MT* p. 79.
62 Dawson, *Records* p. 207.
63 Craig, *Corpus Christi Plays* p. 85.
64 See Lebègue, *Actes des Apôtres* p. 22.
65 See *MeS* p. 217; *MS* II. 370; *MES* p. 201; Craig, *Corpus Christi Plays*, *passim*.
66 See *PPL* p. 176 note 1; Craig, *Corpus Christi Plays* pp. 87, 90, 103; *MeS* p. 226.
67 The Lincoln edict of 1515 is taken from Stanley J. Kahrl (ed.), *Records of Plays and Players in Lincolnshire, 1300–1585*, Malone Society *Collections* VIII, Oxford, 1969 (1974), p. 43; the 1521 reference from *ibid.* p. 49.
68 Craig, *Corpus Christi Plays* p. 105.
69 See *MS* II. 346–8; also Coldewey, 'Digby Plays' pp. 107–8.
70 For Worcester, see *MS* II. 398 and *MT* p. 87; for Lucerne, see *PPL* p. 190.
71 See *MeS* pp. 221, 227–8; for subsequent citations, see Craig, *Corpus*

Christi Plays pp. 86, 96; *PPL* 201–2, 207; K. S. Block (ed.), *Ludus Coventriae or the Plaie called Corpus Christi*, EETS (ES) 120 (1922), p. 230.

72 *PPL* p. 191; Craig, *Corpus Christi Plays* pp. 100, 85–6; Dawson, *Records* p. 208; *MeS* pp. 223, 227; *Mons* pp. lxxvi, cix; Lebègue, *Acts des Apôtres* p. 93.

73 See Johan Huizinga, *The Waning of the Middle Ages*, 1924; Penguin edn, 1955, 314–15; A. M. Nagler, *Theatre Festivals of the Medici, 1539–1637*, New Haven and London, 1964, pp. 10, 18, etc.

74 *MeS* pp. 231–2.

75 M. Blakemore Evans, 'The staging of the Donaueschingen Passion play', *MLR* 15 (1920), 285–6.

76 See *MS* II. 388; *Mons* pp. 11–12; *PPL* pp. 177, 181, 191; Whitley Stokes (ed.), *Gwreans an Bys*, 1864, pp. 28, 70, 78.

77 Lebègue, *Actes des Apôtres* p. 198.

78 *MeS* p. 237.

79 Lebègue, *Actes des Apôtres* p. 197, suggests that lapses in the text of *Les Actes des Apôtres* resulting in ludicrous nonsense bear the Procurator out! For the Bourges compliment, see *ibid.* p. 100; *MeS* p. 235; *MFD* p. 193.

80 *MeS* p. 240.

81 *MeS* pp. 238–9.

82 *MT* p. 83.

83 See *MS* II. 240–8, 329–406 for examples; Dawson, *Records* pp. 1–155.

84 See *MS* II. 338.

85 Dawson, *Records* pp. x–xiii.

86 For Selby Abbey accounts, see *EES* I. 332–9.

87 Stanley J. Kahrl, *Traditions of Medieval English Drama*, 1974, pp. 100–1.

88 *Ibid.* pp. 100–1.

89 *Ibid.* pp. 101–2; *MS* II. 256–7.

90 Lucy Toulmin Smith (ed.), *The York Plays*, p. xxxviii.

91 Dawson, *Records* p. 26, 98.

92 See *MS* II. 256.

93 Norman Davis (ed.), *The Paston Letters*, Oxford, 1971. I. 461 (Letter 275).

94 Quoted in *MT* p. 190.

95 See *MS* II. 244, 247.

96 *MS* II. 191 note 2.

97 *MS* II. 189 note 5; also *ERD* pp. 379–80.

98 See M. C. Bradbrook, *The Rise of the Common Player*, 1962, pp. 17–38; for references, see *MT* pp. 171–99; *MS* II. 257, 251, 187 note 1.

8 Financing the plays

Most general studies of the medieval theatre touch on the financing of plays and on their audiences, but the relative dearth of detail precludes a full-scale treatment. The most useful information is contained in *Mons*, *PPL*, and the two volumes of Malone Society *Collections* cited below. The most valuable general discussions include *CM*, *EES*, *MeS*, and *MT*.

1 See, for examples, Harold C. Gardiner SJ, *Mysteries End*, New Haven, 1946, pp. 1–19; *DMC* II. 416–21; *HSS* pp. 40–1, note 5.
2 *MD* p. 16.
3 *DMC* I. 165.
4 *DMC* I. 363–5; for the Fleury Herod, see *MD* p. 58.
5 *DMC* II. 542.
6 See F. J. Mone (ed.), *Altteutsche Schauspiele*, Quedlinburg and Leipzig, 1841, pp. 145–64.
7 See *A History of Lancashire*, (The Victoria History of the Counties of England), 1914, VIII. 255.
8 For René, see *MeS* pp. 164, 175.
9 *MeS* p. 166.
10 For Romans, see *EES* I. 166; for Mons, see *Mons* pp. lxxviii–ix.
11 For Lucerne, see *PPL* pp. 224–5, 241; for Valenciennes, see *MeS* pp. 176–7.
12 For York, see *EES* I. 294–5; for Coventry, see Hardin Craig (ed.), *Two Coventry Corpus Christi Plays*, EETS (ES) 87 (1902); 2nd edn, 1957, pp. 106, 85, 95; for Lincoln, see Stanley J. Kahrl (ed.), *Records of Plays and Players in Lincolnshire, 1300–1585*, Malone Society *Collections* VIII, Oxford, 1969 (1974), p. 47; for Chester, F. M. Salter, *Mediaeval Drama in Chester*, Toronto, 1955, pp. 63, 50.
13 See Kahrl, *Records* p. 51.
14 For Bassingbourn, see *MS* II. 338; *MT* p. 195 for this and the Suffolk and Essex productions. For New Romney, see Giles E. Dawson (ed.), *Records of Plays and Players in Kent, 1450–1642*, Malone Society *Collections* VII, Oxford, 1965, pp. 207, 205–6.
15 *MeS* p. 175.
16 Kahrl, *Records* p. 84.
17 John Coldewey, 'The Digby Plays and the Chelmsford Records' *RORD* 18 (1975), 103–21, esp. pp. 103–4, 108.
18 For post-performance sales, see Raymond Lebègue, *Le Mystère des Actes des Apôtres*, Paris, 1929, p. 103 note 3, and Dawson, *Records* pp. 207, 198.
19 See *MT* pp. 194–5.
20 Kahrl, *Records* p. 18.
21 *MS* II. 372.
22 *MS* II. 377–8, but also Kahrl, *Records* p. 29 note 1.
23 See *EES* I. 296.
24 For Valenciennes, see Élie Konigson, *La Répresentation d'un Mystère de la Passion à Valenciennes en 1547*, Paris, 1969, p. 19; for Lucerne, *PPL* pp. 92–5.
25 Lebègue, *Actes des Apôtres* p. 81, quoting a German visitor to the Bourges district.
26 *EES* I. 34–8.
27 For French accounts, see *CM* pp. 66–8; for Lucerne, *PPL* p. 173. For the accommodation of important spectators, see *EES* I. 171–2.
28 For France, see *CM* pp. 176–7, 189–93; for Valenciennes, see also Konigson, *La Répresentation* and for Romans, see also *EES* I. 164–6. For the provision of seating and for Neyron's theatre at Lyon, see *CM* pp. 60, 77, 182. For the situation depicted by Fouquet, see *CM* pp. 121–2.

29 See *MS* II. 342 for the Braintree performances; for New Romney, see Dawson, *Records* p. 207; for Sutterton, see Kahrl, *Records* p. 92.

30 On the leasing of the York stations, see Anna J. Mill, 'The Stations of the York Corpus Christi Play', *Yorkshire Archaeological Journal* 37 (1948—51) 497—502; Margaret Dorrell, 'Two studies of the York Corpus Christi play', *Leeds Studies in English* (NS) VI (1972), 63—111; pp. 88—95. The statute of 1554 is given on page 92 of Margaret Dorrell's article.

31 *CM* pp. 38—9.

32 *CM* p. 67 note 2.

33 For the exclusion of certain types of spectator, see *CM* pp. 191, 176; for the *retraicts*, see pp. 171, 174.

34 *CM* p. 70.

35 See *MT* p. 84; *CM* p. 41.

36 For the comment from Autun and for instances of violence, see *CM* p. 282.

37 The affray at York is discussed by Dorrell, 'Two studies' pp. 70—2.

38 Quoted by Howard Meyer Brown, *Music in the French Secular Theater, 1400—1500*, Cambridge, Mass., 1963, p. 6.

39 See *EES* II. 1. 54—97, especially pp. 60—75.

Epilogue

Only a mercifully limited number of books in the colossal library of works devoted to the Renaissance stage discuss the links between medieval and Renaissance principles of staging; apart from *EES*, the most valuable are George R. Kernodle, *From Art to Theatre*, Chicago, 1944; Lily B. Campbell, *Scenes and Machines on the English Stage during the Renaissance*, Cambridge, 1923; Glynne Wickham, *Shakespeare's Dramatic Heritage*, 1969. The best work on early Protestant opposition to religious drama is Harold C. Gardiner SJ, *Mysteries' End. An Investigation of the Last Days of the Medieval Religious Stage*, New Haven, 1946; *CM* (pp. 255—305) contains a stimulating discussion of certain aspects of the demise of the medieval stage.

1 A. M. Nagler, 'Sixteenth-century continental stages', *Shakespeare Quarterly* 5 (1954), 359—60.

2 J. A. Scott in A. J. Krailsheimer (ed.), *The Continental Renaissance, 1500—1600*, Harmondsworth, 1971, p. 247.

3 See Kernodle, *From Art to Théatre, passim*. Vitruvius's treatise is translated by M. H. Morgan as *The Ten Books of Architecture*, Cambridge, Mass., 1926.

4 Kernodle, *From Art to Theatre* p. 14.

5 *Ibid.* p. 51.

6 Nagler, 'continental stages' p. 361. But see also T. E. Lawrenson and Helen Purkis, 'Les Éditions Illustrées de Térence dans l'Histoire du Théâtre,' in Jean Jacquot *et al.* (ed.), *Le Lieu Théâtral à la Renaissance*, Paris, 1964, pp. 1—23 and plates.

7 Translated in A. M. Nagler (ed.), *A Source Book of Theatrical History*, New York, 1959, p. 71.

8   *Ibid.* p. 72, quoted from A. B. Hinds's Everyman Library translation, 1927, II. 297.
9   *Ibid.* p. 77, taken from *The First Book of Architecture*, 1611, II. 3.
10 Quoted by Nagler, 'continental stages', 359.
11 *Ibid.* p. 359.
12 G. Gregory Smith (ed.), *Elizabethan Critical Essays*, Oxford, 1904, I, 197.
13 Gardiner, *Mysteries End* pp. 95–6.
14 *Ibid.* pp. xi–xii.
15 *Ibid.* pp. 98–9, 105.
16 For the full text, see L. Petit de Julleville, *Les Mystères*, Paris, 1880, I. 429.
17 *MES* p. 182.
18 Gardiner, *Mysteries End* p. 61.
19 *MES* p. 59.
20 Gardiner, *Mysteries End* p. 73; see also *MT* pp. 114–15; *MES* pp. 61–2.
21 Gardiner, *Mysteries End* pp. 79–83.
22 *Ibid.* p. 82.
23 *Ibid.* p. 89.
24 *Ibid.* p. 90.
25 *Ibid.* p. 78.
26 *Ibid.* p. 21.
27 On the Counter-Reformation and the Council of Trent, see H. O. Evennett in John Bossy (ed.), *The Spirit of the Counter-Reformation*, Cambridge, Mass., 1968; John C. Olin, *The Catholic Reformation: Savonorola to Ignatius Loyola*, New York, 1969.
28 See Gardiner, *Mysteries End* pp. 108–10, 23–5, 26–7, 25–6.
29 See *HSS* pp. 46–7.
30 On Lope, see *HSS* pp. 153–67.
31 *HSS* pp. 177–80.
32 See Richard Hosley, 'The Playhouse and the Stage' in Kenneth Muir and S. Schoenbaum (ed.), *A New Companion to Shakespeare Studies*, Cambridge, 1971, pp. 15–20. Hosley suggests that the Elizabethan 'game-houses' were also employed as temporary theatres in the same way.
33 On the London inn-playhouses, see *EES* II. 2. 95–109, and C. J. Sisson, *The Boar's Head Theatre*, ed. Stanley Wells, 1972. See also O. L. Brownstein, 'A record of London inn-playhouses, *c.* 1565–1580', *Shakespeare Quarterly*, 22 (1971–2), 17–24.
34 See Gardiner, *Mysteries End.* pp. 26–7. It is curious to note that in 1551 Leicester Borough accounts refer to 'the play that was in the church' (see Richard Leacroft, *The Development of the English Playhouse*, 1973, p. 25), and in 1595 the churchwardens of Winslow, Buckinghamshire, were fined for permitting the performance of an interlude in the parish church (see W. Le Hardy, 'Elizabethan Players in Winslow Church', *TN* 12 (1958), p. 107).

SELECT BIBLIOGRAPHY

The following list of books and articles makes no pretence to completeness: for comprehensive coverage the reader is referred to Carl J. Stratman's *Bibliography of Mediaeval Drama* (Berkeley, 1954; 2nd rev. edn, 2 vols, New York, 1972), and to the reading lists provided in books published since that date. I have listed simply those works which have assisted me most in preparing my survey, citing material written in English wherever possible as being more easily available and comprehensible to the average reader. The place of publication is London unless stated otherwise; titles of periodicals are abbreviated in accordance with pp. 250—1 above.

General works on the medieval stage

Erich Auerbach. *Mimesis. Dargestellte Wirklichkeit in der abendlandischen Literatur.* Bern, 1945. Transl. Willard Trask, New York, 1946.
Richard Axton. *European Drama of the Early Middle Ages.* 1974.
David Bevington (ed.). *Medieval Drama.* Boston, 1975. (The most useful one-volume anthology of texts.)
E. K. Chambers. *The Mediaeval Stage.* 2 vols, Oxford, 1903.
Neville Denny (ed.). *Medieval Drama.* Stratford-on-Avon Studies 16, 1973.
A. M. Kinghorn. *Medieval Drama.* 1968.
Allardyce Nicoll. *Masks, Mimes and Miracles: Studies in the Popular Theatre.* 1931.
Richard Southern. *The Seven Ages of the Theatre.* 1962.
Sandro Sticca (ed.). *The Medieval Drama.* Albany, 1972.
Glynne Wickham. *The Medieval Theatre.* 1974.

Ritual and classical drama

W. Beare. *The Roman Stage.* 1950; 3rd rev. edn, 1964.
Alan Brody. *The English Mummers and their Plays: Traces of Ancient Mystery.* 1970.
Timothy Fry. 'The alleged influence of pagan ritual on the formation of the English mystery plays', *American Benedictine Review* 9 (1958—9), 187—201.
Helena M. Gamer. 'Mimes, musicians and the origin of the mediaeval religious play', *Deutsche Beiträge zur Geistigen Überlieferung* 5 (1965), 9—28.
Theodor Gaster. *Thespis. Ritual, Myth and Drama in the Ancient Near East.* New York, 1950; 2nd rev. edn. New York, 1961.
Jane Ellen Harrison. *Ancient Art and Ritual.* 1913.

Benjamin Hunningher. *The Origin of the Theater*. Amsterdam and the Hague, 1955; New York, 1961.

George La Piana. 'The Byzantine theatre', *Speculum* 11 (1936), 171–211.

Mary H. Marshall, 'Boethius' definition of *persona* and medieval understanding of the Roman theater', *Speculum* 25 (1950), 471–82.

J. D. A. Ogilvy, *'Mimi, scurrae, histriones*: entertainers of the Middle Ages', *Speculum* 38 (1963), 603–19.

Joseph S. Tunnison. *Dramatic Traditions of the Dark Ages*. Chicago, 1907.

Medieval Latin drama

Sister Mary Marguerite Butler. *Hrotswita: The Theatricality of her Plays*. New York, 1960.

Oscar Cargill. *Drama and Liturgy*. New York, 1930.

Fletcher Collins Jr. *The Production of Medieval Church Music-Drama*. Charlottesville, 1972.

Richard B. Donovan. *The Liturgical Drama in Medieval Spain*. Toronto, 1958.

C. Clifford Flanigan. 'The liturgical drama and its tradition: a review of scholarship 1965–75', *RORD* 18 (1975), 81–102.

O. B. Hardison Jr. *Christian Rite and Christian Drama in the Middle Ages*. Baltimore, 1965.

Millett Henshaw. 'The attitude of the Church toward the stage to the end of the Middle Ages', *Medievalia et Humanistica* 7 (1952), 3–17.

Dom Anselm Hughes (ed.). *Early Mediaeval Music up to 1300*. 1954.

Otto Pächt. *The Rise of Pictorial Narrative in Twelfth-Century England*. Oxford, 1962.

Theo Stemmler. *Liturgische Feiern und geistliche Spiele*. Tübingen, 1970.

Sandro Sticca. *The Latin Passion Play: Its Origins and Development*. Albany, 1970.

Edith A. Wright. *The Dissemination of the Liturgical Drama in France*. Bryn Mawr, 1936.

Karl Young. *The Drama of the Medieval Church*. 2 vols, Oxford, 1933.

Works on the staging of vernacular plays

General

Dino Bigongiari. 'Were there theatres in the twelfth and thirteenth centuries?' *Romanic Review* 37 (1946), 201–24.

George R. Kernodle. *From Art to Theatre. Form and Convention in the Renaissance*. Chicago, 1944.

Laura H. Loomis. 'Secular dramatics in the royal palace, Paris 1378, 1389 and Chaucer's "Tregetoures"', *Speculum* 33 (1958), reprinted in Taylor and Nelson (below).

R. S. Loomis. 'Were there theatres in the twelfth and thirteenth centuries?' *Speculum* 20 (1945), 92–8.

Mary H. Marshall. '*Theatre* in the Middle Ages: evidence from dictionaries and glosses', *Symposium* IV (1950), 1–39, 366–89.

Robert Weimann. '*Platea* und *Locus* in Misterienspiel: Zu einem Grundprinzips vorshakespearesches Dramaturgie', *Anglia* 84 (1966), 330–52.

SELECT BIBLIOGRAPHY

Britain

M. D. Anderson. *Drama and Imagery in English Medieval Churches*. Cambridge, 1963.

Sydney Anglo. *Spectacle, Pageantry and Early Tudor Policy*. 1969.

David Bergeron. *English Civic Pageantry 1558–1642*, 1971.

David M. Bevington. *From Mankind to Marlowe: Growth and Structure in the Popular Drama of Tudor England*. Cambridge, Mass., 1962.

Kenneth Cameron and Stanley J. Kahrl. 'Staging the N-Town cycle', *TN* 21 (1967) 122–38, 152–65.

A. C. Cawley (ed.). *The Wakefield Pageants in the Towneley Cycle*. Manchester, 1958.

George R. Coffman. 'A plea for the study of the Corpus Christi plays as drama', *SP* 26 (1929), 411–24.

John C. Coldewey. 'The Digby plays and the Chelmsford records', *RORD* 18 (1975), 103–21.

Fletcher Collins Jr. 'Music in the Craft Cycles', *PMLA* 47 (1932), 613–21.

Hardin Craig. *English Religious Drama of the Middle Ages*. Oxford, 1955.

T. W. Craik. *The Tudor Interlude: Stage, Costume and Acting*. Leicester, 1958.

Giles E. Dawson (ed.) *Records of Plays and Players in Kent, 1450–1642*. Malone Society *Collections* VII, Oxford, 1965.

Margaret Dorrell. 'Two studies of the York Corpus Christi play', *Leeds Studies in English* (NS) VI (1972), 63–111.

Harold C. Gardiner. *Mysteries' End. An Investigation of the Last Days of the Medieval Religious Stage*. Yale Studies in English 103, New Haven, 1946.

Anne Cooper Gay. 'The "stage" and the staging of the N-Town plays', *RORD* 10 (1967), 135–40.

Alfred Harbage (ed.). *Annals of English Drama, 975–1700*. Philadelphia, 1940. Revised S. Schoenbaum, 1964. (Supplements issued periodically to subscribers.)

Markham Harris (transl.). *The Cornish Ordinalia*. Washington, D.C., 1969.

R. W. Ingram, 'The use of music in English miracle plays', *Anglia* 75 (1957), 55–76.

Alexandra F. Johnston and Margaret Dorrell. 'The Doomsday pageant of the York Mercers, 1433', *Leeds Studies in English* (NS) V (1971), 29–34.

'The York Mercers and their Pageant of Doomsday, 1433–1526', *Leeds Studies in English* (NS) VI (1973), 10–35.

Stanley J. Kahrl. (ed.). *Records of Plays and Players in Lincolnshire, 1300–1585*. Malone Society *Collections* VIII, Oxford, 1969 (1974).

'The civic religious drama of medieval England: a review of recent scholarship', *Renaissance Drama* (NS) 6 (1973), 237–48.

Traditions of Medieval English Drama. 1974.

V. A. Kolve. *The Play Called Corpus Christi*. 1966.

Richard Leacroft. *The Development of the English Playhouse*. 1973.

Anna J. Mill. *Medieval Plays in Scotland*. Edinburgh and London, 1927.

'The Stations of the York Corpus Christi play', *Yorkshire Archaeological Journal* 37 (1948–51), 497–502.

Alan H. Nelson. 'Early pictorial analogues of medieval theatre-in-the-round', *RORD* 12 (1969), 93–105.

279

'Some configurations of staging in medieval English drama', in Taylor and Nelson (below).

The Medieval English Stage. Corpus Christi Pageants and Plays. Chicago and London, 1974.

'The Wakefield Corpus Christi play: pageant procession and dramatic cycle', *RORD* 13–14 (1970–1), 221–33.

Robert Potter. *The English Morality Play. Origins, History and Influence of a Dramatic Tradition.* 1975.

Leonard Powlick. 'The staging of the Chester cycle: an alternate theory', *Theatre Survey* (1971), 119–50.

Martial Rose (transl.). *The Wakefield Mystery Plays,* 1961.

A. P. Rossiter. *English Drama from Early Times to the Elizabethans,* 1950.

F. M. Salter. *Mediaeval Drama in Chester,* Toronto, 1955.

Natalie Crohn Schmitt. 'Was there a medieval theatre in the round?' *TN* 23 (1968–9), 130–42; *TN* 24 (1969–70), 18–25; reprinted in Taylor and Nelson (below).

Thomas Sharp. *A Dissertation on the Pageants and Dramatic Mysteries, anciently performed at Coventry.* Coventry, 1825.

Virginia Shull. 'Clerical drama in Lincoln Cathedral, 1318–1561', *PMLA* 52 (1937), 946–66.

Richard Southern. *The Medieval Theatre in the Round.* 1957; 2nd rev. edn, 1975. *The Staging of Plays before Shakespeare.* 1973.

Martin Stevens. 'The staging of the Wakefield plays', *RORD* 11 (1968), 115–28. 'The York cycle: from procession to play', *Leeds Studies in English* (NS) VI (1972), 37–61.

Jerome Taylor and Alan H. Nelson (eds.). *Medieval English Drama: Essays Critical and Contextual.* Chicago and London, 1972.

Glynne Wickham. *Early English Stages, 1300–1660,* 2 vols, 1959–72. *Shakespeare's Dramatic Heritage.* 1969.

Arnold Williams. *The Drama of Medieval England.* East Lansing, 1961.

F. P. Wilson. *The English Drama 1485–1585,* ed. G. K. Hunter. Oxford, 1969.

Robert Withington. *English Pageantry: An Historical Outline.* 2 vols, Cambridge, Mass., 1918–20.

Rosemary Woolf. *The English Mystery Plays,* 1972.

M. James Young. 'The York pageant wagon', *Speech Monographs* 34 (1967), 1–20.

France

Richard Axton and John Stevens (transl.). *Medieval French Plays.* Oxford, 1971.

Neil C. Brooks. 'Notes on the performances of French mystery plays', *MLN* 39 (1924), 276–81.

Howard Meyer Brown. *Music in the French Secular Theater, 1400–1550.* Cambridge, Mass., 1963.

Gustave Cohen. *Histoire de la mise en scène dans le théâtre religieux français du Moyen Age.* Paris 1906; 2nd edn, 1925.

Le Livre de conduite du régisseur et le compte des dépenses pour la mystère de la Passion joué à Mons en 1501. Paris, 1925.

Le Théâtre en France au Moyen Age. 2 vols, Paris, 1928—31.

Grace Frank. *The Medieval French Drama.* Oxford, 1954.

'The genesis and the staging of the *Jeu d'Adam*', *PMLA* 59 (1944), 7—17.

Raymond Lebègue. *Le Mystère des Actes des Apôtres.* Paris, 1929.

Élie Konigson. *La Représentation d'un mystère de la Passion à Valenciennes en 1547.* Editions du Centre Nationale de la Recherche Scientifique, Paris, 1969.

Dorothy Penn. *The Staging of the 'Miracles de Nostre Dame par personnages' of the Ms Cangé.* New York, 1933.

Henri Rey-Flaud. *Le Cercle magique.* Paris, 1973.

Emile Roy. *Le Mystère de la Passion en France du XIVe au XVIe siècle.* Paris and Dijon, 1905.

Donald C. Stuart. *Stage Decoration in France in the Middle Ages.* New York, 1910.

'The stage setting of Hell and the iconography of the Middle Ages', *Romanic Review* 4 (1913), 330—42.

William D. Young. 'Devices and *feintes* of medieval religious theatre in England and France.' Unpublished dissertation, Stanford University, 1959.

Germany

Neil C. Brooks. 'Processional Drama and Dramatic Procession in Germany in the Late Middle Ages', *JEGP* 32 (1933), 141—71.

Wilhelm Creizenach. *Geschichte des neueren Dramas.* Halle, 1911.

M. Blakemore Evans. 'The Staging of the Donaueschingen Passion play', *MLR* 15 (1920), 65—76, 279—97.

The Passion Play of Lucerne. A Historical and Critical Introduction. MLA Monographs 14. New York, 1943.

Richard Froning (ed.). *Das Drama des Mittelalters.* 3 vols, Stuttgart, 1891—2. (Texts and comment).

Eduard Hartl (ed.). *Das Drama des Mittelalters.* 2 vols, Leipzig, 1937. (Texts.).

Wolfgang F. Michael. 'Das deutsche Drama und Theater vor der Reformation', *Deutsche Vierteljahrsschrift* 31 (1957), 106—53.

Franz Joseph Mone (ed.). *Altteutsche Schauspiele.* Quedlinburg and Leipzig, 1841. (Texts.)

Maximilian J. Rudwin. *A Historical and Bibliographical Survey of the German Religious Drama.* Pittsburg, 1924.

The Origin of the German Carnival Comedy. New York and London, 1920.

Rolf Steinbach. *Die deutschen Oster- und Passionsspiele des Mittelalters,* Cologne and Vienna, 1970. (Partly an annotated bibliography.)

A. E. Zucker (transl.). *The Redentin Easter Play.* New York, 1941.

Italy

Mario Apollonio. *Storia del teatro italiano.* 3 vols. Florence, 1943—6.

G. D. Bonino (ed.). *Il teatro italiano.* Vol I (2 vols), Turin, 1975.

Alessandro D'Ancona. *Origini del teatro italiano.* Turin, 1891.

Vincenzo de Bartholomeis (ed.). *Laude drammatiche e rappresentazioni sacre.* 3 vols, Florence, 1943.

Virginia Galante Garrone. *L'apparato scenico del dramma sacro in Italia.* Turin, 1935.

Joseph S. Kennard. *The Italian Theatre.* 2 vols, New York, 1932.

Orville K. Larson. 'Bishop Abraham of Souzdal's description of *Sacre Rappresentazioni'*, *Education Theatre Journal* 9 (1957), 208–13.

Cesare Molinari. *Spettacoli fiorentini del Quattrocento.* Raccolta Pisana 5, Venice, 1961.

Paolo Toschi. *Le origini del teatro italiano.* Turin, 1955.

Spain

J. P. W. Crawford, *Spanish Drama before Lope de Vega.* Philadelphia, 1922; 2nd rev. edn, 1937.

A. Alexander Parker. 'Notes on the religious drama in mediaeval Spain and the origins of the "Auto Sacramental"', *MLR* 30 (1935), 170–82.

N. D. Shergold. *A History of the Spanish Stage from Medieval Times until the End of the Seventeenth Century.* Oxford, 1967.

W. H. Shoemaker. *The Multiple Stage in Spain during the Fifteenth and Sixteenth Centuries.* Princeton, 1935.

Ronald B. Williams. *The Staging of Plays in the Spanish Peninsula Prior to 1555.* Iowa, 1935.

The renaissance stage

Lily B. Campbell. *Scenes and Machines on the English Stage during the Renaissance.* Cambridge, 1923.

Jean Jacquot (ed.). *Les Fêtes de la Renaissance.* 2 vols, Paris, 1956–60.

Jean Jacquot, Élie Konigson, and Marcel Oddon (eds.). *Le Lieu théâtral à la Renaissance.* Éditions du Centre National de la Recherche Scientifique, Paris, 1964.

Gordon Kipling. 'The early Tudor disguising: new research opportunities', *RORD* 17 (1974), 3–8.

A. J. Krailsheimer (ed.). *The Continental Renaissance 1500–1600.* Harmondsworth, 1971.

A. M. Nagler. 'Sixteenth-century continental stages', *Shakespeare Quarterly* 5 (1954), 359–70.

Theatre Festivals of the Medici 1539–1637. New Haven, 1964.

C. J. Sisson. *The Boar's Head Theatre,* ed. Stanley Wells. 1972.

GLOSSARY OF TECHNICAL TERMS

apse: polygonal or semicircular recess in cathedrals and churches, found at the east end of the chancel beyond the presbytery (see Illustration 4).

autos (Sp): one-act vernacular plays, frequently religious moralities, performed in Spain from the fifteenth century onwards. *Autos sacramentales* were plays concerned with the Sacrament played annually at the Feast of Corpus Christi.

basilica: type of rectangular hall with colonnaded aisles, Roman in origin; later a place of Christian worship of a similar type. The term is often loosely applied to any oblong, aisled church building.

booth stage: portable stage consisting of a platform usually mounted on trestles and divided by a traverse curtain to provide a forward playing-area and a concealed changing and assembly area in the rear (see Illustration 13).

chambres (Fr): a less common term for *loges* (see below).

champ (Fr): (1) see *platea*; (2) the enclosure in which the performance took place, and to which the public had to seek admittance (see Illustration 11).

chancel: eastern portion of a church containing choir, high altar, presbytery etc., which lies beyond the nave and is often screened off (see Illustration 4).

choir: that part of the chancel immediately beyond the nave, occupied by the choristers (see Illustration 4).

consueta (Sp): 'customary observance', applied especially to regularly performed dramatic presentations.

corrales (Sp): city courtyards enclosed by blocks of houses, which began to be used as public theatre sites in Spain in the late sixteenth century.

crossing: central area of the nave before the chancel entrance, separating north and south transepts (see Illustration 4).

degrés (Fr): literally 'steps'; usually raked seats where the ordinary public sat, as opposed to the *chambres* or *loges* constructed above them for the use of privileged visitors and the well-to-do (see Illustration 10).

domus (Lat): see *mansion*.

écha(u)faud (-t) (Fr): 'scaffold'; (1) the raised platform on which a player or group of players might perform; (2) the framework of scaffolding built to support seats arranged on several levels (*étages*) (see Illustrations 10 and 13). The term is thus occasionally given to the entire theatre structure.

entremet (Fr), *entremés* (Sp): (1) a banquet 'set-piece' (see Illustration 5) or miniature pageant often involving tableaux mounted on moving vehicles; (2) a pageant-cart or float used in Spanish processions and entries.

étage (Fr): (1) the raised theatre stage itself; (2) an elevated level on which a stage *mansion* might be placed or spectators accommodated. (One *échau-faud* might thus consist of several storeys or *étages*.) (See Illustrations 10 and 13.)

feinte (Fr): (1) stage apparatus devised to accomplish some striking stage effect by means of illusion; (2) the effect itself.

Gloria (Lat): (1) the *Gloria in excelsis Deo* ('Glory to God in the highest'), the angelic hymn at Christ's birth, incorporated in an expanded version into the Mass; (2) the doxology *Gloria Patri* ('Glory be to the Father, and to the Son, and to the Holy Spirit').

hourd, hourdement, hourt (Fr): virtually synonymous with *échaufaud*, a platform occupied by either actors or spectators (see Illustrations 10 and 13).

infernum (Lat): 'the lower place', a frequent term for Hell on the medieval stage (see Illustrations 9, 11 and 14).

interlude: a term with a wide range of meanings, but basically conveying the sense of a short dramatic entertainment or diversion. It could be performed indoors or out, by amateurs or professionals, and serve a didactic or recreative purpose.

Introit: literally 'an entrance', it refers to the opening portion of the Mass service and consists of an antiphon (a short piece of plain-song), a verse from a psalm, and the *Gloria Patri*.

joch (Sp): the Catalan term for 'sport', or 'play'.

jongleur (Fr): a minstrel or entertainer.

juego (Sp): see '*ludus*'.

Kyrie (Gk): the *Kyrie Eleison* ('Lord, have mercy upon us'), a series of choral petitions sung during Mass following the Introit.

Lectio (Lat): 'a reading'; any read portion of the church service, such as the Mass Epistle, the lessons at Matins, etc.

Lent: period of forty days' abstinence observed in the Christian Church, which begins on Ash Wednesday and culminates in Easter.

liturgy: officially authorised forms of Christian public worship, strictly speaking those ordained for the celebration of the Eucharist.

locus (plural *loca*) (Lat): specially designated stage areas at which a particular character is positioned or a particular action takes place (see Illustration 14).

loges (Fr): (1) the separate compartments into which the elevated tiers of seating (sometimes reserved for the affluent or distinguished) were often divided (cf. the modern theatre 'box'): (2) similar structures occupied by performers as their *mansions* as in Illustration 10.

ludus (Lat): generic term for any kind of sport, play, or game, including 'stage-play'.

mansion (Fr): literally 'house', but applied to any scenic structure on the medieval stage, possibly indicating a more elaborate construction than a *sedes*.

Matins: the first service in the daily sequence of eight observed by the Roman Catholic Church and known as the Canonical Office or the *Horae*. It was originally sung at midnight.

mom(m)eries: courtly entertainments performed by amateurs or professionals in which disguise, singing, dancing, and dialogue might play a part.

mon(s)tre (Fr): grand parade of all the participants in a medieval performance, usually preceding the final dress-rehearsal, and serving as a
celebration and a preview of the finished presentation.

mystères mimés (Fr): mute tableaux often performed at French royal entries
on stages along the route, and often elucidated by an 'explicator'.

narthex (Lat): entrance-porch or vestibule at the west end of a medieval
church.

nave: main body of a church or cathedral, from the chancel arch to the west
door, usually divided by pillars into a central area flanked by two side-
aisles (cf. basilica) (see Illustration 4).

officium (Lat): 'the Office', i.e. church service. Often applied to a liturgical
drama indicating its ecclesiastical origins and connotations (cf. *ordo*).

ordo (Lat): 'order' or 'arrangement'; an agreed form of religious observance, hence applied to a liturgical play whose performance had been
sanctioned and adopted into the liturgy (cf. *officium*).

pageant: (1) wheeled vehicle used to transport tableaux (with or without
human figures) about the streets in procession; (2) tableau or play
mounted on such a waggon (see Illustration 8).

pantes, pentes (Fr): rows of seats intended for the general public, either
made up of numerous tiers (*degrés*) or all placed at ground level (see
Illustration 10).

parc (Fr): (1) see *platea*; (2) see *champ* (2) (see Illustration 11).

parloir (Fr): (1) the upper storey of the *Infernum* in plays involving Hell;
(2) an alternative term for the *platea* or *champ*, especially on the indoor
stage.

parterre (Fr): ground-level, where the commons usually stood or sat on
benches, and where some *mansions* might be placed. Frequently the
main playing-area (the *platea*) was also situated at this level (see Illustration 10).

Pastores (Lat): 'shepherds'. A liturgical drama featuring the shepherds at
at the manger.

Peregrinus (plural — *i*) (Lat): 'the traveller(s)' or 'the pilgrim(s)'. Title assigned to liturgical plays involving Christ's appearance to the disciples
on the road to Emmaus.

place (Fr): see *platea*.

platea (Lat): the 'place' or main playing-area, usually but not always at
ground-level and bare of scenery, often employed to represent un-
specified dramatic locations and to present movement taking place
between specified *loca*. (see Illustrations 6, 9, 10, 14 and 15).

presbytery: part of the chancel beyond the choir reserved for the clergy,
generally raised some feet above the rest of the church. Here the high
altar is placed. (see Illustration 4).

Quem quaeritis (Lat): 'whom do you seek?' The opening words of the
angel's address to the three Marys at the empty sepulchre, and of the
trope which formed the text of the *Visitatio Sepulchri* (see Illustration 2).

roc(h)as (Sp): literally 'rocks', but often the term used for pageant-waggons.

sanctuary: another name for the choir of a church, where a criminal might
obtain sanctuary (see Illustration 4).

scaffold: see *échaufaud*.

secret (Fr): see *feinte*.

sedes (Lat): literally 'a seat', and probably originally a bench representing a specific location in a liturgical play. The word still continues to indicate a scenic device of some kind, though it often suggests the presence of a simple platform rather than the possibly more elaborate *domus* or *mansion*.

sequence: *see* trope.

sottie (Fr): a brief comic curtain-raiser performed by *sots* (traditional fools), a form apparently known only in medieval France.

stations: locations in medieval streets and squares often set up with platforms and seats, from which entries or dramatic processions might be watched (cf. US 'bleachers') and at which the passing vehicles or costumed figures might halt from time to time to give performances.

Stella (Lat): 'the star'; applied to liturgical plays featuring the star of Bethlehem, the Magi, Herod, etc.

Te Deum (Lat): *Te Deum laudamus* ('We praise thee, O God'), the celebrated Latin hymn which concluded the Matins service.

transepts: the 'arms' of a cruciform church, set at right angles to the main axis, i.e. 'north' and 'south' transepts (see Illustration 4).

triforium: a gallery usually in the form of an arcade above the nave, choir, and transepts of a church.

trope: a musical or verbal embellishment of the set liturgy. The term 'sequence' denotes the long elaborate tropes originally devised to adorn the final syllable of the word 'Alleluia', from which independent hymns such as the *Dies Irae* were formed.

trouvère (Fr): the northern French equivalent of the Provençal troubadour, or poet-composer-performer.

unguentarius (Lat): the seller of ointments and spices, featured in some plays in which the three Marys visit the tomb on Easter morning.

Visitatio Sepulchri (Lat): (1) the liturgical ceremony often regarded as the germ of medieval religious drama; (2) the dramatic representation of the three Marys and the angel at the sepulchre (see Illustration 2).

voleries (Fr): machines or related devices used to achieve flying effects on stage.

INDEX

287